YALTA

YALTA

DIANE SHAVER CLEMENS

OXFORD UNIVERSITY PRESS

LONDON   OXFORD   NEW YORK

OXFORD UNIVERSITY PRESS
Oxford   London   Glasgow
New York   Toronto   Melbourne   Wellington
Ibadan   Nairobi   Dar es Salaam   Cape Town
Kuala Lumpur   Singapore   Jakarta   Hong Kong   Tokyo
Delhi   Bombay   Calcutta   Madras   Karachi

This reprint, 1978

Printed In The United States of America

FOR

MARTHA DOWNING SCHWAB

ARTHUR FREDRICK SCHWAB

MILLIE ELY SHAVER

HORTIE EVERETT SHAVER

AUTHOR'S NOTES

This work was originally undertaken in 1963 as an analysis of the decision-making process of the Yalta Conference. No historian had undertaken in English a study of the Conference *per se;* indeed, it was only in 1965 that the Soviet Union published its documents on Yalta. For twenty-five years the looming questions of the postwar period have remained polarized: was Yalta a moment of naïve appeasement, a sell-out, on the one hand—or, on the other, was it the price the United States (and Great Britain) paid for a coalition with Russia? The stands taken by analysts have been mostly condemnatory or apologetic. With documents, memoirs, the full minutes of proposals, and statements of each speaker available, I set out to compare and contrast the positions, proposals, agreements, disagreements, and changes of positions of the leading diplomats at the Conference. I hoped thereby to learn what really did and did not happen at Yalta. In doing this, I have uncovered, I believe, the explicit and implicit positions and bargaining weapons utilized by each nation, and have found in the process that commonly accepted hypotheses regarding Yalta bear little real resemblance to the Conference or, indeed, to the dynamics of agreement in diplomacy.

This work analyzes the "zigs" and "zags" of daily diplomacy in the history of the period, yet it is broader in scope. I have tried to view the decisions of Yalta against the larger framework of military-strategic development during the war, the struggle for power in eastern Europe, and the long-range perspectives of Soviet, British, and American policy-makers. The first chapter provides the background of negotiations on the main issues resolved at Yalta. This offers a context for the general reader, but provides little new for the historian who is already familiar with the sources used for that chapter; however, the analysis might suggest a perspective for reappraisal of the Conference.

In this first background chapter I want to draw the reader's attention to the disproportionate amount of evidence from American and British sources compared with that from Soviet sources. This has resulted in the impossibility of subjecting Stalin and his diplomats to the same kind of analysis that Roosevelt and Churchill have undergone. We know to a great extent what the Western leaders were saying in private, what shifts took place in their positions, and in many cases, some of the complex reasons for these shifts. The same cannot be said for available knowledge about Stalin, in terms of internal politics. Despite this shortcoming, I believe that the intentions of the Soviet Union are manifest in the suggestions, proposals, and agreements made by her diplomats during the war and at various conferences, and that we can arrive at valid conclusions about diplomacy during the war and at Yalta by an objective analysis of their actions. The fact that Soviet proposals were frequently incorporations of positions enunciated by the West credits the Soviet Union with a more congenial and compromising position than postwar history has allowed.

I should like to add a note of thanks to the many persons who have been of invaluable help to me in this work. Support and impetus have come over a period of time from many sources. In particular, I owe a debt to the Humanities Department at the Massachusetts Institute of Technology, and especially to Richard M. Douglas and Bruce Mazlish, who have supported projects related to this production. On a grant from the M.I.T. History Program, I visited Moscow in December and January, 1967–68, to do research and to engage in dialogues with Soviet scholars at the University of Moscow Department of History and the Academy of Science. A multi-disciplinary Senior Seminar in Humanities at M.I.T. on "Structure" in 1967 provided me with the opportunity to explore the structure of diplomatic negotiations with a group of competent students and colleagues. M.I.T. made possible the presentation of a paper on Yalta at the September, 1968, Budapest Conference of the Peace Research Society. This opportunity further provided meetings with scholars from different parts of the world from many disciplines. Most recently, an Old Dominion grant for the spring of 1969 facilitated the completion of this manuscript.

Advice, discussions, and suggestions from friends and colleagues have been of substantial value in considering the questions of this period of history. Initially this study of the Yalta decisions was undertaken with the advice of Alexander DeConde of the University of California. I should also like to thank a number of colleagues who have provided stimulating ideas: Theodore Von Laue, William E. Griffith, Edward Chmielewski, Stephen Goodspeed, and Louis Harlan. I gratefully acknowledge the support of and interchange of ideas with my brother, Gilbert Jerome Shaver, of Harpur College, University of New York, and the help of my patient husband, Walter Carl Clemens, of Boston University. My European colleagues have provided interesting rapport and valuable information; among those I wish to thank are Ernst Winter of the Austrian Diplomatic Academy; George Schopflin of Chatham House, Royal Institute of International Affairs; the Department of History, University of Moscow; the Academy of Science, U.S.S.R.; the Lenin Library; as well as various institutes and scholars in Czechoslovakia and Romania.

In the preparation of this manuscript, two former students and research assistants have been generous with their time and effort. Steven Braverman helped accomplish various tasks several years ago when I taught at Boston University. More recently, Robert Supnik has been of invaluable assistance in the final preparation of the manuscript. His original research in my Cold War Seminar provided interesting ideas on the origins of the Polish-Soviet conflict.

I am grateful to the secretarial staff of M.I.T., in particular Mrs. Ruth DuBois and Mrs. Anne Rourke, for their aid and patience in secretarial assistance.

In this work the identifications "Moscow," "Soviet Union," "America," and "London," for example, are used as a con-. venience, to describe the prevalent policy of the nation's leader-. ship at the time. A single policy-maker is frequently designated only as the architect of a particular policy, even though his stand has often bound national policy. Transliterations from the Russian have been given as they appear in a work if it has been translated into English; otherwise the Library of Congress transliteration formula has been followed.

DIANE SHAVER CLEMENS

Cambridge, Mass.
July 1970

CONTENTS

PART I

"THE THREE OF US"

This work will focus primarily on the eight days of the Yalta Conference, concentrating on the main issues resulting in the decisions of the Yalta Protocol. The unfolding of the story of Yalta involves both subjective or voluntaristic determinants—the world views of governmental leaders, their moods, interaction, hopes, fears—and more objective and deterministic forces, such as the inexorable march westward by the Red Army. Like a living organism, the growth and development of proposals, issues, and decisions took place in a climate conditioned by governments and men with certain perceptions and certain vulnerabilities. The significance of the Conference lies partly in the fact that, although the agreements made at Yalta were subsequently abandoned, the decisions made there portended a different course than relationships took after the war.

Let us now turn to a background of these issues on which decisions were made—Poland, the formation of the United Nations, the occupation of Germany (including possible dismemberment, payment of reparations, and the allocation of an occupation zone to France), and the Soviet Union's joining the war in the Far East—for an understanding of the meaning of Yalta.

CHAPTER I

CONFLICTS

AMONG "FRIENDS"

"Today I remember the Crimean Conference with joy and grief. How many hopes, it seems, fully sincere, were expressed in those days, and how many disappointments did we derive from the international situation in the following years." These words, written by a Yalta participant on the twenty-fifth anniversary of the Conference, could have been uttered by any one of a number of men from any one of the three countries. They were written by Soviet Admiral Nicholai Kuznetsov. He concluded, sadly, "But even now, twenty-five years later, I am convinced that the Soviet Union is not to blame for this." This remark suggests the significance of Yalta as the watershed between wartime co-operation and the opening sorties of the postwar era—"the Cold War."

Kuznetsov's statement directs us to the underlying question: why did such a dramatic outward change in the relationships among the "Big Three" (the United States, the Soviet Union, and Great Britain) occur? The West has blamed the Soviet Union, frequently citing as cause the Yalta agreements allegedly broken by the Soviet Union. Whittaker Chambers, with an even more stern appraisal, echoed the perception of the 1950's when he said: "The illusion of Yalta [was] that the Communists yearned for peace if only we'd be kind to them." The Soviet Union has denied this and has blamed the failure on the West. Regardless of these charges, the real test is whether Soviet policy, behavior, and co-operation during the war differed fundamentally or qualitatively from Western policy, behavior, and co-operation.

The diplomatic negotiations on the issues of the Yalta Conference provide one insight into answering this question. The amiability of the Allies and the workability of the wartime coalition reflect what Churchill and Roosevelt called in their correspondence "the three of us." Yet this cohesive structure was built upon fundamental and long-standing conflicts among all three "friends." The paradox of the Yalta Conference was that it convened at a time when the Allies were on the verge of military victory, but fundamentally had resolved little else through diplomatic agreement. At Yalta they made agreements that reflected their mutual interests and embodied traditional compromises. These decisions were later challenged and abandoned, and the world was propelled into the "Cold War."

The Yalta Conference met from February 3 through February 11, 1945. It was designed to co-ordinate policy and strategy as the war drew to an end. Each government was involved, or was prepared to become involved, in the global fighting. The West, after delaying a Second Front in France, was now moving from France toward Germany; the Soviet Union, anticipating the collapse of Germany, was also preparing the equivalent of a Second Front against Japan. Victory was in sight. The struggles, however, were not only against Germany and Japan; they were also among the Allies themselves. The United States had deliberately postponed the settlement of significant political issues—it was thought for the peace conference—but Roosevelt found February 1945 a fateful moment to establish the common ground of agreement and to perpetuate the wartime coalition. Stalin and Churchill agreed.

POLAND

At a critical point in the July 1941 negotiations for the first Polish-Soviet agreement of World War II, British Foreign Secretary Anthony Eden turned to General Wladyslaw Sikorski, Premier of the Polish government in exile in London, and said, "Whether *you* wish it or not, the treaty must be signed." [1]

This attempt to reach a Polish-Soviet understanding had

begun shortly after the German invasion of the Soviet Union. Ivan Maisky, then Soviet Ambassador to Britain, on instructions from Moscow,* approached Eden and asked him to act as an intermediary in negotiation with the Polish government in exile. Russia, Maisky said, wanted to conclude an agreement for the restoration of an "ethnographic" postwar Poland and for the formation of a Polish National Committee and a Polish Army in the Soviet Union. Eden agreed to mediate, and he presented Maisky's proposals to Sikorski that same afternoon.

The London Poles, however, were not enthusiastic. They still remembered the many outrages Poland had suffered at Russia's hands in 1939—the secret Nazi-Soviet agreement to partition Poland; the Soviet invasion on September 17, 1939, and the subsequent annexation of all eastern Poland; the continued imprisonment of 200,000 prisoners of war, and the deportation of 1,000,000 civilians—all of which Maisky had ignored. Sikorski told Eden of Poland's "unnegotiable demands": release of all imprisoned soldiers and civilians, recognition of the Polish government in exile rather than a national committee, and above all, an explicit acknowledgment of the validity of the prewar Polish-Soviet frontier.[2]

The Polish-Soviet frontier was the first and primary cause of antagonism between the two countries. The Polish government in exile clung rigidly to the boundary established by the Treaty of Riga in 1921. The Soviets, on the other hand, wanted that frontier adjusted to reflect more closely the "ethnic balance" of the region. Since the ethnic composition of the region was confused—Poles, Ukrainians, Belorussians, and Jews all jumbled together—what the Soviet government had in mind was not clear at first. Subsequently it clarified its position: the Soviet Union intended to retain western Belorussia and the western Ukraine—that is, all of Poland east of the Curzon Line.† But the Polish

---

* Maisky said in his memoirs these instructions arrived in "mid-July." This must be incorrect, since he made his first official overture to Eden on July 4, 1941. (Maisky, *Memoirs*, p. 169.)

† The Curzon Line was the tentative Polish-Soviet border worked out by the Allied Armistice Commission in 1919. The Molotov-Ribbentrop Line of 1939 followed virtually the same course, but left the Bialystok region in Soviet hands (see map on page 11).

government in exile refused to yield an inch of Polish territory in the east—while, coincidentally, demanding extensive territorial compensation from Germany in the west.

A second cause of antagonism was the Polish government's refusal, or inability, to co-operate according to the Russian idea of "friendly, good-neighborly relations." Again, the Soviet's meaning became clear only with time. The Soviets wanted Poland to forgive Russia's previous offenses and to understand that, for reasons of security, the Soviet Union had a vital interest in both wartime and postwar Polish policy. During the war, the Red Army would be operating in Poland and would require the wholehearted co-operation of the civilian authorities there; after the war, the Soviet Union would be dependent on Poland to police Germany. The London Poles, however, refused to acknowledge the legitimacy of Soviet interests. They believed that to trust the Bear was to be devoured by him, that they had to preserve Poland's sovereignty, win treatment as an equal, and maintain an independent course; in sum, to guard vigilantly against expected incursions on their rights.

The July 1941 negotiations for a Polish-Soviet mutual assistance pact brought these fundamental disagreements into the open. At his first meeting with Maisky, Premier Sikorski demanded explicit recognition of the Riga Treaty frontiers. Maisky demurred; his government favored an independent Poland but would not recognize the prewar boundaries. They compromised on a Soviet denunciation of the 1939 Nazi-Soviet Non-Aggression Pact, but made no new agreement on frontiers. A few general ideas proved mutually acceptable—the re-establishment of diplomatic relations, the formation of a Polish Army on Soviet soil, the liberation of Polish military and political prisoners.

In subsequent negotiations over the proposed treaty, the divergent interpretations of "friendliness" came to the fore. Maisky asked the Poles to "trust" the Soviet government to release the Polish prisoners and to grant the Soviets a veto over the Polish government's candidate for commander of the Polish Army in the U.S.S.R. Sikorski refused; he countered with demands for an explicit promise to liberate prisoners. He even threatened to press reparations claims for damage done in the 1939 invasions.

SWEDEN

LATVIA

Baltic Sea

LITHUANIA

• Vilna

DANZIG

EAST

PRUSSIA

• Bialystok

GERMANY

Berlin •

Oder River

Vistula River

P O L A N D

U.
S.
S.
R.

• Warsaw

Wartha River

• Lublin

Neisse River

C Z E C H O S L O V A K I A

• Prague

• Lvov

AUSTRIA

HUNGARY

ROMANIA

POLAND 1938-1945

POLAND : 1938 ⬜ 1945 ⬜

1938 frontier ▬▪▬▪▬ 1945 frontier changes ▬▬▬ Curzon Line ▬ ▬ ▬

Russo-German frontier, 1939 •••••••••••• Oder-Neisse (W.) Line ▭ ▭ ▭ ▭

Area FDR suggested
Stalin grant to Poland ⬜

Area transferred by
Soviet-Czech treaty, 1945 ⬜

Miles
0   50   100   200

11

Those were harsh words for a prospective ally, and, not surprisingly, the negotiations were quickly deadlocked. Sikorski was pessimistic. With remarkable foresight, he predicted that if no agreement was reached, "the Soviet Government might enforce its will by forming a sort of National Committee assuming the character of a government and entrust the latter with the task of creating a Polish Army. . . ."[3] Still he would not sign an Anglo-Soviet draft agreement.

Britain broke the impasse with a combination of threats and promises. If Poland did not sign, Eden warned, the British government would not issue a proposed declaration in which Britain refused to recognize territorial changes made in Poland since the beginning of the war. On the other hand, the British promised that if the Poles would agree *beforehand* to sign the document, the British government would intercede with Stalin for concessions. Sikorski gave in, but three of his cabinet ministers resigned in protest. In fact, Britain's Ambassador to the Soviet Union, Sir Stafford Cripps, succeeded in ameliorating the terms of the proposed treaty, although not on the sensitive and crucial question of frontiers. Consequently, Sikorski and Maisky signed the Mutual Assistance Pact on July 31, 1941, with suitable pomp and ceremony.[4]

At best, however, this pact represented an "agreement to disagree," and the general attitudes of the governments involved remained the same—Poland cool, the Soviet Union politely interested, Great Britain eager for a façade of Allied solidarity. Indeed, the British were always more eager for a Polish-Soviet understanding than either of the parties involved, who tended to view each other with well-founded suspicion and distrust.

Polish-Soviet relations, never more than cordial, showed a marked proclivity to slide from bad to worse, even during their brief existence. A few incidents illustrate the situation:

By November 25 the Polish Ambassador to Russia, Stanislaw Kot, was declaring that Soviet mistreatment of Polish civilians "constitutes an unfriendly act." Although General Sikorski's visit to Stalin in December 1941 and the resulting "Declaration of Friendship and Mutual Assistance" were hailed throughout the Allied world as milestones in Polish-Soviet relations, no main issues were resolved, nor for that matter, were they even discussed. During the visit, Sikorski declared, "The 1939 frontier must not be questioned." Moving from the verbal arena to the realm of action, Stalin started to pursue Soviet aims unilaterally. When Anthony Eden visited Moscow in late December, Stalin confronted him with a demand for immediate *British* recognition of the 1941 frontiers, or at a minimum, of the Curzon Line.[5]

Again, the Russian government had agreed to allow the formation of a Polish Army on its soil. Yet the project proved of no military value to the Soviets. The Poles constantly complained about the small number of troops allotted them. This number fluctuated in direct proportion to Soviet military success and logistical capacity: the size of the Polish Army was initially set at 30,000 during the disastrous weeks of August 1941; rose to 96,000 during the optimistic days of the Russian winter counteroffensive; and fell to 44,000 with the advent of the German spring offensive. The Poles ignored the Soviets' mounting supply difficulties and demanded permission to recruit and train more troops. The Polish government also refused to allow deployment of its army *except as a unit,* despite Soviet Army Staff pleas for help against the impending German offensive in 1942. Since the Soviets were unable to equip enough Polish troops to satisfy the London government, the Polish Army was never deployed. In effect, it represented a fixed and useless drain on the Soviet logistic system. When the Polish Army Commander, General Anders, (without the consent of his government), requested the evacuation of the army from Russia the Soviet government readily agreed.[6]

The relief program revealed the deep-seated nature of hostility. Under the terms of the Polish-Soviet Pact, a relief system was set up to minister to the needs of the Polish deportees in the Soviet Union. However, a few confirmed instances of espionage by the Polish relief administrators aroused the always-latent Russian xenophobia. In July 1942 the NKVD closed down the Polish Embassy's relief offices, arrested most of the personnel, and expelled the rest.[7]

But the main irritant in this period was the unknown fate of some 8000 Polish Army officers. These men had been captured by the Soviets in 1939 and imprisoned in three prisoner-of-war camps—Kozielsk, Starobielsk, and Ostashkov. As required by the Polish-Soviet Pact, all Polish prisoners were granted amnesty in 1941, yet these officers failed to appear at Polish collection centers. The Polish Embassy addressed repeated queries about their fate to the Soviet Ministry of Foreign Affairs and invariably received evasive or outrageous replies. The Poles soon began to assume the worst: by mid-August 1942 Anders was telling Alan Brooke that he believed the officers "had been murdered" by the Russians.[8]

If these crises embittered Polish-Soviet relations, the re-emergence of the frontier question stretched them to the breaking point. In mid-January 1943, the Soviet Union, encouraged and strengthened by its military success at Stalingrad, openly laid claim to the western Ukraine and western Belorussia. The Poles responded with an adamant refusal to negotiate. However, the evacuation of the Polish Army, which occurred near the height of the Battle of Stalingrad, and the bitter exchanges over the dissolution of the relief system, had undermined the Polish government's political utility, so the Soviets pressed their position vigorously.

Nor did Poland's stock stand much higher with the Western Allies. Although Churchill and Eden had refused throughout 1942 to endorse Russia's demands, they were changing their minds. They showed irritation at the Polish government's hardline stance and at its private ambition to emerge as the most powerful state in East Europe at the expense of the Soviet Union. When Eden visited Washington in March 1943 he told President Roosevelt that Russia's territorial demands were modest and justified, that Stalin genuinely favored a strong Poland, and that Polish aspirations were the primary obstacle to good relations. Rather to Eden's surprise, Roosevelt agreed. The Curzon Line was a good idea. When the time came, the Big Three would provide "a just solution" to the boundary question and present it to the London Poles as a *fait accompli*.[9]

The incipient tragedy lay in the phrase "when the time came." Publicly, Roosevelt was proclaiming that all territorial questions would be resolved after the war. Privately, he was deciding upon, and committing the United States to, the positions he would take at the peace conference, including support for the Curzon Line. Unfortunately, the London Poles assumed—and Roosevelt, hoping to curry favor with Polish-American voters, encouraged this view—that the President's studious public silence on Soviet claims stemmed from disapproval of those claims. Therefore, in the face of British and Soviet opposition, the Poles held rigidly to the prewar frontiers, confident that at the appropriate time Roosevelt would save their borders. When the time came, Roosevelt did nothing of the kind, and the Poles unanimously shouted "betrayal."

By April 1943 the Polish and the Soviet governments were no longer on speaking terms. The Soviet press was filled with references to Poland's "imperialistic" ambitions in Belorussia and the Ukraine, and the Polish exile press in London reciprocated vituperatively. In this state of continuing tension, a brilliant German propaganda coup proved sufficient to sunder the line between the London Poles and Moscow.

On April 13, 1943, Berlin Broadcasting announced that the bodies of 10,000 Polish officers had been found concealed in a great pit in the Katyn Forest, near Smolensk. These men, the broadcast stated, had been taken from Starobielsk prison camp and murdered by the Russians.* The Sikorski government's reaction was immediate and extreme. Without waiting for a Soviet reply, and without consulting either the British or the Soviet government, the Polish government asked the International Red Cross to investigate the massacre. As Sikorski told Churchill on April 15, the Poles would not be dissuaded from a decisive confrontation; they "knew" the Russians were responsible. The Polish press bristled with accusations.

The Polish appeal to the Red Cross happened to coincide *to the hour* with a German invitation to that body, and the Soviet Union reacted with shock and open anger. The question of responsibility for the massacre was conveniently forgotten; the apparent collaboration between the Poles and the Nazis became the primary issue. *Pravda* began rumbling ominously about the

---

* This accusation was probably true. For a summary of evidence pointing to Soviet guilt, see Zawodny, *Death in the Forest*, pp. 77–95.

Poles' "desire to give direct aid to Hitler's forgers and provocateurs." On April 21, Stalin wired Churchill that the Soviet Union was going to sever relations with the Polish government in exile, in view of the apparent Nazi-Polish collusion and the continuing anti-Soviet press campaign. Churchill asked Stalin to wait and promised to muzzle the Poles in London. However, neither Stalin nor Sikorski wavered, and the Soviet Union broke off relations with the Poles on April 25.[10]

The subsequent Anglo-American efforts toward mediation failed to move either side. The Poles issued several "it's-not-our-fault" communiqués and refused either to withdraw their appeal to the Red Cross or to yield on the frontier question. Stalin defined the Soviet position on May 4 in a newspaper interview:

Question 1: Does the Government of the U.S.S.R. desire to see a strong and independent Poland after the defeat of Hitlerite Germany?

Stalin: Unquestionably, it does.

Question 2: On what fundamentals is it your opinion that relations between Poland and the U.S.S.R. should be based after the war?

Stalin: Upon the fundamentals of solid good-neighbourly relations and mutual respect, or, should the Polish people so desire, upon the fundamentals of alliance providing for mutual assistance against the Germans as the chief enemies of the Soviet Union and Poland.[11]

By this time, however, the price of friendliness had risen to include not only recognition of the Curzon Line but also reconstruction of the Polish government in exile on less anti-Soviet lines. In particular, the Russians asked for the dismissal of the Minister of Information, Stanislaw Kot, and the Commander in Chief, Kazimierz Sosnkowski. Premier Sikorski refused, and the Poles maintained their stand through and past Sikorski's death in an airplane crash shortly thereafter, on July 4, 1943.*

* There has been a revival of interest in Sikorski's death, primarily due to Rolf Hochuth's play *Soldiers*, which accused Winston Churchill of arranging the accident. Stalin held the same opinion. He warned Milovan Djilas about British Intelligence: "They were the ones who killed General Sikorski in a plane and then neatly shot down the plane—no proof,

While the new Polish Premier, Stanislaw Mikolajczyk, stood firmly on the crumbling rock of Sikorski's policies, the Allies fenced warily for new positions. In accordance with its announced policy, the United States studiously avoided saying anything about frontiers to anyone. Secretary of State Cordell Hull openly ceded the initiative in a Polish-Soviet *rapprochement* to Britain. On the other hand, he invited Mikolajczyk to come to Washington and covertly encouraged the Polish government in exile on its stand. Churchill had extracted from Stalin a temporary pledge not to form a rival Polish government, but Stalin did not leave his country's interests in Poland unprotected. In May 1943 Moscow announced that the Union of Polish Patriots, a Russian-based Communist émigré circle, was undertaking the organization of a new Polish Army in the Soviet Union.[12]

The British realized that recognition of the Curzon Line was the key to a Polish-Soviet *rapprochement*. Time was running out: the Red Army was driving relentlessly toward the old Polish eastern frontier. The London Poles still seemed to have no conception of the impending shifts in the power balance. During August, the Polish Underground produced, and the Polish government in exile endorsed, a statement on war aims. This "remarkable document" as Mikolajczyk labeled it, called for "a constant watchfulness concerning Soviet influence . . . and a ceaseless recalling . . . of the latent danger in Russian-Communist totalitarian peace aims." In addition, it demanded that Poland receive territorial compensation from Germany, while refusing any such compensation to Russia.

Britain took increasingly desperate measures to force the Poles into a realistic diplomatic stance. On October 5, 1943, just prior to the Big Three Foreign Ministers' Conference in Moscow, Eden visited Premier Mikolajczyk and asked for permission to discuss territorial concessions with the Soviet Foreign Minister, V. M. Molotov. He warned the Polish Premier that without agreement to the Curzon Line there was "scant chance" of a renewal of Polish-Soviet relations. Mikolajczyk refused. In Moscow,

---

no witnesses." (Djilas, *Conversations with Stalin*, p. 73). David Irving, in his book *Accident: The Death of General Sikorski*, reached no final conclusion but advanced a strong theory pointing to a freak accident.

Eden, with Hull's support, urged the restoration of Polish-Soviet relations without prior settlement of the frontier dispute. Molotov in effect dismissed the idea. Eden later told Mikolajczyk, "Since you had bound my hands by refusing to discuss frontiers, I could do nothing more." The Poles considered the frontier deadlock to be Britain's fault and openly criticized the Moscow Conference. The British, in turn, dismissed the Polish government in exile's concerns as a factor in British foreign policy.[13]

The Polish government in exile finally sensed its loss of standing with its Allies. As the first tripartite Chief-of-State meeting approached, Mikolajczyk made frantic efforts to see both Churchill and Roosevelt and to impress the Polish position upon them. He also sent a memorandum emphasizing the sanctity and righteousness of Poland's pre-war eastern frontier. The memo threatened that if the Red Army crossed into Poland without a restoration of Polish-Soviet relations, the Polish Underground would take measures of "self-defence" against "Soviet methods of terror." Both Western leaders were well aware of how Stalin would react to a pre-Teheran meeting with the Poles and refused to see Mikolajczyk. Nonetheless, the United States Ambassador to the Polish government in exile informed the Poles that the President had made "a careful study" of their memorandum.

The United States was in fact pursuing a policy of studied ambiguity. The preservation of inter-Allied unity, especially at Teheran, was indeed important. The November 1944 presidential election was also less than a year away. The attitude of Polish-Americans, to whom the Polish government in exile was a worthy institution, could be crucial to Roosevelt's political future, and the President would not risk upsetting the Polish applecart. As Harry Hopkins confided to Eden, the Polish issue was "political dynamite" for the American elections. The primary aim of American policy was, in Hull's formulation, "to convince the Poles, official and unofficial, that they should take a calmer outlook and not prejudice their case by *undue public agitation against our policies.*" [14] To keep the Polish government in line, the United States dropped hints that the United States supported the Poles' refusal to negotiate on frontiers.

Faced with the exigencies of domestic politics, the United

States proceeded discreetly at Teheran. Roosevelt, in a private meeting with Stalin, spoke vaguely of moving the Polish-Soviet frontier westward and of giving the Poles compensation in Germany. Churchill did not suffer from such inhibitions. He thought the time had come to settle the nagging frontier dispute, and he said so. Stalin was quite accommodating. During the last plenary session, he and Churchill agreed to the Curzon Line (after some dickering about its exact location), and Roosevelt gave the distinct impression that he concurred. However, this tripartite agreement was never put in writing, and in a pinch, the United States could and did claim (as Hull did in his memoirs) that "the conversations at Teheran concerning Poland . . . had no concrete results." [15]

In any case, no one bothered to tell the Poles about the Allied consensus. On December 20, Eden informed Mikolajczyk that Stalin's demands centered on the Curzon Line and that Churchill felt there was a basis for agreement. He did not specify what this basis was. Mikolajczyk was disappointed and expressed his intention of visiting Washington to seek support. Eden objected violently—Mikolajczyk first had to see Churchill, who was at that time recuperating from pneumonia. When the Polish Premier remained obdurate, Churchill had Roosevelt postpone Mikolajczyk's visit until March.[16]

In the meantime, the Soviet Union, bolstered by the apparent tripartite acceptance of its position on frontiers, made a few more attempts to reach a settlement with the London Poles. Around Christmas, the Soviet Embassy in London hinted that the Russians wanted to negotiate directly with the Polish government in exile. Dr. Eduard Beneš, Czech President, received the same impression while visiting Moscow and so informed Mikolajczyk. The Poles ignored these indicators. The Soviet government, in turn, took the next logical step in protecting its interests in Poland by countenancing or authorizing the formation of new, Communist-dominated, Polish Underground institutions—a "representative assembly," the National Council of the Homeland, and the People's Army—though these institutions did not yet assume the character of a government.[17]

When the Red Army crossed the old Polish frontier on January 4, 1944, Mikolajczyk published a declaration affirming the Underground's intention to co-operate with the Red Army—*now on Polish soil*. The Soviets took sharp exception to the implied claim and denounced "imperialistic" Polish designs on western Belorussia and the western Ukraine. Stalin explicitly dismissed the possibility of working with the Polish government in exile. He wrote Churchill that "there are no grounds for thinking that these [Polish] circles can be made to see reason. They are incorrigible."

Churchill and Eden became even more determined to save the Polish government from its folly. On January 20, Churchill told Mikolajczyk point-blank to accept the Curzon Line in return for territorial compensation up to the Oder River in Germany, and on February 6 he reiterated his arguments. The Curzon Line was just, and Britain supported it. He also told Mikolajczyk that haste was needed: "There will be no restoration of Polish-Soviet relations unless you consent to Russia's territorial demands." Mikolajczyk refused, offering instead a temporary demarcation line which would leave Lvov and Vilna in Polish hands. Prime Minister Churchill was infuriated at this lack of co-operation. On February 22, he publicly announced Britain's support for the Curzon Line and ignored the subsequent Polish protests.[18]

Roosevelt was not so forthright. In reply to Mikolajczyk's pleas for concrete help, he offered the "good offices" of the American government to mediate, but he refused to guarantee a solution. At about the same time, he postponed Mikolajczyk's proposed visit to Washington first until May, then until June 1944, since "a visit at this time may bring misunderstanding in public opinion." Nonetheless, the prospect of American support kept the Poles quiet, if not docile. Mikolajczyk still secretly hoped to alter the course of events decisively "if only Roosevelt would support him." The Polish Ambassador to Great Britain, Edward Raczynski, who did not share the Premier's enthusiasm, noted in his diary, "In this way, the weeks go by and nothing at all is achieved." He gloomily predicted that "the Russians [will] cross the Curzon Line and set up a puppet Government in Poland, after which British diplomacy will exert its influence to bring about a 'Russian salad'—that is to say, a Government consisting of Moscow's protégés with the addition of a few of the more 'harmless' elements in London." [19]

The Russians seem not to have given up hope of reaching a *modus vivendi* with the London Poles. The Soviet Ambassador to the various Allied governments in exile, Victor Lebedev, had several secret conversations with the President of the Polish National Council, Grabski, and then asked to see Mikolajczyk. The Polish Premier preferred to postpone the meeting until after a visit to Washington, which he hoped would make negotiations with the Russians unnecessary. But the meetings after Mikolajczyk's return proved sterile.

Mikolajczyk flew to Washington on June 6. He met Roosevelt six days later. The President was in his best personal and diplomatic form, entertaining his visitor with anecdotes of Teheran while concealing the substance of the agreements reached there. Mikolajczyk expressed fears about Stalin's designs on Poland. Roosevelt replied, "Stalin is a realist." He said that the Soviets genuinely favored a strong and independent Poland and were not imperialists. In fact, he went on, at Teheran Churchill had been the first to propose the Curzon Line as the future Polish-Soviet boundary. The President added that he opposed dividing Poland on that line. He did not mention what line he did favor. *At the proper time,* he would mediate the boundary question. Poland should get East Prussia and Silesia in the west, Lvov and Tarnopol in the east.

Roosevelt's apparent disagreement with his Allies seemed a hopeful sign. To probe the President's determination, Mikolajczyk asked whether the Poles should accept the Soviet territorial demands. Roosevelt emphatically favored postponing any settlement of frontiers, but nonetheless he urged Mikolajczyk to visit Stalin in Moscow, a seemingly contradictory stand. The next day Edward Stettinius, the future Secretary of State, indicated why: Although the United States could not for the moment take a firm stand against Russia, "in the not too distant future" American policy would change, would return to its "fundamental moral principles," and would "support Poland strongly and successfully." [20]

Mikolajczyk was highly elated. He was confident that "Poland can count on the support and real friendship of the United States," and that the Polish government in London would not have to concede anything to the Soviet Union despite British pressure. His renewed intransigence manifested itself quickly. He refused to explore the possibilities raised by Oskar Lange, a Polish-American leftist, when the two met in the United States on June 13. Lange had just visited the Union of Polish Patriots and had also talked with Stalin. He told Mikolajczyk that Stalin wished to renew relations with the Polish government. The Soviets favored, but did not insist upon, the Curzon Line, and were anxious for some changes in the makeup of the government in exile. Mikolajczyk ignored virtually everything Lange said. The Polish Premier also refused to bargain with Ambassador Lebedev when they resumed negotiations in London. After two cordial meetings on June 20 and 22, Lebedev presented the Soviet proposals on June 23—first, acceptance of the Curzon Line; second, reconstruction of the Polish government without Kot, Sosnkowski, Raczkiewicz, and Kukiel (Minister of Information, Commander in Chief, President, and Minister of Defense, respectively); and, third, inclusion of members of the Union of Polish Patriots and others in the government. Mikolajczyk did not even explore the possibilities for agreement. He "laughed at" Lebedev and concluded, "Then we have no other business at this time." * [21]

Although Mikolajczyk was encouraged by Roosevelt's predictions and promises, the British were angered by them and by the Poles' renewed stubbornness. Eden bitterly noted, "The poor Poles are sadly deluding themselves if they place any faith in

---

* E. J. Rozek, in *Allied Wartime Diplomacy*, incorrectly stated that these meetings took place before Mikolajczyk's visit to Washington. Mikolajczyk, in his memoirs, stated that the meetings began on June 20. Raczynski, in his diary, recorded that Mikolajczyk met with Lebedev on June 20, 22, and 23, and that all previous meetings had been between Lebedev and Grabski. Eden's recollection that Lebedev broke off the negotiations was incorrect (as both Mikolajczyk and Raczynski admitted). See, Rozek, *Allied Wartime Diplomacy*, p. 219; Mikolajczyk, *The Rape of Poland*, pp. 64–65; Raczynski, *In Allied London*, p. 226; Eden, *The Reckoning*, p. 540.

these vague and generous promises. The President will not be embarrassed by them hereafter, any more than by the specific undertaking he has given to restore the French Empire." In a meeting on June 22, while the talks with Lebedev were still continuing, Churchill warned Mikolajczyk to harbor no illusions about Poland's prospects and reproached him for being less accommodating in negotiations than he had been in January. Nor did the Polish Ambassador to the United States, Ciechanowski, see any cause for rejoicing. He noted that Mikolajczyk's visit and Roosevelt's pledges were being "widely exploited *in this pre-election period.*" Despite this, "official circles" were declaring that there were no "concrete pledges made by the United States toward Poland." Ciechanowski concluded that the Polish question would be subordinated to the needs of Soviet-American relations.[22]

If Mikolajczyk's rebuff to Soviet overtures annoyed Britain, it outraged the Soviet Union. After the unsuccessful meeting between Lange and Mikolajczyk, Stalin wrote to Roosevelt, saying that he would not invite the Polish Premier to Moscow. The collapse of the discussions between Lebedev and Mikolajczyk destroyed the last chances of an accommodation between Russia and the Polish government in exile. On July 22, as Soviet troops crossed the Curzon Line, Radio Moscow announced that the National Council of the Homeland (the Soviet-sponsored assembly in Poland) had formed a Committee for National Liberation, usually known as the "Lublin Committee" or the "Lublin Poles." That same day, the Lublin Committee announced in the "July Manifesto" its recognition of the Curzon Line, and in the following days it signed political and military agreements with the Soviet Union. On July 23, Stalin informed Churchill that he had invited the Lublin Poles to form an administration behind the Red Army in Poland. In response to a strong request from Churchill, Stalin also reluctantly invited Mikolajczyk to Moscow. "I shall certainly not refuse to see him," Stalin promised, but privately preferred that Mikolajczyk meet with the Lublin Poles instead.[23]

With the sudden appearance of a rival Polish government, Mikolajczyk decided to fly to Moscow. When he arrived there, on July 31, 1944, Molotov informed him that Stalin would be busy for three or four days and suggested an interim meeting with the Lublin Committee. Mikolajczyk refused. By the time he saw Stalin on August 3, the Warsaw uprising had broken out, complicating the Polish Premier's already difficult position. Mikolajczyk was torn between trying to obtain Soviet help for the rising and trying to negotiate a political settlement. In the end he achieved neither. Stalin insisted that military aid and political harmony were contingent on an agreement with the Lublin Committee. Mikolajczyk met with the Lublin group on August 6 and 7 but found no basis for agreement. He wanted to postpone negotiation on frontiers; they had already agreed to the Curzon Line. He wanted immediate aid for Warsaw; they denied that significant fighting was taking place. Nor was political unification possible: the Lublin Committee offered Mikolajczyk only four posts in a proposed eighteen-member cabinet.

Mikolajczyk saw Stalin once more, on August 9. He received some encouragement, for Stalin promised to aid the rising in Warsaw *if possible*. Stalin also pointedly countered Mikolajczyk's fear that Russia would impose its social system on postwar Poland. The Soviet Union, he said, needed a strong Poland to prevent German resurgence after the war. Mikolajczyk asked permission to return home for consultation, and Stalin readily agreed.[24]

For the next two months the Polish government in exile was occupied with the desperate and insoluble problem of obtaining aid for Warsaw. Not until the Polish Underground surrendered, on October 2, 1944, could Mikolajczyk turn again to the question of relations with the Soviet Union. Reeling from the disaster in Warsaw, the Polish government in exile had begun the painful process of meeting the Soviet demands—Sosnkowski had been forced to resign as Commander in Chief, and Mikolajczyk was at last prepared to concede most of the Curzon Line. When Churchill visited Stalin in October, he invited Mikolajczyk to Moscow for consultations; the Polish Premier readily accepted. He stipulated only that he meet with Stalin, not with the Lublin Poles.[25]

Mikolajczyk hoped to obtain a compromise whereby the London Poles would receive 80 per cent of the cabinet posts in a reorganized Polish government. At his first meeting with Stalin,

Churchill, and Averell Harriman, he was disabused of the idea. Stalin warned that any proposal which effectively ignored the Lublin Committee, or which failed to recognize the Curzon Line, was unacceptable. Churchill branded Mikolajczyk's 80:20 ratio as inequitable, and vigorously endorsed the Curzon Line. Mikolajczyk objected to a new "partition" of Poland, whereupon Molotov interjected, "But all this was settled at Teheran." Molotov explained that all *three* Allied heads of state had agreed to the Curzon Line as Poland's eastern boundary. Harriman looked at the floor and said nothing. Churchill added quietly, "I confirm this." He then asked Mikolajczyk to agree immediately to the Curzon Line and to a reorganization of the government. Mikolajczyk protested that he had no authority to do so, and the meeting ended.

After the meeting, Churchill prepared a draft statement for Mikolajczyk, accepting the Soviet conditions in return for compensations in the west and guarantees of Polish independence. Mikolajczyk turned it down flatly. On the following day the British and Polish Prime Ministers had a stormy meeting about the progress of negotiations. Churchill warned the Pole to accept Britain's proposal without delay: Polish procrastination had already led to the formation of the Lublin Committee, and further delay would only enhance the Committee's prestige. General Anders was talking of fighting the Russians once Germany was defeated, but that was crazy. In short, Churchill concluded, the London Poles had to accept the British proposal, and at once.

Mikolajczyk demurred. Churchill shouted angrily, "I wash my hands of this business!" He would not allow the peace of Europe to be wrecked because of Poland, he said; the Poles were trying to start another war which would cost 25,000,000 lives. After further exchanges, Eden calmed the discussion and returned to the subject of the Curzon Line. When Mikolajczyk still refused to concede that boundary, Churchill warned, "We will be sick and tired of you if you go on arguing." He added that the reorganized Polish government would be established on a 50:50 basis, or at best 60:40, and left the room to get the draft statement. When he returned, Mikolajczyk declined to sign it, and the Anglo-Polish conversations recessed for an hour.

The resumption of talks found Churchill in a violent mood. Mikolajczyk again explained that he had no authority to accept the Curzon Line. Churchill burst out, "You are no government if you are incapable of taking any decision. You are a callous people who want to wreck Europe. I shall leave you to your own troubles." He threatened to turn to the Lublin Committee and said that Mikolajczyk was making a "criminal attempt to wreck . . . agreement among the Allies." Mikolajczyk objected to this language; Churchill retorted, "If you want to conquer Russia, we shall leave you to do it. I feel like being in a lunatic asylum!" Eden attempted to smooth matters over, but Churchill kept repeating, "You hate the Russians." The Prime Minister left shortly thereafter to confer with Stalin. Stalin desired an understanding with the Poles, but as he told Churchill, "he [Stalin] and Molotov were the only two of those he worked with who were favorable to dealing 'softly' with Mikolajczyk." Churchill was sure that Stalin was under strong pressure from the Party and the military.[26]

The next day, October 15, Churchill talked again with Mikolajczyk. The latter insisted that Poland must retain Lvov and the Galician oil fields. Churchill stormed at this new line of Polish resistance and eventually shouted, "Everything between us is finished." The following day, Churchill wired King George about the Polish discussions, summarizing them as "All Poles Day" and dismissing the London Poles as "decent but feeble." Lord Moran recorded in his diary that Churchill "is apt to lose his temper when Mikolajczyk thinks differently." [27]

Unfortunately, the effectiveness of Churchill's continuing pressure was undermined by the United States. Upon hearing that his Allies endorsed the Curzon Line, Mikolajczyk wrote to Harriman, protesting America's agreement at Teheran to that Line. On October 16 Harriman privately gave support to Mikolajczyk's resistance by replying that Molotov had misinterpreted Roosevelt's position and that Harriman had not corrected Molotov's statement from fear of creating an American-Soviet incident which might cost Roosevelt the election.[28]

The same day Churchill pressed on toward an agreement. He personally presented to Stalin a new but basically unchanged draft Polish-Soviet agreement. Stalin accepted most of it, including territorial compensation for Poland up to the Oder River and Soviet guarantees of Polish independence; he only insisted that the Curzon Line must be the agreed basis for the Polish-Soviet frontier (rather than a line of demarcation), and that Mikolajczyk must reach an agreement with the Lublin Committee. Churchill returned to Mikolajczyk and urged him to accede; instead, the latter replied he would have to consult his government.

After a useless meeting with the Lublin Poles, Mikolajczyk saw Stalin for the last time, on October 18. Stalin again demanded acceptance of the Curzon Line, but he stated, to Mikolajczyk's surprise, that communism did not suit Poland, and that the Soviet Union would not attempt to impose it. Mikolajczyk decided to try to make his colleagues accept the Soviet demands. He returned to London on October 24.[29]

Mikolajczyk had only one last hope—American support for his position on the Polish-Soviet boundary. On October 26, he wired Roosevelt about the Moscow negotiations and asked for the President's help in gaining Lvov and the Galician oil fields for Poland. Churchill let a week pass before he talked with Mikolajczyk. Then he pointedly asked why there was a delay in returning an answer to the Soviet Union. Mikolajczyk still would not move without hearing from Roosevelt, but Roosevelt did not reply until after the presidential elections. By that time, the friendship of the Polish government in exile no longer mattered. On November 17, Roosevelt wired Mikolajczyk that whatever arrangements the Poles made with Russia would be acceptable to the United States, and that, in any case, the United States could not guarantee Poland's frontiers. This left Mikolajczyk isolated and without a choice. He urged immediate acceptance of the Soviet demands, his colleagues refused, and, on November 24, Mikolajczyk resigned the premiership.[30]

Allied reaction to this final instance of Polish obstinacy was swift. When a new Polish government, headed by Tomasz Anciszewski, was formed in London, the British, while maintaining formal relations, broke off all real contact. The United States, which had in general avoided the London Poles, now ignored the

new régime completely. The Soviet Union acted even more decisively. Stalin had lost interest in the London Poles, and he was
even beginning to express doubts about Mikolajczyk both as an
individual and as head of the Polish Peasant Party. Deputy Foreign Minister Ivan Maisky confidentially told Averell Harriman
that the London Poles had "missed the bus" by failing to reach a
compromise in October. Eden put it, "Stalin now had no further
motive to stay his hand." On December 31, 1944, the Lublin
Committee, anxious to ensure its hold on postwar Poland, trans-
formed itself into the "Provisional Government of Poland." Soviet recognition followed on January 5, 1945.[31]

On this question the Western Allies refused to follow suit. By
mid-January, there were two distinct bodies claiming to be the
Polish government, and the Allies were divided over which
claimant to support. Clearly, only the upcoming tripartite Conference at Yalta offered any chance of healing—or alternately ex-
acerbating—this division.

GERMANY: OCCUPATION AND DISMEMBERMENT

For the Soviet Union, the future of Germany was the central and
most critical political issue for the Allies to decide during the
war. Stalin believed that Germany, unless strictly controlled,
would rise again to threaten the Soviet Union. Typical of his frequently expressed concern were his words to Tito: "They will recover. Give them twelve to fifteen years and they'll be on their
feet again." [32] Soviet policy on Germany had three goals: to destroy Germany's ability to wage war, to co-operate with the West
in the suppression of future German ambitions, and to obtain
material recompense from Germany to help in rebuilding the Soviet Union. (The last of the aims—embodied in plans for reparations from Germany—will be examined separately in the next
section.) Despite its overriding interest, the Soviet Union nonetheless usually deferred to the West on questions about Germany.

Stalin immediately raised the problem of the postwar German
state during Eden's visit to Moscow in December 1941. He em-

phasized that the Allies would have to patrol Germany actively and vigilantly. He suggested detaching the German border states, including the Rhineland, Bavaria, Austria, and East Prussia, from the German heartland. Eden cautioned that "the British Government had not taken a decision either way;" still, "there was no objection to it in principle." Austria certainly should be made independent. In any case, Eden said, Britain was "determined that every possible military measure should be taken to prevent Germany breaking the peace again," although "exactly how this was to be done would have to be gone into carefully." Consultation with the United States was a necessity. Stalin replied, "I agree." [33]

Stalin's casual reference to partitioning Germany was taken up enthusiastically by President Roosevelt, who became, until Yalta, the staunchest advocate of dismemberment. During a visit to Washington in March 1943, Eden found that "the President appeared to favor dismemberment as the only wholly satisfactory solution" to the problem of the future security of Europe. Roosevelt and Eden agreed that, under any circumstances, "Germany must be divided into several states."

Tripartite agreement informally existed. Stalin had already spoken in favor of dismemberment; Ivan Maisky had likewise told Eden that "Germany should be broken up," although he did not exclude the possibility of a federal union; and Maxim Litvinoff, the Soviet Ambassador to the United States, confirmed this as the Soviet position. Stalin, however, had only casually mentioned the idea of giving East Prussia to Poland. In their March 1943 talks Roosevelt and Eden went beyond this and decided that Prussia must be completely separated from Germany. These views were not binding because Ivan Maisky had requested that the Eden-Roosevelt conversations be "entirely exploratory," and the President agreed. Nonetheless, Roosevelt thought that agreement was so close that he stated to the press: "I would say that so far . . . we are about ninety-five percent together." [34]

This unanimity proved only apparent. At the Anglo-American Quebec Conference in August 1943, Eden and Hull had to confess that their respective governments were in fact divided on the question of dismemberment. Hull thought that forced dis-

memberment could only lead to a resurgence of German nationalism. Dismemberment was still possible, but only in the form of
voluntary separation or economic decentralization. But if Hull
had his doubts, Roosevelt did not. Prior to the Moscow Conference of October 1943, the President told Hull "categorically he
favored the partition of that country into three or more states,"
all of which would be disarmed. When Hull argued against partition, Roosevelt "insisted that partition was the solution." [35]

Unfortunately, the agreement between the Western Allies and
the Soviet Union did not last long. The West's unilateral handling of the Italian surrender was a blow to tripartite agreement
on a uniform policy toward the Axis nations. American policy toward the European Advisory Commission (the E.A.C.) was the
deathblow.

The Italian government surrendered to the Allies in September 1943. The United States, while lecturing the Soviets on "preserving the peace by . . . international cooperation after the
war," systematically excluded the Soviet Union from Italy. The
Western Allies cabled vague plans to Stalin, thus keeping him informed at least technically; but control of the surrender operations, and control of the conquered portions of Italy, remained
in Anglo-American hands. Stalin pointedly complained of the
West's exclusive action. He suggested a tripartite commission in
Italy to co-ordinate policy. Churchill promptly accepted Stalin's
idea *in form;* on the side he made concrete arrangements to deprive the commission of all real power. He confided to Roosevelt,
"We are in fact rejecting the Soviet proposal." [36] Despite Stalin's
continuing protests, Italian policy remained an Anglo-American
monopoly. When Stalin eventually mimicked the West and dictated the surrenders in Rumania, Bulgaria, and Hungary, the
Western Powers, whose policy he was merely copying, protested
loudly and eloquently over these breaches of tripartite unity.

The European Advisory Commission was born under only
slightly more auspicious circumstances. Eden and Roosevelt had
first discussed the idea of an inter-Allied policy-making commission in March 1943. They expected Soviet troops to control part
or all of Germany at the end of the war. Therefore, since the
Soviet Union could not be excluded from the peace, plans were

developed to contain Soviet policy within the framework of Anglo-American policy. Harry Hopkins, adviser and assistant to the President, thought it essential to reach an understanding "as to which armies would be where and what kind of administration should be developed." For Hopkins, the alternative was a chaotic or even communist Germany. Roosevelt and Eden decided "that the State Department should work out the plan with the British and the one agreed upon between the two of us should be discussed with the Russians." [37]

At the Moscow Foreign Ministers' Conference, Eden brought up the suggested commission but neglected to define its powers. At a private meeting with Molotov, Hull presented what was actually a joint Anglo-American proposal; however, he claimed it as only "a personal suggestion" which, if acceptable, could be coordinated with Eden later. Besides creating a European Advisory Commission, the proposal called for the unconditional surrender of Germany to the United Nations. Germany would be occupied by forces of the Big Three and administered by a tripartite Allied Control Commission. Molotov, after conferring with Stalin, returned, "his face radiant," and exclaimed, "I have shown this to Stalin and he is enthusiastic." He went on, "It expresses Russia's thoughts about Germany exactly as if we had expressed them." The Russians were so enthusiastic, in fact, that Stalin wanted to make Hull's program a Russian suggestion. Hull assented. (Later he was pleased that he had, because the United States began to retreat from this position.[38])

In addition to proposing the E.A.C. and an Allied Control Commission, Hull and Eden explained the official Western position on dismemberment. Hull suggested that "the potential threat of Germany to general security might be lessened through decentralization of the German political structure." Specifically, Prussia, "the tap root of all evil," should be severed from the rest of Germany. Eden remarked that Britain "would prefer to see [Germany] divided into separate states," and he, too, supported splitting Prussia from Germany. Molotov accepted their ideas without exception: "The Soviet government gave its full approval to all measures that would render Germany harmless in the future." He saw dismemberment as a possible method of repression, provided it was "regarded as a minimum and not a maximum proposal."

While the Soviets were accepting dismemberment, the West was developing doubts about it. Eden confessed openly that his government "was divided in its opinion" about partitioning Germany. Hull was more vague in conveying current governmental thought. Publicly he proclaimed that in the United States "dismemberment was still in favor"; in his memoirs he recalled his private thoughts and the basis of his own policy recommendations: "I myself had been opposed to dismemberment from the beginning." He did not mention this personal opposition to Molotov.[39]

The Soviets' impression that the West favored dismemberment was confirmed at Teheran in late 1943. Stalin reiterated his acceptance of the Western proposals from the Moscow conference, but he commented that the measures envisioned were "inadequate." He feared that unconditional surrender, and dismemberment as well, "merely served to unite the German people." Besides, what did unconditional surrender mean? Roosevelt did not want to discuss the question; it would be clarified when it happened. The Soviets were concerned—they had no guarantee that the German surrender would be controlled by all three powers. It might become an exclusively Western affair, just as the Italian surrender had been.

To satisfy Stalin's call for concrete measures, Roosevelt produced a fairly complete program for dismembering Germany. After the war, five autonomous states would be formed: (1) a reduced Prussia; (2) Hanover and the Northwest; (3) Saxony and Leipzig; (4) Hesse-Darmstadt, Hesse-Kassel, and the area south of the Rhine; (5) Bavaria, Baden, and Wurtemberg. He also recommended tripartite control of the Kiel Canal, Hamburg, the Ruhr, and the Saar. This proposal was not greeted enthusiastically by either Britain or the Soviet Union.

Churchill thought the proposal went too far. He exclaimed, "To use an American expression, the President has said a mouthful." In his view, Prussia should be isolated and reduced, and Bavaria, Austria, and Hungary should be allowed to form a "broad, peaceful, unaggressive confederation."

Stalin on the other hand, commented, "All very good, but insufficient." He did not like either the American or the British proposal, but of the two he preferred Roosevelt's. To Stalin, "dismemberment meant dismemberment," simply the elimination of the Prussian officers corps and staffs, which was not far-reaching. The fundamental problem was more complex—to neutralize the Germans' tendency to unite—and this he recommended be accomplished through an international organization which would apply economic and even forceful measures. Playing down Stalin's call for strong measures, Churchill retorted, "Nothing is final." Instead, he advocated disarmament, prevention of rearmament, supervision of factories, and "territorial changes of a far-reaching character." After further altercation the three agreed that dismemberment in some form, coupled with preservation of Allied unity over Germany, would suffice to render Germany harmless. Still, this consensus they admitted was only "preliminary"—Stalin added "very preliminary"—and all the questions related to Germany were handed over to the E.A.C.[40]

Tripartite co-operation died in that body. Roosevelt's advisers at the War Department, Henry Stimson and John J. McCloy, had been warning that the British intended to use the London-based E.A.C. to "give orders" to Eisenhower and to pre-empt American political supremacy in the postwar world. Although the President had agreed to give the problem of dismembering Germany to the E.A.C., once away from Teheran he attempted to undermine the Commission's authority and undo its decisions. George F. Kennan, assigned by the State Department to the European Advisory Commission, vividly recalled the results: "So far as I could learn from my superiors in the department, their attitude toward the commission was dominated primarily by a lively concern lest the new body should at some point and by some mischance actually do something." The State Department was particularly nervous "lest the American delegation, through over-eagerness or inadvertence, contribute to so unfortunate an occurrence." [41]

The logic of postponement manifested itself in the appointment of John G. Winant, already American Ambassador to Britain, as United States representative to the E.A.C. Instead of

being given extra staff, Winant was instructed to limit the scope
of the Commission to technical details of the surrender. Washington, despite the façade of Allied co-operation, intended to use
the Combined Chiefs of Staff or regular diplomatic channels to
make decisions. As a result, the E.A.C. decided only two issues—
the terms of occupation and the allocation of zones.[42] Dismemberment and reparations were left to the heads of state.

Even the zonal agreement ran into trouble. The War Department claimed that the E.A.C. had no "right" to negotiate zones,
which would be "determined by the location of troops at the
time of Germany's surrender or collapse." The War Department
believed that by the end of the war all of Germany up to the
Rhine would be under Soviet control and, as one participant
summarized the government's view in his memoirs: "Therefore it
was useless to expect the Soviet government to carry out any
agreement regarding the division of Germany." (The planners of
Washington might have consulted the Russians instead of theo-
rizing about them: the American Army met the Russians far to
the east, at Torgau, on the Elbe.)

In January 1944, Britain, left to its own devices, proposed dividing Germany into three approximately equal zones. The British would have the northwestern industrial area and the Americans the southwest region bordering on France. The Soviet zone,
in the east, would contain 40 per cent of the territory, 36 per
cent of the population, and 33 per cent of the productive resources. A month later the Soviets accepted the British proposal
and further suggested that Berlin be a separate zone of joint occupation. According to an American negotiator on the Commission, Philip Mosely, the Soviets' acceptance "appeared a sign of a
moderate and conciliatory approach to the problem" of postwar
Germany, since "in terms of war effort and of war-inflicted suf-
ferings, the Soviet Union might have claimed a larger share."
The Soviet representative to the E.A.C. urged that prompt action
be taken.[43]

Washington responded in March, not with agreement but
with a counterproposal. The American representatives on the
Commission were ordered by the Joint Chiefs of Staff to present
a new zonal formula and to "demand its acceptance." The new

PROPOSALS AND FINAL ZONES OF OCCUPATION IN GERMANY

•••••• Original British proposal of January, 1944, accepted by USSR

———— U.S. counterproposal for an American northwest zone

Final zones of occupation, including allotment to France

BRITISH | FRENCH | U.S. | RUSSIAN | POLISH ADMIN.

scheme reduced the Soviet zone to 22 per cent of the area, population, and productive resources of Germany but increased the American share to 46 per cent of the land and over half the population. No background information was provided to justify the proposed division, which, quite illogically, cut across all existing lines of communication and administration. American officials on the E.A.C. were aghast at the new proposal. George Kennan, who had heard a rumor that the new proposal had no formal basis, flew to Washington to explain to the President exactly how disastrous it was. Roosevelt merely laughed about the Joint Chiefs' proposal, and said, "Why that's just something I once drew on the back of an envelope" while en route to Cairo. On May 1 he gave orders to approve the Soviet zone, but he then tried to obtain the northeast zone of occupation for the United States. The British refused. They pointed out that under the proposed plan for the invasion of France, British troops would end up in the north of Germany, American troops in the south. Any attempt to switch places would result in vast administrative confusion. The American government still refused to accept the proposed zones.[44]

Ambassador Winant eventually used Washington's fear of the Soviet Union to force a decision. Winant warned "that the Russians might reach the border of their zone and then keep on going." This made an impression on Washington. Hopkins reported Winant's message to Stettinius, and at last the Joint Chiefs of Staff accepted the Anglo-Soviet proposal as the only way to contain Russian ambitions. Ironically, at the same time, Stalin was calling off the final Soviet offensive on Berlin, which would in fact have placed Soviet troops just where the Joint Chiefs feared they might be. The zonal agreement was finally signed at Yalta.[45]

Although the problem of zones was resolved, the question of dismemberment continued to be an issue. By 1944, another American scheme for dismemberment, the Morgenthau plan, had been officially placed before the Allies. Since this plan had repercussions on the reparations issue, it is necessary to trace the history of that question before returning to the problem of dismemberment.

GERMANY: REPARATIONS

Stalin had initiated discussion of reparations at the Tripartite Conference on Supplies in Moscow during September 1941. He asked Lord Beaverbrook point-blank, "What about getting the Germans to pay for the damage?" but received no answer. During Eden's visit to Moscow, Stalin raised the question again. Eden replied that the British, due to "our experience after the last war," opposed reparations in cash; however, "the restitution by Germany of goods taken away from occupied territories was another matter." Stalin evidently agreed—all subsequent Soviet reparations schemes were based on restitution in kind rather than in currency.

The West, for the most part, paid lip service to the Soviet reparations requests. Just before Eden's departure for Washington in March 1943, Soviet Ambassador to Britain Ivan Maisky visited him to stress that the Soviet Union "would certainly want reparations." The Russians, he conceded, were willing to defer to Western objections: reparations would be "not in money but in kind." But Eden and Roosevelt were less interested in the reparations issue and dealt primarily with matters closer to their own hearts, among which were American relations with Vichy, the dismemberment and policing of Germany, the Soviet interest in Poland, and, as Anthony Eden recorded, "whether it was possible to work with Russia now and after the war." [46]

The subject of reparations was taken up once again at the Moscow Foreign Ministers' Conference of October 1943. At that conference Cordell Hull presented a plan for reparations; the Soviets assumed that it represented the final Western position and they based all their subsequent plans for reparations on it. In a written proposal Hull stated that "Germany would pay reparations for the physical damage inflicted upon the U.S.S.R." The amount of repayment would be determined "through a Commission on German Reparations consisting initially of representatives of the three Powers." Hull also presented some guiding principles, which the Soviet Union adopted as a part of future proposals. Reparations should be "in terms of goods and services, not money." Further, they should be awarded "in proportion to the losses of nonmilitary property suffered through the German action." Hull urged and invited the Soviets "to work out the magnitude and the character of the material and equipment needed" to rehabilitate the Russian economy. Hull's recommendations, became the kernel of the Soviet reparations program as constructed and presented at Yalta by Ivan Maisky.[47]

These conciliatory gestures on reparations were soon lost in "a policy of 'no policy' towards Germany" which paralyzed the E.A.C. Despite Winant's pleas for the formation of a reparations policy in August 1944, while there was still time, in September, Roosevelt told Hull "I dislike making plans for a country which we do not yet occupy," and he halted all postwar planning for Germany in the E.A.C. The President was instead becoming interested in a new scheme for dealing with Germany, the Morgenthau plan, devised by Secretary of the Treasury Henry Morgenthau and Harry Dexter White. The plan would have affected the Soviet Union in two respects. First, it called for the dismemberment of Germany, an idea which Secretary Morgenthau feared had been discarded in American planning circles. As in Roosevelt's plan at Teheran, East Prussia, the Saar, the Rhineland, and the Kiel Canal would be separated from Germany. The remaining territory would be divided into two independent states. Second, it severely restricted the amount of reparations the Soviet Union could extract. The Russians intended to take the bulk of reparations from current German production for several years after the war, but the Morgenthau plan restricted reparations to what could be obtained by dismantling industry or from forced labor.

The Morgenthau plan, presented at the second Quebec Conference in September 1944, threw the Western Allies into confusion. The American State Department and War Department were outraged at the Treasury Department's attempt to usurp State's planning prerogative. Cordell Hull wrote, "This whole development at Quebec, I believe, angered me as much as anything that happened during my career as Secretary of State." Hull wrote an angry memo to the President: "No decision should be taken on the possible partition of Germany (as distinguished from territorial amputations) until we see what the internal situation is. . . ." Roosevelt, who had initialed Morgenthau's proposals "OK—F.D.R.," changed his mind after the Quebec Conference. He concluded privately, "Henry Morgenthau pulled a boner." Churchill, for his part, also initially accepted the Morgenthau plan and then changed his mind. At Quebec, the Prime Minister had seen that Morgenthau's scheme would reduce Germany's industrial capacity to compete in the export business. Morgenthau had also included six billion dollars in postwar credits to Britain to make the plan acceptable to the British. However, the British War Cabinet rejected the plan.[48]

The Soviets, of course, saw nothing of the behind-the-scenes maneuvering on the reparations and dismemberment aspects of the Morgenthau plan, nor did the United States deem it necessary to consult them. Although Roosevelt lamented, "In regard to the Soviet Government, it is true that we have no idea as yet what they have in mind," he had no intention of finding out. He wrote Hull: "I do not think that in the present stage any good purpose would be served by having the State Department or any other Department sound out the British and Russian views on the treatment of German industry." The United States extended its studious silence to dismemberment as well as reparations. The United States had discarded the Morgenthau plan, as Hull noted: "We were also agreed at the State Department to oppose Morgenthau's ideas of a partition of Germany." A new policy was formulated: "In place of partition, every effort [should] be made to promote a federal system of government in Germany." No one informed the Soviet Union.[49]

In fact, Churchill was in Moscow cautiously supporting parts of the Morgenthau plan. On the way to the meeting Eden had said, "I'd like to see the Ruhr and the Saar . . . permanently internationalized." Churchill proposed not only this idea, but also internationalization of the Kiel Canal, independence for the Rhineland, and (his pet scheme) a south German federation with its capital at Vienna. Stalin agreed to all these ideas, including the Catholic south German federation, which he had previously opposed. Churchill wrote to Roosevelt about dismember-

ing Germany: "I am not opposed to this line of thought." [50]
However, by now the President was.

Indeed, Roosevelt's position on reparations, and, to a lesser
extent, on dismemberment, was changing with the regularity of a
pendulum. In September 1944 Secretary of State Hull wrote the
President that "this Government has little direct interest in obtaining reparations from Germany," but that the Soviet government did. However, by mid-November there was a new Secretary
of State, Edward Stettinius, and a new assessment of the situation. Stettinius pointed out that the British were interested in
limiting Germany's productive and export ability, while the Russians, on the other hand, wanted to exploit the German economy, for reparations. The State Department had a method of resolving this contradiction. The German economy should conform
not to the needs of the British or the Soviets but "to the general
economic foreign policy of the United States." German industry
would be converted to peacetime purposes for the production of
reparations; however, the goods produced would be used not for
the Soviet Union but "to effect a large, early contribution to the
rehabilitation of liberated countries." Reparations would be
short term, taken in kind from current production or in forced
labor. Interzonal machinery would be established for the easy exchange of foodstuffs and industrial products.[51]

Roosevelt, presented with contradictory advice from Treasury
and State, for the moment took a stand in favor of reparations.
He "was still in a tough mood," he said, and he was "determined
to be tough with Germany." He approved Stettinius's proposals
as "sufficiently tough." Yet by early December he changed his
mind. Shortly after Stettinius noted that the British were beginning to "advocate conversion of the German economy to peacetime purposes and production of reparations in kind," Roosevelt
shot back, "We are against reparations." The Treasury Department actively supported this decision: "We completely reject . . .
the contention that recurring reparations are necessary so that
Germany may be made to pay for the destruction she has
caused." [52]

By the time of the Yalta Conference, it was difficult to dis-
cover what the American attitude on reparations was. In two re-

ports, "Economic Policies Toward Germany" and "Reparation and Restitution Policy Toward Germany," the State Department recommended certain principles which were, as in the Morgenthau plan, antithetical to reparations. Germany must be left enough productive capacity to pay for her imports, to sustain her population, and to recompense the Allies for their expenses in occupying Germany. Reparations had the lowest priority: "German reparation should be supported only to the extent that it does not conflict with more important objectives." Reparations, insofar as they existed, should "be payable 'in kind.'" Yet this minimization of reparations ran contrary to political reality. The State Department knew that the Soviet Union would want reparations, including "the performance of labor services by German manpower in Russia." The Department grudgingly admitted that since "there is no compelling reason for the United States to oppose such claims," it did not oppose "labor service within reasonable limits." [53]

Nor was the American delegation much clearer about dismemberment. The main State Department position paper favored the transfer of East Prussia (excluding Koenigsberg, Danzig, Upper Silesia, and Pomerania) to Poland, as well as the forced transfer of population from this area. On the other hand, the Department stated "that the Government should oppose the forcible partition of Germany." Such "imposed dismemberment" would create difficulties and disrupt the German economy. "A return to federal decentralization" was recommended instead. The American position, vague on both reparations and dismemberment was a mystery to the other Allies.[54]

Britain's position was only a little better defined. Eden gave Churchill a list of questions which might be raised at the Yalta Conference, but Churchill "was still unwilling to take decisions" on Germany, Eden complained. The Prime Minister was worried by Ambassador Clark Kerr's warning that the Russians "fear here that England will be soft over Germany." [55] Trapped between his own commitments and the War Cabinet's opposition to dismemberment and reparations, Churchill worked to maintain the balance between his honor and his authority.

In fact, by January 1945 only the Soviet Union had a clear

view of what the Allies should do with Germany. Ivan Maisky, by then Assistant Commissar for Foreign Affairs, presented in advance the Soviet government's ideas to Ambassador Harriman in Moscow. The Soviet plan was a smooth blend of the themes and thoughts of Western diplomacy on reparations and dismemberment. Maisky emphasized that the "principal objective of the Soviet Government was security." Germany's heavy industry would be stripped of equipment that might be used for rearmament. Reparations would be short term and might include use of labor. The amount of reparations would be adjusted as security demanded. Distribution of reparations should be based essentially on Hull's recommendation of 1943—"the first priority should be for damage caused by enemy action." Maisky rephrased it, "Those who had done the most fighting should get the most."

On dismemberment, Maisky said that Moscow currently favored independence for the Ruhr, the Rhineland, and possibly the Catholic south; and industrial demilitarization. He added that deindustrialization must not preclude Germany from supplying its own needs or paying for its imports. Still, the expansion of light industry and agriculture were to be encouraged.[56]

The Soviets had made a great effort to find common ground with the West's slippery position. At Yalta they presented their plan to the Allies, and to their surprise, most of the items in it were rejected.

FRANCE

The future of France was less a source of conflict between Russia and the West than it was between the Western Allies themselves. Churchill and Eden were determined to resurrect France as a major power in Europe, both as a guardian against Germany and as a constituent of an anti-Soviet West European bloc. To attain this end, they consistently supported Charles de Gaulle, who, precisely on account of his pride and nationalism, stood the best chance of rebuilding France. The United States, on the other hand, was convinced that "no central French authority, recognized as such and able to talk on equal terms with the Governments of the United States and Britain, should be allowed to come into being." [57] Hence, the American government, instead of supporting de Gaulle, backed Henri Giraud, a general of astonishing political naïveté, and it even courted elements of the Vichy régime. Roosevelt mocked de Gaulle's pretensions and aspirations and often told of the occasion when de Gaulle had compared himself to Joan of Arc. Cordell Hull claimed to be offended by de Gaulle's autocratic tendencies. He was also offended by de Gaulle's determination to preserve the French Empire from American encroachment.

The 1943 merger of the de Gaulle and Giraud factions into one Committee of National Liberation, and Giraud's subsequent eclipse, left the Americans no alternative to de Gaulle. Nonetheless, they continued to grumble about him. Hull told Eden he harbored "no ill will toward de Gaulle" but "regretted that he seemed so constituted, tempermentally at least, that he sought political preferment in the main." Eden understood what Roosevelt's opposition really stemmed from: the President "wanted to hold the strings of France's future in his own hands so that he could decide that country's fate." [58] The two Western Allies could not reach any agreement. Britain continued to support and build up the Gaullist régime, the United States to mourn for Giraud and to flirt with Vichy.

Churchill's main tactic was to force the inclusion of France in any and all relevant inter-Allied commissions and councils. When Stalin proposed a tripartite commission for Italy, Churchill, before accepting, asked Stalin whether France could be a member. "If so," he wrote, "I would suggest it here." Stalin, who had been more assiduous than his Allies in recognizing de Gaulle's Committee of National Liberation, immediately cabled back, "I am for having the French National Committee." [59] Churchill had no intention of giving the proposed Italian commission any power, but French participation would give de Gaulle's prestige a useful boost. Operating on the same principle, Churchill obtained for France a permanent seat in the United Nations Security Council, and eventually membership in the European Advisory Commission.

The gradual restoration of French military and political power raised the question of whether France should participate in the occupation in Germany. In November 1944, Churchill went to Paris to confer with de Gaulle, and afterward he informed both Roosevelt and Stalin that de Gaulle "pressed very strongly" for a French zone of occupation. Although Churchill stressed that he had promised nothing, he confessed he had told de Gaulle that "we should be pleased" if the French took some of the responsibility for guarding the German peace. By early 1945 the President favored giving France a portion of the Anglo-American zones, or so it appeared to Stettinius. When the two Western foreign ministers met at Malta, just before the Yalta Conference, Stettinius told Eden "that the President attached great importance to giving the French a zone of occupation in Germany." According to State Department records, the President actually had, in principle, approved a zone for France and French participation on the occupation machinery (the Allied Control Council). This was consistent with previous decisions to place France on the Security Council of the United Nations and give her membership in the European Advisory Commission.[60] But some time prior to the Yalta Conference the President changed his mind, and at the Conference he initially opposed any place for France whatsoever.

THE UNITED NATIONS

Before the German invasion, the Soviet Union had tried to ensure its national security in several ways: first in the League of Nations; then in a system of collective security with France and Britain; finally in an alliance with Germany, based on expediency. These policies all failed. During 1941 the Soviets slowly developed a new concept: security based on postwar Great Power co-operation and underwritten by specific and binding guarantees and treaties. The lofty and ineffective moral precepts of the 1930's and the opportunism of the pact with Germany were abandoned in favor of a permanent alliance with Germany's enemies. When Harry Hopkins visited Moscow in July 1941, Stalin stated the new Soviet aspiration: "Nations must fulfill their treaty obligations or international society could not exist." [61]

Meanwhile, at Augusta Bay, Churchill and Roosevelt were outlining their ideas on the postwar world. The end-product, the Atlantic Charter, endorsed the time-honored and time-worn Western principles: a permanent security system, self-determination, and free trade. Churchill had carefully excluded Roosevelt's anti-colonialism from the Charter, and all that remained was their common opposition to dictatorships such as the Soviet Union. Stalin understood quite well that the Charter was apparently directed against the Soviet Union, and he complained of this to Eden. Nonetheless, he subscribed to the Charter—even after the last-minute insertion of a freedom-of-religion clause—by signing the United Nations Declaration on January 1, 1942. The high morality and vague promises of the Charter committed the Soviet Union—and the West, for that matter—to very little. Stalin was interested in deeds—treaties, pledges, pacts—not in words or morality. As Eden commented, "Soviet policy is amoral: United States policy is exaggeratedly moral, at least where non-American interests are concerned." [62]

Stalin began his drive for a firm postwar system at the Moscow Three Power Conference on Supplies in September 1941. He pointed out to Lord Beaverbrook and Averell Harriman that the current Anglo-Soviet Pact, signed in haste in July 1941, was insufficient. That treaty committed the participants only to mutual aid, with neither party making a separate peace with Germany. A firmer commitment, particularly a postwar alliance, was needed by the Soviet Union. Shortly thereafter Harriman warned Eden that the Russians would be highly offended by a failure to respond to this proposal. Despite this, the British were not willing to negotiate. Eden decided it was impossible "at this stage to formulate our peace aims for discussion with our allies more definitely than had been done in the Atlantic Charter." As Harriman had predicted, Stalin reacted angrily. The question of an alliance became a major threat to Anglo-Soviet relations, and Churchill decided to send Eden to Moscow to soothe the Russians.

During Eden's week in Moscow in mid-December, 1941, Stalin presented two draft Anglo-Soviet treaties to him. One of them concerned the postwar organization of the peace and called for a council of the victorious powers backed up with military forces. Stalin indicated that he had no objections to postwar European federations, which the British were considering. Eden said that Britain and the Soviet Union had similar ideas, but a formal treaty was not possible at that time.[63]

With the entry of the United States into the war in December, the initiative on postwar organization shifted from the Soviet Union to the United States. In May 1942 Molotov visited Washington, seeking an agreement for the West to open a second invasion front. Roosevelt found "the Russians are a bit down in the mouth at present," and advanced various plans to help or placate the Russians. He did not overlook the advantages of an effective postwar security organization for the Soviet Union. Roosevelt explained why the League of Nations had failed and how the new organization would differ: it would have concentrated police power; present enemies would be disarmed; small nations which disturbed the peace, possibly including France, would be controlled. The Soviet Union, Great Britain, the United States, and perhaps China should act jointly to suppress future trouble. Molotov asked whether other countries might not resent this. The President said possibly so, but he did not retract his idea. He pointedly raised the issue of trusteeships, and told Molotov that the islands held by the British should be placed under an international trusteeship, since they "ought not to belong to any one nation." Stalin might "profitably consider the establishment of some form of international trusteeship" over islands controlled by weak nations.

During the conversation, Molotov praised Roosevelt's views as realistic and supported both the postwar organization as outlined and the concept of trusteeships. Stalin, Molotov said, "thoroughly appreciated the role played by the United States in the initiation of such proposals." Indeed, from that point on the Soviet Union deferred to American policy on a postwar organization.[64]

Roosevelt continued to develop his vision. During Eden's visit to Washington in March 1943, the President said that the new world organization should consist of a general assembly, an advisory council of the Great Powers, and an executive council of the Big Three plus China. Roosevelt elaborated his scheme at a private dinner with Eden and Hopkins. After the war, armaments should be concentrated in the hands of Britain, Russia, and the United States. The Big Three would collectively supervise, but individually garrison, bases or "strong points" throughout the world. Eden scorned the idea. Roosevelt, he wrote, "seemed to be ignoring the obvious difficulty of disarming neutral countries, but I did not take this idea as a serious proposal and it passed with little comment." [65]

The British were working on their own scheme. Churchill suggested a system of regional blocs—specifically, one council each for Europe, Asia, and America—under the minimal control of a worldwide supervisory organization. Churchill's system contained a few unstated but important premises: for example, the Council of Europe would consist of a West European bloc led by Britain, and an Eastern European "federation" or *cordon sanitaire* directed against the Soviet Union. Roosevelt, aware of the implications for the United States' sphere of influence in Latin America, showed some interest in the British proposal, but his Secretary of State, Cordell Hull, firmly vetoed it.

Cordell Hull and his advisory subcommittee at the State Department had their own ideas and, what was more, had the stubbornness to see them through. As George Kennan commented, the United Nations "represented, as it seemed, the escape of the Secretary of State from the frustrations occasioned by his exclusion from the province of policy-making while the war was on." Hull felt that the United States should follow "a diplomacy of principle—of moral disinterestedness instead of power politics." To Hull, the "diplomacy of principle" meant Russia's and Britain's submission to American "principle" as interpreted in Washington. Failure to capitulate, or even hesitation, was "unco-operativeness." When Hull unveiled his "Declaration of General Security," the British promptly endorsed it. At the Quebec Conference of August 1943, they accepted it unconditionally. The Soviet Union, however, failed to give an immediate answer. Assuming the worst, Hull set out to slay the suspected evil-doers.

At the October 1943 Foreign Ministers' Conference in Moscow, Hull lectured Molotov on the necessity of international co-operation. He warned that "isolationism" or an attempt to "gobble up your neighbors" would "be your undoing." Instead, the Soviet Union should "co-operate," that is, should acquiesce in American policy (which the Soviets feared was increasingly directed toward negotiating them out of their legitimate interests). Hull's lecture was superfluous and his fear unfounded; Molotov had said at the outset that agreement should be reached on the world organization. Further, to Hull's admitted surprise, Molotov accepted the American Declaration, stating that "The Soviet government was very favorably disposed toward the principles set forth in this Declaration and therefore welcome it."

The real problem was less Russia's intention on this point than it was Hull's. The Soviets saw the world organization as a powerful peace-keeping mechanism, important to the protection of Soviet security and the elevation of the U.S.S.R. to Great Power status; Hull saw it as an instrument of American foreign policy, designed to maintain America's position as a Great Power and to keep the Soviet Union in the position of a lesser power, subordinate to Washington. The difficulties that arose concerning the Declaration were a result of Hull's criteria for measuring "co-operation." For example, one criterion he insisted upon was the Allies' willingness to accept a fourth "world policeman," China. But China was actually a very weak nation, protected largely by American patronage. Even Churchill grumbled: "As to China, I cannot regard the Chungking Government as representing a great world Power. Certainly there would be a faggot vote on the side of the United States in any attempt to liquidate the British overseas Empire." Molotov pointed out that China was weak and could not be counted on to make the Declaration effective. Nonetheless, he and Eden bowed to Hull's demands. China was elevated to Great Power status, and thus the Declaration of the *Four* Nations on General Security could be signed on October 30, 1943. The Soviet Union and Britain both clearly realized that Roosevelt's intent was to bias the central authority of the new organization toward the United States: as Hopkins put it, "The

President feels that China, in any serious conflict of policy with Russia, would undoubtedly line up on our side." [66]

The world organization was again discussed at Teheran. Roosevelt, who had told Churchill "I think I can personally handle Stalin better than either your Foreign Office or my State Department," met privately with Stalin on November 29 to explain his evolving plans. The President suggested that the world organization consist of three main bodies: an Assembly for discussion and recommendations; an Executive Committee—the Soviet Union, the United States, Britain, China, and others—to deal with all nonmilitary questions; and lastly, "The Four Policemen"—America, Russia, Britain, and China—as the enforcing agency against acts of aggression. Stalin did not reject the President's proposals, but he explored their implication. Would the Assembly be European or worldwide? Roosevelt thought the latter. Would the Executive Committee have the right to make binding decisions? Roosevelt had not investigated the question, but he suspected that Congress would not permit the United States to be bound by the Committee's decisions. Most significantly, would the small nations of Europe favor such a scheme, and further, would not Europe resent China as an enforcement authority? * Stalin recommended an alternative plan: that there be one committee for Europe and one for the Far East. Roosevelt said this was similar to Churchill's scheme of regional committees, and he doubted "that the Congress would agree to American participation in a purely European committee which might be able to compel the involvement of American troops." Stalin asked whether American troops would ever be sent overseas as part of the "Four Policemen" concept. Roosevelt replied that, in the future, land armies would have to be provided by Britain and the Soviet Union.

Stalin, although willing to defer to the American plan, was displeased by its vagueness. The President stated prior to the

---

* Churchill, when he heard of the discussion "much later," noted, "in this the Soviet leader certainly showed himself more prescient and possessed of a truer sense of values than the President." Churchill, *Closing the Ring*, p. 363.

Teheran Conference that he would appeal to Stalin "on grounds of high morality." But Stalin pursued specifics, not principles. He seized on the President's own proposal of "strong points," and recommended they be established not only within Germany and Japan but near their borders as "safeguards." Further, the security organization should "have the power not only to make decisions in times of emergency but to have continued military occupation of the necessary bases." Roosevelt replied that his "agreement with Marshal Stalin on this was one hundred per cent."

Trusteeships were not directly discussed, but Churchill, at a dinner discussion about control of strategic bases, felt that there was an implicit threat to the British Empire. Britain did not aspire to gain new territory, he said, but she intended to keep what she had and "reclaim what had been taken from her" and would not be "compelled to give up anything without a war." Stalin complimented Britain on her war contribution: he personally favored gains for Britain. Churchill in turn asked Stalin what territorial interests the Soviet Union might have. Stalin replied, "There is no need to speak at the present time about any Soviet desires—but when the time comes, we will speak." [67]

Throughout the spring of 1944, the Allies circulated ideas about the world organization. Britain continued to worry about the anticolonial implication of Roosevelt's increasingly global concept. In May, Churchill told Eden, "You should make it clear that we have no idea of three or four Great Powers ruling the world," or, in particular, of ruling the British Empire. The British viewpoint was presented in a Foreign Office paper entitled "Future World Organization." It recommended a three-part structure—council, assembly, secretariat—for the "United Nations," as Eden proposed to call the new organization. Further, he advocated a military staff committee as an adjunct to the council. Member states would provide military forces which, at the council's discretion, would be used to garrison or occupy specified areas.[68]

Hull's ideas were essentially the same, and he decided that the moment was propitious "for unity especially among the United States, Russia, and Great Britain." Action seemed vital, because "malcontents in this country were doing their best to drive Russia out of the international movement." Hull wanted "to keep Russia solidly in the international movement" *as he conceived it.*[69] On May 30, 1944, while the State Department was drafting its viewpoint on the United Nations, Hull invited the Allies to a conference (Dumbarton Oaks) to discuss the issues. Britain responded quickly, but the Soviet Union, unimpressed with the generality of ideas emanating from London and Washington and preoccupied with military matters, delayed accepting the invitation until July 9.

The American proposals, circulated in mid-July, gave both Britain and the Soviet Union food for thought. Roosevelt had rejected a Soviet proposal for a political-military commission. He now believed that the United Nations Organization should be a fully representative body rather than a coercive superstate (to which he had agreed and Churchill had objected), and that the Allies, after reaching agreement, should submit their plan to the other United Nations for discussion. The Soviets observed that Roosevelt's opinions had changed, but they did not complain. Instead, they asked for time to study the American proposal. So did the British. By the time the Dumbarton Oaks Conference opened on August 21, 1944, all three Allied governments had prepared tentative drafts.

The decisions taken at Dumbarton Oaks gave the United Nations Organization a final structure—General Assembly, Security Council, Secretariat, International Court of Justice, Economic and Social Council. As Hull noted, the final structure incorporated "all the essential points" of the American proposal, and yet "was not dissimilar from the original views of the British and the Russians either." Roosevelt's "Executive Council" emerged as the Security Council, which had the power to investigate disputes and also to recommend or undertake action against disturbances of the peace. The Security Council would consist of permanent members who had veto powers, and non-permanent members, elected in rotating fashion, who did not. The General Assembly was defined as a representative body in which each member nation had one vote. Its function was to discuss and to recommend. The British and Soviet delegations had advocated a lesser role for the Assembly, but, in Hull's words, during the opening days of the conference they "substantially accepted our viewpoint." [70]

On the question of the military structure of the United Nations the United States view prevailed. The Soviet draft had attempted to give some real peace-keeping power to the executive council. The Soviets had tailored their ideas to Roosevelt's previous remarks about "strong points" and the "Four Policemen," and about America's probable inability to contribute land forces to future peace-keeping ventures. Specifically, the Soviet draft called for an international air force commanded by the executive council. Nations unable to contribute armed forces would contribute bases, or "strong points."

Roosevelt and Hull rejected the draft, including the ideas they had previously advocated. They suggested that the United Nations should not have its own air force, but should use instead air contingents provided by member states. They also rejected the "strong point" idea, for reasons similar to Molotov's original doubts: "Both the President and I [Hull] strongly objected to this provision as being an infringement on the sovereign rights of smaller countries." With the rejection of the Soviet proposals (incorporating the previously stated American position), the Soviet representative at Dumbarton Oaks, Ambassador Andrei Gromyko, immediately cabled Moscow for permission to withdraw the Soviet draft. Viewing the withdrawal as "co-operative," Hull hailed this as one of the "decisions by his [Gromyko's] Government which enabled the conference to reach a still further degree of agreement." [71]

Two major issues—membership in the United Nations and a voting formula in the Security Council—were not resolved at Dumbarton Oaks and continued to trouble the Big Three until Yalta. The Western positions, and particularly the American positions, on these two issues raised grave doubts in the Soviet Union regarding Allied intentions. A preliminary question which portended future difficulty was that of permanent membership for the Security Council. Although the Big Three were supposed to be dominant, the United States had been insisting on the inclusion of China. Both Britain and the Soviet Union felt that, on the basis of contribution to the war effort, China had little claim to Great Power status, but both submitted to America's demands. As compensation, Britain had requested permanent membership in the Security Council for France, which Britain hoped to rehabilitate as her dependency in the postwar Western European Bloc. French participation in the Security Council would create equal strength for Britain and the United States, each having what Churchill called a "faggot" vote. Roosevelt agreed to the inclusion of France, on the condition she have a suitable government; the Soviets unconditionally concurred.

Then Roosevelt tried to add one of America's Latin American backers, Brazil, to the Council. The addition of Brazil would have given America one vote more than Britain, and would have left the Soviet Union alone against five Western votes. Roosevelt considered "the Brazilian matter was a card up his sleeve"; actually it only served to arouse the British and, even more, to alarm the Soviets, who began to see in America's version of a "co-operative postwar security organization" the power to isolate the U.S.S.R. just as in the League of Nations. America's attempt to add another "faggot vote" backfired. From this point on the Soviets retreated to an "absolute veto" as the only method of protecting the Soviet Union from potentially hostile action.[72]

Another unsolved question—membership in the General Assembly—provided further evidence to the Soviet Union that she would be isolated in the United Nations. The Soviet Union and the United States agreed that the nations which signed the United Nations Declaration would be members. The Soviet interpretation of the agreement was that only the twenty-six original signatories who were also fighting against Hitler would be included. The United States wanted to add six Latin American Republics as well as Iceland and Egypt, nations that had not declared war against the Axis but that had "associated" themselves with the Allied cause. Britain was already fortified by six Commonwealth votes, and the United States was seeking increased backing at every turn. In defense, and to the American delegation's "shock," Gromyko suddenly proposed including all sixteen of the Soviet Republics. Gromyko and Stalin argued, as the United States had done on Brazil, that the Soviet Republics, through their size and their contribution to the war, had earned a place in the structure of the United Nations. Stalin cabled Roosevelt, "You, of course, know that the Ukraine and Belorussia, which are constituent parts of the Soviet Union, are greater in population and in political importance than certain other countries. . . ." [73]

In any case, Stettinius and Lord Cadogan (then Britain's Foreign Secretary), who had been busily packing the General Assembly with their supporters, were left "breathless" at the Soviets' audacity in trying the same tactic they themselves were attempting. When Hull was informed that the Soviets might suggest new members, he fumed, "Are these Russians going to break up our hope of a world organization?" It was "so explosive an issue" that State called it "the X matter." Roosevelt's reaction was the same as that of his subordinates: the United States "could under no conditions accept such a proposal," especially with the presidential election campaign in full swing. Stettinius was given the job of silencing Gromyko. When Stettinius approached Gromyko on August 29, the Soviet Ambassador "agreed that there should be no further reference to it during the Conference." Hull was delighted that "Gromyko proved most co-operative." Stettinius, hoping to dispose of the question entirely, suggested that the issue be handled by the Security Council itself at a later date, but Gromyko replied "that on some other occasion his Government would probably raise the question again." [74]

A final unresolved issue discussed at Dumbarton Oaks—and one which looked as if it would plague the Yalta Conference—was that of an acceptable voting procedure for the Security Council. The three powers had similar ideas. Each nation wanted to retain the right of veto, which meant that each nation insisted on unanimity among the Great Powers in questions of security—according to Hull, "We were no less resolute than the Russians in adhering to this principle." (One of the great difficulties, which has caused a good deal of name-calling ever since, was that the Allies made no clear distinction between a "vote" and a "veto" in the Security Council. Today, the closest equivalent to a negative "vote" by one of the Great Powers would be an "abstention," but at the time of these first discussions—and decisions—the words "vote" and "veto" were used interchange-ably, and their precise meaning was left ambiguous.)

The question was to what extent the veto should apply in the discussions and decisions of the Council. Two days before the Dumbarton Oaks Conference opened, Hull and Roosevelt agreed that "the Executive Council should not be given the right to im-pose the terms of settlement of a dispute." The British and Rus-sians, on the other hand, wanted a firmer guarantee of peace, while, at the same time, they sought to protect themselves from adverse action.

In his July 18 draft Roosevelt had adopted the British argu-ment that the votes of nations involved in cases before the Coun-cil should not be counted in the Council's decisions. It was not clear under this formula whether a permanent member could veto enforcement action against his own nation. Britain and the United States sought a clarification, but Gromyko rejected the entire idea, especially after he saw the heavily stacked Assembly and the predominantly Western Security Council replace the original tripartite unit. He told Stettinius, "The Russian posi-tion on voting in the Council will never be departed from." [75]

The dispute over the veto produced some sharp disagree-ments. None of the Allies was willing to submit to a decision against itself; therefore, they all agreed that 'substantive deci-sions" would require a majority of the Security Council, includ-ing the concurring votes of all the permanent members. (Of course, the nagging problem of what constituted a "substantive decision" also arose.) A majority, without distinction between permanent and non-permanent members, would suffice for proce-dural questions. But what *was* a majority? The British favored a two-thirds majority, the Russians a simple majority. Roosevelt also favored a two-thirds majority, even though he had earlier recommended a simple majority. By the end of the Conference, this question of "majority," along with the problems of the mem-bership and the right of disputants to veto action in cases involv-ing themselves, was left unresolved.

As the participants left Dumbarton Oaks, Hull stated that "all the essential points in the tentative draft" of July 18 had been accepted by the Conference. The Secretary complimented Gromyko "very highly on his excellent showing as head of his delegation. I expressed this compliment in all sincerity, for the Russians had in general shown an admirable co-operation from the first day of the conference." Yet Hull by no means had forgiven the Soviet Union for daring to have its own ideas. He soon cabled Harriman to ask why the Soviets had decided "to reverse the policies 'apparently' decided on at Moscow and Teheran of co-operation with the Western Allies and to pursue a contrary course." [76]

Indeed, the Soviet government decided by mid-September that "the principle of the unanimity of the four Great Powers was inviolable," and concluded that, even if a permanent member were party to a dispute, that member's vote or veto should count. While the State Department continued to agonize about this insistence on an "absolute veto," Prime Minister Churchill and President Roosevelt came to the same conclusion as the Soviets had. After Dumbarton Oaks, Churchill cabled the President: "The point of Dumbarton Oaks will certainly come up, and I must tell you that we are pretty clear that the only hope is that the Great Powers are agreed, i.e., unanimous. It is with regret that I have come to this conclusion, contrary to my first thought." Roosevelt asked Churchill, who was about to go to Moscow, not to discuss this change of heart with Stalin, and the Prime Minister agreed. But Roosevelt had also changed his mind. By November 15, he concluded "that it is necessary for us to accept a compromise solution, in view of the fact that it is unlikely that this country, in the final analysis, would agree to our not having a vote on any serious or acute situation in which we may be involved." [77]

In early December the United States dealt with the offending issue and proposed that a permanent member of the Council be allowed to use his veto in determining actions against a threat to peace even if that member were involved in the dispute. Harriman reported from Moscow that the "Foreign Office is evidently trying to puzzle out and understand the meaning and implications of the proposals." By this time such a modification still did not dispose of Soviet objections, because unanimity of the Great

Powers was violated in the case of recommendations for peaceful settlements if a permanent member were party to the dispute, in which instance that Power could not vote. Stalin wired Roosevelt, "I have, to my regret, to inform you . . . that I see no possibility of agreeing." The Marshal insisted, and Churchill now agreed, on not violating the unanimity rule. Stalin warned, "Such a situation is in contradiction with the principle of agreement and unanimity of decisions." [78]

Within two weeks, Roosevelt was echoing Stalin's concern over the inadequacy of even the revised American formula. In a conversation with Stettinius's special assistant, Pasvolsky, the President asked what would happen in the United Nations in "a dispute between us and Mexico over oil." The American formula, in the process of refinement, confused everyone but the State Department, which understood fully what the American proposal meant and had, for its own consideration, separated out the issues. Pasvolsky explained to the President how the United States was protected against possible action against her in a dispute with Mexico. Roosevelt thereupon replied "that the formula should take care not only of our position, but of the Soviet position as well." [79]

Meanwhile, the State Department attempted to convince Ambassador Gromyko of what the formula would mean in practice. Pasvolsky told Gromyko that "from our point of view the President's formula represents a substantial modification of the position which we took at Dumbarton Oaks." Yet he also said, "it is true that the President's formula is very similar to the formula which was tentatively worked out at Dumbarton Oaks." Gromyko was satisfied by these lengthy discussions: he was assured that both sides held more or less the same ideas. The State Department recognized "that the Ambassador's mind was not closed on this subject and that he was quite anxious to be in a position to present the matter fully to his government." [80]

The British government, after inquiring into the seemingly ambiguous American proposal, produced an ambiguous response. Washington was notified that Britain accepted the American revision, but actually Churchill rejected it. Stettinius admitted that on the eve of Yalta Churchill was still wavering: "The Prime

Minister had made it plain that he himself was not committed to the American proposal." Stettinius considered this evidence that "the Prime Minister had not as yet applied his mind to this difficult problem." The Cabinet and Foreign Office were also in conflict. Sir Stafford Cripps argued that the Soviet formula of complete unanimity offered more protection to British interests, and Churchill agreed.[81] All these ambiguities, doubts, and divisions would have to be worked out around the council table at Yalta.

RUSSIA AND JAPAN

From the onset of fighting in 1941 Stalin considered joining the war against Japan. The clearest indication of his intention came in December 1941, during Eden's visit to Moscow. At one point Eden confessed that Britain faced grave difficulties in the Far East. Stalin correctly interpreted this statement as a request for help in the war with Japan. He immediately apologized for not being able at the moment to do anything. Eden, who wanted to avoid negotiating a *quid pro quo*, said he was not suggesting that. Stalin replied: "I appreciate your attitude. We can do nothing now, but in the spring we shall be ready, and will then help." At this moment Soviet armies had the Germans temporarily on the defensive and enthusiastic estimates predicting Soviet success were running high. Stalin was even proclaiming "Victory in 1942," with more than just propaganda in mind.

At another session, Eden asked if it was correct that, although the Soviet Union could do nothing now, her position would be different in the spring. Stalin replied that the real variable was lack of preparedness. When Russia declared war it would wage more than a token fight. Since Soviet troops had been withdrawn from the Far East in order to fight on the western front, four months would be needed to supply replacements on the Chinese border. Stalin emphasized that a Japanese attack on the Soviet Union would ease matters from a legal standpoint. "We would prefer that Japan should attack us, and I think it very probable that she will do so—not just yet, but later." Stalin anticipated that by the middle of next year, the hard-pressed Germans would most likely urge Japan to attack in order to force Russia into a two-front war.[82]

Stalin gave similar assurances to the Americans. In Moscow, during Cordell Hull's visit in October 1943, Stalin raised the topic of his own volition, "unequivocally" promising to join the war. He told Hull he could "inform President Roosevelt of this in the strictest confidence." Hull was so overwhelmed by this information that he decided to send half of his message to Roosevelt by Army code and half by Navy code to protect its secrecy. At the same time, Molotov assured Eden that the Russians expected only a short interval between the collapse of Germany and the defeat of Japan. Eden foresaw (as the Americans did) a much longer struggle, but Molotov was persistent and, as subsequent events were to prove, correct. Eden left Moscow with the impression that Britain and America could rely on Russia's forthcoming participation.[83]

The culmination came at Teheran in December 1943. When the wartime leaders met together for the first time at this tripartite gathering, Stalin confirmed his pledge to join the war against Japan once Germany was defeated. "We shall be able by our common front to beat Japan," he said. Roosevelt took the initiative by proposing that the Soviets might thereby gain access to Darien in Manchuria. Unknown to Stalin, Roosevelt had already cleared this with Chiang, but Stalin, to lay a correct basis for agreement, asked the President whether the Chinese would approve this and Roosevelt said he thought so. Territorial arrangements were then dropped, but once broached, the subject would arise again.[84]

After the Teheran Conference, Stalin immediately began preparations for the war. According to Chief Marshal of the Artillery N. N. Voronov, Stalin's "important news" from Teheran for the Soviet military was his acceptance of Churchill's and Roosevelt's proposal to participate in the war against imperialist Japan three or four months after the completion of the war in Europe. Stalin had begun to formulate his terms: "He told us that we had to utilize the favorable international situation to regain everything that Japan had grabbed as a result of the Russo-Japanese War." Stalin added, "However, we don't want anything that does not belong to us." He insisted that this decision must remain secret and forbade anyone to speak of it from then on, but, to facilitate preparations, he began piecemeal shipments of ammunition to places on the Amur River, "evoking great wonder among the people who participated in any way in its shipment." Voronov recorded that the Far East command, unaware of the purpose of the build-up, complained of the large supplies wasted in shipment to the Far East instead of to the German front. This flow of supplies continued during the year and a half before the Soviet entry into the Far East war.[85]

In February 1944, Harriman again pressed Stalin to set a date for the entry of the Soviets into the war against Japan, but Stalin said the Soviet Union dare not attack prematurely, suffer a rebuff, and lose bases.[86] When Churchill and Eden visited Moscow in October 1944, the war in the Far East was discussed once more. Churchill was ill (the British delegation feared pneumonia, but the Prime Minister "rallied splendidly") so Eden replaced him in a session with Stalin, Antonov, Harriman, and Deane to discuss the Far East. Stalin announced specific requirements for the Soviet land attack, which he estimated would occur about three months after Germany was finished. General Antonov, who, Eden said, "always looked to Stalin for confirmation," talked of using the Trans-Siberian Railway for transfers to the Far East without mentioning the fact that shipments had already been started. Stalin obviously did not believe that the Japanese would stand by idly while the Russians carried out a heavy build-up: "If they do attack, they will at least solve what will be my most difficult problem with my own people. It will be obvious who is the aggressor." Stalin made specific conditions for participating in the war against Japan: a solution to the problem of stocking weapons and supplies for Russia, and clarification of political terms.[87]

Eden agreed that there was no need for Britain to sit in on the later discussion of the specific requirements of Soviet troops in the East. Harriman noted that, during this second session, on October 17, "Stalin gave us in considerably greater detail the Soviet strategy, indicating quite frankly his weakness in certain areas." Stalin further reminded his American Allies of a recent conversation between Gromyko and Hopkins, in which Hopkins had indicated that Stalin and Roosevelt could "come to a definite agreement on the political as well as the military aspects." * Stalin agreed with the Americans that planning should start immediately for a final settlement at the forthcoming tripartite conference. He displayed a tough attitude toward Japan; according to Harriman, he "spoke emphatically about his determination" and used terms like "break Japan's spine." [88]

As fate had it, Churchill did not participate in either of the two Moscow sessions devoted to the subject, yet his observations corroborated Stalin's eagerness to prepare for war. He cabled Roosevelt from Moscow that he found "an extraordinary atmosphere of goodwill" and that Stalin in a luncheon speech "animadverted harshly upon Japan as being an aggressor nation." The Prime Minister concluded, "I have little doubt from our talks that he will declare war upon them as soon as Germany is beaten."

Churchill had other matters on his mind as well, among them Britain's share in the Far Eastern preparations and political spoils. He admonished Roosevelt: "Surely Averell and Deane should be in a position not merely to ask him [Stalin] to do certain things, but also to tell him," for example, "the kind of things you are going to do yourself, and *we are going to help you to do*." But General Marshall, on behalf of the Joint Chiefs of Staff, had concluded two months before that England would not emerge from the war as a major military power in the Far East. Eden, who in July had admitted he wanted to find "the best way of bringing our weight to bear" had to recognize that this "is not a heavy weight in the Far East." Hence, in July and August, Churchill and Eden, with their Defence Committee, had formulated plans to participate actively in the Far East, and by August 10 Eden could write in his diary, "We are, I think, 'home' as far

* As will be noted again (p. 107), Sherwood incorrectly placed the Gromyko-Hopkins conversation in November. Harriman's memorandum to Roosevelt also placed that conversation in November. This is clearly an editing error, since the memorandum itself is dated October 17, 1944. See *YD*, Harriman to Roosevelt, p. 370; Sherwood, *Roosevelt and Hopkins*, pp. 843–45.

as our plans are concerned. . . . But we are very late." [89] As Churchill feared, Roosevelt continued to consult with Stalin as if Britain had—or would have after the war—little interest in the Far East.

By December, only a few weeks before the Yalta Conference, Stalin was prepared to put his commitment and his political demands in writing. He showed Ambassador Harriman a map and told him what Russia wanted. The items were basically those mentioned at the time of Teheran—the Kurile Islands, Southern Sakhalin, a lease on Port Arthur and Darien, and a lease on the Chinese-Eastern Railway, plus maintenance of the status quo in Outer Mongolia. Stalin was quite willing to modify his demands. He assured Harriman that he deferred to the American desire to preserve China intact (including her reactionary institutions), and that he had no intention of infringing on Chinese sovereignty by encroaching on Manchuria. When Harriman remarked that President Roosevelt preferred an international port rather than a lease in the Liaotung Peninsula, Stalin agreed, "(This can be discussed.) " [90] At Yalta, this issue and the others relating to the Far East were discussed and amicably settled.

CHAPTER 2

THE SETTING

"We Three Should Meet"

"I do think it important that we three should meet in the near future," [1] Roosevelt wrote Churchill in November 1944. This idea had been on the President's mind and in his communications to Stalin and Churchill since July, when the Soviets launched a major offensive to relieve the newly opened Normandy front. The Red Army, marching through Belorussia (White Russia) at a rate of ten or fifteen miles a day, had inflicted the gravest defeat in the history of the eastern front—according to the official German account—"a greater catastrophe than Stalingrad." [2] Soviet forces were in Poland, and the President was suddenly face to face with the political confusion created by the purposeful ambiguity of American policy, which Cordell Hull had once described as a policy of "no discussion . . . at this stage." [3] Allied diplomacy confronted a dilemma of its own making: how to engage Soviet troops in support of Western military measures and yet prevent the Soviet Union from reaping the natural rewards of its action. Clearly it would be impossible to resolve such a dilemma without the willing co-operation of the stronger partner. Secretary of War Stimson had said as much in mid-1943, when he wrote that if the Russians did most of the fighting "I think that will be dangerous business for us at the end of the war. Stalin won't have much of an opinion of people who have done that and we will not be able to share much of the postwar world with him." [4]

Despite the West's claim to having done its share (or more) through Lend-Lease aid to Russia, or through the campaigns in North Africa, Italy, and Normandy, the burden of the war in fact fell disproportionately on the Soviet Union. Andrei Grechko, Marshal of the Soviet Union, summed up the facts in *Pravda* on May 9, 1969, the twenty-fourth anniversary of V-E Day: "The Soviet-German Front was the most active, principal front of the Second World War. Pinned down here were *up to 70 per cent of the total combat-worthy forces* of the fascist bloc. It was on this front that enemy armies sustained the greatest losses, *nearly four times* as great as those incurred on all other fighting fronts." He also showed that no fundamental shift of forces took place after the Allied invasion of France. "Even after the second front was opened in Europe in June of 1944, most of the German fascist divisions were still on the Soviet-German front, as hitherto. . . ."

The dilemma posed by the offensive illustrated the Soviet Union's changed position during the last eighteen months of the war. The June military and July diplomatic offensives were direct outgrowths of the political commitment Stalin made at Teheran, to launch a major offensive against Germany at the time of the opening of the Anglo-American second front, "Operation Overlord."

Roosevelt placed singular importance on Russia's keeping this commitment and diverting the German armies in the east sufficiently to prevent troop transfers to the newly opened and initially weak western front. In accordance with this idea, Major General John Deane (in command of the special military mission to the Soviet Union) maintained pressure on Moscow to assure that nothing would go wrong. The Soviets were most co-operative and moved swiftly to fulfill their obligations. When General Deane informed the Red Army General Staff on April 7 that the invasion would take place on May 31, 1944, Chief of Staff Antonov guaranteed that the Red Army would attack on the same day.

Indeed, the question became how co-operative the West would be. Deane sensed and tried to combat the suspicion that the Western invasion would be postponed—as it had been twice before. In fact, during May and June 1944, Deane had to tell Antonov three times that the date had been changed. He recalled in his memoirs, "Each time I announced a postponement of even a day, my stock reached a new low." [5]

The Soviet command waited for confirmation of the Western offensive and then acted on Deane's information. Soviet General Vasili Chuikov, commander of the 8th Guards Army which later spearheaded the assault on Berlin, vividly described the sudden change at the end of May. His army had just completed its sweep from Stalingrad to a new bridgehead on the western bank of the Dniester. Chuikov's plans were to continue the successful move southward against the retreating Germans. On the night of May 27, a coded radio signal, "autumn, autumn," verified that no fresh German forces had appeared. Unexpectedly, without warning, everything changed. "What was being decided at G.H.Q., and how, was not known to me. Then suddenly the official decision: 'The Army is being transferred to one of the main lines of advance.'" The original campaign plan was scrapped, the troops were pulled back northward to join the First Belorussian Front, and on July 14, as Stalin had promised, a major offensive was started.[6]

This offensive generated political questions which America, reluctantly followed by Britain, had maneuvered to postpone until a general peace conference after the war. Stalin's armies were now in a position to decide unnegotiated issues virtually at will. The Red Army reoccupied the territory seized in 1939, including prewar eastern Poland. Despite Russia's unilateral incorporation of this territory into the Soviet Union in November 1939, the Polish government in exile had refused to deal with the fact. What Molotov had failed to gain by diplomatic means due to Polish opposition as well as Western postponement—namely, recognition of Russian gains from the Molotov-Ribbentrop Pact —the Red Army now achieved.

Skilled in sensing a shift in political power, Franklin D. Roosevelt did not overlook the political-military importance of the Soviet accomplishment. Earlier in the war he had told the British Ambassador to Washington outright that the future of such territories as the Baltic states clearly depended on Russian military progress.[7] That future was now clear. In July 1944 the Russians took Vilna, began the liberation of the rest of Poland, and scheduled operations in eastern Europe and the Balkans.

The President, then on a Pacific tour, moved quickly. On

July 17 he sent an enthusiastic cable to Stalin via Averell Harriman, the American Ambassador to Moscow, requesting a conference: "Your armies are doing so magnificently, . . ." he underlined in his cable. Harriman cautiously deleted this praise.[8] He had revised his estimate of Soviet intentions. In November 1941, Harriman had told the Polish Ambassador, Jan Ciechanowski, that his recent trip to Moscow proved to him that world revolution was no longer an aim of Russia, that Stalin was not a revolutionary communist but a Russian nationalist, and that Stalin's statements to the contrary were for domestic consumption.[9] Now Harriman was alarmed by Soviet successes outside the Soviet borders. He saw a pattern of conquest emerging in eastern Europe. He expressed his concern in a secret telegram to Secretary of State Stettinius on December 19, 1944, warning the American government of possible Soviet motives. On December 28, he again cabled the Secretary of State his view of Soviet designs.[10]

Despite Harriman's misgivings, Roosevelt suggested in his July message that a meeting must take place: "Things are moving so fast and so successfully that I feel there should be a meeting between you and Mr. Churchill and me in the reasonably near future." Churchill also wrote to Stalin, supporting the President's decision, but with less enthusiasm. The Prime Minister, in his letter of July 24, wrote as if he were host and—despite Stalin's reply—said there would be a meeting between himself and Roosevelt: "I need not say how earnestly His Majesty's Government and I personally hope you will be able to come. I know well your difficulties and how your movements must depend upon the situation at the front. . . . I am making preparations for the President and myself. . . ." [11]

Stalin responded hesitantly to the idea of a meeting. Negotiating with his Allies over questions they had formerly refused to decide was a poor substitute for the settlement of those questions by the Red Army. Stalin delayed any meeting. In the interim, the newly formed Provisional government of Poland had issued (on July 22) the "July Manifesto," which established the Curzon and Oder-Neisse lines as Poland's postwar boundaries. The day of the Manifesto, Stalin reiterated to Roosevelt his reason for declining an immediate meeting. "When the Soviet Armies are involved in battles on such a wide front, it would be impossible for me to leave the country"—he could not be distracted from matters at the front. He concluded, "All my colleagues consider it absolutely impossible." [12]

The offensive which Stalin mentioned substantially altered the future of eastern Europe. Unexpectedly, the central eastern front—the shortest route to Berlin—quieted, and the brunt of the Soviet attack was redirected toward the Soviet-Rumanian border. What might have been the deathblow to the German Reich before the end of 1944 became a widespread advance to liberate the Balkans from the Nazi grip. In effect, the Red Army, not the British, fulfilled Churchill's cherished dream: a sweep across the Balkans to destroy the Nazis in their satellite dependencies. The Soviet decision paralleled previous Allied decisions —all politically motivated—to fight the Germans in the furthermost Nazi outposts in North Africa, Sicily, and southern Italy. Now, in 1944, the West helplessly observed the inevitable: Soviet troops ensured the success of politically compatible indigenous forces, just as the Allies had done in their spheres of fighting.

The Red Army encountered a unique opportunity as it approached Warsaw in July. Although Soviet lines were overextended and the troops due for a rest, the Polish Home Army under Bor-Komorowski attempted, despite the misgivings of some members of the Polish exile government, to liberate Warsaw before the Red Army could reach the city. The Germans retaliated on a monumental scale: they annihilated the flower of Poland's old order, the supporters of the London government, and most of the citizens of Warsaw. The Soviets refused to alter their plans and become involved in the carnage.* They sent supplies and some Polish Communist brigades (most of which were destroyed, as Stalin had foreseen), and withstood the wrath of the West, which demanded that Soviet forces sacrifice themselves for a militarily unfeasible venture. The upshot was that the

---

* For the Soviet account of the considerations that went into these decisions, see *Istoriia velikoi otechestvennoi voiny*, IV, 243–52. Alexander Werth records his interview of August 26, 1944, with Marshal Rokossovsky on the Soviet armies' halt in his book, *Russia At War, 1941–1945*, pp. 795–97.

staunchest opposition to the Lublin Committee disappeared along with Warsaw. Although Stalin undoubtedly did not foresee or plan this, the Soviet Union was the sole beneficiary. Sizing up events as they unfolded, Stalin made the most of his opportunities. He allegedly told Tito eight months later: "This war is not as in the past; whoever occupies a territory also imposes his own social system. Everyone imposes his own system as far as his army can reach. It cannot be otherwise." [13]

At the time of the Warsaw uprising, Generals Ivan Petrov, Rodin Malinovsky, and F. I. Tolbukhin unleashed tremendous advances through Rumania in the direction of Bulgaria and Yugoslavia. The Germans were shocked; they had expected a continued attack along the Polish route. Within three days Hitler's quislings in Rumania were ousted. In a bold decision, switching allegiance from Germany to Russia, King Michael appointed a new government which readily accepted Moscow's armistice terms. The West, with propriety, did not intervene in Moscow's arrangements. Rumania declared war on Germany, and the Rumanian Army attached itself to the Red Army. Bulgaria, which had not even been at war with the Soviet Union, decided on immediate neutrality. Undeterred, the Soviets made a last-minute declaration of war and they invaded Bulgaria on September 5.[14]

As these events unfolded, Churchill and Roosevelt became increasingly apprehensive. Churchill told Lord Moran in August, 1944: "Good God, can't you see that the Russians are spreading across Europe like a tide." The Prime Minister feared the possible political consequences for Britain's Mediterranean and Near Eastern policy. He exclaimed, "There is nothing to prevent them from marching into Turkey and Greece." [15]

Roosevelt saw the necessity for action. Secretary of State Stettinius recorded in his memoirs the thinking in American circles: "By 1944, . . . the progress of the war, particularly in the Balkans, made it clear that some agreement on specific details regarding Europe's postwar problems had to be made." He recalled that "for months" Roosevelt thought there must be another meeting of the three leaders because "by late 1944 the course of the war had undergone drastic changes. . . . The second front was now a reality. The Red Army had driven the Germans from

Russian soil and were *now well into the fortress of Europe."* Stettinius knew that it was not only a question of the emerging power of the Soviet Union. The President also wanted military concessions from Russia: "Planning was vital for the final attack on Germany and to bring the Soviet Union into the Far Eastern war." [16] At the end of September, Roosevelt made his second serious bid for a Big Three conference. Stalin, although not so adamant in his refusal as he had been prior to the Balkan offensive, still hedged. Ambassador Harriman conveyed the President's request and pointed out that the proposed meeting was two months away. Stalin replied that a meeting was "very desirable," but unfortunately not likely, since his health did not permit travel. Stalin did not refuse a meeting outright; instead, he suggested that Churchill and Roosevelt meet with Molotov rather than with him,[17] which would have meant discussions, but no binding decisions. In this way Stalin catered to the Allied request for a conference without incurring a commitment.

The Allies next presented an apparent variation: a request that Churchill visit Russia and settle the political issues of eastern Europe. Stalin knew that the Prime Minister and the President had conferred two weeks earlier in Quebec, with a view to co-ordinating strategy, and (to Stalin) suspiciously close to the end of the meeting, Roosevelt requested a Big Three conference. On September 27 Roosevelt's request was followed by a letter from Churchill, who wrote Stalin that "on the agreement of our three nations, Britain, United States of America and U.S.S.R. stand the hopes of the world." He also invited himself to Moscow.

It was natural for Stalin to assume that Churchill was coming to Moscow as the representative of both British and American interests. Accordingly, he replied to Churchill: "I share your conviction that firm agreement between the *three* leading powers constitutes a true guarantee of future peace. . . . Certainly I should like very much to meet you and the President. . . . I wholeheartedly welcome your desire to come to Moscow in October. . . ." [18]

The first hint Stalin had that his assumption was incorrect came in a baffling communication from the President, just as the

Red Army reached the Danube. Roosevelt strongly urged Stalin that Russia should join in the war against Japan at that time. With greater relevance, Roosevelt expressed reserve, if not dismay, over the forthcoming visit of the Prime Minister. He wrote "I am firmly convinced that the three of us, and only the three of us, can find the solution to the still unresolved questions." Although he appreciated Churchill's desire for a meeting, the United States could not be bound by the discussion. He preferred to consider the talks a "preliminary" to a meeting of "the three of us." [19]

Clearly, there was no accord between the Atlantic partners. Stalin realized this, and he wrote Roosevelt that the President's message "somewhat puzzled me. . . . It is unknown to me with what questions Mr. Churchill and Mr. Eden are going to Moscow." Stalin continued to profess ignorance, as if both he and Roosevelt had to wait to learn the purpose of the British visit. With the propriety of a tripartite partner, he concluded: "In the future I will keep you informed about the matter, after the meeting with Mr. Churchill." [20] Stalin may have been baffled, but he was not entirely in the dark about what issues were urgent enough to bring the Prime Minister to Moscow on the spur of the moment. Foreign Secretary Eden recorded in his diary that he and Churchill had communicated to Stalin the necessity to meet and to discuss "both Poland and the Balkans, as well as war plans." [21]

The October meeting in Moscow between Stalin and Churchill was the critical turning point in Stalin's attitude toward a general tripartite conference. If Stalin had qualms that a conference would complicate his unilateral arrangements for the Balkans and eastern Europe, the meeting with Churchill dispelled them. At Moscow, "capitalist" Britain and "communist" Russia entered into an arrangement which, from Roosevelt's point of view, was most unusual. Churchill, who thought at that time that "it was natural that Russian ambitions should grow," proposed to draw a line in the Balkans, dividing spheres of responsibility. Stalin, whose attempt by diplomacy to obtain a much smaller geographic area had proved abortive in 1941 and 1942, was co-operative, despite his realization that the United States opposed such territorial sanctions.

An agreement was reached quite simply. The Prime Minister found the moment "apt for business," and said: "Let us settle about our affairs in the Balkans. Your armies are in Rumania and Bulgaria. We have interests, missions, and agents there. Don't let us get at cross-purposes in small ways." He proceeded to suggest that Soviet Russia's interest predominate in 90 per cent of Rumania and 75 per cent of Bulgaria, and that Great Britain have a 90 per cent "say" in Greece. Finally he suggested that both "go fifty-fifty" in Yugoslavia and Hungary.

Churchill shoved a piece of paper in Stalin's direction, and Stalin checked his approval with a mark. As Churchill described the occurrence: "After this there was a long silence. The pencilled paper lay in the center of the table. At length I said 'Might it not be thought rather cynical if it seemed we had disposed of these issues, so fateful to millions of people, in such an offhand manner? Let us burn the paper.' 'No, you keep it,' said Stalin." [22]

On the basis of the mutually satisfactory October meeting, Stalin began to see that the three leaders could perhaps resolve outstanding conflicts. Toward the end of the Prime Minister's visit, Stalin wrote Roosevelt with renewed warmth and open eagerness in favor of a Big Three conference: he "would extremely welcome the realization of this intention." He informed the President that "it has been clarified that we can, without great difficulties, adjust our policy on all questions standing before us." Stalin now saw the "definite" solution of "all urgent questions of our mutual interest" based on the pattern of the Moscow conversations.[23] Coalition diplomacy was at last working.

Roosevelt's favorable response reinforced Stalin's interpretation: "I am sure that the progress made during your conversations in Moscow will facilitate and expedite our work in the next meeting when the three of us should come to a full agreement on our future activities and policies and mutual interests." Stalin's enthusiasm grew. By October 28, he found it "extremely desirable to realize this plan for a meeting," and he stated unreservedly, "The conditions for a meeting there are absolutely favorable." [24]

Now Roosevelt interposed a delay. In the face of domestic considerations—the November elections—Roosevelt's interest was waning. He and Churchill dickered throughout the fall about the timing and location of the Conference.* In October Roosevelt had written, "I am prepared for a meeting of the three of us any time after the elections here. . . ." After the election, he changed his mind. "The more I think it over," he cabled, "the more I get convinced that a meeting of the three of us just now may be a little less valuable than it would be after I am inaugurated. . . . What do you think of postponement? It appeals to me greatly." Churchill replied simply, "I am very sorry that you are inclined to make no further effort to procure a triple meeting in December." † Eden considered Roosevelt's message to be "bad" and "unhelpful," as did Lord Moran. Churchill, according to Moran, was "unable to hide his irritation. 'The Red Army would not stand still awaiting the result of the election,'" the Prime Minister bellowed.[25]

Stalin also worried about the delay. Foreign Minister Molotov hastened to assure Ambassador Harriman that Stalin was not personally responsible for requesting a meeting in the Crimea: his doctors opposed a long trip. In a cable to Washington Harriman appraised the reason as legitimate. Stalin seemed to be trying to elicit a favorable response from his doctors, who pointed to the damage to his health on the long flight back from Teheran after the last conference. Harriman reported to Roose-

---

* For a detailed treatment of the selection of the Conference site, see Chapter 3, pp. 107–11.

† Roosevelt was not so magnanimous when his British colleague was in a similar political situation. At the plenary session on February 7, Roosevelt proposed that the United Nations conference be convoked in March. Churchill replied this was too early; the British would be engaged in fighting the enemy, and domestic politics would be occupying all their time in Parliament. Hopkins passed Roosevelt a note saying, "There is something behind this talk that we do not know of its basis." The President wrote, "All this is rot," crossed out the last word, and substituted "local politics." *Yalta Documents*, Bohlen minutes, p. 714; ibid., Hopkins to President and reply, p. 729.

velt his "definite impression that he [Stalin] wanted to accede to
your request, and he spoke rather regretfully when he said he
would have to consult his doctors again." [26] The Soviet Marshal's mood had definitely changed. The meeting was made definite, and lower echelon personnel took over the specific arrangements.

The participants in the conference were hopeful of its results.
Churchill and Roosevelt showed eagerness to resolve difficulties
that might undermine their conception of the foundations of the
postwar world. Stalin also favored a meeting, since his Allies
seemed ready at last to consider the unresolved issues that had divided them since the beginning of the war. In the meantime, the
Red Army went about its business of liberating Europe and im-
posing its own social system. The activities of the Red Army,
rather than the decisions of the forthcoming Yalta Conference,
held assurance for Moscow that there would be no "bourgeois"
anti-Soviet governments on the periphery of the Soviet Union
after World War II. The single socialist nation would have company.

POWER AND INFLUENCE

The type of government and social system emerging in the wake
of all three Allied armies in Europe was, as Roosevelt, Stalin,
and Churchill had repeatedly stated, a function of the military-
strategic position of their respective troops during and after the
defeat of the Axis nations. Yet scholarly emphasis upon the
purely military has overlooked a critical factor coloring the Allied mood at the end of 1944 and in early 1945. William Strang
has theorized that a nation can have power without influence, or
influence without power. The Soviet Union in the early stages of
the war had neither. She attempted to use influence without
power and was rebuffed by the West. But by the end of the war,
Russia had both: her armies smashed through eastern Europe,
and Soviet influence, denied throughout the years, was suddenly
given weight.

Philip E. Mosely, Professor of International Relations and

Director of the European Institute at Columbia, vividly recalled this mood in an interview. He stated that top-level thinking in America at the end of the war reflected a "bad conscience" over leaving the Russians to carry the main brunt of the fighting. Professor Mosely, who at the close of the war had been chief of the Division of Territorial Studies at the Department of State and Political Advisor to the United States Delegation of the European Advisory Commission, noted that American officials did not feel they were in any position to tell the Soviets what the United States would or would not agree to after the war.[27] A leading French commentator, writing for *Combat* approximately one week before Yalta, was close to the truth: "America is repenting an excess of prudence." The United States had to scramble to devise a relevant policy "aimed at the partner to the east who, by arms and diplomacy, has acquired excellent cards. England follows the United States in this reversal of attitude." [28]

When the Soviet successes in eastern Europe and the Balkans first stunned the West, Churchill's first reaction was horror. A confidant wrote "Winston never talks of Hitler these days; he is always harping on the dangers of Communism. He dreams of the Red Army spreading like a cancer from one country to another. It has become an obsession, and he seems to think of little else." By the end of September, the Prime Minister saw more clearly the shape of things to come. Moran wrote in his diary, "The advance of the Red Army has taken possession of his mind. Once they got into a country, it would not be easy to get them out. Our army in Italy was too weak to keep them in check." Churchill concluded that "Stalin will get what he wants. The Americans have seen to that." [29]

The Soviet hypothesis, which so affected the Western mood, was that the Soviet Union had fought against Germany almost single-handedly; the corollary was that the peace should be a Soviet peace. The staggering Soviet contribution to the victory, which the Western Allies had postponed recognizing, was the irreducible fact of the war. Marshal Zakharov, in a V-E Day broadcast over Radio Moscow, brought the shocking facts to public attention: "The Soviet people bore the brunt of struggle against Nazi Germany. A total of 607 divisions of Germany and its allies were destroyed, taken prisoner, or disbanded as a result of losses on the Soviet-German front. The Allies' contribution was only 176 [German] divisions destroyed in western Europe and North Africa." He admitted what for many years had not been revealed, "The Soviet Union paid a heavy price for victory—over 20 million killed and thousands of destroyed towns and villages." [30]

Stalin tallied the score each year during the annual anniversary celebration of the Bolshevik revolution. While the battle for Stalingrad raged, Stalin disclosed that 240 German and eastern European divisions were engaged on the eastern front, including 179 of Germany's 256 divisions. In contrast, Great Britain was diverting only four German divisions and eleven Italian divisions. Stalin did not have to elaborate on this disparity.

The following year Stalin reported that the Red Army faced 257 divisions, of which 207 were German. By November 1944 Stalin proclaimed (without taking into account the German transfer of troops after the Normandy invasion) that as a result of the operations of the Red Army, 120 enemy divisions had been defeated, reducing the total number of enemy divisions on the eastern front to 204. Of these, 180 were German.[31]

At the beginning of 1945, according to the prominent Soviet historian V. L. Isrealian, Soviet experts estimated that the German Army totaled 313 divisions and 32 brigades. Of these, 185 divisions and 21 brigades fought on the Soviet front, and only 108 divisions and 7 brigades on the western front, including Italy.[32] At the height of the Anglo-American effort on the Continent the Western Allies *engaged only 33 per cent* of the total German forces.

Very early in the war Stalin began to articulate the thesis that Soviet Russia was singlehandedly fighting Nazi Germany. This formulation became highly useful, and the Marshal did not hesitate to capitalize on it for both internal consumption and international diplomacy. In the latter case, it served two purposes. First, it created constant pressure on the Allies to relieve the Soviet front by opening an early second front. Second, it placed the Western Allies in an extremely uncomfortable negotiating position.

The origins of the Soviet campaign to use Allied embarrassment in order to extract *any* advantage, rather than fail completely, lay in Ivan Maisky's maneuvers in August and September, 1941. In his memoirs Maisky recalled how he agonized over the gloomy reports of Soviet retreat. When he heard Radio Moscow report "mortal danger threatening Leningrad," he resolved to act even without instructions from Moscow. He asked for an interview with Eden on August 26 and told the Foreign Secretary, "In this terrible war the USSR and Britain are Allies, but what help is our British Ally giving us at present? In fact, none!" Maisky lamented that the British refused a second front; that when the Soviets asked urgently for sixty bombs, a lengthy correspondence finally yielded only six; that there was some aircraft help, but not enough. Maisky pleaded, "Begin to give us help immediately, even bit by bit, even as an advance. . . . If that is not done, Soviet people may lose faith in their British ally."

Maisky astutely perceived the impact of the conversation. "My words made their impression on Eden. He became very worried." But the Foreign Secretary countered that "geography imposed difficulties which could not simply be dismissed. . . . We then doubled the number of Hurricanes." * Maisky integrated his impressions into a diplomatic principle of operation. "In my conversation with Eden I was struck by one trait which I had never noticed before: the Foreign Secretary felt embarrassed at the refusal of the British Government to organize a second front in France, and strove to soften our disappointment at this by underlining British readiness to give us help on a large scale in the form of military supplies and otherwise." Maisky soon realized that this attitude was not confined to Eden. "I felt the same note of apology in the statements of other highly placed British people with whom I had to deal in the days that followed." His conclusion: "I 'made a record' in my head that such was the frame of mind in Government and began thinking how best I could make use of them in the interests of my country."

This observation became a point of Soviet policy in the days

* The Hurricane was considered one of the best of the British fighter planes, but not up to the calibre of the Spitfire.

and years that followed. Maisky reported his *démarche* to Moscow but expected no response. However, in this case "quite unexpectedly, in reply to my report on the talk with Eden, I received a telegram signed by J. V. Stalin. Such things happened very rarely. . . . Stalin wrote in it that he approved my *démarche* to Eden." Maisky followed his ploy by asking Stalin to send Churchill a message about a second front. Maisky used this message, and the very real need for a second front, to negotiate other issues.

Anthony Eden was quite unhappy about the extreme pressure that Maisky was putting on them. On September 5, he summoned Maisky and complained "about Soviet propaganda here in favour of second front," which threatened him with "rough reaction and recrimination all would wish to avoid." Maisky said he understood the Anglo-American reaction and managed to secure for Russia tanks and aircraft instead of the second front. He also requested 30,000 tons of aluminum. Eden remained concerned that "the Russians believed, or affected to believe, that it was possible for us to make an important diversion by landing at some point . . ." and that "all our explanations about action on our own account on the continent of Europe, though often repeated to Mr. Maisky in London, failed to shake the Kremlin." [33]

By his own account, the Russian Ambassador repeated the same tactic in March 1942, when he delivered a message in person from Stalin to Churchill. Again Stalin's request for a second front launched Churchill into a defense. Maisky noted "Churchill clearly felt embarrassed. . . . Then I thought: 'These arguments about a second front lead nowhere. Would it not be better to try now, *taking advantage of the Premier's embarrassment to secure some real step on his part?*' " [34]

Stalin also pressured the Allies by asserting that Russia was winning the war alone and that the eastern front would determine the outcome of the war. In a press interview on October 3, 1942, Stalin lamented the absence of a second front and the forced one-sidedness of the Soviet contribution: "As compared with the aid which the Soviet Union is giving to the Allies by drawing upon itself the main forces of the German fascist armies, the aid of the Allies to the Soviet Union has so far been little

effective." A month later the Marshal publicly charged the Allies
with responsibility for Soviet reverses following the successful defense of Moscow. The Germans could take "advantage of the absence of a second front in Europe." If only the Allies engaged
sixty to eighty German divisions, the German "position would
have been deplorable." Stalin repeated the same charge the following day, as well as early the next year.[35]

Molotov's negotiations in 1942 for a second front placed even
more pressure on the Allies, for the Foreign Minister gained the
tactical advantage of winning a promise which was not fulfilled
by the West. By this broken promise the West incurred its first
obligation to prove to the Soviet Union its reliability as an ally.
Invited by Roosevelt, Molotov journeyed to London and Washington in late May and early June of 1942, expecting to arrange
for the second front. Despite protests from the British that a
landing in Europe was not feasible at that time, the Soviet Foreign Minister won a commitment for a second front from Roosevelt. Molotov taunted the British with this. They felt compelled
to support the United States in a communiqué but ominously
warned Molotov that a landing in Europe was quite impossible.
Undaunted, the Foreign Minister returned to Moscow, knowing
that the Soviet government could do nothing except pressure for
a second front; but it could cash in on the breaking of the promise.

Churchill was given the burden of going to Moscow in August 1942 to inform Stalin that there would be no second front
in the coming year. Stalin did not hide his anger and disappointment: "When are you going to start fighting? Are you going to
let us do all the work whilst you look on? Are you never going to
start fighting? You will find it is not too bad if you once start."
Stalin sent a memorandum to Churchill stressing the promise
that had been given and the Soviet Command's reliance upon it.
He concluded that the refusal of the British government to carry
it out "delivers a moral blow to the Soviet public opinion." Stalin knew from Maisky and Molotov that Britain had initiated
the reversal, and he mentioned only in passing that the American Ambassador to Moscow, Averell Harriman, supported the
Prime Minister.[36]

After the victory at Stalingrad, but prior to the Teheran Conference of November 1943, Stalin publicly enunciated the impact
which the hard-won victory would have: "The Red Army's victories have still further strengthened the international position of
the Soviet Union." He referred to the Allied campaign in North
Africa as "backing" for the main Soviet offensive and as support
for the serious blows the Soviets were inflicting on the Germans.
In February 1944, after the liberation of Leningrad and another
Allied promise to invade Europe, Stalin still said the Soviet
Union was "fighting singlehanded." He made pointed comparisons to World War I, when Germany had to fight on two fronts.
He concluded, "The Red Army has achieved a decisive turning
point." One month before the Normandy invasion Stalin again
lauded the singular success of the Red Army. He cited its supplies of "first rate Soviet material," which were "facilitated" by
the Allies.[37]

Perhaps Stalin's implied doubts of his Allies' reliability reflected the expectations of the Soviet military. General John
Deane recalled that "the [Russian] General Staff had never been
convinced that the May data [for Overlord] agreed upon in Teheran was not part of a deception plan that the western powers
were using against their Russian ally." His problem became "to
convince them of our sincerity." Although at the time of the
landing in France the news of the invasion was publicized by the
Soviet press and radio, Deane found "there was no demonstrative
outburst of enthusiasm." Finally, to arouse some interest, he invited the Red Army General Staff to see films of the invasion.
"Their eyes were on their cheeks with amazement at the magnitude of the invasion. It was a phase of war [invasion by sea
against an entrenched enemy] with which the Russians were totally unfamiliar. The pictures definitely changed their previous
attitude. . . ." A change in attitude actually did occur. On June
28, 1944, Stalin commented to Ambassador Averell Harriman
that the crossing and landings were "an unheard of achievement,
the magnitude of which had never been undertaken in the history of warfare. . . ."[38]

While BBC announced "but for the Russians, D-Day would
have been impossible," Stalin set a kinder official line in *Pravda*

and reiterated it personally to Harriman later. In his statement to the Soviet nation, he said: "After seven days' fighting in Northern France one may say without hesitation that the forcing of the Channel along a wide front and the mass-landings of the Allies in Northern France have completely succeeded." He concluded, "This is unquestionably a brilliant success for our Allies." [39]

Soviet Russia suddenly seemed to relax. With the two-front war a reality, and an unexpected agreement with Churchill behind him, Stalin suddenly made a major speech in November 1944, publicly proclaiming the virtues of international conferences (in particular, Teheran, Dumbarton Oaks, and Moscow). He extolled the unity of the coalition and the mutual hopes for the future peace, and he labeled both Japan (with whom the Soviet Union then had a non-aggression pact) and Germany aggressors.[40] Stalin was setting the mood for effective coalition diplomacy. The tone of bitter criticism yielded to friendly and hopeful co-operation.

A Soviet "Second Front"

The Soviet military position at the end of the war represented more than the sum of the victories and sacrifices of the Red Army, the debt the West sensed it owed Russia for her sacrifices, the finesse of Soviet diplomacy in dealing with her Allies, and the strategic location of Soviet forces by 1945. There was, in addition, the West's continuing need for Soviet help to guard against unexpected German strategic maneuvers. The great irony of the military situation in 1944 was that the Allied landing, which Russia had repeatedly sought and finally witnessed after three years, had led to urgent Anglo-American requests for the Soviet equivalent of a "second front."

Soviet forces had already embarked upon an offensive to support the Normandy landings.* On June 6 Stalin informed the President that "the summer offensive of the Soviet troops, to be launched in keeping with the agreement reached at Teheran Conference, will begin in mid-June in one of the vital sectors of

* See above, pp. 63–65.

the front." That offensive opened on a 450-mile front, which extended to 600 miles as it developed. One American expert who observed it stated: "This looked, indeed, like 1941 the other way round!" In one week encirclements of German forces yielded tens of thousands of Germans killed, and 20,000 taken prisoner. In the following week, by another encirclement, the Soviets captured 100,000 at Minsk, of which 57,000 were paraded through Moscow. A 250-mile hole was torn in the German line, clearing the road to Poland and Lithuania.[41]

The West's next urgent request to Stalin came a month before the Yalta Conference. The Germans started a counteroffensive against Eisenhower's forces in the Ardennes, in the Battle of the Bulge. Three German armies overwhelmed one American corps and raced toward Antwerp, the Allies' vulnerable supply base. As Eisenhower recalled, the German advance "was very rapid through the center of the break-through." There was "sudden panic" and "strain and worry throughout the first week of the Ardennes attack." Eisenhower's difficulties were compounded when Montgomery, his self-styled rival, raised the question of a unified ground command and de Gaulle threatened "to act independently unless I [Eisenhower] made disposition for last-ditch defense of Strasbourg." Eisenhower felt he faced revolt behind the lines that "would defeat us on the front." [42]

Churchill, who had visited Eisenhower and, unlike Montgomery, had given him every encouragement, wrote in his memoirs: "At this time Eisenhower and his staff were of course acutely anxious to know whether the Russians could do anything from their side to take off some of the pressure against us in the West." Eisenhower prepared to send his Deputy, Air Marshal Tedder, directly to Moscow to seek help. Bad weather delayed Tedder's departure, and the Prime Minister moved to circumvent this delay: "I said to Eisenhower, 'You may find delays on the staff level, but I expect Stalin would tell me if I asked him. Shall I try?' " [43] Eisenhower approved, and on January 6 Churchill cabled Stalin: "The battle in the West is very heavy. . . . I regard the matter as urgent." The very next day Stalin replied that "in view of the position of our Allies on the western front, Headquarters of the Supreme Command has decided to complete the preparations at a forced pace and, disregarding weather, to launch widescale offensive operations." Churchill replied: "I am most grateful to you for your thrilling message. . . . German reinforcements will have to be split." [44]

Stalin had promised to launch an offensive "not later than the second half of January. You may rest assured that we shall do everything possible to render assistance to the glorious forces of our Allies." The Soviet offensive began even earlier than promised—three days, in fact, before Tedder reached Moscow. Stalin told the Air Marshal "that it had been started on January 12 because he knew of President Roosevelt's and Prime Minister Churchill's worry over the situation on the western front." Deane, who in his book, *The Strange Alliance,* held to the thesis that the Russians were consistently unhelpful, reported to the contrary: "Tedder's meeting with Stalin was highly successful." Characteristically, Deane complained that, "He was not informed how Stalin proposed to carry out his promises. . . ." Eisenhower, in *Crusade in Europe,* merely mentioned, "This was very important—the Russians had opened their long-awaited and powerful winter offensive. . . ." Only Churchill appreciated the position the Red Army had accepted. "It was a fine deed of the Russians and their chief to hasten their vast offensive, no doubt at a heavy cost in life." [45]

One of the leading Soviet field commanders, Marshal I. S. Konev, commander of the First Ukrainian Front, provided an objective appraisal. His army group had received orders from Supreme Headquarters for a January 20 offensive. The plans were developed over a two-and-a-half-month period and finished in November. On January 9, a little more than twenty-four hours after Stalin had received Churchill's message, Konev was suddenly called by the acting Chief of the General Staff. He was informed of "the grave situation which had taken shape in the Ardennes," and told that "following the Allied request, Supreme Headquarters had reviewed the opening date of the offensive." The offensive was to be launched on January 12, according to Stalin's orders. Konev said in his memoirs, "With the benefit of hindsight I have no intention either to minimize or to exaggerate the difficulties this created for us." He was distressed that "the more than eight days of which we had now been deprived, had, of course, to be compensated for by the most intense effort squeezed into the remaining two and a half days." There was very real danger: "Apart from everything else, we were not happy about the earlier date of the offensive because of the weather forecasts." Indeed, the offensive was launched under abominable conditions: "Visibility was virtually down to zero . . . the air was thick with falling snow . . . [tanks] could be distinguished only because they moved." [46]

Stalin was able to write Roosevelt on January 15, 1945, that the Soviet offensive was again forcing the Germans to fight on two fronts and to "relinquish the offensive on the western front. I am glad that this circumstance will ease the position of the Allied troops in the west." The President replied to Stalin with his thanks: "Your heroic soldiers' past performance and the efficiency they have already demonstrated in this offensive give high promise of an early success to our armies." [47]

Toward the end of the war Stalin summed matters up: "The first consequence of our winter offensive had undoubtedly saved the situation in the west . . . the armies of our allies, in their turn, [could] launch an offensive against the Germans." Stalin's appraisal has been reaffirmed by Soviet historians, particularly by V. L. Israelian, in his *Anti-Hitler Coalition*. Using Stalin's correspondence with Churchill and Roosevelt and the military evidence, he concluded that the "great difficulty at Ardennes was relieved by Soviet force." [48]

American sources in retrospect have tended to eliminate the role of the Soviet forces or disparage Soviet support. Chester Wilmot, for example, claimed that the Russian offensive was not a significant factor in aiding the situation on the western front.[49] The reaction in the press at the time of the offensive was a more accurate gauge of the Western and Soviet perception of this event. The Soviet offensive was greeted as a decisive factor in the outcome of the war. News of the offensive found its way into reports by January 13 and 14. *Pravda,* on January 14, 1945, hinted that the war might be shorter than reports from the West indicated. It scorned suggestions that the war would be prolonged into 1946 and told the Soviet people that the Red Army was achieving the victory. Further, the paper attacked Hanson Baldwin, the American military expert and *New York Times* columnist, "who aimed at delay of battle operations on the western front," and yet in this instance had "clamored for abrupt action by the Red Army. These warriors are very brave at others' expense." The general attitude prevailed—and still prevails in Soviet circles—that the West was asking the Red Army to win the war for them.

Soviet propagandist and wartime journalist Ilya Ehrenburg wrote in *Pravda* on January 15, 1945, that the Allies' battles in the Ardennes and the Vosges were no more than skirmishes in comparison to the Soviet engagements on the eastern front. He quoted German sources that the battle in Belgium was nothing but an "ersatz offensive."

Despite *Pravda's* criticism, Hanson Baldwin was both relieved and grateful. In a special to *The New York Times* on January 17, 1945, he lauded the new Soviet offensive: "A weight has been lifted from the minds of those who direct our strategy. . . . The start of the Russian winter offensive transcends in strategic importance both the fighting in western Europe and the invasion of the Philippines." Baldwin referred to the Soviet front as "the principal land front of this global war," where "the bulk of the German Army has been, and still is, facing the Red Army in the east." Military estimates of that time suggested that the Soviets were engaging 110 German and 40 satellite divisions, while the combined Western armies were encountering "perhaps" 70 German divisions. "The comparative figures are the background for the satisfaction and relief with which the long expected and long hoped for Russian winter offensive has been greeted in Washington."

Apologetically, Baldwin regretted that the United States and Great Britain could not reciprocate the Soviets' favor. "The offensive now started comes at a time when the Allies are not in position immediately to launch a correspondingly powerful complementary blow in the west." It was, as usual, the same old "second front" story.

STALIN'S UNPLAYED TRUMP

The German journalist Erich Kuby, in his study of the Soviet battle for Berlin, reached a startling conclusion. He wrote that, at Yalta, "Stalin held a trump card that might easily have won him the game for Germany: he was in a position to order the occupation of Berlin by Soviet forces. But Stalin chose not to play it." [50] Kuby was right. Recently published Soviet military accounts substantiate the view widely held at the time of the Yalta Conference—that the Red Army was ready to take Berlin and end the war. This was not propaganda. The evidence shows that the original battle plan should have put the Red Army in Berlin by the time of Yalta. This would very probably have happened, except for Stalin's fiat.

An American military observer wrote, five days after the 1945 Soviet January offensive opened: "Both Russian and Germans spokesmen seem to agree that this 'general offensive' is not merely a drive for tactical gains or terrain positions, *but is intended to end the war*." This meant that "the battle of the Titans—the clash of the two largest armies in the world—has again been resumed and overnight the strategic complexion of the war has been altered." [51]

Indeed, Western leaders speculated on the possibility of a rapid end to the war. According to Elliot Roosevelt, "The Red Army was chewing up Nazis at an unprecedented rate," and the British and American military were wondering "whether the Russians had not irrevocably broken the German lines in the east, and the collapse of the world's most powerful fascist state might not take place even before the conference was adjourned." [52]

From the middle of January to and through the Yalta Conference, American newspapers not only gave prominent treatment to the news of Soviet victories, but concluded, as did *The New York Times* on January 30, "Berlin's doom seemed conceded." This was typical of the climate of those days. On January 31, in a front-page story, *The New York Times* noted, "The Red Army was twenty miles nearer Berlin yesterday than the day before," while an adjacent article, covering Anglo-American successes, said that American forces had made a four-mile gain against the German Siegfried line.

As the American and British leaders were en route to Yalta, the reading public was given the impression that Germany's demise was imminent. The front page of *The New York Times* on February 2 reported Berlin "feverishly placed in a state of siege," with Soviet forces only fifty-seven miles away; American troops were reported to be breaking through the Siegfried line only in areas of "spotty defenses." By the opening of the Yalta Conference, the Soviet forces were only forty-four miles from Berlin and were capturing Frankfurt and Stettin, while press reports credited American forces with the auxiliary function of bombing Berlin, thus preventing the dispatch of troop transports to the vital eastern front. French observers were predicting that the German surrender "may come at any moment." Rumors abounded in government circles and in the press.

The primary questions which vitally affect any appraisal of the Yalta Conference are what factual basis there was for these reports, and, if there was one, why the Soviets did not take Berlin when they could have. The first serious criticism of Stalin's attack on Berlin in April, rather than in February, came nineteen years later, in 1964, from Marshall Vasili I. Chuikov, former Supreme Commander of Soviet Land Forces. In 1945 he commanded the 8th Guards Army, which, as part of Marshal Zhukov's First Belorussian Army Group, spearheaded the assault on Berlin. In 1965 Chuikov asked, in *Novaia i Noveishaia Istoriia*, "Why did the command element of the First Belorussian Front, after reaching the Oder in the first days of February, not secure permission from Headquarters to continue the offensive toward Berlin without stopping?" Most significantly, Marshal Chuikov judged that "Berlin could have been taken as early as February. This, naturally, would have brought an earlier end to the war." [53]

Chuikov's assessment first appeared in *Oktiabr*, in 1964. In that article the Marshal explored his position judiciously, yet with pointed criticism: "Was not our Supreme High Command being overly cautious. . . . And then the fate of Berlin—and of all fascist Germany with it—could have been decided as early as February." He singled out the planning group: "Supreme Headquarters should have thought the situation through and assessed it properly." In his book, published from the magazine articles, Marshal Chuikov reasserted his arguments (with some minor changes, as we shall see): the armies that later took Berlin (the First Belorussian and First Ukrainian Fronts) could have taken Berlin in February, "and it was the fall of Berlin that decided the outcome of the war . . . I repeat, the capture of Berlin in February 1945 would have meant the end of the war. And the victims claimed would have been fewer than those we lost in April." After Chuikov had been attacked in military circles for defying the official interpretation of the glorious last battle, he concluded even more decisively: "The issue need never have been in doubt: Berlin would have been taken in about ten days." [54]

What *did* happen in scheduling the Battle of Berlin? Should Berlin have fallen in February? The evidence, although not conclusive, suggests that Stalin interfered in the execution of a pre-set plan and stopped the advance on Berlin while he was at Yalta. To date, Western analyses of this final campaign have been based largely on Stalin's decision of early February, rather than on the original battle plan, which he had abandoned at that time, and thus they overlook the political-military significance of a decision that Stalin alone made at Yalta.

According to Colonel General S. M. Shtemenko, Chief of Operations of the Soviet General Staff, by October and November of 1944 Chief of Staff Antonov and the Staff operations officers had worked out the details of the January 20 offensive. Shtemenko wrote: "It was conjectured that defeat could be achieved in 45 days of offensive operations, to a depth of 600–700 km. by means of two consecutive efforts [stages] *with no operational halt between them*." The first stage would commence January 20 and continue approximately fifteen days, covering 250–300 km. The final stage, the "defeat of Germany and the capture of Berlin," would take another thirty days. Shtemenko considered this a conservative plan: "The pace was not fast, since fierce resistance was expected in the final fighting," and he admitted, "In actuality, heroic Soviet troops fulfilled all these plans ahead of schedule." [55] According to this plan, Soviet troops would have reached the approaches to Berlin and would have begun the last battle during the Yalta Conference. The city should have fallen by March 5 according to this schedule.

The schedule, however, was upset in two ways. First, the Allies requested an offensive *earlier than January 20*. Since the Army was basically ready for the January offensive, acceding to this request probably did not retard the execution of the plan. It should, if anything, have speeded it up, and Berlin should have fallen about February 25. Second, the main Armies destined to attack Berlin covered *more than* 500 kilometers in eighteen days —in other words, almost the entire distance projected for the whole operation and almost twice the distance planned for the first stage.

By January 29 the Armies that eventually took Berlin were approaching or had reached the Oder. According to the original operational scheme, there was to be no halt between phases of the attack. The First Belorussian Front and the First Ukrainian Front should have continued the advance against Berlin, and they continued preparations to do so. They would have been fighting in Berlin, therefore, during Yalta. But at this point Stalin arbitrarily ordered a pause, and the advance stopped unexpectedly from Februray 3 to April 16.

How definite was the November plan, and how committed were the Soviet commanders to its execution? By the time of the Yalta Conference, the plans for this operation had existed for three months and had been approved by Stalin for over one month. Shtemenko related, "Many of the operations had already been cleared with the Supreme Commander in Chief even before they were discussed with the Army Group commanders." Commander Marshal Konev relates that he received his briefing on the operation at the end of November. By then the plan was considered finished. "Many clarifications" had been made in November; after the November 7 holidays * the draft had been fully dis-

* The October Revolution is celebrated on November 7 because of the change in the Russian calendar.

cussed but not "given final approval, so directives were not issued to the Army Groups." Shtemenko concluded that "by November 1944, the picture of the Soviet Army's forthcoming winter offensive was fully drawn, even though Supreme Headquarters did not confirm the plan of operations until the end of December. Subsequently, no more than partial amendments were made to the plan of the campaign and of the initial operations." His account is substantiated by two corroborating pieces of evidence; first, the Commanders had received orders according to schedule at the end of November; and second, as Marshal Zhukov recalled, Supreme Headquarters as late as January 27 had *approved* his battle plan to begin on February 1 to 2 to force the Oder and "develop a fast moving offensive toward Berlin." [56]

Then why did Soviet troops not enter Berlin in early February? The answer lies in Stalin's change of mind at the end of January or early February. Shtemenko in his account overlooked the fact that Stalin made two decisive alterations that gave him total control when he reviewed the operational scheme in November. First, he handpicked G. K. Zhukov to capture Berlin. Zhukov's career during the war had blossomed under Stalin, who could rely on Zhukov's extraordinary ability. Zhukov had emerged as the hero of the Battles of Moscow, Stalingrad, and Kursk-Orel; by November–December 1944, Stalin slated him to be the conqueror of Berlin. (Stalin modified even that decision in April.*) Zhukov had never failed Stalin in battle. Stalin could count on him to execute his orders faithfully, and intended that their military glory should again be linked in this final battle. The seriousness of Stalin's intention to execute the battle plan can be seen by his action in November, which changed Army Group commanders, rather than the plan for the last battle.

The approved plan called for the First Belorussian Front, commanded since 1943 by Marshal Rokossovky, to spearhead the

---

* Possibly this change in April resulted from Zhukov's opposition to Stalin's delay in capturing Berlin, a decision which Zhukov resented, although he followed Stalin's orders. Also, Stalin's subsequent decision to take Berlin swiftly could have encouraged him to use the rivalry between Zhukov and Konev to spur the competitors on to vie for the city's capture. These questions are considered later.

attack. In order to pave the way for Zhukov, Stalin transferred Rokossovky in November to the Second Belorussian Front. Rokossovky protested such extraordinary action, saying this was "very unexpected," and crying in dismay, "Why am I being penalized?" [57] Then Stalin gained complete control over the plan itself—and hence the opportunity to change it at will. He assumed the task of co-ordinating the activities of the four Army Groups in the Berlin operation which otherwise would have fallen to Chief of the General Staff. Shtemenko wryly observed: "This rendered superfluous the task of the Chief of the General Staff, A. M. Vasilevskii. . . ." [58]

On January 25, only nine days before Yalta, Stalin telephoned Zhukov, who had just surrounded a large enemy grouping in Poznan, and asked what his plans were. Zhukov advised him that "the enemy was demoralized and no longer able to offer serious resistance." Stalin expressed concern that the rapid advance had separated Zhukov's Army Group from the Second Belorussian Front: "This cannot be permitted now." But he did not pose this as a serious obstacle, estimating that they would regroup in ten to fifteen days.

In this January 25 talk Stalin showed the first signs of postponing the imminent Berlin offensive. He suddenly advised Zhukov that "the First Ukrainian Army Group is now unable to move any farther and to protect your left flank since it will be busy for some time liquidating the enemy." Stalin's statement was not a correct assessment of the situation. As Chuikov wrote, "The enemy did not have sufficient reserves with which to launch a serious counterblow (this is acknowledged, incidentally by Guderian himself)." Stalin presumably believed this as well, because *four days after this conversation,* he approved the First Ukrainian Front's plan to take Berlin with its right flank, which would have been unthinkable were the entire Army Group "unable to move any farther," as he told Zhukov. [59]

Zhukov clearly sensed Stalin's hedging, for in his memoirs in 1965 he wrote, "I asked the Supreme Commander in Chief not to stop the advance of the Army Group." On January 26, the day following Stalin's peculiar conversation, Zhukov made a formal proposal to Headquarters to take Berlin in accordance with the original, and as yet, unaltered plan of assault; he received approval on January 27. Zhukov related, "Stalin agreed with the proposal . . . but he refused to assign additional forces, which were needed for the plan." On January 29 Supreme Headquarters also approved Konev's plan for the capture of Berlin, in accordance with the operational plan adopted in November.

Zhukov began his offensive toward Berlin, and he considered it highly successful up to February 3: "The main force . . . brilliantly completed its march. . . ." [60] But on February 2 and February 4, two directives were issued to the Armies attacking Berlin. The first commanded Zhukov to revert to the defensive; the second, issued by Zhukov in response to the first, wavered between consolidating "achieved successes" and "active operations," and basically contradicted the first. Marshal Chuikov lauded Zhukov's foresight to this point: "For the sake of objectivity it must be said that Marshal G. K. Zhukov, commander of the First Belorussian Army Group, had properly assessed the situation in instructing his troops to consolidate the successes they had won and then to 'take Berlin on February 15–16, 1945 with a lightning thrust.' " [61]

Stalin no longer agreed. For a week the Armies had not been supplied with the necessary stockpiles of munitions and fuel—according to Chuikov, because the high command had failed to think through the operation. Zhukov had not received replacements, and he may have overstepped his orders. Stalin, then at Yalta, picked up the telephone and called Zhukov, probably on February 6.* Stalin asked, "Where are you, what are you doing?" Zhukov answered, "We are planning the Berlin operation." Stalin responded, "You are wasting your time," and issued new orders. Chuikov recalled the disappointment of the assembled staff: "Georgi Konstantinovich [Zhukov] put down the receiver, got up from the table, made his farewells to us, and drove off to his headquarters. We realized that the advance on Berlin was postponed indefinitely." [61]

Instead, the attacking Armies were diverted to Pomerania to

* Chuikov's first account in *Oktiabr* said February 4, but Marshal Zhukov, in his attempt to refute Chuikov's credibility, claimed "no such meeting ever occurred on February 4." In Chuikov's memoirs, republished as a book, the date was revised to February 6, which Zhukov seemed not to have refuted.

clear out the remaining German troops. A few days before Stalin had flattered Roosevelt, assuring him that American troops would reach Manila before Russian troops reached Berlin! Stalin knew whereof he spoke—he was in the process of terminating Zhukov's offensive and postponing the capture of Berlin.

In recent years Shtemenko and Zhukov (as well as other military men) have vehemently opposed Chuikov's argument that Berlin could have been taken in February. The evidence supports Chuikov: Soviet troops could have been in Berlin at least during the Yalta Conference, if not earlier. Erich Kuby put it: "It would certainly have been possible to take Berlin as early as February. That it was not taken then was Stalin's fault, and his fault alone. Politically, this mistake was of the same order as Hitler's decision to halt his Panzer Divisions near the Channel coast in 1940." Seweryn Bialer, who compiled and translated many of the military accounts of this period, concluded: "Chuikov's arguments are persuasive as far as the possibility, albeit the risky possibility, of seizing Berlin in February." Harrison Salisbury called Stalin's reversal of plans "one of the major enigmas of the last days of the war," and speculated on Stalin's motives: "The suspicion is strong that he was politically rather than militarily motivated."

Our basic question remains: what influenced Stalin to call the operation off, just at the time of Yalta? Had the advance continued, even in the face of severe German resistance, the Red Army would have been in Berlin, giving credence to Stalin's argument that the Soviet Union was winning the war alone. Politically, his bargaining position would have been unassailable. Kuby argued that, at Yalta, "Stalin gave Germany away by vetoing the immediate capture of Berlin." [62]

Several considerations probably caused Stalin to rethink the Berlin offensive.

First, Stalin was often cautious in military matters. He frequently reverted to a pet military formulation—the "Permanently Operating Factors"—among which protection for the rear of the Red Army was always primary. At Yalta he spoke about this requirement at great length. According to Stalin's information, the Second Belorussian Front could not advance into Pomerania and hence could not protect the right flank of the main force—the First Belorussian Army Group. Chuikov believed that "this was what caused Stalin to issue his order at the beginning of February . . . to go over to the defensive." Further, the advance had outdistanced its supplies. Zhukov's deputy related that the shortage of ammunition and fuel was due to the unexpected release of transport units to join the offensive on Berlin, leaving supplies behind without suppliers.[63]

In effect, Stalin's resolve may have failed. As in July 1944, when Rokossovky reached the Vistula, before Warsaw, and Stalin halted him, the Soviet command rated German resistance as formidable. In the case of Warsaw this view had proved correct; in the case of Berlin, it was not. The route to Berlin was open, since Hitler stubbornly refused to believe the Russians would continue the advance. Berlin would, therefore, have been an easier target in February than in April.

Second, Stalin's decision may well have been colored by political considerations. The Russians believed it had been agreed that Soviet forces were slated to take Berlin. Eisenhower and the Combined Chiefs of Staff approved the general battle plan in January, and Berlin was left to the Red Army to capture. Eisenhower communicated these plans directly to Stalin at the time.[64] From this point of view, with the zones of occupation already agreed upon by the European Advisory Commission and sanctioned at Yalta,* Stalin behaved like Eisenhower: he decided to save lives and not to extend his forces beyond the zonal lines already defined in tripartite policy.

Only after the Soviets suddenly concluded that not only were the Allies planning to take Berlin, but also that they wanted to beat the Russians there, did Stalin return to the operational scheme for the Berlin offensive. By April the Soviet command felt betrayed: "There remained no doubt whatsoever that the Allies intended to capture Berlin before us, even though, according to the Yalta Agreements, the city fell within the zone designated for occupation by Soviet troops." The Soviet commanders met immediately: "The situation on the front and the operations of the Allies and their plans were reported in detail." On April 1,

---

* For zones of occupation, see pp. 28–36.

"Stalin concluded that it was necessary to take Berlin in the shortest possible time; and therefore, the time remaining to prepare the operation was extremely curtailed. It was necessary to begin not later than April 16 and to finish everything in not more than 12 to 15 days." In other words, when Stalin feared treachery from the West,* the Red Army's difficulties suddenly dissolved, and the original thirty-day estimated assault period was condensed into twelve to fifteen days. Stalin dropped the First Belorussian Front as the sole captor for Berlin and fostered competition between his generals by announcing to both Zhukov and Konev: "Whoever reaches Berlin first—let him take it." [65] Zhukov thus lost his central role in capturing Berlin, and now Konev could vie for and finally did share in the triumph.

Finally, the imminence of the Yalta Conference probably deterred Stalin from moving too rapidly against Berlin. Although Soviet negotiating strength might have been enhanced by a stronger military position, such a decisive action just as well might have provoked the West against the Soviet Union. The wartime alliance, often shaken by Western efforts to contain the Soviet Union, gave Moscow constant reminders of Western animosity. For example, in November 1943, Roosevelt had announced: "There would definitely be a race for Berlin." The Americans had devised a "super-secret" plan, RANKIN, to ensure that the Soviet Union would not defeat Germany alone: in case of sudden German collapse, American troops would be parachuted into the heart of Germany. Churchill had also spent much of the war trying to put Anglo-American forces into the Balkans. In 1954 Churchill admitted what he had had in mind in 1945: toward the end of the war he had ordered Montgomery to keep German arms intact, in case they had to be used against the Russians. Montgomery confirmed this.[66]

In all probability, Stalin played down his military hand in an effort to avert suspicion, discord, lack of co-operation, and, at worst, military retaliation. Marshal Konev, the Soviet Com-

---

* And not without foundation. Churchill was urging Eisenhower to push a strong Anglo-American column across the Elbe and into Berlin as fast as possible, in order to seize the political advantage over the Soviet Union.

mander, described the distrust which top Soviet military circles had about Western intentions: "At that time, during the war, we did not want to believe our Allies capable of entering into any separate agreements with the German command. But the atmosphere in those days was full not only of facts, but also of rumors, and we had absolutely no right to preclude that contingency." [67] Stalin's negotiating stance at Yalta emphasized the necessity of the three nations jointly defeating Germany and jointly ensuring the peace; it paid off in Roosevelt's backing the Soviet plan of controlling Germany. (Would this have been the case if the Soviet military position gave the impression of defeating Germany alone?)

In retrospect, no judgment can be definitive on Stalin's decision, either from a political or military viewpoint. Clearly, the Soviet Union could have achieved an even stronger position prior to Yalta had it been prepared to function unilaterally. Its failure to try for such a position should at least have indicated to the West that their assumptions about Soviet intentions were as ill-founded as Konev's suspicions were of the West. One might as well permit a final view by another commander, Field Marshal Viscount Montgomery, who believed that Stalin's military judgment was sound: "Now consider Stalin. A great leader, ruthless maybe, and no kind of gentleman. . . . Stalin made almost no mistakes; he had a clear-cut political strategy and he pursued it relentlessly. . . . He had an amazing strategical sense and I cannot recall that he put a foot wrong in our discussions on strategical matters. . . ." [68]

Adapting to the "Unavoidable"

Roosevelt enunciated one of his major pre-Yalta themes in a telegram to Marshal Stalin in November 1944: "All three of us are of one mind. . . ." Although the President was referring specifically to the coming conference, this theme was not new. Stettinius recalled, "It was President Roosevelt's belief, and he expressed it to me many times, that if he and the Prime Minister could sit around a conference table again with Marshal Stalin, not only would the war be brought to a speedier conclusion, but plans could also be laid to solve these problems and to create the basis for an enduring peace." Roosevelt had also told the previous Secretary of State, Cordell Hull, essentially the same thing: "My thought is, if we get a substantial meeting of the minds with the British, that we should, then, take it up with the Russians." [69]

Churchill's thoughts were running the same way. He told his friend and physician, Lord Moran, in October: "If we three come together everything is possible—absolutely anything." The Prime Minister confided that he could talk to Stalin as one human being to another, that he was after all sensible. "I don't want the U.S.S.R. to feel it is just an Anglo-Saxon affair. I want them to know it's the three of us. . . . We can settle everything, we three, if we come together." [70]

Stalin, for his part, had consistently opposed the advance co-operation between the British and Americans and pleaded for tripartite planning rather than bilateral or unilateral action. Harriman had advised Roosevelt: "They never like to be faced with Anglo-American decisions already taken," and Clark Kerr and John Winant had said the same. By the time the President decided upon a Big Three conference, he was openly cautious not to alarm the Soviets. Publicly and among his fellow heads of state, Roosevelt resolutely avoided giving any impression that the Soviets would face an Anglo-American bloc at the Yalta Confer- ence. In accordance with this decision, he refused to meet pri- vately with Churchill before the conference between the Western Allies at Malta, and even there he avoided political issues.

Roosevelt also kept Stalin informed of diplomatic negotia- tions with Britain. When his personal envoy, Harry Hopkins, was traveling through European capitals on his way to the Yalta Conference, Hopkins made a particular point of stating for the record that he might even go to Moscow. This was in London, on January 29. By the opening day of the Yalta Conference, *The New York Times* assured the public that those "in close touch with inter-Allied diplomatic relations" could say that "President Roosevelt and Prime Minister Churchill did not meet before the Big Three conference to agree on an agenda or policies." [71]

Once at Yalta, Roosevelt pointedly avoided seeing Churchill alone, particularly at the outset. He tried to befriend Stalin by making snide remarks about Britain. In fact, Hopkins admitted to Lord Moran during the Conference that the President was especially concerned not to "fall out with Stalin." Hopkins confided, "He is quite sure that Russia will work with him after the war to build a better world." Hopkins further related that Roosevelt had informed Stalin of disagreements between himself and Churchill.[72]

For Roosevelt the friendly stance related to his political belief that through friendship he could establish a working relationship. But the British felt left out. Eden wrote: "The President, mistakenly as I believe, moved out of step with us, influenced by his conviction that he could get better results with Stalin direct than could the three countries negotiating together." Roosevelt felt that when he talked personally to Molotov (whom he found cold) or Gromyko, they became "friendlier and more cooperative." [73]

Churchill's attitude of Allied amicability was rooted in his vast human dimension, especially his emotional and sentimental disposition. While Churchill was basking in visions of harmony after the war, he remained fearful of Stalin and the Soviet Union. He was obsessed with communism and thought mainly of stopping Russia. Therefore, at the same time he talked of "the Bear" (as he called Stalin) and referred to the Soviets as "villains," he was writing Stalin: "There are no matters that cannot be adjusted between us," and he repeated that sentiment the next day in the House of Commons. Moran noted, "The Prime Minister wants nothing except Stalin's friendship." Or again: "Whenever the P.M. sees Stalin he seems to come back in a good mood" and delighted in "fresh proof of Stalin's friendship." Churchill began to deny "with great earnestness that Russia wished to convert the world to Communism, as many people feared."

Yet weariness had set in. In September 1944 Churchill admitted moodily, "I have a very strong feeling that my work is done. I have no message, I had a message. Now I only say 'fight the damned socialists.' I do not believe in this brave new world." [74]

As the Yalta Conference approached, and as the Soviet Armies swept into the Balkans, Churchill began to express indifference to the areas of the Balkans he had formerly thought vital to Britain's interests, and he also became indifferent to his own October agreement. When Anthony Eden informed him of difficulty with Molotov over Bulgaria, and told the Prime Minister, "They don't want us to have any finger in Bulgaria," Churchill replied, "There are a lot of things which don't matter." Eden, whose mood had not changed, retorted, "Bulgaria isn't one of them."* Churchill thought differently: "I had never felt that our relations with Rumania and Bulgaria in the past called for any special sacrifices from us." Only two issues still mattered: "the fate of Poland and Greece struck us keenly." [75]

Churchill was even tiring of the Poles. After the failure of his efforts to force the London Poles into a partial reconciliation with the Soviets, Churchill had threatened Mikolajczyk that Britain would abandon the Polish government in exile. He said that "quarrels between the Poles" would "wreck the peace of Europe" and that Mikolajczyk "was out of business forever." But now Churchill knew how the issue could be handled. "I shall say that we can settle everything, we three, if we come together. Then I'll say, there are some small matters to settle." Eden was forced to remind him, "But Winston, Poland is a big, not a small thing." Churchill said a few days later, "It's a tragedy about these Poles. . . . You see what will happen: the advancing Russians will be helped by the Poles. Then these villains will have them completely in their power. Whereas if the Poles are sensible I shall be able to help while they are bargaining with the Russians."

Franklin Roosevelt also began to re-evaluate his still unenunciated but implictly existent policy on Poland. In any case, the President had reached the conclusion that "when a thing becomes unavoidable, one should adapt oneself to it." This was characteristic of Roosevelt's diplomacy, and everyone knew it. At Yalta, when Sir Charles Portal, Marshal of the Royal Air Force,

---

* Eden in his memoirs related that he had a "vigorous exchange" with Molotov. When he tried to explain the difficulties to Churchill, the Prime Minister was disturbed because Eden had bickered. Churchill said it might upset the "good atmosphere" of the percentage deal.

complained to Lord Moran about Churchill who "will fight to the last ditch but not in it. He does not like making decisions," Moran, in turn, revealed his impression of Roosevelt's diplomacy: "He doesn't like thinking things out, but waits for situations to develop and then adapts himself to them." Portal agreed: "That is the exact truth. I never thought of putting it like that." [76]

This inter-Atlantic snappishness extended far beyond the personal retinues of the Western leaders. A quantitative change had recently taken place in America's attitude toward Britain, and in Britain's toward America. Open conflict appeared over the proposal to appoint a deputy for Eisenhower after the invasion at Normandy.* Later, when the British wanted a single northern thrust into Germany instead of an assault on a broad front, Eisenhower gave Montgomery the star role but retained his general strategy. The Chief of the Imperial General Staff, Field Marshal Sir Alan Brooke, was upset. He damned Eisenhower as a "second rate player," and he sulked in his diary, "So we were again stuck." [77]

In the final six weeks before Yalta the newspapers were filled with both subtle and flagrant attacks by the Atlantic partners. The British weekly, *The Economist,* blamed the trouble on Eisenhower's "strategy of an elephant leaning on an obstacle to crush it." The London *News Chronicle* charged that Eisenhower was too busy with "administrative routine" to direct the war and concluded that Montgomery was the "ideal man." When Churchill blew up, it was both at his own failure to divert the Normandy landing into a Balkan offensive and at the strategy the Americans imposed. When American troops landed in southern France in Operation Dragoon, in August 1944, Churchill called it the "last straw," having "no earthly purpose" except "sheer folly." He decided to act, and within a week he went off to Italy to talk to "Alex," to see if the latter could push on through Italy into the Balkans. Eden claimed that Churchill had other motives, among them, to visit with Tito as well as "to see how Al-

* For an account of the struggle between Washington and London for military and political hegemony during the war, see Gabriel Kolko, *The Politics of War.*

exander was preparing for the offensive." Eden lamented in his memoirs: "Both Mr. Churchill and I were unhappy about the reluctance of our American ally to exploit victory in Italy and so enable us to play a more influential part in Central Europe." He saw sinister anti-imperialist motives behind the stand. "Though the United States argued that this was for strategic reasons, we were not convinced that political inhibitions about becoming 'involved in the Balkans' did not play a part." [78]

By the time the Anglo-American military leaders and diplomats met in Malta, an explosion was in the offing. Bedell Smith stopped in one evening to chat with Brooke, who asked if Eisenhower was "strong enough" to be Supreme Commander. General George C. Marshall was becoming increasingly irritated at the suggestions that Montgomery be appointed Deputy to Eisenhower. Marshall told Eisenhower, "As long as I'm Chief of Staff I'll never let them saddle you with the burden of an over-all ground commander." At Malta Bedell Smith complained to Stettinius about the "embarrassment to Eisenhower," and the Secretary determined to take the matter to Roosevelt. He did, but found to his surprise that this was not news to the President. Roosevelt was less concerned than Churchill, since two Americans, Marshall and Eisenhower, were making the decisions.[79]

America had long considered her British ally to be the stronghold of an outdated imperialism. Accusations began to surface. By February 1945, Eden believed "the President shared a widespread American suspicion of the British Empire as it had once been and, despite, his knowledge of world affairs, he was always anxious to make it plain to Stalin that the United States was not 'ganging up' with Britain against Russia." He concluded, "The outcome of this was some confusion in Anglo-American relations which profited the Soviets."

Churchill's impression was similar, and he yielded occasionally to emotional outbursts. The most entertaining to Stalin was his defense of the British Empire on February 9 at Yalta.* But the Prime Minister had already told Roosevelt how he felt: "I believe you are trying to do away with the British Empire," to

* See below, pp. 241–42.

which Roosevelt had responded—not to Churchill but to his own son, Elliot—"The colonial system means war." Eden's judgment was broader: "Roosevelt did not confine his dislike of colonialism to the British Empire alone, for it was a principle with him, not the less cherished for its possible advantages." The Foreign Secretary found the basis of this attitude in Roosevelt's "hope that former colonial territories, once free of their masters, would become politically and economically dependent upon the United States, and had no fear that other powers might fill that role." [80]

Just a week before the leaders left for the conferences, a banner headline on the front page of *The New York Times* labeled British imperialism as the obstacle to peace, proclaiming "U.S. Aim Firm Peace, Churchill Is Told." The London correspondent reported the American attitude "more propitious" toward international collaboration, but warned, "This mood can change as mercurially as the English weather" if the "crusade for freedom ends as just another struggle between rival imperialisms." British "totalitarianism," "specifically . . . events in Greece, and Yugoslavia, and Italy," revealed the British "idea that liberators should impose a government of which they approve on liberated nations and the Washington view that liberated people should choose for themselves." America would not accept the possibility that "a discredited old order rise from the ashes of the old or to see the tyranny of Nazi occupation replaced by some catspaw totalitarianism masquerading behind a native name." [81]

Harry Hopkins, who arrived at Naples to meet State Department officials after his fact-finding tour of European capitals, warned Stettinius and the President that Churchill was in a belligerent mood. He said that Churchill "would beat us all up" at Malta. After the Secretary of State met with Churchill a few days later (in the pre-Conference meetings at Malta, which Stalin had been assured were not sessions co-ordinating strategy), he confirmed that "the Prime Minister was aroused over the sharp differences between the British and American positions on the political situation in Italy." The Prime Minister told Stettinius "in blunt language" that Britain's position had been made quite difficult. In particular, Greece was "causing him great concern."

Churchill said, "The main burden falls on us, and the responsibility is within our sphere . . ." then, correcting himself, "that is the military sphere agreed upon with our principal Allies."

Despite an exchange of viewpoints and some important military co-ordination at Malta, the split in Anglo-American strategy was not healed. Eden said, "There had been no Anglo-American consultation except my meetings with Stettinius. The President was so unpredictable that the Prime Minister and I became uneasy at this void." At a luncheon on the afternoon of February 2, on board the *Quincy*, Churchill and Eden tried to talk politics. Roosevelt resisted, "so a dinner was arranged specifically for this purpose which was no more successful than the luncheon." Eden later approached Harry Hopkins and pointed out "that we were going into a decisive conference and had so far neither agreed what we would discuss nor how to handle matters with a Bear who would certainly know his mind." [82]

Three weeks earlier, Churchill had telegraphed Roosevelt: "This may well be a fateful conference, coming at a moment when the great allies are so divided," and now his prediction was coming true. He began to show signs of depression as well as anger over his increasing lack of directive force. Stettinius noted at Malta that the Prime Minister "expressed utter dismay at the outlook of the world. . . . As he looked out on the world, he added, it was one of sorrow and bloodshed." Churchill was brooding on Atlantic disunity: "It was his opinion that future peace, stability, and progress depended on Great Britain and the United States remaining in close harmony at all times." As the Secretary of State thought about it after this talk, he concluded that Churchill was "very much depressed." Lord Moran evaluated Churchill's disposition on February 1: "his work had deteriorated a lot in the last few months; and that he has become very wordy, irritating his colleagues in the Cabinet by his verbosity. One subject will get in his mind to the exclusion of all others— Greece, for example." Moran saw "waning powers" in the Prime Minister. Even in his telegram to Roosevelt, Churchill betrayed his sense of foreboding: "At the present time I think the end of this war may well prove to be more disappointing than the last." [83]

In contrast, Stettinius found the President, upon his arrival at Malta, "in good spirits." Churchill perked up when he got together with the President, just as he had when he talked with the other Allied leader, Stalin, in October; that left only Eden fretting about the unresolved issues.

But there was more serious concern for the President's health than for the Prime Minister's. Lord Moran recorded, "Everyone was shocked by his appearance and gabbled about it afterwards." He noted, "The President looked old and thin and drawn; he sat looking straight ahead with his mouth open, as if he were not taking things in." Roosevelt admitted he had slept ten hours a night on his sea voyage after leaving Washington but "still couldn't understand why he was not slept out." Stettinius remembered that, during his Inaugural Address two weeks before, the President "had seemed to tremble all over. It was not just his hands that shook, but his whole body as well." The Secretary admitted, "It seemed to me that some kind of deterioration in the President's health had taken place between the middle of December and the inauguration on January 20. . . . In spite of this development, however, I wish to emphasize that at all times from Malta through the Crimean Conference and the Alexandria meeting I always found him to be mentally alert and fully capable of dealing with each situation as it developed."

Lord Moran disagreed with Stettinius's judgment: "To a doctor's eye, the President appears a very sick man. He has all the symptoms of hardening of the arteries of the brain in an advanced stage, so that I give him only a few months to live." He continued, "But men shut their eyes when they do not want to see, and the Americans here cannot bring themselves to believe that he is finished." The day before he and Churchill left England for the conference, Moran had received a disturbing letter from Dr. Roger Lee, the president of the American Medical Association and former president of the American College of Physicians. Dr. Lee reported that Roosevelt had suffered an attack of heart failure eight months before, and described his temperament: "He was irascible and became very irritable if he had to concentrate his mind for long. If anything was brought up that wanted thinking out he would change the subject."

Churchill was also disturbed because Roosevelt did not seem to "take an intelligent interest in the war," and often "he does not seem even to read the papers the P.M. gives him." Churchill became "moody" and gave Moran "a sour look" toward the end of the Conference, saying, "The President is behaving very badly. He won't take an interest in what we are trying to do." Moran replied that "he had lost his grip on things," and Churchill "replied that he thought he had." Moran described Roosevelt as "a passenger at the Conference." This remark was too much for Churchill, who not long before had said of the President, "I love that man." [84]

These were the men with whom Stalin and Molotov negotiated. The question has arisen—usually in the form of a firm assertion one way or another—of whether or not Roosevelt, perhaps Churchill, and even Stalin were capable men by the time of Yalta. In particular, the President's undeniable illness has been cited as the cause of unfavorable or even irresponsible decisions taken at the Conference. No one can prove that Roosevelt's health affected the results of the Yalta Conference, or that it did not. Certainly the President, from all accounts, was not as fit as he could have been, and perhaps his health influenced his judgment. Yet the decisions of the Yalta Conference, analyzed *as decisions,* must provide the answer to this question.

In this sense, it is irrelevant whether Churchill was depressed or Roosevelt sick or Stalin overburdened. Only a critical evaluation of what these men decided and how they decided it can yield an objective judgment of Yalta. Anthony Eden, concerned about Roosevelt's health (and Churchill's moodiness), was essentially correct: "I do not believe that the President's declining health altered his judgment, though his handling of the Conference was less sure than it might have been." [85]

PART II

THE CONFERENCE

CHAPTER 3

THE CONFERENCE OPENS

"OKAY AND ALL GOOD WISHES"

The Yalta Conference was six months in the making, and ultimately the President of the United States chose both the location and the date. Roosevelt first broached the question of location in July 1944. He was thinking about cabling to Stalin that "the hop would be much shorter to Scotland than the one taken by Molotov two years ago." Ambassador Harriman advised the President against this idea, since it required Stalin to fly over enemy-held territory. Harriman warned, "There might be resentment on the part of Stalin's principal advisors which might jeopardize the prospects of the meeting itself." [1] The issue was temporarily put aside.

In October, Roosevelt discussed possible locations with Harry Hopkins, and Hopkins remarked, "We might as well make up our minds first at least to go to some convenient point in Russia —preferably in the Crimea." Roosevelt was amenable, but he wondered about the effect of a trip to Russia on his election campaign. Hopkins heard from Ambassador Gromyko * that Stalin was prepared for a tripartite conference but, in view of the Red

---

* Hopkin's recollections about the origins of the Conference apparently contained some inaccurate dates. He stated that Roosevelt began considering a conference in September; the telegrams among the three leaders indicate that consideration began in July. More importantly, he wrote, *"As soon as the election had taken place* I saw Gromyko . . ." and basically recounted what Deane and Stalin attributed to a Hopkins-Gromyko conversation *in October*. Possibly Hopkins confused the October meeting with a later one. See Sherwood, *Roosevelt and Hopkins*, pp. 843–44, and *Yalta Documents*, Deane to Joint Chiefs of Staff, 10/17/44, p. 8; Stalin to Roosevelt, 10/19/44, p. 9.

Army offensive, was unable to leave the Soviet Union. Hopkins asked Gromyko "whether there was any place in the Crimea at which it was fit to hold a conference." Gromyko said he thought so. Stalin immediately picked up the idea. He told General Deane, Chief of the American military mission in Moscow, that he understood the President wanted to meet him in the Black Sea area. On October 19, Stalin wired Roosevelt that "Ambassador Gromyko has informed me about his recent conversation with Mr. Hopkins in which Mr. Hopkins expressed an idea that you could arrive in the Black Sea at the end of November." Stalin also mentioned to Churchill the possibility of "a triple meeting towards the end of November at a Black Sea port" during the latter's visit to Moscow in October. The Prime Minister, in a telegram to Roosevelt, pronounced it "a very fine idea." [2]

Roosevelt, however, was beginning to have second thoughts, and on October 22 he conveyed his doubts to the Prime Minister: "The selection of a Black Sea port for our next meeting seems to be dependent upon our ability to get through the Dardanelles. . . ." Churchill promptly changed his mind. He wrote back, "From what I saw of the Crimea it seems much shattered and I expect all other Black Sea ports are in a similar state." He recommended Cyprus as an alternative and also asked Eden to look into Athens as a site for the Conference.[3]

Encouraged by Churchill's communiqué, the President cabled Stalin, "I have been thinking about the practicality of Malta, Athens, or Cyprus if my getting into the Black Sea on a ship should be impracticable or too difficult. I prefer traveling and living on a ship." After a few days, Stalin replied that the Black Sea was acceptable, and he hoped the President could arrange "safe entrance of your vessel into the Black Sea." Roosevelt was unhappy at Stalin's failure to take a hint. He informed Churchill that "Uncle Joe"—or, as they abbreviated it in their telegrams, "U.J."—had sent a message "not very helpful in the selection of a place for our next meeting." The President mentioned the possibility of luring "U.J." to Piraeus, Salonica, or Constantinople but doubted the feasibility: "I fear that Uncle Joe will insist on the Black Sea." Churchill, with characteristic suddenness, had made up his mind on one point: "On all this I consider the

Black Sea out of the question and Piraeus very little better." The Prime Minister confessed he was "somewhat attracted by the suggestion of Jerusalem," where there were some very fine hotels.[4]

Roosevelt waited over a week before returning to the question. On November 14, he explained to Churchill, "I am undergoing the throes of the old session [Congress]." He mentioned two alterations to his original plan for the Conference: first, he was postponing the meeting until after the inauguration; second, "All my people advise strongly against the Black Sea." He asked Churchill again whether Stalin could be persuaded to come to Malta, Jerusalem, or Egypt.[5] However, the President did not for the moment raise the question of Stalin's preferences with Stalin himself. He confined himself to addressing rhetorical questions to Churchill.

Hopkins provided the explanation of what was troubling the President. "All of the President's close advisers were opposed to his going to Russia; most did not like or trust the Russians anyway and could not understand why the President of the United States should cart himself all over the world to meet Stalin." Hopkins was subjected to "acid criticism" for having suggested the Crimea in the first place, and Roosevelt was beginning to respond to this criticism: "When they descended on the President to urge him not to go, the President wavered again and cooked up a lot of counter proposals, none of which made any sense." Roosevelt finally repeated some of these proposals to Stalin on November 18. Stalin, in his reply, expressed regret over Roosevelt's doubts about the suitability of the Black Sea coast for a meeting of "the three of us." [6]

Stalin's negative response proved to Roosevelt that Hopkins' theory was correct: any tripartite meeting would have to take place in the Soviet Union. The President told Churchill, "I have a feeling that we will not succeed in getting U.J. to travel beyond the Black Sea. . . . " Churchill wired back, "I agree with your conclusion that U.J. will not travel beyond the Black Sea," but this did not alter the facts: "I am sure the ports there will be unfit for us until the winter has passed" [7]

It is not clear who specifically suggested Yalta as the Conference site. Hopkins wrote that Stalin first recommended Yalta, but none of Stalin's telegrams contained any reference to such a proposal. Gromyko or Harriman may have made the original suggestion. In any case, by December 9, Roosevelt was actively considering Yalta. He cabled Churchill that he was ready to set a date: "I think I can leave after Inauguration Day." He also said that Harriman had suggested Batum as the Conference site; "Yalta is also intact." [8]

Since Roosevelt had not made up his mind, Stalin began his own preparations. On December 14, he told Harriman that the Soviet Union was going to prepare "suitable facilities ashore" at Odessa. The Mediterranean was out of the question, but Stalin was willing to shift the meeting to the Crimea if the President so desired. A week later, Roosevelt cabled his acceptance of Yalta to both Harriman and Churchill, but not to Stalin: "I am prepared to go to the Crimea and have the meeting at Yalta." On December 27, Harriman reported from Moscow that he and Molotov had "discussed in detail the arrangement for the holding of the meeting at Yalta with your ship at Sevastopol." However, this proposal still had not been broached to Stalin. Molotov agreed to secure a definitive reply from the Marshal by the following day.[9]

While Molotov was informing Stalin of the proposed arrangements, Churchill was sending Roosevelt the Admiralty report on Yalta. Churchill concluded, "Stalin will make good arrangements ashore." Almost simultaneously, Harriman reported that the Soviets had accepted the Yalta site and had agreed to prepare the area: "Suitable quarters and staff meeting places can be made available at Yalta where the city was not damaged during the German occupation." [10]

Churchill, mercurial as ever, became enthusiastic about the proposed meeting. "I will certainly meet you at Yalta," he cabled the President, and he suggested that the meeting be designated "Argonaut," which he thought had a "local but not deducible association." Roosevelt asked whether the American party should transfer from ship to plane at Malta. Churchill replied, "I shall be waiting on the quay" there, and proposed the following slogan: "No more let us falter! From Malta to Yalta! Let nobody alter!" The Prime Minister considered a more elaborate version:

"No more let us alter or falter or palter! From Malta to Yalta, and Yalta to Malta!" Upon reflection, he decided, "Perhaps it was just as well that I did not cable it." [11]

Despite the intense correspondence between Churchill and Stalin during late 1944, the two leaders never discussed the question of the site or opening date. The details, decisions, and inter-Allied communication were all handled by the President. On January 3, 1945, Stalin finally broke his silence and cabled Churchill, "I know that the President has your consent to a meeting of the three of us. . . . " Churchill replied, "I look forward very much to this momentous meeting and I am glad that the President of the United States has been willing to make this long journey." Still, no one had formally asked Churchill to attend. Roosevelt finally saw the flaw in the formal preparations, and on January 6 he wrote to Harriman in Moscow, "Stalin may wish to extend an invitation to Churchill." Stalin did so on January 10: "In accordance with the proposal sent by the President, I want your agreement to Yalta as the place and February 2 as the date of the meeting." Churchill cabled back, "Okay and all good wishes." [12] Long before the Yalta Conference opened, the President had set its tone and had become the central figure.

OF PALACES AND PLUMBING

At Malta, beginning the evening of February 2, 700 British and American conferees prepared to board twenty U.S. Skymasters and five British Yorks for the 1400 mile journey to the airfield at Saki. Roosevelt's decision, shared by the Prime Minister, to take only "thirty-five" staff members had obviously been changed. Someone asked if the Russians would not think it an invasion.

Throughout the night, at ten-minute intervals, aircraft took off for the Crimea. Each plane followed the same flight plan: three-and-a-half hours due east, a 90-degree turn to avoid Crete, on to the Black Sea, another 90-degree turn at the radio transmitter near Saki Airport—to indicate that friend rather than foe was approaching—and finally touchdown on the newly constructed concrete block runway. The President's plane left at 3:30 a.m., immediately preceding Churchill's, but the Prime Minister arrived first.

A Red Army band awaiting them played the national anthems of the three countries. Guards with tommy guns were stationed at twenty-foot intervals around the perimeter of the airfield. The welcoming Russian delegation consisted of Molotov, his deputy Commissar Andrei Vyshinsky, Air Marshal Khudvakov, Admiral Kuznetsov, General Antonov, and the Soviet Ambassadors to the two Allied nations, Gromyko and Gusev. The delegation apologized for Stalin's absence: he was still en route from Moscow and had not yet arrived. They invited the Allied leaders into three near-by tents, where they were served lavish refreshments: hot tea with lemon and sugar, vodka, brandy, and champagne, caviar, smoked sturgeon and salmon, white and black bread, fresh butter, cheese, and hard- and soft-boiled eggs. Some of the Conference participants had decided beforehand to begin the six-hour, ninety-mile drive to Yalta at once, and hence missed the feast.

Roosevelt left almost immediately upon arrival, and, traveling over the recently prepared road linking Saki with Yalta, reached the palace of Livadia after six. Armed sentinels lined the road at 100-yard intervals. Each guard executed a rifle salute as the President passed. The woman guards in the contingent, less formal than the men, waved hands and flags. The Prime Minister, who had followed Molotov into a tent for refreshments, passed by somewhat later, and the guards "stood rigidly to attention." Shortly before reaching Yalta, Molotov stopped the Prime Minister's car and invited the group to another sumptuous luncheon, set for ten people. Churchill reflected, "The President's party had apparently slipped past unawares and Molotov was alone with two of his officials." The Prime Minister enjoyed his feast and "soon got into form." He thought Molotov "in the best of humours," and the evening luncheon went well except for a miscalculation by the British group, which had already "duly" lunched on sandwiches in the car. As the delegation descended from the chilly mountains to the sea coast, the change was, as Churchill remembered it, into "warm and brilliant sunshine and a most genial climate." [13]

Yalta was the Soviet Union's first tripartite conference, and despite the devastation in the Crimea, the Russians undertook to provide an atmosphere that would please the President and the Prime Minister. General Deane, who had the job of co-ordinating arrangements for the American delegation with the Soviets, observed, "The preparations for the conference caused them considerable anguish." Tsar Nicholas's more than fifty-room palace, Livadia * was selected as the President's residence and headquarters. It was constructed between April 1910 and September 1911 by the architect Krasnov, at a cost of two million rubles, paid in gold. It was of marble and limestone construction, although Western accounts mistakenly call it a white granite edifice. The view of the sea, 150 feet below, and the mountains behind led Stettinius to proclaim the view "was a breath-taking sight and reminded me of parts of our Pacific coast." The Germans in their retreat had ravaged the area: the delegations were warned that mines still might be present. Much of Livadia had been torn down, including the panelling on the walls, but the Russians had moved quickly to remodel it. Large numbers of plasterers, plumbers, electricians, and painters were brought in from Moscow. Furniture and fixtures were shipped from three Moscow hotels, including the Metropole. Ten days before the Conference, Ambassador Harriman's daughter came down to supervise the refitting and furnishing. The U.S.S. *Catoctin,* a naval auxiliary ship, was sent to exterminate the vermin in the palace.[14]

Roosevelt's personal quarters were on the first floor, within a few steps of the Conference Hall. He lived in one of the Tsar's

---

* Livadia is currently one of 86 sanitoria along the 55 miles of seacoast called Yalta. All these sanitoria accommodate 40,000 people at any given time. Before World War II, there were 36 sanitoria; the Germans destroyed 27 of them. Livadia once had 1000 laborers or staff to work for 7 members of the royal family. In 1925 it became the first sanitorium in the Crimea and catered to poor peasants. Today, 1200 Soviet citizens are accommodated at Livadia, including the adjacent 9 buildings in the Livadia complex, in which Tsar Nicholas housed his government officials. In 1970-71 the Conference Hall of the palace will become a museum of the Yalta Conference, where approximately 40,000 foreign tourists each year can see original documents, photographs, and the Conference Hall itself.

bedrooms, surrounded by orange velvet panels, and used the old billiard room of oak and red velvet as his private dining room. All the plenary sessions were held on the first floor of Livadia, in a long hall with windows facing the courtyard on one side, the front entrance of the palace looking to the woods on the other side, and a great fireplace at the end of the hall. On the same floor a two-room suite, overlooking the sea, was reserved for Stettinius, and there were "comfortable quarters" for Byrnes, Hopkins, Leahy, Harriman, Bohlen, and several others. On the second floor, Marshall had the imperial bedroom and Admiral King the Tsarina's boudoir, which became a favorite joke among the American delegation. The State Department delegation was small enough to be "comfortably housed," but the military contingency was too large—five to seven generals had to share rooms and lived in "overcrowded conditions." Even so, the military got along—they organized a mess hall for themselves on the second floor, where they had both American and Russian food.

In all, the palace had three stories and over four dozen good sized rooms, so space was not lacking. As Stettinius put it, "The only acute shortage was bathrooms." [15] Stalin quipped that the Tsar had a number of bedrooms on the first floor because he changed bedrooms every night—and sometimes during the night! In fact, Stalin remarked with a grin, the only place where one could be sure to find the Tsar was in the bathroom first thing every morning. The Tsar's bathroom was, in a sense, the main source of discomfort for the American delegation: the 215 Americans in the palace shared only a few bathrooms, and Roosevelt had the only private one. Further, Russian chambermaids walked in and out without knocking, to the immense dismay and embarrassment of the delegation.[16]

Churchill found the "very large villa" assigned the British delegation "impressive," but Roosevelt's was "even more splendid* . . . close at hand, and it was here, in order to spare him physical inconvenience, that all our plenary meetings were held."

---

* I personally find Vorontzov an extraordinarily beautiful palace, superior to Livadia in every respect (except perhaps, sheer size of the rooms), and cannot account for the oft-expressed opinions of the British delegation that Livadia was finer.

The Vorontzov Palace (sometimes called "Aliupka" for its location) was ten miles from Livadia and four miles from Stalin's quarters in between. It had been built from 1828 to 1848 by an English architect of diabase stone for the Russian noble family, Vorontzov, one of whom had been Russian Ambassador to England in the early 1800's, and another, his son, the Governor General of the Crimea and a distinguished military officer in the Crimean War. By the fireplace in the dining room Churchill found two paintings which he recognized as portraits of the Herberts of Wilton. Ambassador Vorontzov had brought back the pictures when he married a daughter of the family. These paintings and the palace itself were all the Germans left in the area, and, as with Livadia and Stalin's quarters, everything else was brought in.

The villa has the appearance of a Scottish castle from one side and a Moorish palace from another. (The descriptive plaques in the villa museum call the north and west façades "Nineteenth Century Tudor" and the southern façade "Oriental.") Through a great Moorish archway, a wide flight of steps, flanked by six marble lions, leads to the garden, which descends in terraces to the Black Sea. The first pair of lions is sleeping, the next awakening, and the last roaring. Two old and lovely cypresses stood in the courtyard, and rare subtropical plants had been put in in 1945 for the British.

Churchill, his daughter Sarah, Anthony Eden, Sir Alexander Cadogan, Sir Alan Brooke, Sir Andrew Cunningham, Sir Charles Portal, Field Marshal Alexander, Sir Archibald Clark Kerr, General Ismay, Lord Moran, and a few others stayed at Vorontzov. Churchill was given three rooms. His bedroom, of Oriental decor, opened onto the terrace and faced the sea. Generals, Air Marshals, and Admirals were packed together in a score of open, hotel-like rooms which had once been the servants' quarters. The rest of the British delegation was sent to two rest-houses twenty minutes away, piled five or six in one room. Churchill recalled, "No one seemed to mind," and Moran afterward explained, "Give the Englishman real discomfort, and he becomes cheerful." [17]

The British compared notes with the Americans and found

they had the same difficulties. There were only two baths in the whole villa. Queues formed outside each, and there was only cold water at that. Venturing downstairs once, Lord Moran discovered the military leaders "hunting for a tin to wash in," so that at least a few "could get a wash without lining up for the two communal basins." Moran found "the reception rooms are what might be expected from the gentleman who was responsible for the lions," * but he remarked, "The plumbing and sanitary arrangements are elementary." His professional judgment was acerbic: "In this palace, with its gilt furniture, its lashings of caviar, its grand air of luxury, there is nothing left out but cleanliness."

Bedbugs became an immediate problem. Churchill sent for Moran the first night "because he had been bitten on the feet," and Eden's secretary as well as Churchill's butler "had been eaten up," Moran recorded. The casualties mounted. Moran responded to a call from one of the sanitoria where the bulk of the delegation was housed. There he found "the most elementary bedding arrangements, spread out on the floor, and bugs in all the bedding." He concluded, "Something must be done." He promptly borrowed two sanitary squads from the Americans and proceeded to squirt D.D.T. everywhere. He also took personal precautions: "I haven't unpacked my suitcase, and I have no intention of doing so." [18]

By the time he wrote his memoirs, eight years later, Churchill considered that "every effort was made by our hosts to ensure our comfort, and every chance remark noted with kindly attention." Lord Moran observed that the staff had been specially picked from those who had previously served the British delegations on trips to Moscow: "All my Moscow friends seem to be here in their white coats . . . these waiters are really the only people I recognize when I revisit Russia." General Hastings Ismay, Churchill's chief of staff, recognized his former two waiters from the Hotel Nationale. When alone with him, they fell to their

---

* The reception rooms, which Moran (in his style of understatement) finds acceptable, are a light blue with white moulding, strikingly like Wedgwood porcelain. There are two rooms, full of light, which were often used together, with one as a stage where artists such as Rachmaninov and Chaliapin performed.

knees, kissed his hand, and left. But in general the staff seemed
to be under strict orders to remain formal and efficient. Portal
admired a large glass tank with plants and remarked it contained
no fish; two days later a consignment of goldfish appeared. Another casual remark, about a lack of lemon peel for cocktails, resulted in the arrival of a lemon tree, which was planted in the
hall.

Stalin made a point of hiding the despair of his devastated
nation. He purposely told Roosevelt that all they lacked in Russia was "tin, rubber and pineapples." Churchill checked this line
out personally on a tour as he left Yalta. He slyly asked his guide
whether the Russians were short of glass. The guide, unlike the
Marshal, did not hide the facts. But the official stance prevailed
when Sarah Churchill tried to give chocolates to some friendly
children during the same excursion. A soldier waved her away,
saying they did not need feeding.

The Soviet delegation resided at Koreis Villa, built around
1850, which had belonged to Prince Yusupov, reputedly Raspu-
tin's assassin.* Here Stalin, who arrived the morning of February
4, worked each night, running the government and directing what
Churchill, impressed, called "their immense front, now in violent
action." [19] It was precisely this subject which Stalin arranged to
spend the entire day of February 4 pursuing.

SOME INFORMAL CHATS

Through Molotov, Stalin set up informal conversations with
both Churchill and Roosevelt. The visit to Churchill was arranged for 3:00 p.m., the one to Roosevelt at Livadia for 4:00

---

* Intourist was unable to arrange a tour of Koreis for me, so very little
can be said of the palace since the American and British delegations
record nothing of it either. However, by taking a boat trip and climbing
a small mountain, I finally arrived at a statue of Lenin on top of the
mountain overlooking the palace, and was able to photograph it. For
some reason this seemed to provoke both curiosity and consternation
among a number of Soviet citizens in the area. Westerners are expected—
and encouraged—to visit Livadia or Vorontzov, but it is considered peculiar to be equally interested in the "home" of the Soviet delegation.

p.m. This order was probably a simple matter of convenience, since Stalin's final destination was the plenary session scheduled for 5:00 p.m. at Livadia.

Stalin's talk with Churchill was not particularly significant. They discussed Soviet military successes for the most part. Stalin emphasized the unique Soviet contribution to victory—unwavering determination and the full commitment of manpower. Churchill prodded for more information. He asked what the Russians would do if Adolf Hitler moved south, as the West had predicted he would. Stalin resolutely answered, "We shall follow him!" The Oder River was no longer an obstacle, he claimed. Soviet bridgeheads had already been established, and the Germans were weak everywhere. The current successes were just the beginning. (Stalin neglected to mention that his generals were following the orders of a battle plan that called for the imminent capture of Berlin—a plan he would scrap two days later.)

Stalin suggested, as Churchill had done earlier in the war, that the Allies transfer their forces in Italy into the Balkans and central Europe. By attacking Vienna and simultaneously linking with the Red Army, they could outflank the Germans south of the Alps. Churchill rejected his own scheme: "The Red Army may not give us time to complete the operation." Churchill dismissed the whole incident: "It cost him [Stalin] nothing to say this now, but I made no reproaches." [20]

In contrast, Stalin bypassed the Red Army's successes as far as possible when he talked with Roosevelt. The President complimented the Red Army on its current success and position. Stalin told Roosevelt the opposite of what he said to Churchill. Soviet troops were on the Oder but were encountering great resistance. The Americans would reach Manila, the Marshal predicted, before the Russians reached Berlin. In addition to the authority he had to slow down the Soviet pace, Stalin further knew that Churchill respected power and would bargain accordingly; but with the President it was important not to overplay his hand.

Stalin was far more interested in the situation on the western front. Roosevelt, in response to questioning, confirmed that a Western offensive was in the offing. However, the President later hedged on details of the offensive, claiming that ice on the Rhine might prevent an Allied crossing until March. Further, he admitted that the Americans and British were divided on location of the major crossing. Before Stalin had a chance to comment, Roosevelt changed the subject to military liaison between General Eisenhower, Supreme Commander in the West, and the Red Army. Stalin readily agreed that efficient inter-Allied liaison would expedite Germany's collapse.

Roosevelt then turned to political matters and gave Stalin several valuable hints about the thrust of America's hitherto enigmatic foreign policy. The President indicated that, unlike Britain, the United States favored a harsh policy against Germany. The German destruction of the Crimea, he said, made him more bloodthirsty than he had been a year before, at Teheran. He hoped Stalin would again propose a toast to the execution of 50,000 officers in the German Army! * Stalin interjected that everyone was more bloodthirsty now and that this destruction at Yalta was minor compared with that in the Ukraine.

Roosevelt brought up the Free French and gave a vivid demonstration of his antipathy to Charles de Gaulle. He asked Stalin how the Marshal had gotten along with de Gaulle in Moscow the previous December. Stalin, who (according to de Gaulle's account) complimented the Frenchman in December for his skillful negotiating,† echoed the President's well-known sentiments and labeled de Gaulle naïve and unrealistic. He mocked

---

* At a banquet at Teheran, Stalin, perhaps seriously, proposed executing the German General Staff and 50,000 German officers. When Churchill objected, Roosevelt proposed a compromise—executing only 49,500. The President's son Elliot also supported the joke, whereupon Churchill stormed out of the banquet.

† In Moscow Stalin allegedly told de Gaulle, in a low voice so that no one could overhear him, "You have played well! Well done! I like dealing with someone who knows what he wants, even if he doesn't share my views." de Gaulle, *Salvation*, p. 88. The French and Soviets had just concluded a twenty-year Franco-Russian alliance, but de Gaulle had refused to include a provision recognizing the Polish Lublin Committee as the government of Poland, a reason for which Stalin would not want to compliment his new ally openly.

the French for asking for the same rights as the Big Three even though France had done very little fighting.

The President disparaged the French, telling Stalin that de Gaulle had once compared himself spiritually with Joan of Arc and politically with Clemenceau. Stalin agreed that the French were pretentious. They had not fought in 1940 and at present were making only a small contribution. Roosevelt informed the Marshal that he was arming eight new French divisions; Stalin pointed out that this generosity highlighted French weakness. The President inquired about de Gaulle's territorial plans. He understood that the French had no interest in annexing German territory but only wanted it under international control. Stalin responded that de Gaulle had told a different story in Moscow, claiming the Rhine was the natural boundary of France and wanting troops stationed there permanently.

Roosevelt went on to say "something indiscreet," which he would not want to repeat in front of Churchill. The British, Roosevelt said, wanted to have their cake and eat it too, by building up France artificially into a strong power. In any future war, France would hold the line against Germany with 200,000 troops while the British army reassembled.

The President then changed the subject, and began to discuss the question of tripartite zones, with the possible allocation of a zone to France. He was having a great deal of trouble with the British on zones too, he confessed. The United States preferred the northwestern zone in order not to be dependent on communications through France. Worse yet, the British expected the United States to restore order in France and then turn over political control to the British. Stalin asked specifically whether Roosevelt favored a French zone and for what reasons? Roosevelt vacillated. Giving France a zone was not a bad idea, but, on the other hand, it could only be done out of kindness. Both Stalin and Molotov agreed vociferously. Since it was 4:57, the leaders adjourned to the first plenary session.[21]

Stalin had at last gained some clues to the American position on two key issues. Roosevelt would favor a repressive policy against Germany and he would oppose an equal role for France in the wartime and postwar machinery. Stalin agreed in the first instance and was quite willing to go along in the second. But the British position was not discussed.

THE FIRST SESSION

At the first plenary session of the Yalta Conference, Stalin suggested that Roosevelt—self-appointed moderator of the Allied coalition, and perhaps the greatest source of both strength and uncertainty—make the opening remarks, just as he had done at Teheran. Roosevelt replied that he was honored to do so, and went on to stress unity among leaders who understood each other well. Their only goals were to end the war and to create a stable peace. Already they had seen that "frankness in talks made for an early achievement of good decisions." [22]

The first topic of the Conference, as Stalin had requested the day before, February 3, was the military situation. As previously arranged, Roosevelt asked Antonov to report on the advances of the Soviet forces. Antonov gave a factual account of the offensive which five Red Army groups had begun January 12 on the 700-kilometer front stretching from the Nieman River to the Carpathian mountains. He was careful to emphasize that, because of unfavorable weather, the advance had not been planned for this time, but had been started as a Soviet service to the hard-pressed Western Allies: "However, in view of the alarming situation that had developed on the western front, in connection with the German offensive in the Ardennes, the High Command of the Soviet forces ordered the offensive to be started not later than mid-January, without waiting for the weather to improve."

Antonov then explained the over-all plan. Since the Russian forces were facing the center, the most solid sector of the front, they first had to thin out the enemy grouping. Hence, attacks had been launched on both flanks—in East Prussia and "in Hungary in the direction of Budapest." As the Soviets had hoped, the Germans had withdrawn the bulk of their tank forces—twenty out of twenty-four divisions—from the central sector. In fact, eleven of these divisions now uselessly reinforced the German position around Budapest.

These diversionary maneuvers had notably enhanced Soviet strength. In the central sector the Russians outnumbered the Germans two to one in infantry and had a force "overwhelming in artillery, tanks, and aviation, and artillery density of 220 to 230 pieces per kilometer on the central front." Although weather conditions at the start of the Soviet offensive had been so unfavorable that air operations and artillery observation were ruled out, the Soviets, relying only upon artillery and good preliminary reconnaissance, had pushed forward ten to fifteen kilometers the first day and had broken "the whole tactical depth of the enemy's defenses." In only eighteen days the Red Army had advanced 500 kilometers, an average of twenty to thirty a day, occupying the Silesian industrial area and the east bank of the Oder. East Prussia had been isolated from the rest of Germany, and the Germans had lost 400,000 men, with forty-five divisions routed.

Antonov then outlined future operations and offered to entertain any requests from the West. The Germans would intensify their defense of Berlin, he asserted. They would sacrifice all other fronts in order to amass the maximum strength in front of the capital, and might transfer divisions from western Europe and Italy for this. Vienna would also be defended "as solidly as possible," probably with reinforcements from Italy. Antonov calculated that the Germans could move thirty to thirty-five divisions to the eastern front from other areas. Sixteen divisions had already been transferred, and another five were on the way.

Finally, Antonov broached the possibility of Allied action against the Germans in the first half of February in order to prevent the transfer of further German divisions to the eastern front, particularly from Italy. As a secondary objective, he requested air strikes against the Berlin and Leipzig junctions.[23] Settlement of this question would have been essential if Stalin had decided to strike at Berlin as scheduled.

Eager to evaluate the impact of Antonov's report, Stalin asked the Allies if they had any questions. Roosevelt asked if the Soviet Union intended to change the gauge of the German railroads. Stalin curtly reminded the President that the Soviets had limited resources: what few changes they made were not for pleasure. Roosevelt again suggested liaison and joint planning. Churchill, implying that the West thought the Soviet Union was not co-operative, concurred, and reinforced the President's request. Stalin simply answered, as before, that he agreed.[24]

In response to Antonov's report, Churchill promised that the military staffs would discuss how to prevent the transfer of German divisions from the Italian front. Further, he raised the possibility which Stalin had privately mentioned earlier—the transfer of British forces from Italy to the Ljubljana corridor. This time Stalin did not reply at all.

Following the question period, General George C. Marshall, the American Chief of Staff, reported on the military situation in the West. The German offensive in the Ardennes had been halted. Eisenhower was regrouping his forces for an offensive, which would take place in the north since it was the line of least resistance. Another operation was planned for the southern sector of the front, north of Switzerland. Operations would begin on February 8, in typical Allied fashion (which Stalin considered excessively cautious): as many units would be used as supply facilities permitted; the Rhine would not be crossed until March. Marshall conceded that the operations on the western front had developed slowly because of lack of tonnage, but the opening of Antwerp was "livening up" things. The Germans currently were trying to disrupt this line of supply with flying bombs.

Stalin deprecated this obstacle: "Bombs and rockets rarely hit the target." General Marshall replied that a lucky hit might destroy the Antwerp lock gates, with disastrous consequences. Marshall continued that the Allied air force had always been active when weather permitted. That very day it had destroyed troop trains on their way to the Soviet-German front. By this stage of the war Allied bombing had reduced German oil production to 20 per cent of normal operation. Marshall estimated that the enemy had thirty-two divisions on the Italian front, opposing an equal number of Allied divisions; the Allies' advantage lay in their great air superiority. Finally, Marshall declared that a renewed German submarine offensive could be anticipated because an improved submarine had been perfected. Although there were only thirty German submarines operating at the time, the Allies were encountering difficulty in locating them because of the tide in shallow waters.[25]

Ethnocentrism is rampant in all the various accounts of the military reports. American and British writers generally dismissed Antonov's report and stressed only the fine quality of Marshall's presentation and the favorable impact it supposedly had. Stettinius, after summarily treating Antonov's report, stated, "Marshall thereupon presented extemporaneously one of the clearest and most concise summaries I have ever heard in my life. . . ." Churchill remarked of Antonov's report merely that it was "detailed," but said of Marshall's: "Marshall gave us a brilliantly concise account of Anglo-American operations." Eden noted only that the Russians were pleased to learn of Allied plans from Marshall. The Bohlen minutes omitted the substance of Antonov's report. Of the official Western minutes, only the Combined Chiefs of Staff have a complete account of Antonov's speech.[26]

The Soviet minutes of the Conference display the same tendency: Antonov's statement is recorded in detail, Marshall's is summarized. In addition, there are several discrepancies between the Soviet and American minutes regarding Marshall's presentation. Whether these divergences sprang from mistranslation or from postwar political calculation, the result was that they minimized the Western contribution to the war effort. For example, Marshall stated that Allied bombing had reduced German oil production to 20 per cent of former capacity; the Soviet minutes say to 40 per cent. Marshall listed thirty-two enemy divisions on the Italian front, the Soviets twenty-seven (they omitted five Italian divisions). Marshall mentioned Allied problems in detecting German submarines in shallow waters; the Soviet minutes blame the problem on Allied technological incompetence.[27]

The Soviet secondary histories are even more interesting. They use Antonov's report to stress that the Soviets were bearing the heaviest burden in the war, and, more importantly, that the Soviet offensive of January 1945, stemmed from the general obligation to help one's allies, *an obligation which the West failed to return*. As one historian comments: "When the West was in trouble in January 1945, at the request of Churchill, Stalin ordered an increased tempo of attack all along the Soviet-German front," but that the Allies, for their part, would not or did not thereafter prevent the transfer of German troops from Italy or France to the east.

Returning to the Conference: After Marshall's report, Churchill asked whether the Soviets could offer assistance against German submarines, since Danzig, the principal point of their construction, would soon be approached by the Soviet forces. Stalin inquired about the other locations of production, and Admiral of the Fleet Sir Andrew Cunningham, Chief of Naval Staff, supplied the information. Churchill also asked the Soviets to make available their experience in crossing rivers, but he received no answer at that time.

Instead, Stalin wanted to ask a number of questions about the strength of the impending Western offensive, and he made an implicit comparison between Soviet and Western military strength. What was the length of the breakthrough front? Marshall replied that it was between fifty and sixty miles long (the Russian front, as Antonov had described, was 700 kilometers, or 500 miles). Did the Germans have any fortifications on the breakthrough line? Yes, heavy fortifications had been built. Stalin asked whether the Allies would have the reserves to exploit the success. Marshall's affirmative reply prompted Stalin to stress his own emphasis on reserves, which had proven vitally necessary in the various Russian winter campaigns.

Stalin had many more questions: how many tank divisions were planned for the breakthrough? The Soviets had used 9000 tanks in the central sector of their front, he said. Marshall could not answer specifically—there would be ten to twelve tank divisions for every thirty-five divisions. Stalin was not satisfied: how many tanks were there in an Allied division? Three hundred, answered Marshall, and Churchill interrupted to assert that in the whole theater in western Europe the Allies had 10,000 tanks. Sta-

lin remarked that that was a great many. The Soviets had between 8000 and 9000 planes: how many did the Allies possess? Sir
Charles Portal, Royal Air Force Chief of Staff, replied that the
Allies had nearly as many on the section of the Western Front
designated for the attack. This included 4000 bombers carrying a
load of three to five tons per plane.

Stalin inquired about the Allied superiority in infantry; the
Soviet command on the front of the main attack, he asserted, had
a superiority of 100 divisions to the 80 German divisions. From
this remark Churchill concluded, erroneously, that the Soviet
strength on the fighting front was much greater than it actually
was. Charles Bohlen, the interpreter, reported, and recorded in
his minutes, that *"in Poland* the Soviet Army had enjoyed a
superiority of 100 divisions." The Combined Chiefs of Staff, who
co-ordinated minutes at the end of each session, correctly recorded "the Russians employed 100 divisions, which was 20 more
than the Germans had." Bohlen's translation misled Churchill,
and perhaps the whole delegation, because, according to Bohlen
and Stettinius, Churchill observed that the Russians had 180 Soviet divisions against 80 German divisions. This statement was
not inaccurate; but it was misleading. The Soviet Union did
have 180 divisions, 100 of which were being used in Poland
against 80 German divisions.[28]

Churchill, responding to Stalin's prods, tried to establish Anglo-American superiority. He denied that the Allies had ever possessed an advantage in manpower; what they did have was a
"very great superiority in the air." General Marshall added that
ten days earlier the Germans had seventy-nine divisions opposing
their seventy-eight divisions in the west. Stalin asked no further
questions. He concluded by making one further comparison, that
in the present offensive the Soviets enjoyed artillery supremacy of
four to one.

To soothe ruffled tempers, Stalin revealed one of the Red
Army's operational techniques: "The Soviet people, being the
Allies' comrades-in-arms, can exchange experiences." He described a special breakthrough force which the Soviets had devised a year before. For the breakthrough they had used 230 guns
per kilometer. The special force was quite significant, Stalin said:

it "had opened the gates for the Red Army. From then on, the advance had not been difficult."

Stalin then dealt with questions of Allied military co-operation. The Soviet Union, he declared, always fulfilled its responsibilities with great consideration for the position of its Allies, and, above all, acted out of moral obligation: what wishes did the Allies have? Churchill ignored the question and dealt with the assumption, acknowledging the obvious success of the Soviet Army. He thanked the Soviet Union and expressed the gratitude of England and of America "for the massive power and successes of the Soviet offensive." [29]

Stalin appeared to be quite irritated at Churchill's remark. The Soviet offensive, he tried to indicate, was not dictated by a desire to garner gratitude, nor by formal agreements made at Teheran. The Russians, in attacking, were fulfilling the *moral* obligations of an ally. The Soviet minutes summarized Stalin's remarks: "The Soviet Government considered that to be its duty, the duty of an ally, although it was under no formal obligation on this score." Further, "Stalin would like the leaders of the Allied Powers to take into account that Soviet leaders did not merely fulfill their obligations but were also prepared to fulfill their moral duty as far as possible." Roosevelt immediately said he agreed. There was no obligation binding from the Teheran Conference. The Allies were committed only to move as quickly and as extensively as possible against the common enemy. Having shown his assent, Roosevelt switched from the question of general co-operation to tactical liaison. Earlier, he said, it had not been possible to establish a common plan of operation. But now that the Allied and Soviet armies were approaching Germany together, their operations could be co-ordinated.

Churchill also said he welcomed Stalin's words. It had not been necessary to strike any bargain with the Soviet Union "because of the complete confidence" which the President and he felt in the Marshal, the Russian people, and the efficiency of the Russian military. However, Roosevelt's point was important. There was an advantage to collaboration, for if either army were hampered at its front, the other might operate nevertheless. Stalin pointed out that such a state of affairs constituted *lack* of co-ordination. The Soviet offensive had halted in the autumn just as the Allies had begun theirs. That should not happen again.[30] (The critical reader must bear in mind the possibility that Stalin was evaluating the ability and willingness of his Allies to fight in the West simultaneously with the final Soviet offensive on Berlin, which he was in the process of deciding at this point.)

With the session near its end, the Allies responded to Stalin's request that they state their demands. Admiral Cunningham said he would like the Soviet forces to take Danzig as soon as possible. Roosevelt asked Stalin if Danzig were within Soviet range. Stalin affirmed that Danzig would "hopefully" be within Soviet range. This remark "seemed to cause general hilarity, and the Prime Minister laughed heartily." Admiral Cunningham was quite insulted by it all.[31]

"UNCLE JOE" ON WAR AND PEACE

That evening, Roosevelt gave an intimate dinner at Livadia for Stalin, Churchill, and the main Big Three advisers.[32] Champagne and vodka flowed freely (although Stalin, after a judicious interval, switched to water) while Roosevelt served caviar, consommé, sturgeon, beef with macaroni, chicken salad, fried chicken, and dessert. The Russian secret police planted a man who sat silently at the banquet, partaking only of lemonade and mineral water, "listening to everyone."

Good humor generally prevailed. The repartee was fast, if not witty. Roosevelt, commenting on Stettinius's expressed hope to visit Moscow, asked Stalin, "Do you think Ed will behave in Moscow as Molotov did in New York?" The idea that Molotov, unaffectionately known in the West as "Stone-Ass," might have wildly, or even mildly, indulged himself while touring New York City under benevolent auspices of the White House Secret Service, was beyond possibility, but Stalin fell in with the President's mood and quipped, "He could come to Moscow incognito."

Emboldened by this exchange, Roosevelt confided to Stalin, "There is one thing I want to tell you. The Prime Minister and

I have been cabling back and forth for two years now, and we have a term of endearment by which we call you and that is 'Uncle Joe.' " The term seemed no endearment to Stalin.* He asked just what this meant. The President explained and ordered more champagne. Byrnes suggested that Uncle Joe was no worse than Uncle Sam. Stalin was not mollified and said it was time for him to leave. Roosevelt asked him to stay. Stalin still seemed offended; Molotov stepped in and explained that Stalin was merely pretending. "He is just pulling your leg. We have known this for two years. All of Russia knows that you call him 'Uncle Joe.' " Whether he was pretending or was truly offended at the semi-public airing of such a term, Stalin agreed to stay until 10:30, and actually stayed until 11:30.

Churchill broke the tension with a toast. The whole world had its eyes on this Conference, he said, and if it were successful, there would be peace for a hundred years. Only the three Great Powers who had shed blood and fought the war could maintain the peace.

This toast struck a responsive note in Stalin. He made it quite plain that only the three Great Powers who had borne the brunt of the war and had liberated the small powers from German domination should have the unanimous right to preserve the peace of the world. As an illustration, he selected Albania, the smallest of the eastern European states, and at the same time an unreliable socialist upstart, in his opinion. It would be ridiculous, he said, for Albania to have an equal voice with the three Great Powers who had won the war. The notion, current among the liberated countries, that the Allies had shed their blood to liberate them was absurd. The small powers were now scolding the Allies for not taking their rights into consideration, and this, by implication, was equally absurd. Stalin admitted he could serve no other interest than that of the Soviet state and people, although the Soviet Union was prepared to pay its share in the preservation of peace, and he was prepared, in concert with the

* In Russian, the term "uncle" connotes familiarity and is a colloquial form of address, hardly to be used in relationships where respect and authority predominate.

United States and Great Britain, to protect the rights of the small powers. But he would never allow any Allied action to be submitted to the judgment of the small powers.

Roosevelt and Churchill hastened to agree. Roosevelt stated that the powers who had fought the war must write the peace. Churchill said that there was no question of small powers dictating to the large. Stalin insisted he had in mind the reverse, that the large powers must dictate to the small. Churchill understood this and continued that the great nations had a moral responsibility to exercise their power with moderation and great respect for the rights of the smaller nations. (Off to the side, Vyshinsky argued Stalin's position with Bohlen. The Soviets, Vyshinsky declared, would never permit the small powers to judge the acts of the Big Three. Bohlen replied that the American leaders had to bear in mind American public opinion, which demanded protection for the rights of smaller nations. Vyshinsky remarked that the American people should learn to obey their leaders. Bohlen said he would like to hear Vyshinsky tell that to the American people; Vyshinsky replied he would be only too glad to do so.)

Churchill, still acting as peace-maker, toasted the proletarian masses of the world, and this led to a lively discussion about self-government. Churchill noted that although he was always being "beaten up" as a reactionary, he was the only one present who could be thrown out of office any minute by universal suffrage. Personally, he gloried in that danger. Stalin ironically remarked that the Prime Minister feared such elections. Churchill maintained that he did not; he was proud of the possibility of a change of government. The Prime Minister added that all three governments were moving toward the same goal by different methods.

The discussion reverted to the rights of small nations. Churchill defended the minor powers, remarking with casual eloquence, "The eagle should permit the small birds to sing and care not wherefor they sang." Stalin disagreed: small birds, he implied, had better watch their steps. Argentina, for example, ought to be punished for her failure to co-operate with the Allies. If Argentina were in *his* section of the world, he would make sure of it. But Argentina was in the American sphere, so

Stalin would do nothing. Roosevelt replied that the Argentine people were good but there were some bad men in power for the moment, but he found that Poland was an example of a minor power in Stalin's sphere. There were, the President declared, many Poles in America who were interested in the future of Poland. Stalin immediately replied that of the seven million Poles in America, only seven thousand voted, and he made his statement with particular emphasis, certain that he was right. Stalin always enjoyed making a point. The Soviet Marshal had years of just such points behind him.

On that note the banquet ended. Stettinius and Bohlen apparently enjoyed themselves. Eden, on the other hand, thought the whole affair a disaster. He wrote in his diary:

> Dinner with Americans; a terrible party I thought. President vague and loose and ineffective. W. understanding that business was flagging made desperate efforts and too long speeches to get things going again. Stalin's attitude to small countries struck me as grim, not to say sinister. We were too many and there was no steady flow and brisk exchanges as at Teheran. I was greatly relieved when the whole business was over.[33]

In general, the Western participants attached little significance to this banquet. Actually, Stalin had been extremely frank about his attitude on small countries and spheres of influence, and, had the West listened, some important misunderstandings on Poland and on the United Nations could have been avoided later.

MILITARY MEETINGS

The military issues raised at the first plenary session were discussed at a series of meetings between the Anglo-American Combined Chiefs of Staff and the Soviet General Staff. General Antonov suggested that Field Marshal Sir Alan Brooke serve as chairman for the first combined Staff meeting on February 5. Brooke accepted, and he promptly placed the main Anglo-American request before the Soviets. The British and Americans wanted the Red Army to engage the Germans to the fullest during March and April, while Western troops crossed the Rhine. Brooke acknowledged the difficulties: thaw and mud would be trouble-some during these months, and the Soviets had already outdistanced their own communication lines. General Marshall, while he too appealed to Antonov for Soviet activity during the Rhine crossings, also tried to answer Stalin's implicit criticisms of Allied strength. When appraising the western front, he said, special conditions had to be borne in mind. The Allies did not have superiority in ground forces, and the lines of communication were delicate; their great strength was in air power. The Allies' lack of superior ground forces made Soviet help quite crucial, Marshall went on. The West had a distinct advantage only when air power was usable, that is, when bad weather did not interfere. Soviet help was extremely important to keep the enemy from concentrating his forces during a spell of bad weather.

General Antonov reiterated the promise that the Soviets would continue their offensive so long as the weather permitted. He assured Marshall that the Soviets would take every measure in order to make such interruptions as short as possible and to continue the advance to the limit of Soviet capacity.

In return he had one main request. The Russians wanted the Allies to prevent the Germans from transferring troops from west to east. The Germans had transferred divisions to the western front at the time of the Normandy invasion, and the Soviet military leaders wanted them to be kept there. Antonov specified that the Soviets were most concerned with the Italian front.

Alan Brooke, speaking for the Allies, was not encouraging. He admitted that the Allies had been on the offensive in Italy until the weather had interrupted, and were now preparing another. However, the Allies were going to transfer some of their own divisions from the Italian front. Field Marshal Albert Kesselring, German commander in Italy, could easily do the same, and the West would be helpless to stop it.

Antonov tried to ascertain what this meant for the eastern front. He asked for Allied estimates of German strength in Italy. The West's replies indicated that the Germans could withdraw as many as ten divisions from Italy. The Allied chiefs seemed to realize how disappointing their answers were, for they countered in glowing terms with Western contributions to the air war. Sir Charles Portal declared that the Allies had a total of 14,000 aircraft, and that the air war could continue even if the land war were bogged down. The Allies had already made a major contribution with their aircraft by destroying enemy oil, he said. The Allies would continue using their air superiority for the common cause by attacking German aircraft plants. Field Marshal Alexander added his assurance that Allied air power was the best preventive measure to halt a withdrawal of German divisions from Italy. General Marshall also emphasized the Allied air campaign.

Air Marshal Sergei Khudyakov, after praising the Soviet's own air power, returned to the question of troop transfers. He expressed hope that Alexander would use Allied planes to hamper any transfer of German divisions. Alexander affirmed that this was one of his objectives, and Khudyakov was much relieved. Antonov, however, was disappointed over the Allies' inability to play a larger role on the Austro-Italian front. He had hoped that the Allies would strike toward the Ljubljana Gap and Graz to help the Soviet drive to Vienna. This did not seem possible from what he had just heard.

Brooke repeated Marshall's earlier statement that the Allies had no great superiority in land forces. They were concentrating for a deathblow in western Germany. If the Germans withdrew from Italy, Allied troops were insufficient to take advantage of this withdrawal. Antonov dropped his request and turned to the possibility of halting a German withdrawal from Norway. Again the Allies could not help. German troops were moved by sea, and the Allies were hindered by mines they said. In any case, Allied forces were too weak to engage in a land action in Norway. Antonov, blocked at every turn, ceased inquiring about the prevention of troop transfers.

After a brief and pointed discussion of Western artillery techniques, the staff meeting turned to the highly sensitive question of liaison between the two fronts. Unfortunately, the matter was out of Antonov's hands, for the Soviet Command was highly centralized and operated entirely out of Moscow. Commanders did not make their own decisions on the field, but operated on orders from Moscow. Stalin directed the operations. Alexander, in his memoirs, wrote: "He [Soviet Marshal Tolbukhin] told me that an objective would be given to him in a directive from Moscow, and that the necessary extra formations would be sent to him, administered by Moscow, and maintained from home. All he had to do was to prepare the plan of battle and direct the operations. When the objective had been gained the supplementary shock troops were withdrawn from him." [34]

Fleet Admiral Leahy gave his "very frank" view (which the American staff had not even bothered to discuss with the British): Allied armies should be able to deal rapidly with Soviet commanders through the Military Mission in Moscow. Brooke concurred, and asked if they could also have direct contact between the Soviet and Anglo-American commanders on their respective fronts, in order to co-ordinate day-to-day action.

Antonov agreed there was a need for co-ordination, but said that requests should be handled through the military missions in Moscow, as Leahy had suggested. Marshall objected—why should liaison be so limited? Antonov replied that liaison could be expanded to meet changing conditions but should, in all cases, be limited to the General Staff in Moscow and the missions. Marshall pointed out difficulties such as clashes between planes that had already arisen because of lack of instantaneous co-ordination in bomb raids from Italy over the Balkans. Antonov countered that this clash had stemmed from navigational error rather than a failure of liaison. No tactical co-ordination was necessary. Since the deployment of the Soviet Air Force was arranged from Moscow, decisions on strategic problems should be taken in Moscow through the missions there.

Sir Charles Portal agreed that liaison through Moscow was acceptable for strategic missions, since the Joint Chiefs of Staff were responsible, rather than the front commanders. However, a constant exchange of information was necessary for air operations in Italy and the Balkans, and it was inefficient to make such exchanges through Moscow. Marshall Khudyakov explained that any decision to engage in direct liaison would have to be decided by Stalin. General Antonov tried to be helpful and suggested that a geographical line be established as a limit for Allied bomber raids. The British and Americans asked for time to think that over.

The Allies turned to another difficult issue. Leahy asked the Soviet staff for a planning date for the end of the war. Antonov was vague, warning that there could be no meaningful prediction, and further said he disliked assumptions. Leahy and Marshall insisted that a date was necessary to plan the handling of shipping. The Allies considered the first of July the earliest possible date and December 31 the latest. Following suit, Antonov mentioned summer as the earliest and winter as the latest. With that statement, the first military session adjourned.[35] It is possible that the military information regarding the situation in the West and the Allied inability to prevent troop transfers was a factor—perhaps even a decisive one—in Stalin's call to Zhukov the next day halting the attack on Berlin. At any rate, Stalin was considering, or had decided, to stop the campaign, and any estimates of a schedule for the defeat of Germany would require a re-evaluation.

The second military session was much like the first.[36] The Allies again pressed for Soviet action while the West crossed the Rhine. Marshall betrayed fear that a lull in the fighting might occur on the eastern front at that time. Antonov repeated, for at least the third time, that the Russians would take all possible steps to prevent transfers of German troops from the east to the Rhine, but he received no satisfaction in return on the prevention of transfers from west to east except for continued bombing raids. Indeed, Allied intelligence reports indicated (as Antonov learned as a result of pointed questions) that the troops that had spearheaded the unsuccessful German counteroffensive in the Ardennes had already been pulled out and sent east.

The question of liaison was not resolved. The West rejected Antonov's suggestions for a bombline on the ground that a permanent divider would unnecessarily curtail the actions and effectiveness of the Allied air forces. Antonov explained that the bombline was only a guide, that it would be adjusted daily through liaison in Moscow. In the ensuing discussions, the Soviet Staff asked for twenty-four hours' notice of Allied bombing operations and a deeper buffer zone in front of the Red Army than the Allies had proposed. The West rejected these conditions, and the dispute, now deadlocked, was referred to the military missions in Moscow. Stalin, for his part, refused to reorganize the Soviet military in order to permit direct liaison between Western and Soviet commanders, and Antonov tactfully conveyed this to the Allies.

On other questions, amicability prevailed. The Russians tried to answer all the Allied requests for information, bases, and technical help, but some of these issues had to be referred to Stalin.* The West in turn presented a survey of Allied action in the Pacific and of plans for defeating Japan after the fall of Germany. Finally, the Chiefs of Staff finished ironing out the details of an agreement on the treatment and repatriation of liberated prisoners. The final document, a British redraft of the original Soviet proposal, was signed as part of the protocol of the Yalta Conference.[37]

* See Chapter 7, The Far East and Other Issues, pp. 252–55.

CHAPTER 4

THE FUTURE OF

CENTRAL EUROPE:

GERMANY AND FRANCE

The disagreements at Yalta over Germany stemmed from the three Allies' divergent views about the desirability of measures to prevent a renewal of German aggressiveness, and what form they should take. The Soviet Union, devastated by Germany twice in twenty-five years, had the most direct interest in these issues. Stalin had told the West that the Soviet Union could not be expected to fight Germany once every generation. Guarantees against any German resurgence and for the economic reconstruction of the Soviet Union were essential. Yet, by Yalta, the West was shying away from a harsh policy against postwar Germany and moving toward the idea of reconstructing Germany on prewar lines—minus, of course, the Nazi hierarchy. The Western Allies were worried about the disastrous effect that dismemberment of Germany might have on Western trade.

Stalin apparently did not know that Roosevelt was wavering back and forth, advocating and then rejecting both dismemberment and reparations. Churchill, on the other hand, emerged clearly as an opponent of both, and Stalin was prepared at Yalta to do battle with him. At Teheran Stalin had said to the Prime Minister, "You are pro-German," and he had summarized Churchill's outlook with the aphorism, "The devil is a communist, and my friend God a conservative." He was only half-jesting: Churchill continually expressed doubt about the severity of the proposed peace terms. Further, members of the British government often discussed whether a postwar Anglo-German alliance would be more advantageous than an Anglo-Soviet one.[1]

The Soviets were most worried about Western opposition to reparations. Compensation from Germany was critical to them, especially because the United States had not decided whether to give postwar aid to Russia (which, at Washington's initiative, had been under discussion for a long time). A month before Yalta, Molotov submitted a formal request for postwar aid, but he received no real satisfaction from Ambassador Harriman, who felt, like many others in the American government, that "postwar credits to the USSR can serve as a useful instrument in our over-all relations to the USSR." The Soviets decided to count on nothing from the West and to rely instead on reparations.[2]

On the basis of his limited information about Western negotiating positions, Stalin prepared a virtual *quid pro quo* for Yalta. As far as Stalin knew, the President, through the Morgenthau plan, had apparently decided in favor of dismemberment; Churchill, while in Moscow in October 1944, had spoken of a loose confederation of separate German states. Stalin did not believe that dismemberment, by itself, could contain German expansionism, but he was willing to accept it, provided that he received in return a firm guarantee of reparations from Germany. As matters stood, the occupation zones drawn by the European Advisory Commission left most of German industry in Anglo-American hands. Stalin wanted part of that industry, and he thought that he had an excellent bargaining lever—Soviet acquiescence to dismemberment. The fallacy of this premise only emerged at the conference, when Britain and, to a lesser extent, the United States turned their backs on their own previously enunciated policies toward dismemberment.

The West, while no longer favoring dismemberment, had not formulated any clear substitute policy. Its embarrassment was even greater because the Soviet proposals, both for dismemberment and reparations, were based upon Anglo-American recommendations of the previous three years. Roosevelt and Churchill had given specific, albeit brief, promises of support for reparations for Russia. Yet Roosevelt now vacillated and Churchill had changed his mind. By Yalta, Churchill was firmly opposed to reparations in any form, and he labeled the Soviet reparations plan "madness." Roosevelt, urged by the State Department to support reparations and by the Treasury to oppose them, eventually agreed with Stalin. His decision was based primarily on Harry Hopkins's personal advice—that the Russians had "given way a great deal at the Conference" and had thereby earned continued American support on reparations.[3]

Aside from dismemberment and reparations, the European Advisory Commission had successfully dealt with the questions relating to the collapse of Germany—zones of occupation, the surrender document, formation of an Allied Control Commission. However, the recent addition of France to the E.A.C. and to the proposed Security Council of the United Nations raised the question of French participation in the occupation of Germany. This question had two parts—a French zone of occupation, and a French seat on the Allied Control Commission. The British were particularly anxious to gain agreement on both. They felt that the rehabilitation of France was essential for filling the power vacuum which would follow the defeat of Germany. As Churchill put it, "Britain would be left alone to contain the might of Russia." Eden thought that the hopelessly weak nations of Europe must form a bloc around Britain; otherwise, "their only hope lies in making defence arrangements, not with us, but with the Russians." [4]

For Britain, the very existence of her influence in European politics seemed to be at stake. Eden concluded, "Europe expects us to have a European policy of our own, and to state it . . . we are likely to have to work more closely with France even than with the United States." He and Churchill envisioned a Western European bloc under Britain, aligned against an Eastern Soviet bloc. Throughout the war, they had tried to build up the West and to forestall the formation of a parallel bloc under Soviet influence. Eden believed it necessary to create a strong counter to the Soviet Union, whether or not Russia was contained within its own frontiers. He wrote, "Our treaty with the Soviet Union, which is designed to secure the collaboration of the Soviet Union for this purpose on Germany's eastern flank, *needs to be bal-*

anced by an understanding with a powerful France in the West." [5]

Stalin, although he made a few subtle comparisons between France and Poland, had no real interest in France's formal status in the inter-Allied machinery. Consequently, he followed Roosevelt's lead. When the President, to the shock of the State Department, initially opposed Britain's requests for France, Stalin took the same position, thus building some negotiating reserves against Britain's anti-Soviet positions. Nonetheless, Stalin did not really care. When Roosevelt agreed to a zone for France and her inclusion on the Allied Control Council for Germany, Stalin readily followed suit.

DISMEMBERMENT

Molotov set out immediately, on February 3, 1945, to ensure the primacy of the German question by placing it first on the agenda. At the conclusion of the military session on February 4, Churchill accordingly announced that the topic for consideration the next day would be "the future of Germany, if she had any." Stalin replied with resolution: "Germany will have a future." *

At the first foreign ministers' meeting, on February 5, the discussions were centered on Germany. Selecting a point that had previously been an Anglo-American recommendation, Molotov brought up the division of Germany. Eden was reluctant to take up the matter. Molotov reminded Eden of the Morgenthau plan, and commented that the British and Americans ought to be ready for this discussion because, unlike the Russians, they had already studied the question. Molotov and Eden then agreed that they would have to prepare the way for a general discussion of Germany, because it was unlikely that the heads of state could agree. Molotov came to the point. He listed the Soviet require-

---

* The Soviet minutes are the only ones that have any record of such a remark. It is possible that it was added later for its political value. There are many deletions in the minutes. *Soviet Crimean Documents*, No. 6, p. 97.

ments. The Soviet Union considered reparations and long term credits essential to her own postwar rehabilitation. The foreign ministers decided that the time had come to settle these issues.[6]

Roosevelt opened the second plenary meeting on February 5, announcing that the topic on the agenda was "political aspects of the future treatment of Germany." Informally, Roosevelt said that there ought to be a discussion of the zones approved by the European Advisory Commission, a review of Churchill's plan to create a zone for France, and a subsequent consideration of French participation in the Allied control machinery.

Stalin had a better planned agenda, and he recommended that additional items be added. First, he listed the dismemberment of Germany. Stalin remarked that a formal commitment on the part of the Allies was logical in view of the present Anglo-American position. Already, he emphasized, an indirect commitment existed. At Teheran there had been a preliminary exchange of views; since then, in October, he and Churchill had discussed the issue in Moscow. Because of these precedents, Stalin thought a definite decision should be made on whether to dismember Germany. After that, the form of the dismemberment should be considered.

Second, would it be better to give Germany a central government set up by the Big Three, or simply an administration? More specifically, if the country were dismembered, would each section have a government? Or would it have only an administration? Stalin requested a clarification of these questions.

Third, he asked that the conditions of Germany's surrender be decided. As an example of the problems of their present position, Stalin asked whether the Allies would preserve the Hitler government if it surrendered unconditionally. He had in mind the precedent of Allied support of pro-Fascist factions in Italy after the invasion. His categorical position was that unconditional surrender and the preservation of the former government of Germany were quite mutually exclusive. Citing Italy, he showed by example that "unconditional" surrender did in fact have conditions. Therefore, Germany, like Italy, should have specific terms spelled out.

Fourth, he considered that the time had come to decide whether Germany should pay reparations, and, if so, what the amount of the indemnity should be.[7]

Roosevelt tried to dodge the question of dismemberment by using his agenda rather than Stalin's. The issues raised by the Russians, he said, were subordinate to the questions of zones. In fact, the zones of occupation might prove to be the first step in the dismemberment of Germany.*

Stalin refused to allow his agenda to be discarded. He refused a consideration of zones. Turning to the first of his questions, he insisted upon immediate settlement of dismemberment, claiming it was a primary question that had never really been settled. He repeated Roosevelt's Teheran proposal to divide Germany into five parts. Stalin recalled how he had supported the President at Teheran, and how Churchill had agreed to the principle of dismemberment, although the Marshal had felt there was some hesitation at that time. Stalin recognized that the former three-way agreement had no binding effect but was only an exchange of views.

Stalin pressed on to determine current dispositions. He reminded Churchill that, in their October conversation in Moscow, the Prime Minister had produced a plan for dividing Germany into two states, Prussia and Bavaria, with the Ruhr and West-phalia under international control. Stalin asserted they would have adopted this proposal had the President been there.

Stalin created a situation that made it difficult for the British and Americans to retreat from their own plans. Since Roosevelt and Stalin had clearly been in agreement on dismemberment, and Stalin and Churchill had later concurred, a three-way agreement seemed the logical result. Churchill's hand was forced; and

* This last intention mentioned by Roosevelt is the one stressed in the Soviet minutes, which try to disavow Soviet intentions of German dismemberment. Matthews's notes and Stettinius's recollections indicate that this was Roosevelt's intention. Bohlen records a qualification by the President: "The permanent treatment of Germany might grow out of the question of the zones of occupation, although the two were not directly connected." See Matthews minutes, *Yalta Documents*, p. 624; Stettinius, *Roosevelt and the Russians*, p. 122; Bohlen minutes, *Yalta Documents*, p. 612; *Soviet Crimean Documents*, No. 6, p. 97.

he affirmed that the British government agreed in principle to dismemberment, with one qualification.* He could only permit a most general approach because the matter required detailed study.

At the same time that he verified Stalin's suspicion that Britain was shying away from harsh terms, Churchill affirmed as his *personal* preference the scheme of dismemberment to which Stalin alluded. Prussia, "the tap root of all evil," should be isolated, he said, and he emphasized that another state should be created with Vienna as its capital. Then the Prime Minister moved on, elaborating additional questions for discussion: frontiers, the disposition of the Rhine valley, the Ruhr and Saar areas, and the fragmentation of Prussia. He agreed with Roosevelt that this was not a propitious moment for decision, and reiterated that an apparatus was needed to study these questions. Since the details of surrender had already been worked out and an immediate surrender could therefore be effected, he deduced there remained only the real problem of zones. The Allies could occupy Germany after surrender in accordance with this agreement.

Stalin used Churchill's retreat to surrender terms to keep the discussion directed toward his own goal: the inclusion of dismemberment in the surrender terms. He indicated that the current surrender terms were too imprecise. Claiming that the issue was unclear, at least in his mind, he tested a hypothetical case. What if a group within Germany overthrew Hitler and accepted the terms of unconditional surrender? Were the Allies prepared to treat with that group as they had done in Italy?

Eden promptly responded that such a group would then receive the terms approved by the European Advisory Commission. H. Freeman Matthews, Deputy Director of the Office of European Affairs, assumed that Stalin was unfamiliar with the Euro-

---

* The various minutes differ on who agreed to this. Bohlen and the Soviet minutes link this statement with the British government, but Churchill, Matthews, and Stettinius attribute a "we" all agreeing to dismemberment. See Bohlen minutes, *Yalta Documents*, p. 612; *Soviet Crimean Documents*, No. 6, p. 97; Churchill, *Triumph and Tragedy*, p. 351; Matthews minutes, *Yalta Documents*, p. 625; Stettinius, *Roosevelt and the Russians*, p. 123.

pean Advisory Commission's approved protocol, so he left the room to get a copy. Churchill began outlining theoretical courses the Allies might take, but Stalin's point was not lost on him. He said that if there was an acceptable group willing to sign the terms of surrender, it did not need to know its future. The Allies could add whatever conditions on dismemberment they wished.[8]

Churchill's admission that there yet remained conditions for unconditional surrender gave Stalin his point of departure. Dismemberment, declared Stalin, was not an additional demand; it was an integral part of the terms of surrender. Therefore a clause should be added to the terms, stating that Germany would be dismembered but not giving the details. Churchill agreed that this was important, but insisted it was not the main consideration. For him the Allies' right to impose dismemberment at a later stage, and not have to discuss it with the Germans, was paramount. The Allies should agree on this point. Stalin agreed that it was necessary only to demand dismemberment of Germany. In fact, this was why he had raised the issue.

Churchill then reversed his stand and asked that the ultimate solution be left to the peace conference. After silently observing the argument develop, Roosevelt broke in in the role of moderator. He revived Stalin's original question—whether or not to dismember Germany. The President declared that this important issue should be decided, and the details left to the future. Stalin hastily agreed.

Roosevelt, like Stalin, felt dismemberment was an essential condition of surrender rather than a detail. He agreed in part with the Prime Minister's assertion that further study was required for certain questions which had been raised. But on dismemberment Roosevelt declared that it would be advisable to present the Germans with terms of surrender including the Allied intention to dismember. The President recalled (as Stalin had reminded him) that at Teheran he had favored a decentralized Germany. He had been influenced, he claimed, by a visit to Germany forty years earlier when he saw the country under a decentralized administration, without any concept of a "Reich." The last twenty years had brought greater centralization in Berlin, and decentralized administration no longer existed. As a result, he rejected talk of plans limited to the decentralization of Germany; such talk was utopian. Dismemberment was the only choice. Now that he had worked himself back into his earlier frame of mind, Roosevelt posed a specific question: how many states would emerge? Five or seven might be a good number, he thought. Churchill interrupted to add "or less," in accordance with his former views.

Roosevelt accepted this qualification, repeating that a study was in order, and turned back to Stalin's question—should the Allies tell the Germans that Germany was to be dismembered? [9] Churchill stuck to his position that if the Germans did not know their fate, dismemberment could be ordered any time after the surrender. The Germans should be told only to "Await our decision as to your future." Churchill insisted that a question as important as dismemberment, involving the fate of eighty million people, could not be decided in eighty minutes.[10]

At this point in the discussion Harry Hopkins passed a note to Roosevelt, suggesting that the issue be submitted to the foreign ministers, who could devise a procedural approach to decide on dismemberment. Roosevelt maintained it was necessary to reach an accord at Yalta, since a public debate over the issue would result in hundreds of plans, which would be a mistake. The President then referred the problem to the foreign ministers. He charged them with devising a procedural plan to study dismemberment within twenty-four hours.

Just what the foreign ministers were being told to do was not clear to Churchill. Trying to make sure that Britain was not committed to a plan for dismemberment, he asked if Roosevelt's suggestion was only to plan a study of dismemberment, and not a plan to dismember Germany. Roosevelt reassured Churchill, and since he did not have to approve the *fact* of dismemberment, Churchill agreed to accept the principle, and to set up a commission for a study of procedure.[11]

Stalin was not satisfied. He argued the urgency of the moment. Events were moving so swiftly in Germany that the Allies could be caught unprepared by a sudden collapse. The capture of the coal basin in Silesia by the Red Army and the prospective capture of the Ruhr by the Allies were creating a new situation, he said. (He may have been thinking of his generals, who were still at that moment following the plan to attack Berlin immediately.) But he agreed with Churchill that there need be no comprehensive plan for dismemberment at the time.

Stalin summarized the discussion during the remaining minutes of the session. There had been agreement (1) to dismember, (2) to establish a commission of the foreign ministers to work out the details, and (3) to add to the surrender terms a clause stating that Germany would be dismembered, without giving details. Stressing that there were two against one, he noted that only Churchill remained unconvinced. Stalin pushed his view once more, hoping that Churchill would give in. The surrender terms were vital, he claimed, since whatever group accepted the surrender document would take the responsibility for binding the German people to the dismemberment. It would be risky to follow Churchill's suggestion and say nothing to the Germans. By stating dismemberment in advance, Stalin said, the German people would know what was in store for them.*

Churchill read Article 12 of the terms of surrender, which stated: "The United States of America, the United Kingdom and the Union of Soviet Socialist Republics shall possess supreme authority with respect to Germany. In the exercise of such authority they will take such steps, including the complete disarmament and demilitarisation of Germany, as they deem requisite for future peace and security." In accordance with this the Allies already had full authority, Churchill insisted; further steps would be superfluous. Roosevelt pointed out that dismemberment was not mentioned and stated he shared the Marshal's view that the German people should be informed of what was in store for them.†

Churchill tried a new tack. The addition of dismemberment to the terms should be postponed for military reasons. Stiffening the surrender terms might harden German resistance: General

---

* The Soviet minutes delete this statement, again dissociating the Soviet Union from pushing for dismemberment.

† The Soviet minutes again record only that part of the statement which does not identify Stalin as the main proponent of dismemberment. *Soviet Crimean Documents*, No. 6, p. 99.

Eisenhower wouldn't want that. Churchill concluded: "We should not make this public."

While Roosevelt remarked that the Germans were now beyond the point of psychological warfare, Stalin found the flaw in Churchill's reservation. He reminded the Prime Minister that the conditions of surrender were for the Allies' advantage only, and emphasized that the terms indeed should not be made public. The Soviet chief stressed the propriety of this decision since it followed the same procedure Roosevelt and Churchill had put into effect in Italy.

Stalin did not waste words: "I want it agreed (1) to dismember and (2) to put dismemberment into the surrender terms." He waited for Churchill's response. Churchill still refused to give in. He would go no further than agreement in principle and to a study to find the best method for implementation.

Roosevelt pressed on in behalf of what had become his and Stalin's position: "Would you put in Article 12 in addition the word 'dismemberment'?" Churchill admitted finally, "Yes, I would agree." After the Prime Minister's concession, Eden attempted to avert further discussion, but Churchill went on, "I have no objection to the proposal. It is agreed." * 12

By the end of the discussion, Stalin had gained acquiescence to the principle of dismembering Germany and the inclusion of dismemberment in the terms of surrender. Although all three chiefs *seemed* agreed, a difficult argument had developed: Churchill linked dismemberment to other issues, hoping to avert a decision until later. When Stalin sought an immediate decision, Roosevelt joined him and weighted the argument in favor of including the word "dismemberment" as a principle in the terms of surrender.

The foreign ministers met February 6 with instructions to devise a method to study dismemberment. Molotov was determined, in accordance with the Allies' tentative agreement at the

---

* Matthews's record must be correct, because the foreign ministers acted in accordance with this instruction from all the delegations. The Bohlen and Soviet minutes leave the impression that Churchill wanted this to be studied by the foreign ministers; they omit Roosevelt's pressuring tactics.

previous day's plenary session, to include the definite statement of Allied intention to dismember Germany in the terms of surrender. Eden tried to nullify the commitment which Churchill had reluctantly made.

Secretary Stettinius walked a tightrope between the Soviet and British arguments of the day before. Deferring to the President's recommendation, the Secretary proposed inserting the word "dismemberment" in Article 12 of the surrender terms. To placate the British, Stettinius simultaneously agreed that study was indeed necessary before there could be agreement on how to implement dismemberment. Molotov immediately associated himself with Stettinius's suggestion.

Eden fought. The ensuing verbal battle between the British and Soviet foreign ministers focused on Eden's suggested substitute wording for "dismemberment." He preferred a weaker commitment: "and measures for the dissolution of the German unitary state." Molotov reacted against this generalized statement, first, by reminding Eden that this substitution was too late, since agreement to dismember Germany had already been reached the day before, and second, by threatening that if there were a reconsideration there would also be a harsher Soviet counterproposal. Molotov suddenly demanded more of the surrender terms than simple agreement to dismember (which he had himself just sanctioned). He suggested that Allied intentions be rephrased more explicitly: "In order to secure peace and security of Europe, they will take measures for the dismemberment of Germany." *

Eden hammered away at the more comprehensive phrasing. The British government did not want to be committed before a

---

* Stettinius's recollection leads to some confusion as to what in fact developed. Stettinius mentioned only the Molotov formula and made no reference to the Eden formula which provoked it, or to the obvious intention of the British in putting forth that formula. Stettinius saw the conversation as hostile to Molotov and a gravitation toward his own compromise attempts. See Stettinius, *Roosevelt and the Russians,* pp. 136–37. Since both the Page and Matthews minutes record the same occurrences in the same order, it seems certain that Eden made the first counterproposal, and Molotov responded by pushing his own proposal and trying to force a more definite commitment. See *Yalta Documents:* compare pp. 656 and 658.

thorough study had been made, he insisted. Confronted with an even less desirable wording, Eden refused to consider Molotov's counterpoposal and agreed to what Molotov originally wanted —the simple addition of the word "dismemberment," though he still promoted his own weaker proposal by claiming it had the advantage of covering not only dismemberment but also decentralization.

With Eden committed, one way or another, Molotov pressed for the Soviet draft. This time Eden flatly rejected it: the British delegation would go no further than the addition of the word "dismemberment." Although everyone had already agreed to the inclusion of the word "dismemberment," Stettinius belatedly attempted a compromise between the agreed-upon position and Molotov's new wording. He recommended an alternative phrase: "including dismemberment to the degree necessary to safeguard the peace and security." However, he said he really preferred his own initial suggestion ("dismemberment") to this.

Molotov seized the new opportunity to gain a firmer commitment from the British, and he promptly endorsed Stettinius's second proposal. Eden objected vociferously. Now in command of the situation, Molotov offered as a compromise a slight rewording which excluded any mention of the degree of dismemberment but which stated that dismemberment was necessary "for the future peace and security." Eden rejected this; he supported Stettinius's personal preference, and he endorsed the Secretary's original proposal.

Molotov pursued Eden with Stettinius's substitute, arguing that finally they had a definite statement. He even insisted that the second American proposal was better than the mere inclusion of the word "dismemberment" because it more closely reflected what Churchill himself had said the day before!

The deadlock continued, and tensions escalated. The foreign secretaries concluded their session by noting that they did agree on the addition of the word "dismemberment," and that Eden should consult with Churchill to learn whether the Prime Minister preferred the second Stettinius proposal (which Molotov was backing but which Stettinius really did not prefer).[13] Molotov's adamant negotiating reflected the Soviet perception (not unfounded) that the West—in this instance, the British—would eventually oppose the destruction of German military potential and instead concentrate on re-establishing a favorable British-German trade balance, which would be possible only with an economically strong and Western-supported postwar Germany. To counter this, Molotov sought a strong commitment to dismemberment from the Western Allies, particularly since Roosevelt seemed to waver.

The third plenary session of the Yalta Conference opened on February 6, and again the subject was dismemberment. Molotov dropped his demands after conferring with Stalin, who most likely considered the simpler agreement satisfactory, especially in view of the British objection to any stronger phraseology than inclusion of the word "dismemberment" in the terms of unconditional surrender. It was in Moscow's interest to get *any* written commitment assuring Allied co-operation against a German revival. Therefore, Molotov withdrew the Soviet proposal. Consequently, Churchill willingly accepted the word "dismemberment" in the surrender terms, but he stressed that he did so on his own and without the explicit approval of the War Cabinet.[14]

A French Zone

After Stalin presented his agenda and won a verbal commitment from Churchill on dismemberment, the President turned the attention of the Conference back to the role of France. Where Churchill had been Stalin's antagonist on dismemberment, Stalin now opposed him on France. Stalin employed the same tactic Churchill had used—relating the issue to a spate of concomitant problems in order to delay settlement.

President Roosevelt asked whether a zone should be allocated to France.* He said he understood from Marshal Stalin in their

---

* This issue is entirely omitted from the Soviet minutes. There is no reference whatsoever to its having been discussed. Political considerations of the 1960's, the friendship of de Gaulle for the Soviet Union, and France's independent position regarding her Western commitments, probably determined the exclusion of the publication of material offensive to

talk the day before that the French definitely had no intention of annexing territory on the Rhine. Stalin corrected the President: the French had made the opposite quite plain to him—they *did* want this territory.

Churchill feared the main question was being sidetracked, and he established two specific points for consideration: a zone for France, and a role for France in the control machinery for Germany. To separate these items from related issues, he insisted it was impossible to discuss the frontier question in this connection. He stated his position succinctly: Great Britain was in favor of a French zone and wanted the United States and the Soviet Union to agree to it. He pointed out that the Soviet Union had no real stake in the matter since the Soviet zone would not be affected. The British and Americans only needed Allied consent for the right to carve a French zone from their own.

Stalin immediately inquired whether this would not create a precedent for other states to make similar demands? Churchill dismissed this as beside the point. The proposed decision was a necessity for Britain, a *sine qua non* for Britain's ability to keep the peace. If the occupation were a long one, Britain alone—without the assistance of France—could not bear the burden.

Stalin raised a second objection. Would this not change the tripartite control of Germany to a four-power control? Stalin was speaking under the impression that his opposition was shared by Roosevelt, who had assured him the day before that the United States was unsympathetic to France. Churchill admitted the two questions were interrelated, and that he expected a place for France on the Allied Control Council if she were granted a zone. But he drew the line there. France would be the only power granted a zone: for other countries, like Belgium or Holland, there was only the possibility of assisting in the occupation.

Seizing on Churchill's mention of lesser powers, Stalin suggested that England might permit not only the French, but also the Belgians and Dutch to assist in occupation without participating in decisions. If this procedure were adopted, the Soviet Union would also like to ask other states to help in occupation.

France. Stalin was in fact France's most adamant opponent in granting her equal status in the postwar world.

Stalin said he preferred such a joint occupation to the four nations making separate decisions, a situation which would create
unnecessary complications. Churchill ignored Stalin's recommendation and argued adamantly for the inclusion of France alone.
His position foretold the future role France was to play in Europe. France had traditionally been a check on Germany, and
Great Britain intended that France should again be useful. Since,
by the admission of the President himself, it was uncertain how
long the United States troops would remain in Europe, France
became particularly important.

Roosevelt confirmed Churchill's argument. As Roosevelt saw
it, American troops would not stay in Europe much more than
two years after the war. Congress could be counted on to support
reasonable measures to safeguard the future peace, but this did
not extend to maintaining a large military force in Europe. Surprised at this admission, the Prime Minister's insistence that
France be included became even greater. France had to have a
large army, because France was the only other ally Great Britain
had in the West. Appealing to Stalin on a very sensitive point,
Churchill compared Britain's need of France with the Soviet dependence upon the Poles for support against Germany.[15]

Stalin's attitude changed. A probable withdrawal of American
troops gave validity to Churchill's request; without the United
States, there might not be enough strength in the West to guard
against German resurgence. Churchill's parallel of the French
and Polish roles *vis-à-vis* Germany was not wasted on Stalin, who
was quite willing to recognize that for all practical purposes
there were spheres of influence. A "friendly" Poland would serve
Russia just as a "friendly" France would Britain, one in the Eastern sphere, the other in the Western. Therefore, Stalin dropped
his antipathy and admitted the necessity of a strong France—
which he suddenly recalled had recently signed a treaty of alliance with the Soviet Union!

As Stalin was becoming accustomed to the idea, Roosevelt
openly backed it—France should be given a zone. Further, he
agreed with Churchill that it would be a mistake to bring in any
other nations.

FRANCE AND THE ALLIED CONTROL COUNCIL

With Roosevelt now in agreement with Churchill, Stalin was ready to concur on a zone. But French representation on the Allied control machinery to oversee the occupation of Germany was another question, at least for Stalin, who insisted that the peace must be protected only by those nations which had made the greatest sacrifice and contribution to winning the war. While he claimed to support Britain's desire to see France become a strong power, Stalin refused to implement measures assuring this position, because it did not conform to this basic principle. He lamented that he could not alter the facts, which were that France had contributed little to the war and had opened her gates to the enemy. The Allied Control Council must reflect this. (Yet one set of American conference minutes suggests that even as he said this Stalin may have been prepared to yield on this issue, too.*)

Churchill ignored Stalin's criterion; he repeated that the question was one of the *future* role of France. He argued that temporary conditions did not determine the greatness of a power and that France would take her place in the world again. He concluded that when that time came, Britain wanted France in that place, so she could help ensure the containment of Germany.

Stalin altered his position slightly. France could, he agreed, have a zone; however, the Soviet Union did not want to see her a member of the control machinery.

Roosevelt re-entered the argument. A note from Harry Hopkins to the President encouraged him to remind the group that the French already were involved in guarding Germany, because France was a full member of the European Advisory Commis-

---

* Matthews recorded a more qualified statement by Stalin, leaving the door open to future change. He quoted Stalin as saying that the Control Commission must be composed of nations which opposed Germany firmly from the beginning, and *"so far"* France did not belong to that group. Matthews italicized *"so far."*

sion, the only Allied body aside from the Yalta Conference that was considering the German problem.[16] Having seemingly supported Churchill's conception of the role of France, Roosevelt then backed Stalin. He agreed that France should not be a member of the control machinery. He used Stalin's argument that it would create a precedent. The Dutch, for instance, by virtue of the destruction of their flooded lands, could claim a privileged position similar to that of the French. Prior to this, neither Stalin nor the President had been persuaded by precedent in granting France a zone, but they suddenly saw its political implications.

The British delegation argued that, tactically, France was unlike the other nations. Eden insisted again that there would be no question of granting a zone to any power other than France. He pointed out that agreement to a zone for France already implied agreement to her joining the control machinery, for the French would never accept the zone without a position on the control machinery. Besides, were there only a zone, how could it be controlled? Stalin retorted that Britain would represent France because greater powers should directly control the lesser powers. Clearly, he, at least, intended to control the lesser powers of eastern Europe—including Poland.

Stalin argued that the French precedent distorted the whole perspective of Great Power control. The control machinery was charged with a vital role, the everyday administration of Germany. France's participation would weaken this machinery.

Seeing the futility of conflict in the plenary session, Churchill proposed to hand the issue over to the foreign ministers for study. Molotov protested that no further discussion should take place, since the question had been resolved. The European Advisory Commission had already drawn up a tripartite administration agreement for Germany, and France was not included.

Eden, trying to placate Molotov, agreed that the matter was closed, but he continued to argue his case. He said that, as a practical matter, the relationship of the French zone to the control machinery should be considered, and that there existed an obligation on the part of the British and the Russians to the French. France had pressed the British hard on this before the

Conference, and Eden seized on a delicate point—had not the French similarly pressed the Russians? Stalin said that he had refused to deal with the French on matters that could only be dealt with properly by the Big Three. He then summarized the proceedings. All agreed on a zone for the French; however, France should not receive a place in the control machinery. The foreign ministers would review the relationship of the zone to the Commission.[17]

The foreign ministers met on February 7 at Molotov's villa, where he served both as host and as Chairman. He was meticulously fortified with proposals on each issue of the agenda. His first proposal was to create a subcommittee to redraft Article 12 of the surrender terms, in order to add the word "dismemberment," and it was readily accepted by the ministers.

Molotov's second proposal, incorporating the will of the three leaders as expressed in the plenary session of February 5, was that a special commission be created to study how to proceed in dismembering Germany. This proposal kept the study of dismemberment in the hands of the Big Three, since Molotov suggested that Eden plus the American and Soviet ambassadors to London serve on it. Stettinius reacted negatively to the proposed commission. The European Advisory Commission (which included France) already existed for such purposes, he said. He claimed not to want the E.A.C. bypassed and its prestige undermined.

Eden used Stettinius's statement as a lever to keep French participation in occupation before the ministers. He reminded his colleagues that if the problem were referred to the E.A.C., France, as a member, would already be deciding Germany's fate. Linking dismemberment to the role of France, Eden then called for terms of reference to be established for the body which would make this study. Eden listed some of the particular questions the British government wanted studied, and let the ministers know Britain did not find the proposed commission complete without France.

Molotov was neatly trapped; he retreated to avoid mixing dismemberment with a decision on France. He had called for a study of the procedure to be followed, not for instructions to the study group. Perhaps the entire question of a study should be dropped, he said, or referred to regular diplomatic channels in London instead of the special commission he had just recommended. In any case, he asserted, the foreign ministers had not received instructions to form any such group as he had proposed.

Eden pursued his argument. The ministers did have the power to recommend such a commission. Molotov continued to retreat: the Soviet government was really not insisting on a dismemberment commission at all. Eden put his cards on the table. The British wanted to see the French represented on any commission studying dismemberment. Molotov raised no further objections; he suggested only that this question be decided by the commission when it was set up. Everyone agreed.[18]

Next, Molotov presented a prepared statement on the question of France's relationship to the Allied Control Council. Capitalizing on Soviet-American agreement to exclude France from this body, Molotov proposed that, as agreed, France be given a zone, and that the French zone be placed under the supervision of the Control Council.[19]

Eden avoided any consideration of the Soviet proposal. He reiterated that France must be represented in any control machinery. He repeated his previous arguments. First, the French could not accept a zone without this control, and second, it was logical for France to be represented, since she already was a member of the European Advisory Commission. He added that France still would not participate in vital conferences such as Yalta.

Molotov ignored Eden's remarks and advocated immediate adoption of the Soviet proposals, with a stipulation that, should conditions change, France could be reconsidered. Eden refused. Stettinius proposed that the European Advisory Commission consider French participation and that it not be decided right now. Molotov agreed. This still would have left the role of France undecided, and Eden accordingly refused. The foreign ministers only agreed to submit their differences to the plenary session, with Eden, on the one hand, calling for immediate solution, and Molotov and Stettinius, on the other, seeking to submit the question to the European Advisory Commission. Eden made a last try to change Molotov's opinion, but they could not reach agreement.[20]

Later in the day, at the fourth plenary session, Britain continued battling for equal status for France in the control machinery. Churchill argued the British case once again, using the same arguments as before, with one addition: the French would create problems if they had a zone but did not participate in the control machinery. French participation could not be referred to the European Advisory Commission; it was a weaker body—and it included France already. This would create a division with the Soviet-Americans on one side and the Anglo-French on the other. With postponement making the subsequent rejection of his solution likely, Churchill pressed on. He called on Russia and the United States to reverse their position by transferring the issue back to the foreign ministers for further study.

The other leaders gave him no satisfaction. Roosevelt wanted to postpone a decision for several weeks. Stalin backed the President and mentioned that the three governments had a favorable history of settling questions by correspondence. Taking another turn as a democratic advocate, Stalin claimed the European Advisory Commission itself should make the decision, since everyone would then have the benefit of French opinion, while at Yalta France was not represented.[21] There the issue rested for two days.

The status of France cropped up next on February 9, during a discussion on the Declaration on Liberated Europe. Britain asked that France associate herself with the Declaration. Feeling that France, like Poland, should be subordinate, Stalin retorted, "Three would be better." [22] The next morning France was discussed once more by the foreign ministers. Eden raised the issue of France and the Declaration and found that the tide was turning. Molotov hedged instead of balking. He gave the excuse that he had not had time to consider the inclusion of France and suggested that they wait for the plenary session. Further evidence was provided by Stettinius's new stand. The Secretary of State suddenly claimed that he highly approved the British proposal to associate France with the Declaration on Liberated Europe.[23]

By this time the Soviet government had been informed of the

change in American policy toward the whole question of French participation in the control machinery for Germany. Roosevelt had told Stalin through Ambassador Averell Harriman that the American position would be reversed. Stalin agreed that if this was the considered opinion of the President, he would go along with it.* [24]

Molotov's mild position at the foreign ministers' meeting would seem to indicate that Roosevelt and Stalin co-ordinated their move sometime during the evening of February 9. Further, Alger Hiss's minutes of the foreign ministers' conference at noon of February 10 indicate that Stettinius agreed to France's association with the Declaration. Stettinius said that it was highly desirable, "as stated yesterday." However, there is no record of this point having been discussed by Stettinius previously. Stettinius himself made no reference to his acceptance of the British proposal until noon of February 10.

At the plenary session on February 10, Eden called for a statement that France associate herself with the Declaration. Roosevelt then officially announced that he had changed his mind about the role of the French: he now backed their participation on the Allied Control Council, since there could not be a zone for them without this decision. Further, he too recommended that France should associate herself with the Declaration. Stalin immediately stated that he was in agreement with the President's position.[25] Great Britain had finally succeeded in gaining for France a position which would permit her to help defend against German aggression and, Churchill hoped, would strengthen Britain in Europe.

"TO EACH ACCORDING TO HIS DESERTS"

Among the decisions Stalin wanted made at Yalta was agreement to German reparations, which the Soviets had long requested.

* Stettinius said that Roosevelt changed Stalin's position on this issue, but he did not know how or why. Stettinius, *Roosevelt and the Russians,* p. 262.

The recovery of Soviet Russia from the destruction of war would depend to a large extent upon the material compensation the Kremlin could exact from the remains of the Nazi empire. Stalin had put reparations on the agenda for the February 5 plenary session. Roosevelt as chairman placed this question last on the agenda for that day's discussion.

The President outlined his understanding of the issues. First, small powers had claims against Germany. Second, there was the question of utilizing German manpower. In considering this, they had to determine what the Russians wanted, he said, because the Americans and British had no need for manpower.

Stalin ignored Roosevelt's questions; he indicated that the Soviet Union was not prepared to discuss the manpower issue at that time and suggested instead that they discuss the Soviet reparations plan. Churchill asked to hear the Soviet plan.

Stalin called on the Deputy People's Commissar for Foreign Affairs, Ivan M. Maisky, to explain the Russian plan. Maisky, a popular former Ambassador to Great Britain, commanded the respect of his British colleagues. The Russians hoped his presentation might win sympathy for the plan, which established the principles basic to the whole Soviet reparations scheme. The main points were these:

1. Reparations were to be in kind rather than in money.
2. Germany would pay in two ways: one by withdrawal from her national wealth, the other by payment in goods to be delivered annually after the war.
3. Germany was to be economically disarmed, and 80 per cent of her equipment removed from heavy industry. Aircraft factories, specialized military enterprises, and plants producing synthetic fuel would be totally eliminated. The remaining 20 per cent of her industrial facilities would be adequate to sustain Germany.
4. Reparations would continue for a ten-year period, and withdrawals from German national wealth would be made during the first two years after the war.
5. The German economy had to be controlled for world

safety, and this control must be exercised through joint Anglo-American and Soviet directions. Allied control must continue after the ten-year period.

6. The Nazis had caused unprecedented destruction, and not enough reparations existed to cover this damage. The Soviet government had arrived at a figure which was realistic, and they had a scheme of priorities for division of the repayments. Priorities would be established according to the size of the country's contribution to the victory, and the amount of the loss suffered by the country. Countries best qualified under these criteria would receive reparations first.

7. The Soviet Union estimated that it should receive ten billion dollars compensation for its direct losses, which should be repaid through the means outlined above. Maisky stated again that this constituted only a small part of actual damage, but under the circumstances, the Soviets would have to be satisfied with this minimal recompense.

8. A special Reparations Commission of representatives from the Big Three should meet in Moscow to work out details on the basis of this plan.[26]

The reaction of the Western Allies was ominous. Churchill expressed serious doubts that the Soviet plan could be effected. The Prime Minister tried to play down reparations in general by citing British experience in the First World War. The Allies, he warned, had collected only a part of their reparations, and that only as a result of investments in Germany. Churchill conceded that Russian sacrifices were greater than those of any other country and agreed to the removal of German plants to the Soviet Union. He opposed the Kremlin's fixing an exact amount. He hinted that the Soviet Union should follow the British example and not seek reparations. Churchill agreed Russia had suffered the greatest losses, but Britain faced the most desperate financial and economic consequences.

Churchill appeared more interested in the damage done to other countries than in the devastation of the Soviet Union. Other countries which had suffered great destruction on their own soil had to be considered for reparations, too. What would the Allies do with Germany's starving population—feed the people of Germany out of their own pockets? Stalin, prepared to show that Churchill's objections had already been taken into consideration in the formulation of the Soviet plan, listened calmly. He made a mild counter: there would be food for the Germans, and the problems Churchill envisioned for Britain would exist with or without the Soviet plan for reparations.

Churchill gave an example—if one wanted to ride a horse, one must feed it! Stalin countered with another—the horse should not charge at the feeder! Churchill admitted his metaphor was not a good one: one should substitute a car for a horse. The car had to have petrol. Germans were men, not machines, Stalin retorted. To this Churchill agreed. He then suggested the establishment of a Reparations Committee which would deliberate in secret.[27]

Roosevelt had not decided against reparations. Unlike Churchill, the President remained a potential ally of Stalin against a German revival. He allowed himself to think out loud. The United States had loaned Germany money after the last war, he said, but would not repeat this mistake. After World War I, the United States had returned assets to Germany, but this time the Congress might pass a special law against such a move. Although the United States wanted neither German manpower nor German machine tools, the United States would not help Germany. In fact, the more Roosevelt thought, the more definite he became. Certainly German living standards should not be higher than those of the Soviets, and Russia should get everything it deserved from Germany. Further, America at the same time wanted to help the British find new markets to replace those lost in the event that Germany did not become an industrial giant. Roosevelt accepted the Reparations Commission to study the needs of various countries and agreed that it should be based in Moscow. Churchill acquiesced.[28]

During the discussion, Maisky had been carefully noting the British and American objections. By the time Roosevelt had finished speaking, Maisky was ready with his defense.

He remarked that the Allies' objections were based on their own past disappointments with reparations, but that the Soviet plan, in contrast, was built on an entirely different principle from the reparations claims made after World War I. First, he claimed, the Allies' problems had resulted not from attempting to exact an exorbitant amount, but from using money as the means of payment, and that, therefore, Germany had to obtain foreign currency. Reparations in kind eliminated this difficulty. Second, the very fact that Germany's former enemies had invested in her economy had encouraged the Germans to default on reparations. This could not happen again unless the West financed Germany. Churchill and Roosevelt responded with gestures that they had no such intention.* Maisky advanced the premise that if the proposed reparations were in kind and the Allies were determined not to finance Germany, then the experience of World War I was irrelevant.

Maisky went on to Churchill's statement about the inability of the Germans to pay the sum proposed by the Soviets. He compared the reparations figure with Western budgets. The ten billion dollars suggested by the Soviet government was only 10 per cent of the United States budget for that year. The Soviet conference minutes record that Stettinius enthusiastically endorsed this by exclaiming "Absolutely correct!" If anything, Maisky said, such a requirement was too modest.

Maisky denied, too, that the Germans would starve. Capitalizing on Roosevelt's previous remark that German living standards should be no higher than Soviet standards, Maisky estimated that the German people would enjoy the average European living standard and would have every chance to build a postwar economy rooted in the expansion of agriculture and light industry. If Germany made no military expenditures, she would save a considerable amount of money. After all, the Germans had formerly spent six billion dollars a year on arms alone! Churchill waxed enthusiastic momentarily: "Yes, that is a very important consideration." [29] Still, he suggested that the Conference drop the issue and allow the new Commission to consider it.

Stalin wanted an immediate decision. Minimally, the Soviet proposal and its principles could be a guideline for the Commis-

---

* The Soviet minutes emphasize these assurances by putting them in bold face type.

sion. But before determining what instructions the Commission should receive, the Conference had to create the Commission. Stalin singled out his main opponent; he asked Churchill directly whether there should be a Commission. Churchill cautioned against a hasty decision on reparations and recommended the creation of the Commission. At that time, the governments involved could settle the issues. Roosevelt disengaged the antagonists by changing the subject. He suggested tripartite control over reparations, with representatives of the three governments on the Commission. Churchill readily agreed, but Stalin made no comment for the moment.

Stalin picked up where Maisky left off. Both London and Washington had avowed their desire to see the Soviets receive a fair compensation, and Stalin cited present willingness to establish the Reparations Commission as a beginning. But the conference must provide the Commission with guidelines. Stalin had in mind particular instructions. The nations which had borne the main burden of the war and had organized the victory should be the first nations to receive reparations, he insisted. This definition referred to the Soviet Union, the United States, and Great Britain.* Stalin explained that he did not want Soviet Russia to be the only country to receive compensation. Each should undertake to collect from Germany, and each should find a suitable form of reparation.

Guarding against Britain's asking a disproportionate sum for France, Stalin debunked France's contribution to the war effort. He reminded the Allies that France had contributed a mere eight divisions to the war. Even the Yugoslavs were fighting with twelve, and Stalin would ask nothing for them. The Poles themselves had committed ten divisions. Stalin said: "I do not include France in the first category and certainly France shall not have reparations from us." [30]

Stalin claimed that Germany's resources after the war would exceed her present capacity because the soldiers would be home

---

* The Soviet minutes indicate that Roosevelt and Churchill agreed with Stalin when he stated that the nation that had made the greatest contribution toward winning the war should be granted the first priority in reaping the rewards.

and the factories would be working. He continued to press for immediate agreement. Therefore he suggested handing the particulars of a reparations plan over to the foreign ministers, rather than to the proposed Reparations Commission. Churchill agreed, but said he thought this move was futile. He told Stalin that he [Churchill] would be driven out of office. Stalin had a different concept of the prerogatives created by power: he retorted, "Victors are not driven out."

The Prime Minister objected to the war effort as the only criterion qualifying a nation for reparations. He preferred the Socialist principle: to each according to his needs and from each according to his abilities. Stalin, a lax ideologist in the company of capitalists, did not hesitate to prefer another principle: "To each according to his deserts." * On that note the reparations question was handed to the foreign ministers.[31]

At the foreign ministers' meeting, two days later, Molotov offered a proposal, incorporating agreements reached by the three powers during the plenary session of February 5. These were synthesized into a comprehensive plan embodying Soviet reparations requirements. The Soviet plan stipulated: (1) reparations should be received first by those nations which had borne the burden of the war and had organized the victory; (2) discussion of labor usage would be postponed; estimates of reparations should remain as defined by Maisky in the earlier Soviet statement; (3) a set sum of $8,000,000,000 would be specified for America and Britain, despite their disinterest in receiving reparations (consonant with the Soviet eagerness for the West to share in the reparations and thereby legitimize the Soviet claim while solidifying a three-nation partnership directed against Germany.) [32]

Playing the game Molotov's way, Eden examined the Soviet principles and expanded the basic concept to include more credit for the Allied effort. Reparations payment should be related to

---

* This violation of Marxist-Leninist ideology is included in Soviet minutes, emphasizing the intention of the Soviet Union to demand her share of the victory. Socialist principle would accept the ability of the individual and give to him according to his work (or, perhaps "deserts"); communist principle would accept the ability and return to each "according to his needs."

the suffering endured at the hands of the enemy, he suggested. Molotov agreed readily and turned to Maisky for explication of the Soviet plan's reasonableness. In careful detail Maisky outlined why twenty billion dollars in reparations was not a large sum. Beginning with the prewar national wealth of Germany, i.e. one hundred twenty-five billion dollars, which had been reduced by the war to seventy-five billion dollars, he deduced that analysis of the mobile wealth in other highly industrialized countries demonstrated that it was feasible to transfer 30 per cent, or twenty-two to twenty-three billion dollars of Germany's wealth, without inflicting unnecessary hardship.

Molotov requested that the formal establishment of a Reparations Committee be put in writing. It should be set up in Moscow, and charged with the task of devising a formula on the basis of the guidelines agreed upon at the Yalta Conference.[33] The ministers accepted this proposal but specified that the guidelines had yet to be established by the Conference. In other words, guidelines did not mean implicit acceptance of the Soviet principles. The foreign ministers agreed to report their discussion of reparations, and their agreement on the setting up of a Reparations Commission in Moscow, to the plenary session. Molotov made one final plea. Reparations must be a collaborative effort, he stated. The Soviet Union believed in the interest of justice the United States and Great Britain should decide an amount of compensation.[34] At the foreign ministers' meeting of February 8, Molotov again asked whether the other foreign ministers were prepared to discuss allocation of reparation sums, and Eden and Stettinius replied they were not but would try to be prepared the following day.[35]

At the next foreign ministers' session, on February 9, the American delegation presented its own proposal for reparations. The American draft was not radically different from the Soviet proposal. It incorporated the principles enunciated in plenary session. It also partially sanctioned the Soviet sum with the inclusion of a specific directive to the Reparations Commission to consider the Soviet government's suggested total. This American proposal became the basic document upon which final agreement was reached by the Yalta Conference.

The particulars of the American proposal were these:

1. It incorporated the Soviet principles that reparations should be received by those who had borne the burden of the war and by those nations which organized the victory,* and the recommended British principle that compensation should also be in accordance with the heaviest losses sustained.

2. It included *verbatim* the text of the Soviet proposal, with its suggestion for the removal of national wealth from Germany within two years and annual deliveries covering the next ten years.

3. It directed the Reparations Commission in Moscow to undertake a study of how to reduce and eliminate certain industries "from the standpoint of total decentralization of Germany" and to take into consideration the Soviet government's suggested total of twenty billion dollars for reparations. This combined elements of both Soviet and British demands: the British wanted no definite decision to be made until the questions were studied, and the Soviets wanted a guideline which suggested a specific sum to be given the Commission.[36]

The Soviets were happy to have American support concretely formulated, but the plan met with serious opposition from the British. The Soviet and British delegations clashed over the amount of reparations. Churchill admitted that in principle the Soviet Union should receive compensation from Germany, but he refused to agree to any specifics. Implicit in the ensuing battle was Great Britain's reluctance to sanction reparations for Russia, despite the verbal reassurances. Maisky and Molotov bargained harder and suggested an even more specific agreement than the American proposal—namely, a final commitment to an exact sum. Eden repeated that the British would not agree to any figure, even as a basis for further discussion.

The difference between the American and British positions

---

* Maisky had proposed this formulation to the plenary session on February 5, and Stalin reiterated it in words almost exactly the same as those in the American proposal. *Soviet Crimean Documents*, No. 6, cf. pp. 100 and 102.

came into even sharper relief. Molotov praised Maisky's work on reparations, with an aside that its one blunder was to request only a minimum for the Soviet Union. Stettinius backed Molotov, but emphasized that Maisky's figure was reasonable. Then, in an effort to placate the British, he added that it was preferable to set no definite figure. Molotov retreated to a written confirmation of what had been already conceded and dropped his former request for a three-way division of reparations. He asked the foreign ministers only to approve at least part of the sum; for example, the Soviet Union should receive half of the reparations, or ten billion dollars. Stettinius acquiesced: half of an unspecified sum should go to Russia. Molotov agreed to this but asked that the amount be specified. Eden continued to demand prior study by the Commission.

The ministers finally recorded that two of the three Allies had agreed to consider the Soviet sum, with Britain dissenting.[37] At the plenary session the same afternoon Stettinius reported unanimity on the first two points of the American proposal; however, only the Americans and Russians could agree to recommend a fixed sum as the basis for discussion by the Moscow Reparations Commission.[38]

On the morning of February 10, in a last-minute maneuver, Eden confronted the foreign ministers with a British substitute for the American-Soviet reparations agreement. It entirely rejected the Soviet principle that the spoils should be divided by those bearing the greatest burden of the war. The Foreign Secretary proposed classifying reparations according to three categories: (1) national wealth to be removed during the first two years after the war for the purpose of destroying German war capacity, provided this would not endanger Germany's economic existence or render her unable to fulfill her obligations; (2) annual deliveries according to a time schedule; and (3) use of German labor.[39]

In effect, this plan revealed that Britain did not oppose reparations if they provided no interference with the recovery of Germany. This was tantamount to outright opposition to the theory behind reparations. Eden gave further evidence of his ultimate concern: "Germany's need from time to time to acquire sufficient foreign currency from her export trade to pay for her current imports." Eden accused the Russians of taking a contradictory position, one which would bleed Germany economically while forcing her to pay. Maisky confessed bitter disappointment with Eden's statement, which the Soviets saw was designed to preserve Germany as far as possible. Eden denied this, yet he warned the Russians that the Prime Minister did not think they would receive what they hoped for. Maisky made one last attempt to reconcile the two positions. He claimed that the reparations plan complemented the needs of the dismemberment agreement. The foreign ministers' last problem was to approve a basis of discussion for the Commission. Specific British proposals, such as Eden's current plan, could be made later.

Eden raised some objections to the instructions recommended for the Commission. He preferred reparation payments be made over five years rather than ten. Stettinius interrupted to argue in favor of the Soviet-American formula. Maisky argued that specifics could be adjusted later, and the Secretary of State agreed. Maisky stressed that the ten-year period was only one basis for discussion; in fact, the removal of heavy industry might take only seven years. Even the Soviet government was not committing itself to any particular schedule. Eden turned the tables: if that were the case, then why mention any time limit in the formula at all? Maisky responded that the purpose was to find a common basis for discussion.[40]

The culmination of the battle over reparations took place at the plenary session of February 10. Churchill stated with finality that instructions from the War Cabinet made it impossible for the British government to mention any specific figures for reparations. Unexpectedly for the Soviets, the President backed Churchill, observing that if any figures for reparations were mentioned, then the American people would think it meant money. The Soviet notes for this session quote Roosevelt as straying even farther from his former position. He recommended that nothing be said in the Conference protocol and that the Moscow Reparations Commission should make a study of the questions before determining the amount of reparations.*

* This is the only record of such a statement by Roosevelt. *Soviet Crimean Documents*, No. 8, p. 113.

At this point Andrei Gromyko, Soviet Ambassador to Washington, in an unprecedented appeal, confided to Harry Hopkins that Stalin thought the Americans had turned against the Russians and sold out to the British. As a result Hopkins passed the following note to Roosevelt: "Gromyko just told me that the Marshal thinks you did not back up with Ed [Stettinius] relative to Reparations—and that you sided with the British—and he is disturbed about it. Perhaps you could tell him privately later." [41]

Stalin tried to save the situation. Assuming the British estimates were based on their World War I experience, Stalin pointed to the difference: it was not money, but goods in kind which the Soviets wanted in reparations. Churchill countered that the Moscow Reparations Committee could issue an interim report which would make it possible for the Soviet government to remove certain goods from Germany.

Stalin became quite excited and got up from his chair. He would be quite frank. Whatever Russia took from Germany could never compensate for her losses. He agreed that Russia could, as Churchill suggested, take factories and lands, but it was preferable to arrive at a tripartite formula for reparations and not resort to unilateral action. There was no question of money. The treaties which the Soviet Union recently made with Finland, Rumania, and Hungary already set a precedent by specifying reparations in kind.

Stalin asked for an acceptable tripartiate formula. He suggested that the Yalta Conference affirm the principle that Germany must pay reparations, and that the Moscow Commission set the amount of the payment. The Soviet-American proposal of twenty billion dollars with 50 per cent for Russia should be the Commission's basic document.

Stalin resorted to harsh words in his disappointment. If the British opposed reparations for Russia, he admonished them to be honest now. He reminded the Americans they had already agreed to accept the sum of twenty billion dollars for discussion. He asked if the United States had withdrawn this agreement. He looked around to see the reaction to his open charge.[42]

Challenged indirectly by Gromyko and now face to face with Stalin, Roosevelt reassured the Marshal that no change had occured in the American position at all. The President said, "I am completely in agreement." He asked only to alter the word "reparations," which incorrectly implied money rather than goods, in their protocol. In this way, Roosevelt explained his earlier apparent wavering. Stalin remained suspicious and reminded Roosevelt that since the proposal would not be published, it could not mislead the American public. Roosevelt nevertheless contended that while the United States was prepared to discuss sums as well as principles, it objected to the word "reparations." Stalin acceded, substituting "compensation for losses."

Churchill and Eden emphatically rejected this agreement. Stalin reminded them that a consideration of the Soviet figure was not a binding commitment. Churchill replied with a final note of refusal. A cable had come from the War Cabinet which reaffirmed Eden's position in the foreign ministers' meeting: England attached great importance to Germany's ability to pay for her imports and trade after the war.

In view of this, Stalin tried to determine what the British would be willing to grant Russia. Russia bargained. Let Churchill name his figure, for the Soviet figure was not sacrosanct, said Stalin. A new figure could be discussed. "It is necessary that things move forward," said Stalin. Roosevelt nervously suggested that the whole issue be reviewed by the Commission later. This was precisely what the British wanted, and Molotov instantly condemned the suggestion. Only yesterday Stettinius had announced agreement to the sum, he said, and he quoted the text of the previous agreement. Both Maisky and Molotov presented arguments against referring this question to the Commission —it was a lesser body, and the important decisions had to be taken in the main Conference.

Eden recommended that the Commission "take into consideration" the Soviet report to the Conference, rather than agree to it as a basis for discussion. Molotov charged that this was backtracking: "Eden's proposal ignores the fact this question has been discussed at the . . . Conference." When this failed to move the British, Stalin gave up. He asked for a minimal formula, stating, first, that the heads of government agreed that Germany should pay compensation for the damages caused as a result of the war, and, second, that the Moscow Reparations Commission be instructed to determine the amount. Churchill readily agreed, and turned to Roosevelt, who replied, "Judge Roosevelt approves and the document is accepted." [43]

After Stalin had time to reflect, he changed his mind. He brought the matter up again at the tripartite dinner that evening. One possible explanation for this reversal is that both Molotov and Maisky were clearly unhappy about the lack of support for the Soviet position and they conveyed their disappointment to Stalin. Another is that Stalin may have suggested a minimal formula to shame Britain into something stronger, and when this failed, he tried to recapture the stronger American-Soviet formula. In any case, he tried once more to persuade Churchill. Stalin said he was dissatisfied and disappointed with the reparations agreement. He must return to Russia to tell the Soviet people that they were not going to get any reparations because the British opposed it. Repeating his verbal assurances, Churchill said that, on the contrary, he hoped Russia would receive reparations in large quantities. His only concern was that they not be beyond the capacity of Germany to pay.

Stalin restated his position. He wanted the communiqué to indicate agreement on Germany's responsibility to pay for its damage and the creation of a Reparations Commission. In addition, he hoped the protocol would state that the United States and the Soviet Union agreed to consider the sum of twenty billion dollars, 50 per cent to go to Russia. It would be stated that Britain could mention no figures. Everyone agreed.[44]

The final protocol, which the Conference approved the next day, was prepared by Molotov.* He used as his basis the American proposal to the foreign ministers of February 9, which, as mentioned before, was close to the original Soviet proposal. Certain changes were incorporated in it which reflected the expressed desire of the last plenary session on February 10; for example, Stalin's request for an explicit statement that Germany must pay for losses in the war, and Roosevelt's request for explication that payment would be in kind rather than money. Molotov took the liberty of adding the use of labor as an accepted

---

* Byrnes suggests that the Soviet delegation put "use of labor" into the statement without its having been previously considered or discussed. This, however, as the foregoing indicates, is incorrect. See Byrnes, *Speaking Frankly*, p. 29.

form of reparations (although he had barred it as an issue at the Conference) by including the British categorical breakdown on reparations from Eden's counterproposal the previous day. Because of Eden's objection to a ten-year reparation term, the draft stated the period of payment was "to be fixed" later. The draft indicated that there was American-Soviet backing for, and British abstinence from, twenty billion dollars as the basis for discussion by the Moscow Reparations Commission.[45]

On February 11 the protocol was finally agreed upon in a working session of the foreign ministers and approved by the heads of government. It reflected the Allies' agreement and disagreement. The United States was committed to the guidelines of twenty billion dollars suggested as the reparations sum from Germany, of which 50 per cent would go to Russia. Nowhere in the Soviet minutes is there any indication that this was a commitment beyond a basis for discussion at the Reparations Commission's sessions.

Yet one lingering disagreement from the Yalta days is whether or not the United States agreed to support Russia in her request for ten billion dollars in reparations. The American willingness to agree to the Soviet proposal—the incorporation of this sum into the American proposal itself, the verbal assurances from Stettinius that he considered this reasonable, and the explicit reaffirmation of American backing on this sum as a basis for discussion despite British intransigence—all of these factors implied a continuing moral commitment to back the Soviet Union. The Soviet Union had every reason to assume that American support at the Yalta Conference indeed *did* mean the Americans agreed that the Russians should receive a specific amount of compensation for the extensive damage which all knew the Soviet Union had suffered (and to which Roosevelt on numerous occasions purposely alluded). The only reason the American commitment at Yalta was *not* firmer was that British objections led the Soviet delegation to ask only for instructions to the Commission. Had circumstances been slightly different, the United States would have acceded to the Soviet request for ten billion dollars in reparations.

CHAPTER 5

POLAND:

THE BEST HE COULD GET

In one way or another, Poland figured in virtually every inter-Allied dispute during and after the war. Winston Churchill later commented, "Poland had indeed been the most urgent reason for the Yalta Conference." [1] At the Conference itself, Poland was the subject of a prolonged and acrimonious debate, just as the Conference decisions on Poland were bitterly debated after the war. Yalta was labeled a "sell-out": one prominent historian claimed that the cause of Polish freedom suffered its "ultimate adversity" at Yalta. [2] The central position of the Poland question among all the inter-Allied troubles, and the controversy over it after the war, make a re-examination of the discussions and decisions on Poland crucial to any evaluation of the Conference.

The background to the Polish dispute has been presented earlier. It can be summarized as follows: Britain and the United States recognized the Polish government in exile in London; the Soviet Union recognized the Polish Provisional Government in Warsaw. The Soviet Union, and the Warsaw (Lublin) Poles, had decreed the boundaries of Poland to be the Curzon Line on the east and the Oder–Western-Neisse Line on the west. Britain supported the Curzon Line but not the Oder-Neisse; the London Poles' position was precisely the opposite. The United States half-heartedly agreed with Britain but covertly encouraged the London Poles to maintain their stand.

In this welter of opinions, only the Soviet position was internally consistent. Stalin had repeatedly elucidated two principles as a basis for Soviet policy toward Poland: first, during the war, the Red Army's lines of communication and supply in Poland must be protected; second, after the war, Poland must be "friendly" to and dependent on the Soviet Union and must act as a bulwark against German aggression. Stalin told Roosevelt as much in a letter in December 1944:

> It should be borne in mind that the Soviet Union, more than any other power, has a stake in strengthening a pro-Ally and democratic Poland . . . because the Polish problem is inseparable from that of the security of the Soviet Union. To this I should like to add that the Red Army's success in fighting the Germans in Poland largely depends on a tranquil and reliable rear in Poland. . . .[3]

The Soviet principles, in application, meant support for the Curzon and Oder-Neisse lines and for the Lublin government. The insistence on the Curzon and Oder-Neisse lines stemmed directly from Stalin's vision of the Soviet Union's postwar security system and the role Poland would play in it. He intended to put as many obstacles as possible between the Soviet Union and the resurrected capitalist Germany, which he suspected both Churchill and, to a lesser extent, Roosevelt were maneuvering for. To this end Stalin had been pressing for Allied recognition of Russia's pre-1941 acquisitions in Poland, Rumania, Finland, and the Baltic. He had also insisted that the postwar governments in eastern Europe must co-operate with the Soviet Union against any rebirth of German aggressiveness. In particular, he vehemently opposed an independent east European federation, such as the London Poles advocated, which could easily become a *cordon sanitaire* directed not against Germany but against the Soviet Union.

In Stalin's view, the Curzon Line was the cornerstone of the future Soviet security system: it moved the Soviet Armies 150 miles closer to Berlin. Recognition of the Curzon Line signified adherence to the Soviets' concept of collective security with Soviet power in eastern Europe concomitant with Western power in Western Europe. Recognition of the Soviet's Great Power role became the key criterion for determining the "friendliness" of any Polish faction. The Oder-Neisse Line was a rather more subtle bit of policy. The Russians assumed that their support for large-scale Polish expansion would earn, if not the undying gratitude, at least the temporary friendship of a dependent future Polish government. Also, since the Germans would presumably resent the loss of most of old Prussia to the "traditional enemy," Polish-German collaboration would be discouraged, while Polish-Soviet relations (and the dependence of Poland) would be promoted.

In choosing a government for Poland, the needs of the Red Army as well as the requirements of Soviet security dictated the direction of Soviet policy. The Polish government in exile was unsatisfactory in both respects. First, the London Poles, by their words and deeds on the frontiers question and the Katyn incident, indicated a total disinclination to co-operate with Russia on terms of "solid good-neighborly relations and mutual respect," to use Stalin's phrasing.[4] Second, their partisans and their official underground Army in Poland, the *Armia Krajowa,* were continually harassing Red Army units on Polish soil. Stalin complained to Roosevelt in his December 1944 letter that "terrorists, instigated by Polish émigrés, assassinate Red Army soldiers and officers in Poland, wage a criminal struggle against the Soviet forces engaged in liberating Poland and directly aid our enemies, with whom they are virtually in league." The Marshal concluded, "There are no grounds for continuing to support the émigré Government, which . . . threatens civil war in the rear of the Red Army, thereby injuring our common interest in the success of the struggle we are waging against the Germans." [5]

On the other hand, the Russians considered that the Polish Provisional Government was behaving splendidly. It had restored order (except for the sporadic banditry of the London-sponsored brigands); its army was fighting "shoulder-to-shoulder" with the Red Army; it had signed binding economic and military agreements with the Soviet Union; it scrupulously (or slavishly) observed Soviet preferences on such issues as frontiers. This government had been established under Soviet auspices, virtually without regard for Polish popular feelings; and it was restoring calm, but by an orgy of bloodshed. These facts were irrelevant. The government did its job; therefore Stalin gave it his support and urged his Allies to do the same.

The Western position on Poland was not nearly so lucid. Roosevelt and Churchill frequently granted that during the war the needs of the Red Army in Poland were paramount. But they believed that after the war Poland should be "democratic" and Western-oriented, yet nonetheless cooperative toward Russia —despite differing social systems and five hundred years of enmity. The Western Allies indicated that the government in exile, because it was already in existence, best fit their vision, although not very well. The Lublin government was out of the question. Roosevelt, replying to Stalin's letter of December 1944, wrote that there was no evidence "to justify the conclusion that the Lublin Committee as at present constituted represents the people of Poland." [6] Perhaps a new government could be formed. In any case, the West by 1944-45 retained only one cardinal principle: the question of Poland could not be allowed to disrupt the unity of the wartime coalition.

It was easier to determine what the Western leaders did *not* want rather than what they did. First, they did *not* want an obvious "sell-out" to the Soviet Union, or, in other words, Soviet policy prevailing over Western policy. Churchill was under pressure from the Polish community and government in London and their supporters in Parliament, all of whom urged a strong line against the Soviet Union. Roosevelt (as he put it) had to think of the six or seven million Polish-Americans, many of whom considered the Polish government in exile, not to mention the Allies, dangerously lenient toward Russia. Second, the Western leaders did *not* want the London Poles, particularly the liberal-nationalist Mikolajczyk, to go down the drain. Some method of "saving face" for the "honest" members of the London régime was needed. Third, they did *not* want the Polish question to linger as a divisive issue among the Allies. Any tripartite agreement was better than none. (The Soviets, as will be seen, played quite effectively on this fear of permanent disagreement.)

Finally, Churchill and Roosevelt, especially Churchill, were not reconciled to the thought of Soviet hegemony in Poland. They had still not resolved in their own minds the question of whether the Soviet Union had, or should be allowed to have, legitimate interests outside its own borders. By all their previous actions—by their repeated approval of Stalin's principles; by their acknowledgment that Poland played an analagous role to France as a watchdog against Germany for a larger protector (Poland for the Soviet Union, France for Great Britain); by their disavowals of the leaders and policies of the Polish government in exile—by all these admissions and agreements Churchill and Roosevelt should have been ready to accept Stalin's proposals on Poland. But they were still uneasy—Churchill because of his phobia about the "Bolsheviks," Roosevelt because of his own enigmatic vision of the postwar world. The undoing of the Soviet Union's favorable situation in Poland, although it was never mentioned, remained an underlying goal of Anglo-American diplomacy.

It was questionable, however, whether such a reversal could be achieved at Yalta. Stalin held the upper hand on every issue. His troops were occupying Poland, his protégés effectively controlled the reins of government in Poland. Stalin had only to wait for the government and the boundaries which he supported to become irreversible facts. Worse yet, he could profess a desire for agreement and then have the allegedly independent Lublin government block any undesirable changes. The West needed specific and binding concessions and had little to bargain with —at most, the threat of maintaining a rival Polish government and thereby complicating, although not unduly, the Soviet Union's foreign relations. The Western leaders understood the weakness of their position: as Churchill remarked to Molotov, while munching caviar at his first meal at Yalta, "I don't think much of the Lublin government, but I suppose they are the best you can get." [7]

THE ANGLO-AMERICAN POSITION

One reflection of the weakness of their bargaining stance was that Churchill and Roosevelt had to raise the issue of Poland themselves. Stalin, for whom the status quo in Poland was en-

tirely satisfactory, waited through two plenary sessions until the
West made the first move on February 6. Even while the Western
leaders presented their positions, he remained patient and quiet.
By remaining silent he was able to observe, as he subsequently
pointed out, that American and British interests were marginal
compared to the Soviet Union's, and to base his own response on
what the British and American heads of state conceded or demanded.

Roosevelt, in his capacity as chairman, spoke first. He said he
was objective about the issue because of "a more distant point of
view of the problem." His commitment was to the six or seven
million Poles in the United States, with whom his position corre-
sponded. Their main concern, he said, was "losing face."

Churchill summed up Britain's interest in Poland by stating,
"the question was one of honor." In the name of Britain, he disavowed any material interest in Poland, and described the interest
of His Majesty's Government as a matter of chivalry. His flair for
words compensated for his bargaining weakness: "Honor was the
sole reason why we had drawn the sword to help Poland," and
for reasons of honor, "Poland must be mistress in her own house
and captain of her own soul." [8] From the viewpoint of Soviet diplomacy, both British honor and America's plea for saving face,
given as disclaimers of any selfish interest in the Polish state,
could be accommodated in a Soviet solution.

(It is interesting that the Soviet minutes include an editorial
footnote discrediting Churchill's claim that Great Britain entered
the war to help Poland. This footnote states that Britain's declaration of war against Germany did not lead her to implement
her guarantees to Poland. It cites as proof Churchill's memoirs,
in which the British leader stated that Britain and France con-
tented themselves with a pause while Poland was attacked. The
Soviets charge that they remained impassive and left Hitler with
no complaints.[9])

After abjuring any materialistic designs on Poland, the President raised the question of the Polish-Soviet frontier. Both he
and Churchill had agreed at Teheran, and in subsequent correspondence, to the Curzon Line, but now he wanted Stalin to con-

cede a deviation from that line. Casually phrasing his request as a personal favor, Roosevelt said, "It would make it easier for me at home if the Soviet Government could give something to Poland. . . . I hope that Marshal Stalin can make a gesture in this direction." The President suggested that Lvov should be conceded to Poland by the Soviet Union.

The President and the Prime Minister admitted that they were not offering opposition to the Curzon Line, but were only making personal pleas for Soviet magnanimity. Roosevelt explained that one-sided settlement of the boundary issue in favor of the Soviet Union was indicative of how the Poles, meaning the Polish government in exile, might "lose face." Stalin interrupted to excoriate even this argument. The only "Poles" in the opinion of the Soviet Union were the Lublin Poles, who were on record as favoring the Curzon Line. There were "real" Poles and "émigré" Poles, and the "real" Poles lived in Poland. The implication was that the President sought a concession for émigré Poles who no longer had any power in Poland.

Roosevelt retreated from Polish honor to personal considerations. He asked the Soviet government to ease *his* position as President by giving the Poles something to "save face." As if in answer to Stalin's distinction between "real" and "émigré" he contended that *all* Poles wanted to maintain face. He hoped that Lvov and the oil lands southwest of that city could be considered by the Soviets as an offering to all the Poles. At the same time, Roosevelt said he would not insist upon that concession.

Churchill, hastening to show British solidarity with the President in dealing with the Soviet Union, assured Stalin that the British government had already given its word to back the Curzon Line, including the loss of Lvov. This boundary was based on Russian right instead of might, the Prime Minister said. He seemed adamant, promising to hold to that view despite criticism. On the other hand he too suggested that if the mighty Soviet Union wanted to make some gesture of magnanimity to the weaker Poland, the Prime Minister would welcome it.[10]

The Allies, having taken a mild stand on an important issue, admitted that the question of a Polish government which would ensure Polish sovereignty was far more important than Lvov and the surrounding oil fields. Roosevelt bluntly stated that American opinion did not support the Lublin government. Churchill emphasized that Britain recognized the Polish government in exile. Yet both men, anxious to avoid offending Stalin, and not really satisfied with the current leadership of the government in exile, set forth their opposition to the Lublin Poles cautiously, and simultaneously insisted that they really did not associate themselves with the London Poles at all.

Roosevelt remarked that personally he was not acquainted with any member of the government in exile, although he had known and respected Stanislaw Mikolajczyk. Churchill assured Stalin that his hands were clean: although the British government continued to recognize the London Poles, the Prime Minister also had no direct contact with its members. The British no longer considered it necessary to meet with the members of the government in exile. However, Churchill considered some persons among the London Poles respectable, such as Mikolajczyk, Tadeusz Romer, and Stanislaw Grabski, whom he recommended as intelligent and honest men.

The Anglo-American opposition to Stalin's Lublin Committee rested on a tenuous base, since both the President and the Prime Minister only minimally supported the alternative Polish government in London. Despite Roosevelt's encouragement to the members of the government in exile, the President viewed developments in Poland as remote from American interests. Even American public interest, generated by the publications media, underwent a dramatic change in the five weeks before Yalta—a change that in fact portended the conclusion reached by the Conference. One indication of this change can be seen by reading *The New York Times* of that period, which provides a useful index of the shift in attitude. The chart on p. 181 shows how support for the London government, which coincided with opposition to the Soviet-sponsored Lublin Committee in the month before Yalta, changed into open praise for the Lublin Committee as the Conference approached, and how neutrality—or even hostility—toward the London government predominated by the time of the Yalta Conference.

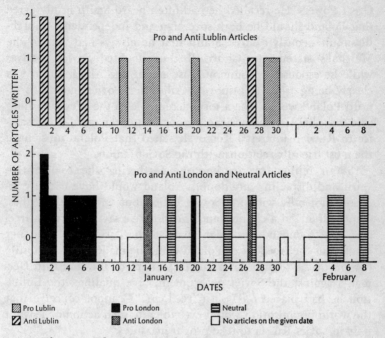

Fig. I: *The New York Times* Coverage on Poland

In contrast, Stalin was prepared to argue that the Lublin government had been instrumental in the war against Germany. The justification for the Lublin government became greater as the support for the government in exile diminished.

In a bid to drop both the Lublin and London Poles in favor of a new government, Roosevelt said that he primarily sought assurance from Stalin that the Polish government really "represented the people." Churchill reinforced Roosevelt's request, insisting that the sovereignty, freedom, and independence of Poland were at stake. The Poles had to have a homeland where they could live as they thought best.

Once having implied that the Soviet sponsorship of the Lublin government endangered the Poland that the West wanted to preserve, Churchill disassociated himself from this inference, stressing good faith and mutual moral obligation among the Great Powers. He recalled he had often heard Stalin firmly agree that Poland should be both sovereign and independent. Churchill simultaneously assured Stalin that he always had trusted the Marshal's statements. Churchill thus doubted Soviet motives while he espoused a common trust among the Allies. Stalin was clearly being asked to assure his Allies that Soviet intentions toward Poland would take a form acceptable to the West. To indicate that the Anglo-American proposals countenanced no disservice to Russian interests, Roosevelt stated that Poland must have the most friendly relations with the Soviet Union.

Stalin replied magnanimously, furthering the co-operative spirit and dispelling any doubts. Poland would have friendly relations not only with the Soviet Union but with all the Allies. Churchill added a circumstance in which he saw that Polish freedom and independence might have to be curtailed: "I do not think that the freedom of Poland could be made to cover hostile designs by any Polish government, perhaps by intrigue with Germany, against the Soviet government." He qualified the limitation he had placed on Polish freedom: "I cannot conceive that the world organization would ever tolerate such action or leave it only to Soviet Russia to take proper measures."

Churchill granted another principle as a guide in dealing with Poland. He admitted that any proposal for a government in Poland would have to take into consideration the securing of the Red Army lines of communication.

After all these statements about amity and principles, about frontiers and philosophies of government, Roosevelt finally stated the core of the Anglo-American position—a proposal to establish a new government. He recommended that a presidential council of outstanding Poles be formed to appoint a provisional government. Churchill immediately supported this proposal. Great Britain and the United States were again confronting Stalin with a plan which would force him to abandon the Lublin government and to risk the favorable situation existing in Poland. Stalin had now heard the British-American case. Seeking time to organize and prepare his own statement, he requested a ten minute recess.[11]

The Soviet Rebuttal

Stalin's lengthy and complete statement defined the Soviet position quite clearly and shrewdly, structuring the arguments parallel to the Anglo-American case. It was not a position that would be negotiable. Nor did it have to be, for its base was a *de facto* situation. Stalin addressed himself throughout to Churchill, whom he still considered his main antagonist, despite the fact that Roosevelt had accepted the burden of the opposition in the preceding hours. He used Churchill's and Roosevelt's arguments as his starting point. By comparing the Soviet and Western arguments on each issue, he used the weakness of the West's position in order to enhance Soviet strength.

Agreeing that Poland was a point of honor for the British government, Stalin said honor was only a part of the real question. Not entirely allowing the matter to drop there, Stalin announced that honor was involved for Russia too, because of "Tsarist sins" against Poland. Becoming as much a moralist as Churchill, and using language reminiscent of his days in a seminary, he insisted the Soviet government intended to atone for these sins.

But, Stalin went on, for Russia, the question of security, the life and death of the Soviet Union itself, was more crucial than honor. Twice in the past thirty years the Germans had crossed Poland to attack Russia. Stalin credited the success of the Germans in crossing Poland to the inability of the Polish state to defend itself, with the Soviet Union powerless to help. He concluded that the solution best serving Soviet security was the creation of a powerful, free, and independent Poland. Thus, Stalin implied that Russia's security *was synonymous* with Poland's freedom and independence.

With the implication that Poland had only the Tsars to fear, the Marshal emphasized the difference between Soviet policy and Tsarist policy. The Tsars had attempted to assimilate Poland. In contrast, the Soviets abandoned such an inhuman policy and followed the road of friendship with Poland. In atonement for the

Tsars' transgressions, Russia wanted to be the protector of Polish independence.

Stalin turned next to an impassioned defense of the Curzon Line. He argued that the Curzon Line was the minimum the Soviet Union could accept and suggested that if there were any revisions to be made, they should be made in the Soviets' favor to include the Russian area of Bialystok. The West was lucky that the Soviet Union accepted even the Curzon Line. It was a boundary drawn by foreigners without the presence of the Russians and without the consent of or consultation with the Russians. Stalin claimed that he was already departing from the strict Soviet position. He alleged that Lenin would not have conceded the Curzon Line; he would not have relinquished Bialystok.

Stalin played on the Western concern for honor. He lamented that the Allies were putting him in the position of being less Russian than Curzon or Clemenceau. That would disgrace him; he would be criticized, for example, by the Ukrainians. Rising from the table (he did this rarely during the Conference), he asked, how could he even return to the capital of Moscow? [12]

Stalin had reasons he had not mentioned for taking such a firm stand. The boundary settlement was to be a package deal. Once the Curzon Line was established in the east, a concession would be made on the western Polish frontier at the expense of Germany. The Marshal offered Soviet blood to compensate the Poles: "I prefer that the war continue a little longer and give Poland compensation in the west at the expense of Germany." Stalin even incorporated the opinion of ex-Premier Mikolajczyk— whom he disinherited on all other occasions—to prove the desirability of the Oder-Neisse frontier which the Soviet government already recognized as the future boundary. Stalin interjected that, of the two Neisse rivers, it was the Western Neisse which he backed. He called upon Roosevelt and Churchill to support this position.

Without waiting for an answer, Stalin went on to the question of a Polish government. Avoiding a reply to the Roosevelt and Churchill proposal for a presidential council to form a new government, Stalin concentrated on exposing Churchill who, he thought, was veiling imperialistic deeds with democratic talk. Stalin admonished Churchill: "hopefully the Prime Minister had only engaged in a slip of the tongue by proposing the establishment of a Polish government." Playing out his role, Stalin remarked that certainly he had been called a dictator, but at least he had enough democratic feeling to refrain from setting up a Polish government without consulting the Poles. Outdoing the Allies, he lectured that only by the consent and participation of the Poles could any Polish government be established.

Stalin closed the door to any solution other than the one the Soviet Union had already effected. He blamed the London Poles for making any discussion of a new government pointless. Churchill had seen that when he brought the London Poles to Moscow, Stalin said, subtly reminding Churchill that the Prime Minister had divorced himself from them ever since. Since the Lublin régime had also been invited to Moscow at that time, Stalin asserted that that had been the proper moment for a solution. The London Poles had been hostile and now the Lublin Poles were repaying them. That unsuccessful meeting had eliminated any opportunity for a coalition. Because the London Poles had not compromised, the Lublin Poles would not agree to any new solution. (This was the keynote for future discussions, when Stalin would fall back upon the threat of freezing the status quo. At the same time he would disclaim Soviet responsibility for a deadlock while "democratically" transferring the burden to the shoulders of the Lublin Poles.)

Having ruled out the possibility of an intra-Polish solution, Stalin suggested an inter-Allied one. He stressed that he personally would be glad to unite the Poles if there were any chance of success. Suddenly Stalin inquired whether the Warsaw Poles should come to the conference or, alternatively, whether talks should be resumed in Moscow?

Stalin concluded his statement by calling for Allied support of the principle which justified any Soviet unilateral action, a principle, in fact, already granted by Churchill and Roosevelt— the necessity of protecting the communication lines of the Red Army at all costs. Stalin made this the *raison d'être* for backing the Lublin Poles. So long as the Red Army had to protect its rear and ensure order behind the front lines, Stalin refused to permit London Poles in Poland. He disclaimed political motives for this, assuring the Allies that the Red Army was not interested in what kind of government existed. The Red Army's concern was purely military, and in particular it could not condone being attacked from behind the lines. The Lublin government helped keep order, while the London Poles formed "forces of internal resistance" which had already killed 212 Red Army men and broken the laws. Therefore, announced Stalin, if this continued, these Poles, even though recognized by the West, would be shot. In any case, support of the Lublin government would continue. In summary, Marshal Stalin stated he had no alternative. On the basis of military demands alone, the Warsaw Poles were necessary for the success of the Red Army. "Such is the situation," Stalin concluded.[13]

Churchill interjected that he and Stalin must be supplied with information from different sources. Britain could not accept the Lublin government, for it was not backed by the majority of the electorate. On the other hand, Britain wanted to eliminate the possibility of conflict and bloodshed in Poland, and agreed that attacks on the Red Army were inadmissible.

The session ended with Roosevelt, Churchill, and Stalin lamenting that the Polish problem was such a headache but resolving to make every effort to solve it.[14]

QUID PRO QUO

On February 7, at the beginning of the fourth plenary session, the discussion returned to the Polish issue. Stalin said he had received a letter from Roosevelt with suggestions on Poland. The letter embodied Stalin's own suggestion of bringing the London and Lublin groups to Yalta, but Stalin saw it for what it was: a maneuver to pressure him to moderate his position on Poland, accept a compromise government which both sides could recognize, and, by reviving a semblance of the prewar status quo, demonstrate Allied unity. Roosevelt professed that he was greatly disturbed that the Big Three had had no meeting of minds on the political situation in Poland. "I am sure this state of affairs should not continue and that if it does it can only lead our people to think there is a breach between us, which is not the case."

At the same time he made this proposal, Roosevelt reiterated the Western assurances to the Soviet Union. He indicated he was impressed with Stalin's need for stability in the wake of the Red Army, and he agreed that the establishment of any government in Poland was conditional upon creating this stability. Roosevelt was in agreement with Stalin's own pet thesis—there must be a present understanding for the sake of future unity.

But the President went on to make specific recommendations that would have put an end to the Lublin government. In a more concrete proposal than the one he had made the previous day, he asked that two members of the Lublin government, plus two other Poles from a list submitted to Stalin, be invited to Yalta to try to establish a provisional government which the British and American governments would then be prepared to recognize. He had taken into account Stalin's accusation—a democratic process would be assured because this new government would hold free elections at the earliest date. As Roosevelt reassured Stalin, "I know this is completely consistent with your desire to see a new free and democratic Poland." [15]

Stalin had little choice. Through this letter, Roosevelt was challenging him with a specific proposal to help implement his own democratic statement of the day before, when the Soviet leader had admonished Churchill for suggesting the creation of a Polish government without the consent of the Poles. Moreover, Stalin, who had used the issue of preserving Allied unity in his opposition to the inclusion of France in the control machinery, as well as in his objections to the American voting formula, was being asked to show that he intended to perpetuate Allied unity on Poland.

The Soviet Union maneuvered adroitly. Stalin turned first to Roosevelt's letter. He claimed that he had received the letter just an hour and a half before the meeting, and that he had immediatley set out to locate the Poles to bring them to the Yalta Conference in accordance with the President's request. But, Stalin asked, "Where could these Poles be found?" He could not reach the Lublin Poles by telephone. When he had tried, he had been informed that they were away in the cities of Cracow and Lodz. As a result, he had little hope of finding them. He would still try to reach someone to help find the other Poles. Once communications were established, the Conference would be told how soon the Poles would arrive.

To placate his Allies, Stalin announced that he thought it would be helpful to bring a Western-supported Pole still in Poland, like Wincenty Witos or Adam Sapieha, to the Conference.* Yet this was difficult; unfortunately, he did not know their addresses.

Stalin's statement, softening an otherwise outright rejection of Roosevelt's request by giving implausible excuses on the one hand while holding out some possibility of implementation on the other, concluded with a final note of despair. It appeared there was not enough time anyhow to bring the Poles to the Conference.[16] This meant, in effect, that Stalin had no intention of trying to form a "new" Polish government at Yalta.

It seems likely that the Soviet delegation placed no telephone calls and made no effort to reach either the Lublin Poles or to trace any other persons whose presence Roosevelt requested. First, the Soviet minutes of the Conference conveniently deleted all reference to Stalin's attempt to reach Polish leaders. It is not at all inconceivable that the present government would find it embarrassing to have Stalin's assertion aired within East European circles. Second, Stalin had never had any trouble previously in arranging the comings and goings of the Lublin Poles. When Charles de Gaulle visited Moscow in December 1944, the chief members of the Lublin Committee appeared at the French Embassy in Moscow to be received by de Gaulle "on matters of intelligence." [17] They had also been available for the Mikolajczyk and Churchill visits of August and October of 1944. Third, this sort of melodramatic maneuver was not at all new for Stalin. He was fully capable of making a dramatic act or obviously fraudulent statement to demonstrate a co-operative spirit, while in reality entirely rejecting a proposal. A similar interpre-

* Witos was leader of the pre-1939 Polish Peasant Party; Sapieha was Archbishop of Cracow; both remained in Poland during the war.

tation might be given to a meeting in 1941, when Stanislaw Kot, Polish Ambassador to the Soviet Union, asked Stalin for information about 8000 "lost" Polish officers. Stalin, apparently trying to convince the Polish Ambassador of the Soviets' good intentions, immediately telephoned the NKVD to inquire about the missing men. During the phone conversation Stalin muttered, loud enough for Kot to hear, "They say they have all been released," and said nothing further on the issue. Kot dismissed the entire incident as "obvious play-acting." * [18] On another occasion, Stalin tried to divert Polish concern about these officers by stating that they had all escaped to Manchuria.[19]

Before Roosevelt or Churchill could raise questions or present alternative suggestions, Stalin announced that Molotov would present a draft proposal on Poland which met the President's requests, but it was being translated and had not arrived yet. In the meantime, Stalin made ready to announce a concession on the voting procedure in the proposed United Nations. Referring to the recent meeting in the United States on the United Nations Charter, Stalin suggested that "We might talk of Dumbarton Oaks." [20]

Stalin had conceived of a counter-maneuver. Suddenly the Soviet delegation was prepared to accept the American voting formula, at last convinced that Soviet interests would be safeguarded thereby and that the formula furthered the collaboration of the Big Three in keeping German peace. In the eyes of the West, because Stalin had withheld agreement on such formulas at Dumbarton Oaks and at the previous plenary session, this appeared to be a major concession. In addition, the Soviets set aside the previous request that *all* Soviet Republics be granted membership in the General Assembly and asked for the admittance of only two or three separate Republics of the Soviet Union.

---

* Mikolajczyk, on the other hand, was not so sure. He believed that the NKVD informed Stalin of the liquidation of these officers, thus accounting for Stalin's studious silence about the officers thereafter. Mikolajczyk, *The Rape of Poland,* p. 381. In either case, Stalin exhibited a facility to play out the role the Allies expected of him, despite the harsh reality he was hiding.

There was a suggestion implicit in the timing of this concession and in Stalin's statements: both questions—a voting
formula for the United Nations and the formation of the Polish
government—could be solved at the same time. Stalin linked his
concession on the voting formula to the request for American acceptance of the Molotov draft on Poland.

The Soviet delegation had already provided a clue to its intention. Word was leaked to the British, and Churchill informed
Roosevelt and Stettinius just before the opening of the session,
"Uncle Joe will take Dumbarton Oaks." [21] Molotov, just a few
hours before, had declined an offer made by Stettinius to discuss
the American voting formula, and had mentioned that he would
raise a few questions later. Now, at the plenary session, Molotov
accepted the voting formula unconditionally. He stated that the
Soviet government, having heard Secretary Stettinius' full report
the day before, and Mr. Churchill's explanations, found the question considerably clarified. "We paid much attention to what
Churchill told us."

Since Roosevelt had questioned the Soviet intention to preserve Allied unity over the issue of Poland, Molotov again insisted
that the desire to preserve this unity was the cornerstone of the
Soviet acceptance of the American voting formula. "In the light
of these explanations," Molotov said, "we believe it would secure
the unanimity of the three powers in guaranteeing the peace and
security after the war. Our position in the questions of the Dumbarton Oaks essentially was to secure the maximum of unity
among the three great powers in the question of peace and security after the war." [22]

The Soviet proposal on Poland was then officially placed before the Conference. It put into writing the essence of Stalin's demands of the day before and included token concessions in accordance with Western demands. The proposal took into
consideration Allied objections to the present form of the Lublin
government; it catered to the Allied plea to stress free elections
and responded in a minor way to the request for magnanimity in
the drawing of the Curzon Line. The Soviet plan set aside Roosevelt's proposal for a provisional government and forced a deci-

sion on the basis of Soviet terms. It implied a flat rejection of any other solution.

The aim of the Soviet proposal can best be evaluated by examining its specific provisions, which are summarized here. Stalin's primary concessions are italicized. The Molotov draft: (1) set the Curzon Line as the eastern frontier of Poland *with digressions up to eight kilometers in Poland's favor;* (2) created the western Polish frontier from the city of Stettin along the Oder River to and along the Western Neisse River; (3) agreed *it was desirable to enlarge the currently functioning provisional Polish government with democratic leaders from Polish émigré circles, and that this enlarged government should be recognized by the Allies;* (4) placed the responsibility upon the provisional government to call the population of Poland to elections; and (5) set up a commission in Moscow, composed of Foreign Minister Molotov plus the British and American ambassadors, which would enlarge the government and consider the proposals of their governments.[23]

This Soviet proposal represented a compromise and concessions to Britain and America on Stalin's former position on Poland, but the particular compromises were inconsequential except for the possibility of enlarging the government. Roosevelt and Churchill had pleaded for a face-saving formula, and the Russians, to accommodate them, had contrived one. The frontier in which both Churchill and Roosevelt had expressed a secondary interest, and for which they merely requested Soviet magnanimity, remained essentially the same, with a possible token change to satisfy this Allied request. The Soviet draft stood firm on the question of the government: the Lublin government had to be the basis for reorganization. The real concession was the admission that it was desirable to enlarge the government. (The proposal could be subjected to the criticism Stalin had made of Roosevelt's former proposal—i.e., the Great Powers and not the Poles were deciding what kind of government Poland should have.)

The distinction between the Lublin and London Poles was set down in writing. Implying, as Stalin had said the day before, that the Lublin Poles were the "real" Poles, the Soviet draft stated that men added to the government could come from émigré circles. There was no guarantee that this enlargement would automatically take place. The commission, composed of Molotov and the ambassadors, would discuss how this proposal might be carried out. (This parallels Churchill's insistence that a group should study *how* to dismember Germany. If Britain could later backtrack by this device, so could Russia.)

The Soviet proposal indicated that the Russians did not intend to go very far in modifying their favorable situation in Poland. They had put into writing their desire for elections, their willingness to include the Allies in a commission to work out the problem of creating a provisional government, their acceptance of the desirability of an enlarged government, and a boundary concession of five to eight kilometers to Poland on the Russo-Polish frontier. It was in the Soviet interest to grant these concessions. The Soviet government needed Allied unity to keep the peace against Germany, and an unresolved conflict over Poland could become a major threat to this unity. In essence, the Soviet compromise satisfied the Soviet aims while saving face for the Allies.

Before the American or British delegations had a chance to react to the Soviet draft, Molotov dealt a deathblow to Roosevelt's proposal of an alternative solution. With finality, Molotov informed the plenary session that the Soviets had again attempted to reach the Poles by telephone but had been unsuccessful. Molotov announced that the failure of this second telephone call made it obviously *and finally* impossible to summon the Poles to the Crimea. The Soviet Conference minutes again have no reference to any attempt by the Russians to reach the Poles by telephone.[24]

Molotov appealed to the President for acceptance of the Soviet draft. Without referring directly to the United Nations, he stressed that these proposals had been put forward to help meet the President's wishes. Roosevelt responded properly. He had been mollified by the Soviet acceptance of his pet scheme, the American voting procedure, and further saw a Soviet compromise proposal on Poland designed to "meet the President's wishes." He graciously acknowledged that progress had been made in the light of Mr. Molotov's suggestions. Neither he nor Churchill raised substantial objections. Stalin and Molotov took careful note of the criticisms and tried to reconcile them as they were raised. For example, Roosevelt objected to the use of the term "émigré." Churchill supported Roosevelt and suggested the term "Poles temporarily abroad." The Prime Minister was also disturbed that the Soviet draft made reference only to democratic leaders *outside* Poland. Stalin was eager to incorporate these moderate changes and agreed that the words "and from inside Poland" should be added to Molotov's proposal.

Churchill returned to the boundary question. Conceding that he raised it not because he objected directly to the boundary suggested by Molotov and Stalin, but because he had qualms about the problem of the transfer of population, he questioned the wisdom of making the Neisse River the boundary: "It would be a pity to stuff the Polish goose so full of German food that it got indigestion." On the other hand, he did not mind the transfer of populations if there was a capability to receive them. There were those in Britain who objected, but he professed not to be among them. For example, he felt that the absorption of East Prussia could be handled, but the extension of Poland's western boundary to the Neisse River would create a new problem.

Churchill's objection was easily dismissed by Stalin's assurance that the problem no longer existed. Churchill need have no worries because, Stalin said, at the present time there were few Germans in these areas. They had run away from the Soviet troops, leaving the areas vacated. Indeed, at that moment several million refugees were in flight westward.[25]

Churchill was left without an argument and conceded that this certainly made things easier. Gathering enthusiasm, he suddenly went on to support Stalin. The problem was even simpler, since there had been six to seven million German casualties in the war and there would probably be another million, making assimilation easier. Stalin asked whether that would be one or two million, and Churchill replied sportingly that he was not proposing any limit on the destruction of Germans.

Roosevelt remained silent during the friendly interchange be-

tween the Prime Minister and the Marshal. Earlier he had proposed to put the Soviet draft aside until it could be studied, and
Stalin had readily agreed; when Churchill finished his chat with
Stalin on transfer of population, he too agreed to postpone
discussion.[26]

The Soviet delegation left the plenary session without receiving any real challenge to their Polish proposal. The spirit of the
session portended imminent resolution. Stalin had dispensed
with the only substantive objections. The problem of terminology
over the word "émigré" had quickly been resolved by Soviet
agreement to reword the Soviet proposal; Churchill's concern
over transferring populations was relieved by Stalin's assurance
that only a limited population would remain to be transferred;
and, finally, Churchill himself had provided valuable statistics
which indicated that Germany could, because of her population
losses in the war, absorb a Soviet transfer of Germans into her reduced territory.

On the surface, by the close of the session on February 7,
1945, there appeared to be no serious obstacles to the Soviet compromise solution.

A WESTERN REJECTION

At the fifth plenary session, on February 8, Roosevelt and
Churchill rejected Molotov's compromise draft on Poland by offering a counter proposal. Stalin, however, benefited from the
lack of co-ordination between the two. An awkward situation was
created when Britain and America tried to present separate proposals. Churchill finally rescued the situation by reluctantly
agreeing to back the American proposal with minor reservations.

With this qualified support, Roosevelt proposed the creation
of a *new government* in Poland. A presidential council appointed by Molotov and the British and American ambassadors
in Moscow would set up a provisional government. The three
members to serve on the presidential council would be selected
from the Lublin government, democratic elements inside Poland,
and democratic elements abroad. The provisional government
would hold elections for a constituent assembly, which then

would elect a permanent government. The Three Powers that had established the presidential council would recognize the provisional government as soon as it was formed. Roosevelt also accepted the Curzon Line, but followed Churchill's stance in rejecting the Soviet proposed western frontier.[27]

Stalin was certain of what Roosevelt was trying to do, namely, to break the Soviet hold on Poland. The problem was to counter it. His first supposition was that if Washington and London admitted their abandonment of the Polish government in exile, that admission would bring them one step closer to accepting the other existing government.

Stalin asked his question directly: were the British and Americans ready to abandon the government in exile? Churchill and Roosevelt answered that when a provisional government could be created, they would end their recognition of the London Poles. Unsatisfied, Stalin pressed further, testing their intentions with details. What would happen to the property of that government? Roosevelt stated that it would pass to the new government.

Stalin sat back and let Molotov take over.[28] The Foreign Minister undertook to make the American proposal look ridiculous and impossible to carry out. By implication, the Soviet proposal would still remain the only basis of agreement. Molotov threatened that any program ignoring the existing government at Warsaw—democratically backed by the Polish people—was unacceptable. "If we start on the basis that the present Government could be enlarged, the basis of probable success is more secure." He discredited any other plan, alleging that only the Warsaw Poles were connected with decisive events in Poland. Molotov defined what appeared to him the only remaining problem: "How many and who should be taken in by us."

According to Molotov, the government of Poland *already* existed and functioned. He ridiculed the President's proposal, which, were it put into effect, would result in the side-by-side existence of two governments—the presidential committee and the Lublin government. Molotov further complicated the situation by setting up a decoy for the presidential committee. A national council already existed in Poland and was similar to a presidential committee. This national council could be expanded, he suggested. Roosevelt objected, insisting on his presidential committee, which would have a different composition. Molotov countered with a demand for the expansion of the national council. Clearly, expansion of a Soviet-backed government or committee was the only road to agreement.

Molotov, who earlier had proclaimed that the Poles must speak for themselves, now spoke for them. Creating bargaining leverage for himself, the Foreign Minister threatened that the Western-backed Polish leader Mikolajczyk (whom the Soviet government had not yet accepted in any capacity) might become unacceptable to the Lublin government. Molotov therefore proposed, as if everyone agreed on expanding the Lublin government, that two other Poles from the outside join three leaders from the Lublin government to discuss expansion with the ambassadors and himself.

Churchill up to that point had tried to remain controlled, but he then steered a collision course. The Prime Minister declared that the formation of the Polish government was the crucial point of the Conference. He exhorted the Soviet Union to be guided by the necessity for unity (meaning an Anglo-American solution) and threatened that "the world" would see this issue as indicative of fundamental differences.

So far the problem was insoluble, the Prime Minister warned. Great Britain operated from "facts" which differed basically from the Soviets'. In the eyes of Great Britain, the Lublin government did not represent the Polish people. Great Britain refused to abandon her Polish Ally, who had fought Germany, and would not accept the Lublin government, the Prime Minister said, as he turned from his previous and frequent disavowals of support for the London Poles. Since Great Britain had already given in on the issue of boundaries, she would not capitulate on the question of the Polish government as well. Calming himself, he admitted that, personally, he thought the Polish government in exile had been "unwise"; on the other hand, he would not recognize any government of Poland until he saw that it represented the Polish people. Only a free election would accomplish that.[29]

Molotov offered Churchill no satisfaction. Molotov's tactic was to threaten that in this event there could be no agreement over Poland. Perhaps discussions in Moscow later would be useful, he suggested. Parodying Churchill's plea for a democratic solution, he reminded everyone that it was hard to settle the issue, since the Poles were not at Yalta. The West wanted and needed an agreement, and Churchill pushed for an immediate settlement. Roosevelt followed, stressing that they really did have a common viewpoint: the desire for a general election as soon as possible. Western concern centered only on the interim solution.[30]

Stalin had let Molotov pave the way. Now he added authority to Molotov's negative pronouncements. Intent on keeping the focus on the lack of agreement, the Marshal took Churchill's own arguments and used them against a settlement. He reminded Roosevelt that Churchill did not have any information on Poland and found it impossible to get any. Churchill rejoined, "I have a certain amount!" to which Stalin replied, "It doesn't agree with mine!" Churchill heartily agreed to that.

Stalin burst into a monologue: The Soviet armies controlled the situation, not Britain or America; the Lublin government was currently in power in Poland; and the Red Army had already "revolutionized" the Polish mind. A democratic government already existed and it was in control, he said. The Polish government recognized by the Soviet Union met the criteria his Allies advanced, i.e., it was democratic, representative, and popular. The Marshal introduced his proof. First, the basis of the popularity of the government lay in the fact that it had remained in Poland and had not abandoned the people in their hour of need. Second, Stalin reasserted that the action of the Red Army had brought about "a great revolution in the Polish people's minds." The Soviet Army was reversing former Polish suspicions of Russia which had stemmed from the Tsarist division of Poland. The Poles now were celebrating the Russian success, and, if anything, they were surprised by the London Poles' lack of participation in this moment of victory.

Stalin threw the burden for agreement on Churchill. "You are afraid also that we may separate before agreement. We have different information and have reached different conclusions." Having threatened no agreement, Stalin explained how the West could have one. Molotov was right, he began, there could be no presidential committee. But the situation was not so tragic as Churchill depicted it. There was a way out if everyone realized the necessity for one thing: the reconstruction of the existing government.[31]

Roosevelt, perhaps worn down by this point, focused on elections, the democratic process he believed would determine the future of Poland. The President asked how long it might be before general elections took place. Stalin guessed only a month, accepting Roosevelt's hint that the arguments over the composition of an interim government were unimportant since the future would be decided by free elections. Responding positively, Churchill declared that this would certainly set British minds at rest. The Prime Minister tried to restore the equilibrium which he, Molotov, and Stalin had upset. He reassured the Russians that the British would not ask for anything that might hamper the military operations of the Soviet forces.

Roosevelt still wanted to be rid of the problem, and he asked that the Polish issue be referred to the foreign ministers. Molotov, observing the effect of his tactics, indulged in a brief moment of levity: "The other two will outvote me." [32]

With a congenial mood re-established, Stalin took advantage of the remaining moments of the session to introduce a couple of questions designed to remind the Allies that, in their respective spheres of influence, the Soviets had kept their side of the bargain. Stalin's insinuation was that if anyone had violated agreements, it was the British.

Implicit in Stalin's argument was his assumption that Poland was an unrecognized Soviet sphere of influence, and he reminded everyone of it. Comparing Poland to Western-supported France, Stalin raised the telling point: "Why was more to be demanded of Poland than of France?" He pointed out that de Gaulle had not been elected, and yet the Soviets recognized his government and concluded agreements with him! Stalin thought there should be reciprocal treatment for the Soviet sphere of influence.

This conversation provided evidence that the Western Allies were keenly aware of their own spheres of influence, although they denied it publicly. Roosevelt automatically thought of his difficulty in arranging for the American Secretary of State to meet with the British and Soviet foreign ministers, because "my Foreign Secretary has all South America to take care of." This remark provided a springboard from which Stalin could again remind Churchill of their respective spheres. Churchill had complained of an inability to get information from Stalin's sphere, and Stalin now paid him back. The Soviet leader informally raised two barbed questions. First, he wanted to know why the new United Government in Yugoslavia had been delayed, when the British had already agreed to it. Second, there were so many rumors on Greece—not that he had any criticism, he emphasized —but he just wanted to know what was going on. Churchill gave a brief answer and Stalin hastened to reassure him: "On Greece I only wanted to know for information. We have no intention of intervening there in any way." [33]

Stalin was reminding Churchill that the British sphere of influence in Greece was safe because Stalin permitted it to be. He had also dropped an unsubtle hint about Yugoslavia—if Churchill were to challenge Soviet good faith in Poland, Stalin would reciprocate in Yugoslavia. On this note, the discussion of Poland at the fifth plenary session ended.

THE AMERICAN PROPOSAL

At the foreign ministers' conference at noon February 9, Stettinius made an effort to tie together the varying attitudes on a Polish government. He agreed to drop the idea of a presidential council. Like Roosevelt, he insisted that the Allied governments were not actually so far apart on the question of a Polish government because, first, everyone agreed that the Poles themselves had to have elections to determine their government, and second, all wanted a provisional government composed of members of the present Polish provisional government along with representatives of democratic elements inside Poland and abroad.

The Americans offered a formal compromise. Roosevelt felt secure in the belief that elections would guarantee the emergence of what the West meant by a "democratic" government, especially since Stalin said the elections could take place within a month. Given that, the American government was prepared to overlook the particulars of an interim solution. Molotov capitalized on this concession. He agreed wholeheartedly that the most important issue was the holding of elections "as soon as practical." Now the interim solution could more firmly reflect military considerations, in particular, measures to protect the rear of the Red Army. Molotov insisted that if this were not given proper attention, "an impossible situation would arise."

Stettinius made a proposal * which was acceptable to the Soviet government, primarily because it acceded to a reorganization of the Lublin government as the basis of the "new" government. There were changes Molotov wanted to make, but for the time being he withheld an official response pending discussion with Stalin. But this American proposal provided a tentative American-Soviet understanding, leaving only Great Britain, through Eden, still objecting to an expansion of the Lublin government. Even Eden's arguments were beginning to weaken. He admitted the possibility of error, but he thought most people felt that the Lublin government did not represent Poland. It would be much easier for Britain to abandon the government in exile if the new government were more neutral than Lublin.[34]

When the plenary session convened the same afternoon, Stettinius reported on the foreign ministers' meeting. He was interrupted the moment he mentioned Poland. Churchill requested a discussion of Poland before proceeding. Molotov hastened to announce that the Soviet Union accepted the American proposal made by Stettinius as the basis for discussion.[35] This put the Soviet Union and the United States together. In fact, the American proposal embodied most of the Soviet prerequisites for a solution to the Polish government, with the addition of a guarantee of democratic implementation.

Putting the British, now isolated, on the defensive, Molotov accepted Churchill's challenge of the previous day, to consider Allied unity, and justified Soviet acceptance of the American pro-

* It is analyzed below.

posal in terms of a prime concern for unity. Should there be no agreement, the onus would be on Britain. Churchill stood alone, blocking unity by not accepting the U.S.-Soviet solution.

Molotov still wanted to make several changes in the American proposal which would weaken any commitment to the creation of a more Western-oriented government in Poland. What he hoped to accomplish becomes clear as one compares the American proposal from the foreign minister's session with the particular substitutions he now offered at the plenary session. These substitutions brought the latest proposal on Poland closer to the original Soviet demands. The phrases Molotov wanted changed, and the substitutions he offered, are italicized.

Molotov proposed the following specific changes: [36]

1. The American proposal stated "that the present Polish Provisional Government be reorganized into a *fully representative Government* based on *all democratic forces* in Poland and including democratic leaders from Poland and abroad, to be termed *'The Provisional Government of National Unity.'* " Molotov preferred it to read: "The present Provisional Government of Poland should be reorganized on *a wider democratic basis* with the *inclusion of democratic leaders* from Poland itself and from those living abroad, and in this connection this Government would be called the *National Provisional Government of Poland.*" Molotov sought thereby to limit the concept of fully representative government with all democratic elements included and, further, to use a name as close as possible to that of the Soviet-recognized Lublin government, known already as the Provisional Government of Poland.

2. Molotov sought the inclusion of the words *"non-Fascist and anti-Fascist"* in the clause permitting democratic parties the right to participate in elections. The Soviet Union accepted the rest of the paragraph, which charged Molotov, Harriman, and Clark Kerr to consult in Moscow with the leaders of the present provisional government and other democratic leaders within Poland and abroad for the reorganization. This government would then be pledged to the holding of "free and unfettered elections

as soon as practicable on the basis of universal suffrage and secret ballot in which all democratic parties would have the right
to participate and to put forward candidates."

3. Molotov wanted to delete the last sentence of the proposal,
which stipulated that the ambassadors in Warsaw would observe
and report on the carrying out of free elections. Molotov rea-
soned with the Allies that this was, on the one hand, offensive to
the Poles and, on the other hand, superfluous because it is the
duty of ambassadors to observe.

Molotov did not then relinquish the floor; instead he moved
on to discredit British intentions in Yugoslavia before Churchill
had a chance to discredit Soviet motives in Poland. Great Britain
would be on the defensive and have to prove that developments
in Yugoslavia, over which Britain exercised control, were taking
place in accordance with promises. Molotov turned the knife: "I
have one more request to make. The carrying out of the Yugoslav settlement has been delayed. Since Mr. Churchill agreed on
this settlement we feel that it should be carried out immediately." [37]

Churchill would not permit himself to be trapped; he waived
consideration of Yugoslavia until Poland was discussed. But he
did commend the Soviet delegation on the great step forward indicated in their new position.[38] This strengthened the Soviet
position momentarily, and it appeared the Soviets were on the
verge of gaining Allied backing for the Soviet position on Poland. However, Churchill did not succumb to Molotov's charges,
and he warned against decisions taken too hastily just because
agreement seemed at hand. If twenty-four more hours were
needed to attain agreement, then those twenty-four hours should
be found. He saw the success or failure of the Conference resting
on agreement on Poland.[39]

After Stettinius finished presenting the foreign ministers' report, there was a thirty-minute recess, during which the British
and American delegations considered the Molotov amendments.
Afterward, the Anglo-Americans gave up demanding guarantees
to ensure a representative democratic provisional government
and negotiated instead for a guarantee of free elections, on the

assumption that this would create a new democratic government. This shift, which harmonized the British and American policies, recognized the expansion of the Lublin government but requested democratic elections.

Roosevelt optimistically opened the discussion by saying that a close look at Molotov's proposals showed that agreement was in sight and that differences at this point were "only a matter of words." The President suggested certain changes which would align the Soviet and Anglo-American positions. One of the "words" Roosevelt objected to was the name of the government. He asked Stalin to consider that the wording "the present Provisional Polish Government" was embarrassing to the London Poles. So perhaps one could rephrase this to read "the Provisional Government now functioning in Poland."

The President then moved to a more crucial question that tested the avowed intention of the Soviet Union to carry out free elections. He protested the omission of ambassadorial observations to ensure free elections. Roosevelt advised against this deletion on the ground that the six million Poles in the United States still wanted some gesture of reassurance.[40] These criticisms did not seriously challenge the Molotov amendments to the American proposal.

Churchill's criticisms were more barbed than Roosevelt's, and Stalin pitted himself directly against his main antagonist after Churchill exhausted his arguments. Churchill credited the Red Army with creating a "new situation" by "the liberation of Poland," and he urged a concurrent responsibility to create a new and more broadly based government. He requested that the draft of the proposal include reference to this "new situation." Then he turned to the question of whether the ambassadors should report on the elections. As supplicant, he showed caution in wording his concern. It was really a question of getting information, he said. He begged Stalin to take into account the difficulty of the British government's position; the British were at a disadvantage in negotiating over Poland because they had little knowledge of what was going on. The British government, for instance, had heard that the Lublin government intended to try members of the Polish Home Army as traitors, and this rumor had caused great anxiety and distress. Churchill said he objected to relying upon information gained from parachutists and the underground. How could this be remedied without hampering the Soviet troop movements? Was there no way that the British and Americans could see for themselves how the Polish problem was being settled?

Churchill suggested that the British and Americans already observed this principle in their military spheres. He challenged Stalin by citing one communist who agreeed—Tito would not bar foreign observers from assuring the world that elections were impartial. Offering reciprocity, he stated that the British would welcome observers to the elections to be held in Greece, and that the United States, Britain, and Russia should all be observers in Italy. Churchill said this was no idle request and cited Egypt, where the benefits of observation revealed that the elections were controlled by the government in power. Stalin immediately rejected comparison between Poland and Egypt. There could be no real election in Egypt, he said, because of bribery and corruption. Churchill did not argue that point. He tried to turn the discussion back to his plea for observation of the elections, but Stalin persisted. What was the percentage of those in Egypt who could read and write? In Poland, he triumphantly announced, 70 per cent of the people were literate, and the people could voice their opinion.

Churchill had to admit he did not know the literacy rate in Egypt.* He backed down, insisting he had intended no comparison between Egypt and Poland. His only interest was in fair elections, and how free would the elections be? Would Mikolajczyk be allowed to take part in the election? Resorting to the formula that enabled him to play democrat while, in effect, answering "no," Stalin replied that this was a question that would have to be discussed with the Poles. Churchill tried an alternative approach: ought the ambassadors to discuss the question in Moscow? Stalin answered that this seemed acceptable provided it was approved by this Conference. The Prime Minister, irate at Sta-

---

* The Soviet Conference minutes boast triumphantly in bold face type in an editorial note: "None of the British delegation was able to answer the question."

lin's refusal to give him satisfaction, abruptly announced that he had no desire to continue discussing the matter. He said he wanted only to be able to tell Parliament that elections would be free.[41]

Stalin did not want Churchill to give up, but just to give way. Seeing that Churchill was ready to close the matter, Stalin answered Churchill's inquiry about Mikolajczyk in reassuring terms. Since Mikolajczyk represented the Peasant Party, which was not a fascist party, his party could take part in the election. Some of the candidates of this party would enter the government. That this promised nothing was clear when Stalin returned to his original premise: the settlement of this question had to be left for discussion by the Poles.

Churchill bargained hard and alone, threatening to withhold the concession he had made on the Polish boundary. The Prime Minister reminded the Marshal that upon his return he would face a grave situation with Parliament in battling for acceptance of Poland's eastern boundary. Parliament would accept the boundary were it assured that the Poles would decide their own government.

Churchill weakened his argument by repeated disavowals of personal interest. He remarked that he did not have a high opinion of the Poles: "I do not care much about Poles myself." Stalin responded as if this were a trap to get him also to undermine the groups he was trying to build up. He defended the "real" Poles. There were good men among the Poles. Some were good fighters; however, they did fight among themselves. Churchill proclaimed antipathy for this division and suggested equal opportunities for all Poles. Stalin answered that there would be equal opportunities for those Poles who were "non-Fascists or anti-Fascists." The Prime Minister, who had been categorized several years earlier by the Soviets as a Fascist, preferred instead the terminology, "democratic parties."[42]

As an anchor for his Polish policy, Stalin seized upon the American-generated Declaration on Liberated Europe. This document, which had been conceived as an extension of the Atlantic Charter and a guarantee that America's principles of morality and democracy would prevail in Eastern Europe, explicitly charged the Allies with the obligation of eradicating "fascism" in the creation of democracy. Stalin said it had "good words" in it, which proved the necessity of obliterating the last traces of "Fascism and Nazism" and thereby creating democratic order, which he said was just what Soviet troops were doing in Poland. Roosevelt related the two issues. The Polish elections must be the first example of the implementation of the Declaration on Liberated Europe; and further, Roosevelt submitted, they must be like Caesar's wife—above suspicion. Stalin relaxed momentarily, joking that she may have had that reputation, but actually she was not so lily-white. Roosevelt ignored the imputation and repeated the Polish election at least should be above reproach.*

Molotov sprang back into the argument and rejected observers as unacceptable; they would undermine the confidence of the Poles. The issue was deadlocked, and it was growing late. Roosevelt again suggested submitting the unresolved question to the foreign ministers.

Stalin did not want the debate to end without indicating that Russia could compromise. In the final moments of talks over Poland, he accepted Roosevelt's preferred name for the Lublin government, the "Provisional Government now functioning in Poland." [43]

By the end of the session the Soviets had accepted the American compromise proposal, which established the Lublin Committee as the basis for expanding the government of Poland. The British and American representatives now were asking only for the right to observe the elections in order to ensure their "democratic" character. Stalin and Molotov argued that this was superfluous and an insult to the Polish government. Churchill insisted that the position of the Red Army had created a "new situation," perhaps hoping thereby to elicit from Stalin reciprocal usage of democratic terminology, thus committing the Soviet Union to a Western-style government in Poland.

Stalin had no qualm about giving *verbal* guarantees of a "democratic" solution for Poland, but he refused to allow Western democratic methods to provide the ground rules for bringing

* For further discussion of the Declaration on Liberated Europe, see pp. 262–64.

this democracy into existence. He rejected any special agreement with the heads of state that would guarantee observation of the elections, thus preventing Anglo-American intervention in the internal affairs of Poland. He also rejected the implication that the Soviets were not acting in good faith. But to avoid a breach with the West, Stalin, in a reversal of his former position, held out to Churchill the hope that Mikolajczyk might, after all, come into the government. Molotov had hinted the same thing earlier in the day at the foreign minister's meeting.

Only two major unresolved issues concerning Poland remained: guarantees for observation of elections, and Western support for a Polish boundary on the Oder-Western-Neisse River.

BRITAIN COUNTERATTACKS

There were, however, a few surprises yet to come. That same evening, at a special meeting of the foreign ministers, Eden announced that a strong cable from the War Cabinet prevented the British from agreeing to the proposed Polish settlement unless it conformed more closely to the British proposal of the previous day. Eden submitted a drastic revision of the American formula. The foreign ministers had to discuss it as a proposed amendment to the American formula, since agreement had already been reached on that. This already weakened Eden's chances of success.

The British draft attempted to appease Russia by incorporating Churchill's statement on the new situation created by the victory of the Red Army. Yet it threatened the decisions taken at the plenary session. It asked for the creation of a *new* government (rather than the reorganization of the Lublin government) and the reinstatement of the democratic guarantees which would ensure a government "fully representative of the Polish people." Lastly, it requested that the ambassadors be responsible for observing and reporting on the fulfillment of the pledge for free and unfettered elections.[44]

Unfortunately, there is no complete record of the conversation which took place in the foreign ministers' conference concerning the British revisions. Charles Bohlen, H. Freeman Matthews, and Edward Stettinius all state only that the meeting was held, and documentary accounts include the approved text. Opinions differ as to the tenor of the meeting. Stettinius describes the argument which ensued over the text as "lengthy and grueling," but Bohlen refers to the discussion as "lengthy and amicable." [45]

What happened can best be deduced from a comparison of the original British proposal with the final text presented to the plenary session the next afternoon.* In the following examination the passages of the British draft which Molotov succeeded in changing for the final text are numbered and italicized.

A new situation has been created by the complete liberation of Poland by the Red Army. This calls for the establishment of a (1) *fully representative* (2) *provisional Polish Government* which can be more broadly based than was possible before the recent liberation of Western Poland. (3) *This Government should be based upon the Provisional Government now functioning in Poland and upon other democratic Polish leaders* from within Poland and from abroad. This new Government should be called the Polish Provisional Government of National Unity.

Mr. Molotov, Mr. Harriman and Sir A. Clark Kerr should be authorized to consult in the first instance in Moscow with members of the present Provisional Government and with other democratic leaders from within Poland and from abroad with a view to the reorganization of the present Government along the above lines. This (4) *"Provisional Government of National Unity"* would be pledged to the holding of free and unfettered elections as soon as practicable on the basis of universal suffrage and secret ballot. In these elections all (5) *democratic* parties shall have the right to take part and to put forward candidates.

When a Polish Provisional Government of National Unity has been *formed*, (6) *which the three Governments can regard as fully representative of the Polish people,* the three Governments will ac-

---

* The reader may find it helpful to turn to the final document on Poland, included among the trilateral documents in Appendix A.

cord it recognition. *The Ambassadors of the three powers in Warsaw,
following such recognition, would be charged with the responsibility
of observing and reporting to their respective Governments on the
carrying out of the pledge in regard to free and unfettered elections.*[46]

Using the American proposal (agreed to by the Soviet
Union) as a lever, Molotov succeeded in bringing the British
proposal into line with the American draft. Thus the final Polish
agreement at Yalta was not seriously altered by Eden's last-minute attempt to reverse the impending Polish solution. A closer
look at the changes Molotov effected substantiates this.

Molotov accomplished the removal of (1) "fully representative" from the text and thereby obviated any written Soviet obligation to undertake a Western democratization of Poland. Molotov was openly opposed to including democratic terminology. He
continued to demand equal consideration for Russia: Poland
should receive the same treatment as France. "Representative
government" required too much explanation, Molotov charged,
citing de Gaulle as a case in point. Was de Gaulle's government
a representative one? he asked rhetorically.

Molotov's rewording read (2) "Polish Provisional Government" instead of "Provisional Polish Government." The former
had been agreed upon at one point in the Conference and was
also the same name as the existing Lublin government.

Molotov refused to create a *new* government and returned to
the Allies' earlier acceptance of (3) *reorganizing* the existing
Lublin government. The final draft read: "The Provisional Government which is now functioning in Poland should therefore be
reorganized on a broader democratic basis with the inclusion of
democratic leaders from Poland itself and from Poles abroad." [47]

Molotov had the word "Polish" inserted in the phrase (4)
"Provisional Government," as in (2).

(5)   The Soviet Foreign Minister (fortified by the Declaration on Liberated Europe which explicitly stated the need to destroy Nazism) inserted "anti-Nazi" *in addition to* Eden's "democratic parties." Molotov compromised in selecting this word
rather than his preferred term "anti-Fascist," which was more
objectionable to the West and had been personally offensive to

Churchill. Molotov thereby gained acquiescence to another principle which made a distinction among peoples and which gave the Soviet Union authority to discriminate among parties and interfere in Poland's internal affairs. The final text therefore read, "In these elections all democratic and anti-Nazi parties shall have the right to take part and to put forward candidates."

Agreement could not be reached by the foreign ministers on (6) "recognition" of what their Governments might "regard as fully representative," but on the following day there was agreement on this alternate wording:

> . . . [When a Polish Provisional Government of National Unity has been] properly formed in conformity with the above, the Government of the U.S.S.R., which now maintains diplomatic relations with the present Provisional Government of Poland, and the Government of the U.S.A. will establish diplomatic relations with the new Polish Provisional Government of National Unity, and will exchange Ambassadors by whose reports the respective Governments will be kept informed about the situation in Poland.[48]

The main argument among the foreign ministers was over the creation of a "new" government as opposed to expansion of the Lublin government. Molotov used the American formula as an operating principle, and reminded his colleagues of the "new situation" which the document had to reflect. Thereby he won reacceptance of the wording which stated there would be a reorganization of the Lublin government. Great Britain fought; Eden argued that there must be a new government to which recognition could be transferred. Stettinius agreed. But in the deadlock, the foreign ministers reverted to the language of the former American proposal which reorganized the Lublin government. This temporarily set aside the question of whether this compromise, i.e. an expanded government, was or was not a new government. Falling back on the fact that they had already agreed, the foreign ministers avoided divergent interpretations.

The wording of the final draft stated that the Lublin government would be reorganized. The British and American delegations preferred to interpret this to mean that a new government would emerge from the reorganization. The Soviets looked at it differently. For them, the statement meant what it said. The next day Molotov tried to get the West to admit that the Polish government was already in existence. He wanted to add: "The Governments of the United States of America and Great Britain will establish diplomatic relations with the Polish Government as has been done by the Soviet Union." Stettinius and Eden refused.

There had been no agreement on Anglo-American principles. Each side was aware that a different interpretation prevailed. Molotov had even pointed out that the document upon which they had agreed reflected this difference and suggested that the matter be discussed. Apparently, however, the question was not taken up again.

Observation of elections by the ambassadors of the Great Powers was not settled at this meeting. The British and American delegations continued to seek assurances of a free election, and Eden and Stettinius appealed to Molotov to consider the wishes of the British and the American Poles. Molotov insisted that even the methods of election could be decided upon only by the Poles. The unarticulated message was that the Soviet delegation granted no guarantee and had little use for another pro-Western government in Poland. Stettinius wanted a written guarantee that the Poles had the right to decide their own election. Molotov would not even hear of that.[49] Finally, frustrated by Molotov's rebuffs, the American delegation gave in. It changed its position the next day and offered to withdraw the statement in the American proposal that the ambassadors ought to observe the elections. The American delegation was willing to accept a guarantee that *in effect* the ambassadors would observe and report on elections. Eden took strong exception to the American concession. The British outburst provoked Stettinius to say that he really preferred to retain the original formula but wanted to hasten agreement. In effect, the United States, for the second time, supported the solution offered by the Soviet Union. The United States was willing to drop a written commitment if she could have a vague oral promise.

In the morning Britain made one last move to gain a guarantee. Churchill and Eden met with Stalin and Molotov shortly before the plenary session on February 10. Churchill impressed upon Stalin the fact that he had to give Parliament a guarantee that the elections in Poland would be fair. At present, Churchill insisted that he was unable to keep watch over events in Poland. Stalin pointed out that if Churchill recognized the Polish government, there should be no problem, for then the ambassadors would be free to observe and report. Churchill inquired about the inhibitions on freedom of movement for his staff, and Stalin promised that, as far as the Red Army was concerned, there would be no interference in observing. He would give instructions. Then he added: "But you will have to make your own arrangements with the Polish Government." [50]

Both Churchill and Stalin were late for the plenary session as a result of this last-minute talk. Churchill approached Roosevelt before the meeting began and said, "I believe that I have succeeded in retrieving the situation." [51] In his memoirs, he commented, "This was the best I could get." [52] As a result, the final agreement mentioned observation by ambassadors. This was actually a gain for the Soviets, because, incorporating Stalin's position, it postulated that there must be recognition of the Polish government first, after which there could be an exchange of ambassadors and then observation and reporting.

Again agreement was superficial. Soviet intentions differed entirely from those of the West and from those of the British in particular. There could be little doubt about that.

At the plenary session on February 10, Eden presented to the Big Three the final version of the agreement on Poland. It bore the evidence of a complex series of meetings and discussions. It was the American proposal (which paralleled the original Soviet proposal), amended by Molotov, redrafted by the British, and then further amended by Molotov. It also showed the revisions of two foreign ministers' meetings, and of Churchill's private talk with Stalin.

Roosevelt gave his approval. Churchill, however, pressed for the inclusion of a resolution of the last remaining question—the frontiers. All were in agreement on Poland's eastern frontier, but on the western frontier there was concurrence on compensation for Poland only up to the Oder River, not to the Neisse which the Soviets supported. Churchill stood firm on his inability to go any further on this question by explaining that he had received a cable from the War Cabinet saying they were against a settlement if the boundary were extended to the Neisse.

At this point Roosevelt, who had opposed territorial settlements until the peace conference, turned the tables on Stalin and argued that this question should be discussed first with the Poles. Ironically, both Stalin and Churchill pressed for immediate settlement of the issue. Roosevelt, however, did not want frontiers mentioned; he claimed that question had to be put before the United States Senate—which was true, as the U.S. Constitution requires it. But whether Roosevelt was actually concerned with his constitutional authority, or simply wanted to delay, is unknown. Stalin undoubtedly assumed the latter.

Ignoring the President, Churchill insisted that the three were close to agreement on a boundary formula. They had already agreed to the principle of compensation for Poland in the west. Molotov supported an immediate solution: it would quiet the Poles by clarifying their territorial status. He proposed that the foreign ministers should draft a statement and include it as the final sentence of the Polish statement.[53]

Roosevelt threw his support to Churchill after he received a note from Harry Hopkins. Hopkins said Churchill was in difficulty because of a "bad" telegram from the War Cabinet, which considered that he had conceded too much on the Polish issue. When Churchill persisted in trying to clarify the frontier, Roosevelt went along and insisted that Churchill himself be authorized to draw up the draft statement on the Polish borders.[54]

In the course of this session and during its adjournments, the final paragraph on Polish frontiers was drafted. Eden presented it at the very end of the meeting. Roosevelt remained wary of any commitment by the United States to frontiers before a peace treaty. Therefore, he asked that the statement read "Heads of Three Governments" (instead of "the Three Governments") "feel" (instead of "recognize") that there should be consideration of the Curzon Line and compensation in the west for Poland.

Molotov also had an amendment to recommend. He wanted to include "with the return to Poland of her ancient frontiers in

East Prussia and on the Oder." [55] Having agreed to Russia's historical right to the territories lost in the Russo-Japanese war in the Far Eastern Agreement, Roosevelt asked how long ago these lands had been Polish. Molotov replied: "Very long ago." Roosevelt, turning to Churchill, quipped: "Perhaps you would want us back?" Churchill answered that America might be as indigestible for Britain as the Germans for Poland. Stalin, not to be outdone, remarked that there was no problem there because the ocean separated the two of them.[56]

Stalin pressed on for the Oder–Western-Neisse boundary he had promised the Lublin government. Churchill refused to discuss the question. He claimed that, like the President, he could not commit his government. Stalin withdrew his proposal, and the British draft was included in the protocol and communiqué of the conference.

Stalin and Molotov had pushed the frontier issue up to the very end, but they had failed to get Western backing for the frontier they had already recognized. The statement adopted by the conference read:

> The three Heads of Government consider that the Eastern frontier of Poland should follow the Curzon Line with digressions from it in some regions of five to eight kilometers in favor of Poland. It is recognized that Poland must receive substantial accessions of territory in the North and West. They feel that the opinion of the new Polish Provisional Government of National Unity should be sought in due course on the extent of these accessions and that the final delimitation of the Western frontier of Poland should thereafter await the Peace Conference.[57]

This statement, although not entirely satisfactory to the Soviet Union, was more acceptable than no agreement; it represented, at last, a definite written commitment to the Curzon Line as part of the eastern boundary of Russia, for which the Soviets had constantly sought confirmation since the German attack in 1941.

The Polish problem appeared solved by February 11, 1945. But the solution did not wear well with time. At the beginning of the Conference, Churchill had needled Molotov, saying that the Lublin Poles were not much, but were "the best you could get." By the end of the Conference, Churchill admitted to Roosevelt that the election provision for Poland was "the best *I* could get," and that actually the remark could extend to his own attitude toward the whole Polish agreement. The agreement at Yalta was basically a Soviet-American proposal. Even so, after Yalta, the President of the United States, using interpretations that were buried by the time of the final agreement, decided that the Yalta decision was not the best *he* could get. There have been many maneuvers over and attempts to undo this Yalta decision ever since.

CHAPTER 6

THE UNITED NATIONS

The American delegation at Yalta considered the United Nations to be the crucial issue of the Conference. They felt that the maintenance of peace after the war depended upon acceptance of the American proposals for a world organization, proposals which balanced the security requirements of the Great Powers against the rights of small nations. In particular, the American delegation claimed that its plan for the United Nations adhered rigorously to three principles: equality of all nations in discussion; preservation of Great Power unity; self-determination for liberated nations and colonies. However, only the Americans detected a contradiction between the first principle and the second, or, perhaps, considered it important—if the Great Powers unduly dominated the executive section of the United Nations, the smaller powers might feel offended and deprived. Hence the American voting formula was devised, giving the small nations a voice in the Security Council without interfering with the Great Power veto.

In theory, the American proposals on the Security Council, membership, and trusteeships represented compromises between Allied principles and the exigencies of world politics. Actually, several of these proposals were stratagems which assured Western control over the world organization. These had been slipped in under the guise of appeasing world opinion or of guaranteeing the rights of small nations. For example, the principle of self-determination for liberated colonies, to be implemented through the Trusteeship Council, was one such disguise, and a thin one at that, for American anti-colonialism. From the American perspective, European colonial domination was bad: it would be uprooted and replaced with conditions opening the door to American economic domination—which was, of course, entirely different. According to the British Colonial Secretary, John Foster Dulles told the British Colonial Office in 1942 that "We [the British] should realize that deeply embedded in the mind of most Americans was a fundamental distrust of what they [the Americans] called 'British Imperialism.' . . . The only way in which we could remove this deep-seated prejudice would be to invite the co-operation of the United States in the development of our Colonies after the war." [1]

Similarly, the principle of equality among nations concealed the practice of the stacked deck. Every nation that had contributed to the Allied war effort, including the six Latin American "Associated Nations," should be represented in the General Assembly. Just coincidentally, this assured the West a decisive majority in the General Assembly as originally constituted. Or again, the major partners in the anti-Axis coalition, including France and China, should be given permanent seats on the Security Council. Quite incidentally, this gave Britain and the United States one puppet vote each in the Council; it also left the Soviet Union isolated and outnumbered four to one. Since the terms of the American voting formula were incomprehensible to everyone except the State Department by the time of the Yalta Conference, the Soviets feared that under this formula the Security Council might be able to vote sanctions or action against the Soviet Union. Big Three unanimity was a stated principle; it was not a fact.

The Soviet Union was quite cognizant of the reality underlying the American proposals, and acted accordingly. The Russians countered Western attempts to pack the General Assembly by demanding Assembly membership for all sixteen Soviet Republics. Still, at Dumbarton Oaks it had been decided that the Assembly would not possess any significant powers, and Stalin, always emphasizing the practical, was willing to drop his demand if by doing so he could gain something concrete, such as agreement on Poland. The admission of a few Republics to the General Assembly would be useful for prestige and for domestic reasons; beyond that, the General Assembly was hardly critical to the decision-making process. Stalin saw no reason to press his original demands.

But the possible ramifications of the American voting formula was entirely another question. Since the Security Council was so heavily weighted in favor of the West, Stalin considered an absolute veto essential to the protection of Soviet interests. Not until he was entirely convinced that the American formula permitted each Great Power to veto possible proposals contrary to its own interest did he cease his opposition. If the Soviet Union were protected, the right of discussion in the Security Council, like the composition of the General Assembly, did not matter to Stalin.

The British were as concerned as the Russians about the gap between American principles and practices. Churchill feared, with reason, that the United States wanted to dismantle the British Empire. He was particularly worried about American attempts to "internationalize" British possessions which had fallen to the Japanese, such as Hong Kong. Indeed, during Eden's visit to Washington in March 1943, Roosevelt urged the British to "give up Hong Kong as a gesture of good will." Eden replied that he had not heard the President suggest any reciprocal gestures by the United States.[2] Roosevelt continued to propound his idea up to and throughout the Yalta Conference, suggesting in addition various schemes to deprive France of Indochina and to promote the independence of India.[3] The British reacted with a fierce defense of their Empire. Churchill became frantic at the mere mention of trusteeships. He fought vigorously to exclude the Empire from the scope of the American trusteeship concept. He succeeded; the sanctity of the Empire was preserved for a few more years.

THE AMERICAN VOTING FORMULA

At Yalta, on February 6, Roosevelt initiated discussion of the Security Council voting formula. Using carrot-and-stick diplomacy, he issued a sharp warning—if the American voting formula were not accepted, the Allies might find themselves without American help in keeping the German peace. Stettinius then formally presented a detailed report on the Articles which the United States proposed to include in the United Nations Charter. These Articles explained the means by which the Security Council would arrive at decisions and act upon them. At the beginning of the session, the American delegation circulated a memorandum which, for the first time, put into writing America's listing of what constituted a substantive decision and the specifying of those which required the unanimous consent of the permanent members (or, in other words, which could be vetoed). The delegations had this memorandum before them as Stettinius read the American proposal.* He referred briefly to a "minor clarification" of Chapter VIII, Section C, of the United Nations Charter, the very section over which Great Britain and the Soviet Union had professed confusion.

The sudden appearance of a "minor clarification" made Stalin wonder whether the Americans were maneuvering for last-minute changes. Accordingly, he inquired whether this "clarification" embodied any changes. Stettinius and the interpreters began trying to explain that the changes were of a minor nature. Stalin and Molotov evidenced unfamiliarity with the subject, venting suspicions that this was an American technique "to slip something over them," as Stettinius later phrased it. From the ensuing confusion, the American delegation rapidly concluded that only Andrei Gromyko, Soviet Ambassador to the United States, was familiar with the American proposal and understood the intent of the change.[4]

Gromyko helped mollify Stalin's and Molotov's initial hostility by explaining that there was no real basic alteration; only four words—"under the second sentence"—had been added to Paragraph I, Chapter VIII, Section C. After the atmosphere calmed, Stettinius then continued with his analysis of the voting formula, emphasizing the responsibility and desirability for states besides the Great Powers to set forth their views in the Security Council without any limitation. To Stalin, this portended doubts about Allied unity, granting disproportionate power to small states dependent on the West. Stettinius and the Americans

* For Stettinius' report, see Appendix B.

countered that a guarantee to minor states was an important consideration—without it the United Nations Organization might prove impossible. Stettinius described this proposal as a fair compromise between two conflicting responsibilities: on the one hand, the maintenance of universal peace through Great Power unanimity; and on the other, fair treatment for all members of the organization, a matter which "for the people of the United States was of exceptional importance." He concluded by outlining the questions which would require the affirmative votes of seven members, and agreement among the permanent members, in order to pass.

Stalin and Molotov were unprepared at that time to take a position on the American voting formula. However, they *were* certain that it would work against the Soviet Union, and they were quite suspicious of it at first. They stated that the Soviet Union considered the voting method vital and therefore wanted to study the proposal before continuing discussion, perhaps on the following day.

To the surprise of the Soviet delegation, Churchill backed the President's proposal wholeheartedly and encouraged Stalin to do likewise. Anticipating Stalin's objections, which were similar to Britain's pre-conference reservations, Churchill stressed that the American proposal preserved the special position of the three Great Powers; in the case of Britain, it guaranteed protection of the interests of the British Commonwealth. Stalin might surmise, Churchill hinted, that if British interests were protected, Soviet interests would similarly be secure.

Churchill next argued that the three Great Powers had to forgo their exclusive role in part or else be vulnerable to charges of attempting to rule the world by not extending to the small states the right of free expression. Stalin inferred that Churchill was singling out the Soviet Union as the prime suspect, since Roosevelt proposed and Churchill endorsed a formula which would prove that the Great Powers did not desire to "rule the world." By a process of elimination, this left only the Soviet Union. Stalin listened closely as Churchill used the British Empire, specifically Hong Kong, to prove his argument about the limited and benign function of discussion in the United Nations.

If China aspired to recover Hong Kong from Britain, she was free to express this opinion before the Assembly. In this instance, as an interested party, the British could not take part in the Security Council voting.

Stalin interrupted Churchill to substitute the more critical case of Egypt, and her claim to the Suez Canal, for Hong Kong. He asked the Prime Minister whether Egypt would be a member of the Assembly. Churchill answered affirmatively, and Stalin insisted that Churchill use Egypt in his argument.

Churchill persisted in discussing Hong Kong. Whatever China said, if Great Britain considered the question an infringement of her sovereignty, Britain could veto any action. He next took up Egypt, claiming not to fear the votes of any smaller powers under this voting formula. Finally, Churchill mentioned that Argentina might have possible claims against the United States and that the United States was equally protected and could veto any action under the Monroe Doctrine.

His penchant for idealism coming to the fore, Roosevelt diverted the discussion from national interest to higher moral issues. It was an Allied responsibility to protect the smaller nations. The Big Three had promised as much in the Teheran Declaration when they accepted responsibility for a peace acceptable to the "peoples of the world." Churchill returned to his point: it was undesirable to create the impression that the Big Three sought to dominate the world and to prevent the other countries from expressing their opinion.[5]

Stalin was ready to reply. First, he admitted that the proposals had to be studied thoroughly by the Soviet government and that they could not understand everything simply by hearing it. Stalin requested a copy of Stettinius's document and tried to analyze what he thought it meant. It appeared to Stalin that the right of various countries simply to voice an opinion could not be so important on the basis of Churchill's own argument. "That right is not worth much." Besides, it was a false issue: no one, including Stalin, challenged this right to an *opinion*. The heart of the problem lay in making viable decisions. Alluding to Churchill's attempt to reconcile democracy and privilege, Stalin expressed doubt that either China or Egypt would be content with merely voicing an opinion. They would demand an effective part in the decision-making.

Stalin exposed Churchill's implication that the Soviet Union was seeking world domination by not agreeing on the spur of the moment to the American voting formula as Britain had done.* The Marshal rhetorically challenged Churchill to name the power that was trying to dominate the world. The United States? Stalin said he could not conceive of that. The President made an eloquent gesture, disavowing such an intention. Stalin continued, Britain? No, he answered. Churchill followed Roosevelt's example with a gesture. This left only the Soviet Union. So Russia was striving for world domination, he asked? The Soviet Conference minutes indicate that by this time general laughter prevailed. Stalin played further: maybe China was a possibility. He concluded that it was pointless to talk of such an ambition when his friend Churchill could not name a single power with this goal.[6]

Churchill denied Stalin's perception. He assured the Marshal that he entertained no such notion. The point was to take preventive measures in order that other nations would not think so. Stalin ironically reminded Churchill that "the others" would certainly not find the United States and Great Britain guilty of an intention to dominate the world, since they had adopted the proposed voting procedure for the United Nations Charter. By process of elimination, this left only the third, unnamed power as a suspect. Stalin sarcastically let Churchill off the hook. When he too had studied the proposal, he said, perhaps he would see the point more clearly, since Churchill was persuading him the point was something other than it seemed.

Churchill was quite right, Stalin conceded. There did exist a problem, but it was more serious than the right of nations to express opinions or than an accusation of world domination. The real responsibility was to preserve peace after this war, which only Allied unity through the maintenance of a permanent united front could do. Stalin said this was the real purpose of the

* The Soviet Conference minutes record the interchanges at great length, and the Soviet delegation obviously felt the impact of this charge keenly. See *Soviet Crimean Documents*, No. 6, p. 105.

Conference and its deliberations. He sensed that these decisions must account for future developments and said that the real challenge (since the present leaders could rely upon one another) was to guard against disunity when they were gone and another generation replaced them.

Following this key statement of principle, Stalin apologized for his unfamiliarity with the Dumbarton Oaks proposals. He stressed that this did not reflect a lack of interest; it was because he had other commitments. The questions of the United Nations Charter were highly important, he said, because their resolution would ensure a minimal difference in opinion among the three, and this was of primary concern for the Soviet Union.

After this preliminary endorsement of the President's scheme for postwar co-operation, Stalin grew magnanimous regarding America's vested interest in Asia. He suggested that China be added to the powers accorded a special position. Vigilant lest America gain disproportionate representation, Churchill quickly amended Stalin's idea to include France.[7]

Was it correct, Stalin went on, that, according to the present proposal, there were two categories of disputes that the Security Council would handle—those requiring settlement by coercion and those demanding peaceful solutions? Receiving an affirmative reply, he asked whether it was also correct that, when sanctions were being considered by the Council, all permanent members could vote, even if a member were a party to a dispute; while, if a peaceful settlement (which did not involve force) were being considered, the party to the dispute, even if a permanent member of the Council, must refrain from voting? Again he received an affirmative answer.

Stalin was gaining confidence in his interpretation. Before setting forth his argument, he solemnly reminded the Allies that if the Soviet Union appeared to place too much emphasis on voting in the Security Council, it was "because the Soviet Union was, most of all, interested in the decisions to be adopted by the Security Council." Stalin reminded the West that "after all, the decisions would be adopted by a vote. Discussions could go on for a hundred years without deciding anything. But, it was the decisions that mattered."[8]

Stalin tested the voting formula with Churchill's own examples. It was possible that China (which Stalin had just recommended for membership on the Security Council) might demand Hong Kong, and Egypt ask for the return of the Suez Canal. These countries would not be alone in their voting. They would have friends, and the voting would reflect this fact. Stalin was greatly surprised when Churchill assured him that Britain could still veto any action against her and that the authority of the United Nations Organization could not be used against any one of the three Great Powers.

Stalin asked in disbelief whether this could in fact be the case. Eden emphasized that all the member nations could argue but could not take a decision. Still doubtful, Stalin asked a second time if this were actually the case. Both Churchill and Roosevelt hastened to assure him that this interpretation was correct. Stettinius added that even economic sanctions could not be applied without unanimity of the permanent members.

With Stalin confused by this unexpected guarantee, Molotov stepped in. He tried to ascertain in what way the Big Three were vulnerable under this formula, and inquired whether this unanimity was obligatory even for recommendations in peaceful settlement of disputes. Maisky phrased the question more specifically —were the five points which Stettinius listed as types of decisions requiring peaceful settlement subjects on which decision could be taken, or were they only items for discussion? Stettinius indicated that they were items for discussion.

Stalin did not believe it. He voiced his fear that any authority not exclusively reserved for the Big Three would serve to destroy their unity. Further, if this unity ceased to exist, world opinion might be mobilized against certain Powers in an effort to ostracize them from the world community. Judiciously sticking to examples affecting Britain, Stalin revived Hong Kong and asserted that discussion of such an issue might dissipate Allied unity. Stalin's implication that the United States or the Soviet Union could oppose British imperialism was not lost on Churchill. The latter retorted that the regular avenues of diplomacy would function, and would be the special responsibility of the Big Three to try to settle their mutual problems without raising issues which would divide them.

Stalin stopped using theoretical examples and came to the point. He reminded his colleagues that in the Russo-Finnish War, the British and French had succeeded in mobilizing the League of Nations against Soviet Russia, and the League had then isolated and expelled her. Churchill replied that England had an entirely different attitude then and had been "very angry" with the Russians. Stalin could not rely on a change of attitude—what could be done to prevent a similar recurrence? Eden and Churchill answered that under the American formula isolation of the Soviet Union was impossible. Molotov said this was "the first time the Soviet side heard of that." Not wanting to be dependent on the absence of British "anger," Stalin asked if the Conference could not put more obstacles in the way of a similar attempt.

Churchill explained that the Soviet Union could not be expelled from the United Nations as she had been from the League, since expulsion required unanimous action and any one of the great Powers could veto it. Stalin was genuinely surprised. Roosevelt confirmed that this was what the veto meant. Stalin dwelt on possible pressure to mobilize anti-Soviet opinion and worried that the Soviet Union would be the target of Western hostility in the future as she had been in the past. Churchill assured him that diplomacy would attempt to solve problems; for instance, Roosevelt would not resort to a public attack on Britain—and neither would Stalin—without attempting first to resolve the conflict through diplomacy. The Prime Minister confidently announced that there was always a way to settle disputes through diplomacy. Churchill vouched for himself in this.

Stalin quickly added himself to Churchill's list of those who could vouch for their effort to promote unity. But the club of the good-intentioned was limited, he pointed out: who would vouch for Maisky? Roosevelt was uncomfortable with the personal nature of the dialogue. He observed that disunity could not be obviated by any voting formula. In contrast, freedom of discussion in the Security Council, guaranteed by the United States proposal, would demonstrate before the world the faith the Big Three had in one another. Stalin supported Roosevelt's analysis but recommended continuing the discussion the next day.[9]

When the next plenary session convened, on February 7, the Soviet delegation had prepared to accept the American voting formula and to concentrate its effort on gaining a place in the United Nations General Assembly for a reduced number of Soviet Republics. The Americans were very surprised at the Soviet move, the British less so. Churchill had learned of the change in Soviet policy before the session opened and had confidently told the President, "Uncle Joe will take Dumbarton Oaks."

In the middle of the crisis over Poland, Molotov announced the Soviets' acceptance of the voting formula. He explained: "We paid much attention to what Churchill told us." Churchill, in his memoirs, suggested that both the Soviet reversal on the voting formula and a consequent willingness to reduce the number of Republics in the United Nations were due to Britain's influence, although he did not specify precisely the role His Majesty's Government played.[10]

THE BATTLE FOR TWO REPUBLICS

With agreement to the American voting formula, inclusion of some Soviet Republics as original members of the United Nations Organization became the important issue. One motivation was undoubtedly domestic: a concession by the Soviet government to the Republics for their patriotic response to the war was important. This was the case especially in Belorussia, the Ukraine, and Lithuania, where strong resistance to centrism had often combined with separatist tendencies, resulting in revolts and, at times, even in independent status. Pressure for domestic concessions had already found expression in the constitutional changes of 1944, in which the central government extended to the Republics the power to conduct foreign relations. Admittance to the United Nations would have been another instance of repaying these Republics. The Soviet delegation anticipated the granting of their request: first, because the support of Great Britain seemed forthcoming; and, second, because the Soviets had modified their position to request membership for only two or three Republics rather than all sixteen.

Molotov began by arguing that the Soviet Republics should be included on the basis of their own merits. He stressed that a legal claim to separate representation logically followed from the constitutional reforms of the year before. Molotov said the Soviets were not raising the question of admittance in the same form as they had at Dumbarton Oaks; rather they would now accept admission for three or at least two of the Republics—particularly White Russia, the Ukraine, and Lithuania. Mentioning their importance in size, population, and role in foreign affairs, he primarily applied the principle the Soviets had used as a yardstick for other issues: the role of these Republics, or any nation, in winning in war. He argued that "these three Republics had borne the greatest sacrifices in the war and were the first to be invaded by the enemy," and asked accordingly for favorable consideration of this proposal.

Roosevelt's response was disappointing. The President wanted to bypass the Soviet request in order to move directly into the issue of second greatest importance to the American delegation: selecting the nations to attend the United Nations Conference. This Conference ought to take place in a month if possible, Roosevelt said, and any decision on the Soviet request for seating two or three Republics should be postponed until they met. Pressuring for an early Conference, the President added that the sooner the Conference met, the sooner this question could be examined.

Roosevelt criticized the Soviet request in a vague, negative way. He articulated problems he suddenly foresaw: nations were of different sizes and structures; should each nation have one vote, or should the Great Powers have more than one vote? If they should have more than one, that would violate the rule they had just agreed upon. The President concluded that the foreign ministers should study this issue and also decide when and where the United Nations Conference should meet and what nations should be invited.

Churchill did not permit Roosevelt to sidestep the question so easily. He lined up forcefully and squarely behind Molotov's request that the United Nations accept two or three Republics as initial members. Appealing to Roosevelt, the Prime Minister made an eloquent gesture of appreciation for the Soviet concession on the American voting formula and then suggested Britain's experience helped bridge the difficulties Roosevelt mentioned. The United States and Great Britain already had different national structures, for Britain, unlike the United States, was an Empire or Commonwealth in which "self-governing dominions had, for a quarter of a century, played a notable part in the international security organisation" of the League of Nations. Since Great Britain could never allow the existence of an international organization which did not accept the Empire's Dominions, Churchill said he had "great sympathy for the Soviet request."

Churchill launched upon a peculiar argument—a nation like Russia, which was larger than the Commonwealth and "was bleeding but smiting the tyrant on her path," must certainly "look askance" at Great Britain which had secured votes for her Dominions. Pushing Roosevelt gently, he thanked the President for not giving a negative answer to the Soviet request. Churchill then announced he had gone as far as his authority permitted; he would have to consult the War Cabinet in London. He asked, therefore, to be excused from giving an immediate answer to the Soviets.[11]

Ignoring Churchill's unexpected pronouncement, Roosevelt again attempted to refer the issues to the foreign ministers. But Churchill would not stop. And, again unexpectedly, he opposed the calling of the United Nations Conference in March, as Roosevelt wanted. This would be the height of the war on the one hand, and domestic problems would require the presence of the Foreign Secretary in Parliament, on the other; therefore, an immediate resolution of the question of admitting the Republics was necessary. Anthony Eden was taken aback by this emphasis on domestic politics and recorded in his diary: "Mr. Churchill unexpectedly spoke up against such a meeting in wartime. This was another example of the Prime Minister's reluctance to see any energies diverted to peacetime tasks. . . ."[12]

Churchill defended the Soviet case. Roosevelt insisted that

the proposed United Nations Conference was not too momentous a step to take immediately, since it would not be a convocation of the Assembly, but a meeting to organize the security organization, in fulfillment of the Dumbarton Oaks pledge. Churchill answered that he did not understand how they could "undertake the immense task" at a time when attending nations would be in dissimiliar positions—some would be under German occupation, some would have participated in the war, some would not have fought at all. It was by no means clear that the participating delegations would be representative of their constituent populations. Great Britain's election would put England in a difficult position. France "would be there with a loud voice." Churchill went back to the point: "I should be very disappointed if the settlement of the membership of the Assembly was postponed until a new meeting of the United Nations can be held."

While Churchill was speaking, Roosevelt was receiving different messages from his own advisers. Harry Hopkins, special assistant to the President and active in United Nations planning, scribbled a note that "There is something behind this talk that we do not know of its basis," and that they should find out that evening "what is on his mind." Stettinius wrote Roosevelt that Secretary of War Stimson "takes this same view" as Churchill.

Hopkins advised the President "to try to get this referred to the foreign ministers before there is trouble." Roosevelt, for the third time during the discussion on the United Nations, begged the question and demanded that the foreign ministers should handle these issues. This time Stalin agreed, and Churchill consequently acquiesced, but not without one last sally: this, he concluded, was "no technical question but one of great decision."

After an intermission to calm the atmosphere, Roosevelt introduced a diversion. In an appeal to the Soviet Union, the President tried to explain that Russia and America had a common economic interest in bringing small nations into the United Nations. He remarked that the early establishment of the United Nations would give countries like Iran a way of gaining purchasing power so there could be an expansion of world trade with greater exchange in volume of goods. His magnanimity flowing over to other states, the President expressed hope that these countries would be helped by the new organization. Roosevelt tried to reconcile socialist and capitalist economic goals by announcing a similarity between Soviet and American approaches to economic planning. The Soviets considered the problem of economy as a whole, he observed, and that was just what the American Tennessee Valley Authority did. By this time, Molotov had in hand the English translation of the Soviet proposal on Poland, and the conference set aside the discussion of the United Nations until the following day.[13]

At the foreign ministers' session on February 8, the dominant issue was the admission of two or three Soviet Republics to the General Assembly. Foreign Secretary Anthony Eden, in his capacity as chairman for the day's session, kept the issue fairly well focused. Stettinius tried to alter the agenda to coincide with Roosevelt's priorities and asked what nations should be invited to the initial United Nations Conference. He invited the Allies to a Conference in the United States, which would be held perhaps in March as Roosevelt had said, but no later than April, if other considerations warranted a delay. Stettinius stated that only the nations which had signed the United Nations Declaration should be officially invited to the Conference. Yet prior to Yalta, the United States had told the Soviet Union that it had no fixed concept of which nations should be invited to the United Nations Conference. The Soviet Union assumed, apparently, that whatever Republics—either all sixteen or the reduced number—would become initial members and would also be invited.

Echoing the President, Stettinius said Molotov's request for multiple membership of Soviet Republics could be sympathetically considered when the Conference met. Yet simultaneously Stettinius foresaw a difficulty in accommodating additional votes for the Soviet Union; the "one state–one vote" formula would have to be changed. Stettinius offered to refer the question back to the President. (Molotov did not remind him that the President had just referred it to the foreign ministers.) The Secretary of State said that he expected it would receive favorable action, because the President "had said that the subject was most interesting and deserved sympathetic consideration."

Molotov asked Britain to state her views on the Republics, reminding Stettinius that the Soviet Union's position was already clear. Eden first satisfied Stettinius's request to complete arrangements for the United Nations Conference and agreed to a Conference in the United States, with a strong preference for the latter part of April. Stettinius moved on to set possible dates; Eden asked for a postponement each time; Molotov said each time that he was in agreement with whatever date was set. The date finally agreed upon was April 25, whereupon Molotov pointedly made a friendly and unconditional promise to attend the Conference on that date.[14]

With Stettinius satisfied, Eden again took up the Soviet Republics. He was sympathetic to the Soviet proposal, he said, and he was ready to say so at the appropriate moment. Molotov approved wholeheartedly: "The sooner the better."

Eden's statement failed to elicit stronger support from Stettinius, and Molotov took over. He disagreed with the American assertion that the question involved giving more than a single vote to each country. He advanced Churchill's analogy of the previous day: just as the component members of the British Empire—Canada and Australia, for instance—would have separate status in the Assembly, so the constitutionally separate members of the Soviet Union could. The Soviet government had accorded more individual rights to each of the Republics. They were beginning to develop their own foreign relations, which made the similarity with Britain's Dominions more striking. Further, the size and importance of the three Republics warranted such a position both economically and militarily.

Molotov concluded that immediate agreement on this question was important, and a postponed settlement highly undesirable. Otherwise, there might be "difficulties" in determining which nations should attend the conference. For example, which Polish government would attend? The Soviets might also object to inviting those countries which had no diplomatic relations with the Soviet Union. Thereupon, Molotov demanded to see the list of countries to be invited. Stettinius promptly presented it both orally and in written form. With no actual rejection of the American list, Molotov warned that if agreement was not reached on the list, the foreign ministers must take note of that difference.

Eden quickly stated that everything had been agreed except the question of the Soviet Republics. Stettinius hastened to assure Molotov that he was seeking a way to "arrange for consideration of the Soviet request before the first meeting of the Assembly." He defined the problem only as a procedural one. When the United Nations met to adopt the Charter, it would at that time elect its members.

Eden had a more acceptable proposal: namely, that the United Nations include membership for the Soviet Republics as a formal item on the Conference agenda. Molotov readily accepted this proposal, with an amendment that the foreign secretaries go on record as favoring the admission of the two or three Republics to the Assembly.

Stettinius considered this argument impressive, but he said that, since he had not discussed it with the President, he could make no commitment. He promised to take up the issue with Roosevelt and anticipated a favorable reply before the end of the day.[15] The combination of Soviet and British pressure had finally maneuvered the reluctant American leadership into immediate consideration of the Soviet request.

The foreign ministers' report from the noon meeting was rewritten by a special subcommittee which met after that meeting but before the plenary session.* At the subcommittee meeting the Soviet Union agreed to reduce its request for three Republics in the Assembly to two. The United States delegation still did not endorse the Soviet proposal, but, as the foreign ministers' report indicated, by the time the plenary session convened at 4:00 p.m., American backing had been given. In the interim, Roosevelt, who was about to meet privately with Stalin, had been informed of the British-Soviet concurrence. The President told Stettinius that because of strong British backing for the Soviet proposal, the Americans would have to go along. The President

---

* A subcommittee had been created that afternoon at the foreign ministers' meeting to deal with a number of these details. The subcommittee consisted of Alger Hiss, Andrei Gromyko, and Gladwyn Jebb.

communicated this to Stalin directly. In addition, Roosevelt had a private talk with the British in which he indicated support for the Anglo-Soviet proposal.

The rest of the American delegation was shocked to see this report placed before the plenary session, and they blamed the British delegation for overextending its authority and committing the United States. Anthony Eden had to tell them, "You don't know what has taken place." [16]

ORIGINS OF A MISUNDERSTANDING: "ORIGINAL MEMBERS"

An important problem which would plague inter-Allied relations from the Yalta Conference up to the United Nations Conference had its origins in this plenary session. The point at issue was whether or not the White Russian and Ukrainian delegations would be represented at the San Francisco Conference. After the Yalta Conference, the United States took the position that it had been clearly understood there that these two Soviet Republics would *not* be separately represented, and that the Soviet Union, by bringing extra delegations to San Francisco, had broken the agreement reached at Yalta. In his memoirs, Secretary of State Stettinius professed shock when Gromyko spoke of attendance by *two* Soviet delegations besides the main one. The Secretary recorded that the British and American positions, in contrast, remained "as agreed at Yalta." [17]

Actually, the problem was that Roosevelt had in mind his own particular concept of which nations should attend the San Francisco Conference—mainly those that had signed the United Nations Declaration and were on the list he brought to Yalta. At the same time that the President wanted to keep the Soviet Republics from attending (which he never made explicit), he granted to the Republics the rights and privileges which qualified them for equal status.

Stalin and Churchill, on the other hand, understood that invitations would be extended to those nations that had declared war against Germany, and, on this basis, the Soviet Republics qualified. An alternate formulation said that "original members" would attend the San Francisco Conference. Since the two Republics had been accepted as original members, Churchill and Stalin logically assumed again that the two Republics would attend the meeting. The San Francisco Conference in theory would decide the membership of the United Nations (although Roosevelt's list in fact was the basic document), and those nations attending that Conference would declare themselves original members. Those not present would not be considered original members.

Roosevelt was not bothered by consistency. The list the American delegation had drawn up of nations to be invited included the Commonwealth nations, which would be original members. The "Associated Nations"—six nations in Latin America within the American sphere of influence—were also to be invited. These nations had "associated" themselves with the United Nations Declaration but had not signed it. The President, however, did *not* include the Soviet Republics, which both Churchill and Stalin considered analogous with the British Commonwealth, in his list. In view of the Soviet Republics' war record compared with the marginal efforts of the "Associated Nations," Churchill and Stalin protested Roosevelt's rationale.

The foreign ministers' report, presented to the fifth plenary session, on the afternoon of February 8, indicated agreement on the details related to convening the first United Nations Conference. In particular, the report proposed to summon those nations that were signatories of United Nations Declaration for a Conference in the United States of America starting Wednesday, April 25, 1945. At that time the Conference would determine the original membership of the Organization, and the United Kingdom and the United States of America would support original membership for two of the Soviet Republics.[18]

At this session the United States operated on the basis of a premise which had been explained neither to Russia nor to England. It was a refinement of the American formula which made it possible to bring the "Associated Nations" into the United Nations as original members by defining original membership in terms of signing the Declaration of the United Nations and joining the war against Germany. The President hoped to postpone the question of including the Soviet Republics until *after* the United Nations Conference opened. Basic to Roosevelt's position was his belief that the two Soviet Republics functioned as dependent *states,* similiar to the forty-eight American states, rather than functioning as the Commonwealth *nations* did. Neither Stalin nor Churchill accepted this interpretation.

Eden opened the debate on the report. He condemned Roosevelt's formula. The British delegation did not accept the easy access afforded nations that signed the United Nations Declaration and thereby gained the status of United Nations members as if they were in fact fighting against Germany. This alone was hardly sufficient for participation in the Conference. In effect, he was arguing that the United Nations membership should be confined to those nations which had borne the brunt of the war against Germany. This position coincided with the Soviet principle: those nations contributing the most to victory should participate proportionately in the peace.

Stalin followed Eden's example and questioned the right of some of the nations the President had selected to share equal status with the Allies. Stalin advanced Molotov's argument to the foreign ministers: ten of the states slated to attend the Conference had not given the Soviet Union diplomatic recognition. It was difficult to understand, Stalin said, how the President planned to foster world security while supporting nations which had failed to recognize Soviet Russia.

Roosevelt attempted to explain—as if it were an oversight—that these nations had wanted to establish relations with the Soviet Union, "but had just not gotten around to doing anything about it." Others were following the line of the Catholic Church, and the best way to effect recognition was to bring them all together at the Conference. He reminded Stalin that the Russians had already met directly with these nations at Bretton Woods and at the United Nations Relief and Rehabilitation Administration conferences.

Roosevelt admitted that the United States was in an embarrassing situation. She had advised a few of the American Republics *not* to declare war. Now she was asking them to do the opposite. He lamented that these countries would be in good standing had they not accepted American advice.

Stalin did not reject Roosevelt's plea for special consideration of the United States' position in what Roosevelt had effectively called America's sphere of influence. However, Stalin's yardstick, like Eden's, was different from Roosevelt's. Stalin asked what principle Roosevelt used for inviting nations to the Conference. Membership in the United Nations or as an Associated Nation sufficed, the President answered. Stalin disagreed. This was not satisfactory. Some nations had fought hard, while others like Argentina and Turkey had wavered, speculating on the winning side. Alluding to the Soviet Republics which bore the main thrust of the war in Europe, Stalin said the combatants would resent sitting next to those who had simply "associated" themselves.[19]

Roosevelt asked for Stalin's support as a personal favor, telling the Marshal how important the issue was to him: "My idea, and it would save my life, would be to invite those who are on the list who have helped us *on condition* that they declare war." The President thought March 1 could be a deadline for this action, and Stalin again assented to the President's explicit will.

Churchill returned to Stalin's point that some countries had played a poor part in the war and were joining the Allies only now, when it was safe. But at the same time Churchill thought the entrance of new nations into the war could only put more pressure on Germany, and so had a hidden advantage.

There was general confusion during the discussion over joint acceptance of criteria qualifying a nation to receive an invitation to the April Conference and thereby obtain original membership. According to the President, original members of the United Nations were to be those nations invited to the Conference, and those nations invited were supposed to have signed the United Nations Declaration. Further, the British and Russians used active participation in the war as a condition, but there was no tripartite agreement to that. In fact, there was no tripartite agreement to Roosevelt's formula, either, but the President continued discussion as if there were. Roosevelt's authority, although unclear in its application to policy, was paramount because the invitation list and proposals for the Conference had been drawn up by the Americans.

Finally, the heads of state used original membership and attendance at the United Nations Conference interchangeably without any attempt to distinguish the categories. Different conditions were applied to the nations discussed for original membership. The Soviet Republics were supposed to be original members, but the United States and Great Britain, while sponsoring other candidates for the United Nations Conference, did not add the Republics to the invitation list. Each time a different set of criteria prevailed as a nation was added to the list. Roosevelt announced he wanted Iceland in the United Nations. Churchill supported this candidacy, but also wanted Egypt, whose non-belligerency he claimed had been of service to the British, to be a member.

The Prime Minister suddenly confessed he did not have a firm idea of what the guiding principle was. Would any nation that declared war on Germany before March 1 be extended an invitation? The Soviet minutes recorded that Stalin answered in the affirmative. The Marshal thought that any nation which made a declaration of war would be entitled to attend the Conference and to become an original member of the United Nations. The Hiss minutes, however, indicated that Roosevelt mentioned that only "Associated Nations" which declared war qualified. This was not generally understood or agreed upon.

Stalin requested that former enemy states which subsequently declared war on Germany should be excluded; Roosevelt and Churchill readily agreed. Churchill asked that Ireland be excluded from membership because she maintained German and Japanese missions but recommended that Turkey be admitted since her position had been "friendly and useful." Stalin was the first to agree, and Churchill (not without cause) expressed gratitude to the Marshal for his position. Roosevelt asked what should be done about Denmark; she had succumbed to German occupation. Since Iceland had ended its union with Denmark in 1944 and had been occupied by the British and Americans during the war, Churchill asked whether Denmark had recognized the independence of Iceland. Stalin immediately answered that it had not.[20]

Churchill did not see any difficulty over the question of initial members, because, as he observed, he agreed with Stalin and Roosevelt that any nation declaring war before the end of the month could "come to the party." Quite obviously, Churchill and Stalin shared the same interpretation—a declaration of war before the deadline determined United Nations membership. Only Roosevelt continued—and silently, at that—to distinguish between a declaration of war and signing the United Nations Declaration as one set of conditions, and appearing on the American list of nations to be invited as another. For Roosevelt, who held the prepared list—from which he did not plan to deviate— *both* were necessary.

Stalin said that Denmark should wait before becoming a member. Roosevelt agreed. Churchill said that Denmark would have a perfect right to attend the Conference (in Churchill's interpretation, this meant that Denmark would, therefore, be an original member) were she able to "speak on her own behalf." Churchill then repeated, as if this were the agreed upon formula, that all who declared war had this right! Eden apparently grasped the American refinement, and he said that the selection principles admitted those nations which signed the United Nations Declaration before March 1.[21]

The example of Denmark had clarified Roosevelt's view that signing the United Nations Declaration was the *sine qua non* for a nation to be invited to the Conference and thereby to become an "original member." When the Soviets perceived this refinement, they sought to include White Russia and the Ukraine in this category. Molotov was quick to ask—should not the Soviet Republics also sign the Declaration before March 1? Roosevelt hedged with an imprecise yet negative response: he thought they should keep the list they had (it was really the list *he* had), which now included the United Nations, "Associated Nations," and Turkey. Roosevelt said he feared that tiny countries like Andorra and San Marino might try to sign if other exceptions were made. Implicitly, the President was vetoing a Conference invitation for the two Republics.

Churchill, grasping the President's rejection, protested the logic that allowed small countries "that had done next to nothing for victory" to attend simply because they declared war, while postponing the invitation of the two Soviet Republics. Churchill argued once again that the Republics had borne great sacrifices, and if they signed the Declaration, they also should be invited.

Roosevelt tried to divert the issue from attendance at the Conference to guarantees of original membership. He pointed out to Stalin that, by the formula devised, original membership for the two Republics would be supported by the Big Three. He neglected to mention that they would not be invited to the Conference. Stalin, trying to align the position of the Republics to conform correctly with the general formula for members, proposed that the Ukraine and White Russia be named in the protocol, invited to the Conference, and allowed to sign the United Nations Declaration.

Churchill agreed with Roosevelt's concern about nations like Andorra and San Marino; but, since other exceptions were being made, he saw no reason why the Soviet Republics should not be added. Stalin found it illogical that the Soviet Republics should become members of the Assembly just as other states, and yet not sign the Declaration. It seemed to him that the Republics might encounter difficulties for this inconsistency. Stalin voiced his fear that a failure to sign the Declaration could be construed negatively and could damage the status of the Republics both at home and abroad.

Roosevelt and Stettinius rejected Stalin's and Churchill's arguments, and asked Stalin to take their word that this would not happen. Churchill disagreed and backed Stalin. Roosevelt became visibly disturbed by the Anglo-Soviet challenge to his personal formulation. Finally, in exasperation, Stalin brought his perplexity into the open: "I don't want to embarrass the President, but if he will explain his difficulties we will see what can be done."

Roosevelt said that this was a technical question which forced a whole new concept on the United States. The other states they had discussed were separate nations, but the Soviet Union would be one state with three votes. This problem should properly be placed before the Conference in April, at which time the United States and Great Britain agreed to support the Republics. Stalin asked again if this would not work to the disadvantage of the two Republics. Roosevelt said no. Stalin accepted the President's word and withdrew his proposal for the Republics to sign the United Nations Declaration, but he asked that the Republics be named in the text of the foreign ministers' decisions.[22]

In sum, the Republics were left in an ambiguous position. *The question of whether there would be delegations for these original members was never discussed at Yalta.* Roosevelt's aversion to receive the Republics as signatories to the Declaration implied, for him, that there would be no separate delegations. Yet, since the Republics would achieve status as separate nations at the time of the Conference, it was reasonable to infer that their delegations should be present at the Conference at which they became original members. Stalin certainly received every assurance that by the time of the Conference the Republics would be accorded the same treatment as other Assembly members. Roosevelt nonetheless continued to treat them as special cases, without giving the Soviet Union an explanation. There may have been domestic considerations behind this. Some members of the American delegation were afraid that granting the Soviet Union three votes would have adverse political repercussions at home. As compensation and preparation against an adverse reaction, Roosevelt requested three votes in the General Assembly for the United States. Both Churchill and Stalin readily agreed, but the President ultimately decided not to make use of this concession.[23]

TRUSTEESHIPS: "NOT ONE SCRAP OF BRITISH TERRITORY . . ."

The question of United Nations trusteeships led to another clash. In the foreign ministers' session on February 9 the Americans proposed to include in the United Nations Conference invitation a paragraph asking for an exchange of opinions on trusteeships prior to the Conference in April. This was rejected. Then Stettinius mentioned that the United Nations Organization would have the right to deal with trusteeships and to set up appropriate machinery to implement decisions. Eden asked why this should receive mention. Stettinius said it would not because the paragraph had just been eliminated from the invitation. He thought the problem of trusteeships could be taken up by the Conference and at the diplomatic level.

The foreign ministers accordingly agreed to consult on trusteeships prior to the Conference but not to mention it in the invitation. Recalling Churchill's sensitivity on this subject, Stettinius emphasized that he did not expect detailed discussions of what islands or territories would be placed under trusteeship. Eden's interpretation of American intentions was less sinister than Churchill's, and he readily agreed to discuss Allied policy on this issue later.[24]

When the plenary session convened the same afternoon, Stettinius reported on the foreign ministers' meeting. The report on Yugoslavia touched off a bitter discussion between Churchill and Stalin.* Stettinius brought up the trusteeships over colonial and dependent peoples. Churchill thought the trusteeships were a device whereby the Americans would dismantle the Empire, and he replied in great agitation, confirming Stalin's view that an imperialist would rather fight than relinquish his empire: "I absolutely disagree. I will not have one scrap of British Territory flung into that area. After we have done our best to fight in this war and have done no crime to anyone. I will have no suggestion that the British Empire is to be put into the dock and examined by everybody to see whether it is up to their standard." In heated fury, he continued, "No one will induce me as long as I am Prime Minister to let any representative of Great Britain go to a conference where we will be placed in the dock and asked to justify our right to live in a world we have tried to save."[25]

Stalin relished every word. Eden was the only one to recall Stalin's reaction:

> Though the Prime Minister's vehemence was a warning signal to the Americans, it appeared to give the most pleasure to Stalin. He got up from his chair, walked up and down, beamed, and at intervals

* See Chapter 7, "The Far East and Other Issues," pp. 260–61.

broke into applause. This embarrassed Roosevelt and did not really profit anybody, except perhaps Stalin, who was able to please himself and to point to the division of his Allies at the same time.[26]

Stalin's delight may have yet had another source—with Soviet military control over Poland an accomplished fact, and with part of eastern Europe secured after years of unsuccessful negotiations with the Allies, Stalin too had an empire to lose. While Britain and the Soviet Union shared some conditions of empire, their leaders approached the matter from differing points of view. Resting on the respectable tradition of empire, Churchill refused to submit Great Britain to scrutiny. Stalin was both a newcomer to the Tsarist inheritance and was still undecided about the degree and methods of Soviet control; accordingly, he had based his defense on previously articulated Allied principles. For example, Soviet control would assure military success by stabilizing the Red Army's lines of communication and supply. His projections for after the war were also based on current Allied agreements— democratic procedure would be allowed free reign.

Roosevelt was embarrassed by Churchill's tirade. He asked the Prime Minister to wait until Stettinius was finished, because the trusteeship report did not cover the British Empire. Churchill refused to be quieted: "If we are out, I have nothing to say. As long as every bit of land over which the British flag flies is to be brought into the dock, I shall object so long as I live."

Stettinius felt compelled to explain that the trusteeships would apply only to former enemy territory. He assured Churchill: "We have had nothing in mind with reference to the British Empire." Churchill agreed he had no objection to enemy territories coming under trusteeship, but he insisted it would be better then to state once and for all that the trusteeships had nothing to do with the British Empire.

Churchill, recognizing the similarity of his and Stalin's situation, tried to enlist Stalin's aid against the American encroachment. He asked Stalin how he would feel if the international organization wanted to make the Crimea into a holiday resort. Stalin did not deign to give Churchill any comfort: he would be delighted to make the Crimea available for Three Power conferences! [27]

Eventually, Churchill's objections to territorial trusteeships found expression in the following clarification of the Conference protocol: trusteeships would apply only to existing League Mandates, former enemy territories, and territories voluntarily offered. In addition, the protocol incorporated the following decisions—that the United States should consult France and China, that the agreed upon invitation be sent to the United Nations, and that the permanent members of the Security Council should consult prior to the United Nations Conference.[28]

CHAPTER 7

THE FAR EAST

AND OTHER ISSUES

The Soviets had many of the same territorial ambitions as the Tsars had had. Spheres of influence in the Far East and Iran, control of the Straits of the Dardanelles, a protectorate in the Balkans—all these grand designs of the Tsars had their counterparts in the Soviets' aims, although generally in less grandiose form. As Harold Macmillan noted, "All through its history, the landlocked Russia Empire has sought two main objectives: outlet to the warm seas and a defensive ring of territory on its western borders. The revolutionary Government pursued the same aims as its predecessor." [1]

In the Far East the Soviet Union by the end of the war intended to regain everything the Tsars had lost or traded to the Japanese—the Kurile Islands, Southern Sakhalin, control of the Manchurian railways. To the Soviets, the Kuriles and Sakhalin were essential outposts for protecting the Maritime Provinces, which, as the Japanese intervention of 1919-21 had shown, were exceptionally vulnerable to invasion and occupation. The Manchurian railways formed a vital link in the Trans-Siberian railway to Vladivostok and were crucial to the preservation of the Soviet Union's tenuous east-west lines of communication and transport.

Elsewhere, Soviet policy was cautious and often conservative. Russia wished to revise the Straits Convention in order to guarantee that Turkey would not arbitrarily close the Dardanelles and thereby immobilize Soviet naval forces in the Black Sea. In

Iran, Russia had established a sphere of occupation, and she intended to preserve it, especially because the Iranian government appeared subservient to American economic interests. Finally, Stalin was keeping a wary eye on Yugoslavia, and especially on that "upstart socialist," Marshal Tito, to make sure that British influence did not gain the upper hand and also, paradoxically, that British desires were not completely ignored.

These Soviet policies interacted with Britain's defense of the Empire and, more spectacularly, with America's burgeoning overseas economic plans. As we have seen, the extent of Soviet claims in the Far East was continually being adjusted to American plans and ideas. Roosevelt hoped to expell the "imperialists"—Britain, France, and Japan—from China and Korea, and possibly from Indochina and Hong Kong, and to substitute American economic hegemony. The President realized that the United States alone could not fill the vacuum left by the collapse of Japan and the debilitation of France and Britain. To fill the gap, he sought to promote the Soviet Union as America's junior partner in Asia. After the war, the United States would control China and occupy Japan; the Soviet Union would receive territorial concessions from Japan and a share in Manchuria and Korea. The British were to be left out entirely. Churchill and Eden perceived Roosevelt's aims; nonetheless, aside from trying to rehabilitate the principle of colonialism by advocating the restoration of French rule in Indochina, they could do little. The war against Japan was for the most part an American effort, and the United States had made clear its intention to retain the spoils of victory.

In contrast, American policy in Iran excluded the Soviet Union and hence produced conflict rather than co-operation. Great Britain and the Soviet Union had invaded Iran in 1941 and established spheres of occupation in order to overthrow the pro-Nazi regime of Riza Shah. They signed a treaty promising to withdraw their troops shortly after the end of the war, and Britain solemnly pledged not to seek any advantage in Iran at Russia's expense.[2] The United States, which entered Iran in 1942 with troops and advisers to facilitate Lend-Lease shipments to the Soviet Union, was not so fastidious. By November 1943, the United States had established a virtual protectorate in Iran, and

American companies were pressing for oil concessions. The British, who had traditional interests in Iran, disregarded their pledge to the Soviet Union and followed suit. As the wheels of British imperialism and of "unselfish American policy" (Hull's phrase), which in this case amounted to the same thing, rolled forward, the Soviets became alarmed for their interests in northern Iran, and, in September 1944, they dispatched a negotiating team to Iran to secure a five-year oil concession in the north.

To the United States, the sudden entrance of the Soviet Union into the concession game, and the long-range threat to American ascendancy in Iran which this posed, far outweighed immediate economic considerations for American oil companies. The American government promptly reversed itself and advised the Iranians to postpone consideration of *any* concessions for six months or so. The Iranian government quickly adopted the idea and announced that it was deferring all negotiations until the end of the war. The Russians, caught by surprise, continued their pressure for a concession and even forced a change of government in November. The Iranian parliament retaliated by passing a law virtually barring any concessions.[3]

At this point, the United States virtuously stepped in on Iran's behalf to protest Soviet "intervention" in Iran. Ambassador Harriman informed the Soviet government that the United States had taken note of Iranian, not to mention American, anger over the proposed Soviet oil concession and had called off negotiations for its own concession. Harriman warned that the American government insisted on strict observance of Iranian sovereignty. The Declaration of Teheran had to guide Allied action. Therefore the United States would not permit interference in Iranian affairs. The British also made several requests that the Soviets cease their activities in Iran.[4] The Iranian controversy vividly illustrated the double standard which Washington applied to international affairs—Soviet demands for a concession were "interference," Western demands were not. The Russians were baffled. They left their negotiating team in Iran and tried in vain to follow the rules established by the West. They did not yet realize that the Allies' rules were for the Allies' exclusive benefit.

The United States was less concerned about Yugoslavia, another issue broached at Yalta. American policy-makers had backed the wrong horse for leadership of the Yugoslav resistance. When their choice, Draza Mihailovic, lost out to Tito, they left Yugoslavia to Britain and the Soviet Union. Both countries had their hands full. Churchill had to cope with the demands of King Peter, the Yugoslav monarch, and with the Yugoslav government in exile in London, for full restoration of their prewar status; Stalin had to cope with Tito's refusal to deal with any of the "fascist" elements of the exile régime. In October 1944, Churchill and Stalin agreed to split influence and responsibility in Yugoslavia fifty-fifty. They tried to unify the Yugoslav factions, while viewing each other's designs with suspicion. After protracted negotiations, Subasic, premier of the exile government, and Tito signed an agreement establishing a new coalition government, with Tito's followers receiving 80 per cent of the cabinet posts. By the time of the Yalta Conference, Subasic was preparing to fly to Yugoslavia to assume his new position as foreign minister.

The United States was not really worried by the apparent Communist domination of Yugoslavia, nor by the disappointing result of negotiations on Poland. Roosevelt and the State Department had prepared a declaration on eastern Europe guaranteeing the creation of democratic, anti-German régimes in liberated countries. They hoped that adherence to this declaration of principles would force the Soviet Union to follow democratic procedures in Poland and the Balkans. Actually, Stalin had no qualms about signing a high-minded endorsement of democratic principles. He was much more interested in the declaration's anti-fascist implications, which he considered worthy of approval. The British, quite understandably, took the opposite view.

THE FAR EAST: POLITICAL SETTLEMENT

On February 8, Roosevelt and Stalin discussed the Far Eastern war in a private meeting at Yalta.[5] Before turning to Soviet political aims, Roosevelt cast aspersions on both Britain and France and questioned their right to have any influence in Asia after the war. In particular, he undercut Britain wherever possible. Referring to a proposed sale of ships to the Soviet Union after the war, Roosevelt told Stalin that the British never sold anything without demanding interest for it. The President suggested that he handled things differently. Stalin was duly grateful. The President expressed hope that the Soviet Union "would interest itself in a large way in the shipping game"; Great Britain's interest in shipping was traditional and well-known. Also, he commented that Great Britain should give Hong Kong to China. Although he realized Churchill would have strong objections to this, Roosevelt preferred to see Hong Kong under international control, which was, as Stalin knew, the President's plan for the port of Darien.

Roosevelt then proposed that the Soviets, the Chinese, and the Americans share a trusteeship over Korea. The President mentioned this might last twenty to thirty years while the Koreans prepared themselves for self-government. Stalin, interested in the extent of commitment this would involve, asked if troops would be used. When the President said no, Stalin approved. The Far East had clearly become a sphere of American military power, and the Soviet Union accepted Roosevelt's vision. Churchill had admitted to Stalin in October that the war against Japan was primarily an American responsibility,[6] and Stalin could see that the President had his own ideas about the roles the respective nations would play.

The President had more to say. There was one question related to Korea which was rather delicate: he did not want the British to share in the trusteeship there. Yet he was caught because the British would resent their exclusion. Taking his cue from Roosevelt, Stalin argued that the British would certainly be offended. In fact, "the Prime Minister might kill us." Stalin recommended that the British, therefore, be invited.

It was clear by the end of the conversation that Roosevelt planned to exclude Britain from any sphere of influence in north Asia. The Soviet Union would probably have sway over Manchuria as a result of her control of the railroads and two ports on the Liaotung Peninsula (Darien and Port Arthur). The President planned to share the trusteeship of Korea with the Soviet Union, and to exclude the British from this area.

Yet Roosevelt's desire to remove the British competition from Asia went even further. The President said he wanted to see Indochina under a trusteeship; he admitted that this would upset Britain, which was worried about its position in Burma and therefore anxious to rehabilitate France in Asia. Stalin sided with the President and remarked that Britain already had once lost Burma by relying on Indochina. Britain was not the country to protect this area. In essence, Stalin was asking Roosevelt to consider a southward extension of influence for both the United States and the Soviet Union.

The President continued with criticism of French rule in Indochina. France had done nothing to help the natives since taking over the colony. The United States found itself in an embarrassing situation because de Gaulle was now asking for American ships to transport French forces to Indochina. Stalin asked where someone like de Gaulle was going to get even the troops to put in the ships. The President answered that de Gaulle had promised to find the troops whenever the President found the ships, but up to that moment he just did not seem able to find the ships!

Stalin and Roosevelt had found agreement on Asia an easy matter. Britain and France would be excluded, and the entire Far East would be opened to American influence. The Soviet Union would help fill in the vacuum left by the withdrawal of Japan and the exclusion of the Western imperialists. In this relaxed atmosphere, Stalin brought up the political conditions under which Russia would enter the war against Japan. Roosevelt was well aware of the Soviet conditions for entry into the war; he immediately conceded that the southern part of Sakhalin Island and the Kurile Islands, which at one time or another had belonged to Tsarist Russia, should go to the Soviet Union. In the case of the two ports—Darien and Port Arthur—and the Chinese-Eastern and Southern-Manchurian Railroads, the President said he could not make a commitment. His agreement to Stalin's stipulations would be conditional upon Chinese acceptance of the status of these areas. Nonetheless, he considered the possible resolutions. The Russians might arrange to lease Port Arthur, but the President wanted Darien internationalized to buttress his plan of similarly neutralizing Hong Kong. In the case of the two railroads connected with the Soviet railway system, there could be a lease placing them under Soviet operation, or possibly a Sino-Soviet Commission to oversee them.

Stalin pushed slightly. He said that if leases to both Darien and Port Arthur were not granted, he could not justify war against Japan to the Soviet people. If his political conditions were met, there would be no problem. Roosevelt stood firm on talking to Chiang Kai-shek first, indicating it would be difficult to do this immediately without endangering secrecy about Soviet intentions. Stalin agreed but wanted these Soviet conditions put in writing before leaving Yalta. The President indicated that this could be done.

Stalin understood well that once Japan was defeated, her hegemony over the Asian mainland was to be taken over by China, and that the United States planned to control China. Under these circumstances Russia's position rested on her ability to accommodate the Chinese as well as the Americans. Stalin reassured the President that the Soviet Union had the best intentions regarding China and would not upset America's plans. The Chinese Prime Minister, T. V. Soong, was expected to come to Moscow at the end of April, Stalin said. The Chinese could be consulted as soon as it was possible to free Soviet troops from the west to move eastward. Roosevelt remarked that he had been trying for some time "to keep China alive," and Stalin promised Roosevelt that the China of Chiang Kai-shek would remain alive. He suggested only that Chiang lacked good leaders around him: the good men in the Kuomintang had been overlooked, he said. Roosevelt brushed aside Stalin's praise for the Chiang government and stressed that he was trying, with increasing success, to bring the Communists and the Chungking government together. His failure was more Chiang's fault than it was the Communists'. Stalin confirmed that his own preference was for just such a policy as Roosevelt espoused—a united front. Stalin said he could not understand why, confronted with a war, the Chinese had failed to unite against the Japanese. He reminded the President that he consistently backed a united front policy, and (as far back as the 1920's, in fact) had insisted on it. He assured Roosevelt that he had never agreed with its dissolution.[7]

The details of the Far East settlement were worked out on the last day of the Conference, at a meeting between Harriman and Molotov, held at the latter's request. The Soviet delegation had drafted an agreement based on the Stalin-Roosevelt conversation, and they gave Harriman an English translation. The proposal included the specific territorial conditions laid down for the entry of the Soviet Union into the war, so phrased that the transfer of Japanese-held territory constituted a Russian "right": "The former rights of Russia violated by the treacherous attack of Japan in 1904 should be returned." Specifically, the draft agreement mentioned the return of the southern part of Sakhalin Island to Soviet Russia, the "restoration" of Port Arthur and Darien, and the "restoration" of Russia's right to operate the Chinese-Eastern and Southern-Manchurian Railroads. In accordance with the understanding on China, the draft stated that China would possess full sovereignty in Manchuria and that the Soviet Union was willing to conclude a pact of friendship and alliance with the National Government of China.[3]

Ambassador Harriman was not satisfied with the Soviet draft, since Molotov had taken the liberty of including the ports and railroads as leases, to which Roosevelt had objected. The Ambassador made three suggestions: Darien and Port Arthur should be confirmed as free ports rather than leases; the railways should be operated by a joint Chinese-Soviet commission; and the concurrence of Chiang Kai-shek should be stated as a prerequisite for the agreement. Molotov knew that Stalin had already agreed to all three conditions. Even so, he did not hesitate to argue the last point with Harriman. Possibly he feared that America might use "China" as a pretext to cancel the agreement.

Roosevelt gave his assent to the Russian draft, pending the acceptance of the American amendments. The draft was re-submitted to Molotov. Stalin was also willing to accept the written conditions, but he told Harriman later in the day there was a problem over Port Arthur; he did not want it internationalized because he needed it for a Soviet naval base. Harriman directed him to Roosevelt, who agreed to this alteration. Stalin then accepted joint Chinese-Soviet control over the railroads as the most appropriate means of handling them. Stalin further suggested the Chinese might want to concur on the status of Outer Mongolia.

Roosevelt brought up one last technicality. Should he approach Chiang or would Stalin prefer to do it during the visit of Prime Minister Soong? Stalin recommended the President contact Chiang, since Stalin was the interested party. Roosevelt agreed to send an officer from Washington through Moscow to Chungking with a letter of instructions.[9] Finally, the Far East agreement was shown to the British, and Churchill readily agreed. As the Prime Minister had told Stalin on the afternoon of February 8, Great Britain welcomed the appearance of Russian ships in the Pacific and supported the restoration of Russia's former losses in the Pacific.[10]

The Far East: Military Co-operation

After (and only after) the political issues were settled, the Soviet Union proved exceptionally willing to co-operate in making Russia a military power in the Far East. Soviet and American military leaders met for two days (February 8 and 9) to discuss plans and problems caused by Soviet entry into the war with Japan. On February 8 the American staff presented to the Soviet staff a series of written questions. Even though some of the questions had been asked before, the Soviet staff would not or could not define policy or commit Soviet Russia without the consent of Stalin. General Antonov stated that he could not give authoritative answers before conferring with Marshal Stalin, but said he would give his personal views on the questions placed before him. Antonov stressed that overall Soviet plans had undergone no change since he presented them to General Deane and Ambassador Harriman in October.[11]

All the questions raised on February 8 were answered by the Russians on the next day, with Stalin himself deciding the most sensitive issues. In sum, the following issues were discussed and settled:

1. The Americans asked the Soviets whether they wanted a supply line across the Pacific to Siberia. Previous talks in Moscow had indicated the desirability of such a line. On February 8 Antonov pointed out that the Trans-Siberian Railway could be disrupted by a Japanese attack; hence, sea and air routes were necessary to assure deliveries. Soviet planning for war with Japan was based on the assumption that the Japanese would put up a hard fight against the Russians. On February 9, Antonov affirmed his earlier statement that the sustained pressure on the eastern front in Europe had so far prevented troop transfers to Siberia.

2. The United States had previously requested air bases at Komsomolsk and Nikolaevsk or in any suitable area which would not hamper Russian operations. Antonov admitted he could not authorize this personally. Consequently, Roosevelt raised the issue with Stalin, who obligingly approved the location of these bases. Antonov confirmed Stalin's decision on February 9.[12]

3. The Americans requested information of possible effects of Siberian weather on operations. Antonov provided a lengthy report indicating what time of the year would be best for certain operations and what time would be most undesirable.[13]

4. The American staff asked whether the Soviets wanted American help in the defense of the Kamchatka Peninsula, whether bases could be built there by the Soviets prior to their entrance into the war, and whether an American survey party could enter the area. Antonov stated that "American help would be useful," and confirmed this acceptance the following day. He gave a detailed picture of the Soviet Union's current difficulties in preparing the area and concluded that it was presently impossible to make an estimate of Soviet requirements.

Stalin told Roosevelt on February 8 that the establishment of American air bases was deemed very important. On February 9 Antonov indicated that the Soviets would prepare bases, and that Stalin approved the American survey party. The Soviets, however, did not want the Americans to begin survey operations until the last minute, in order to preserve secrecy and to avoid provoking the Japanese at a time when the Red Army was concentrating its total force against Germany.[14]

5. The American Chiefs of Staff asked if the Soviet Union would capture Southern Sakhalin. Antonov indicated in the February 8 meeting that it would be done immediately after joining the war. The next day he stressed again that the conquest of Sakhalin was one of the primary aims in the war against Japan and that the Soviet Union could undertake it without American help. The Americans asked if La Pérouse Strait, which separates Sakhalin from the Japanese main islands, would be open to shipping. Antonov's answer on both days indicated that once control of Sakhalin was secured, the Strait would be closed to the Japanese, but it would not be open to the Allies until a base could be constructed.[15]

6. The Americans asked, "Are we assured that combined planning in Moscow will be vigorously pursued?" implying that the Soviet staff shared no real interest in co-ordinating actions. General Antonov and Marshal Stalin had agreed insofar as possible to Allied requests for limited combined planning. Antonov felt insulted by the phrasing of the question. He explained that since Soviet troops had not arrived in the Far East, there could be no combined planning until the Soviets had bases of operations there. General Marshall persisted. The American staff required firm data on which to base their own future plans. He reiterated that "specific and constructive planning must be pursued." Responding to the repeated criticism, General Antonov promised to do his best to improve the planning situation in Moscow.

Roosevelt raised the problem personally with Stalin, who again agreed on February 8 to combined planning and said he would give the necessary instruction in Moscow. On February 9, General Antonov, dismayed by the Americans' apparent refusal to believe his repeated promises, stated, "We shall fulfill on our side the plan which was made." He implied that if planning broke down, it would not be the fault of the Soviets. General Marshall attempted to smooth over the unpleasantness; the Americans were not questioning either Soviet good faith or ability to carry out plans, he said. Antonov was mollified, and he immediately became more amiable. He confirmed the agreement that combined planning would proceed vigorously in Moscow.[16]

7. The Americans requested weather stations in Siberia to provide more weather information. Antonov had to clear this with Stalin; on February 9 he replied that the request was approved.[17]

In addition to these specific questions raised in writing by the American Chiefs of Staff, the military delegations exchanged information about supplies for the proposed air bases. Stalin granted every request pertaining to military liaison. He approved the construction of American airfields in the Budapest area, which would allow American bombers to avoid the hazardous trip from Italy to Germany. He also agreed to allow an American strategic bombing survey team to work in eastern Europe; however, Soviet Air Marshal Sergei Khuydyakov requested that Soviet bomb experts be permitted to accompany them.

Stalin, in turn, wanted to purchase ships for the Soviet Union after the war. Roosevelt gave every assurance that this probably could be arranged. The President hoped to change American legislation so that surplus shipping could be transferred on credit and without interest, thus avoiding the problems that had arisen in World War I. Roosevelt proposed charging a fixed sum on credit (cost plus depreciation), so that in twenty years the entire credit would be extinguished. Stalin praised the President for his handling of such economic problems. In particular, Stalin lauded Lend-Lease as an extraordinary contribution, without which the war could not have been won so quickly.[18] On issues related to the Far East, Allied amity reigned unimpaired.

IRAN

On the other goals which the Soviets had lifted from the portfolios of Tsarist policy—Iran, the Dardanelles, the Balkans—no such unanimity was possible. At Yalta, Iran first came up during the foreign ministers' meeting on February 8.[19] Eden lectured on acceptable bases of Allied policy in Iran. He reminded his colleagues of the legal obligation incurred by the Allies under the Declaration of Iran and the British-Soviet-Iranian Treaty. In a statement reminiscent of Churchill's lecture on Poland, he said: "The Iranian government should be the master in its own house and free to make its own decisions." This principle might prevent competition among the Allies in Iran. He recommended, therefore, that all the Allies refrain from interfering in Iran's internal affairs. The Soviet desire for oil was understandable, Eden continued, and the Soviet Union was a natural market for Iranian oil. However, the Allies ought not to press for oil concessions until their troops had been withdrawn. In any case, the Allies at the Yalta Conference had to make a declaration promising the withdrawal of their troops earlier than stated in the Declaration of Iran. This withdrawal could begin as soon as the supply route to Russia through Iran was closed.

Molotov undertook to delay any decision. He expressed surprise that troop withdrawals was at issue. As a new question, it would require some (indefinite, perhaps infinite) time for study. Turning to pressure for an oil concession, Molotov claimed that the Soviet Union was the aggrieved party. The Soviet government had merely asked the Iranians what their attitude would be toward an oil concession. It had received a favorable reply from both the Iranian government and from Foreign Minister Saed. Both Iran and Russia profited from such an arrangement; therefore, an oil concession would fulfill the terms of the Declaration of Teheran, in which the Soviet Union promised to grant assistance to the Iranian economy. However, Molotov continued, the situation had changed. The Iranians suddenly refused to negotiate and insisted there should be no concessions during the war. In refusing negotiations, the Iranian government was not acting in the interest of the people, Molotov declared. Many Iranian officials and citizens had informed the Russians that the decision against negotiations had been taken in a hurry and was unwise. The Soviet government, Molotov concluded, saw no reason why the decision could not be reversed again. In any case, the matter should rest since the situation was not acute: "It should take its own course."

Stettinius and Eden argued that the West also had a stake in oil concessions and yet was willing to respect the decision of the Iranian government to postpone concessions until the troops were withdrawn. Stettinius reminded Molotov that American troops were in Iran only to maintain a supply line to the U.S.S.R. Eden recommended that these troops be withdrawn as soon as the supply route was no longer needed. Both Eden and Stettinius insisted that they had no opposition to a Soviet oil concession per se.

Molotov had his own recommendations. It was advisable to stop with a mere exchange of views on the subject, he said. The most he would offer was to summon the head of the Soviet negotiating team in Iran to Yalta. Since the Conference had at most two remaining days, Molotov's suggestion amounted, in effect, to an indefinite postponement of the entire question.

Stettinius and Eden refused to drop the question. At the foreign ministers' meeting at noon, February 9, they reminded Molotov that the issues raised by the British paper on Iran had still not been discussed. Stettinius said the United States backed Britain wholeheartedly. Molotov retorted that the Soviet delegation had not had time to study the paper and would not discuss it.[20]

The next day Eden made another attempt to discuss Iran. Trying to commit the Soviet delegation to the Teheran Declaration, he inquired whether it would be advisable to issue a communiqué on Iran. Molotov said flatly that it would not be. Stettinius spoke up for Eden and attested that a communiqué clarifying the Allied viewpoint was desirable. Molotov rejected this idea again. Eden suggested they make a statement that the Declaration of Iran had been re-examined and reaffirmed at Yalta. Molotov refused.[21]

In the face of Molotov's obstinacy, discussions over Iran were entirely futile, and Stettinius followed Molotov in favor of dropping the whole issue. Churchill considered the matter unimportant and refused to bring it up in a plenary session. Eden, however, particularly exasperated by Molotov's intransigent stance, raised the issue with Stalin personally. He got no further than the word "Iran." Stalin began to laugh: "You should never talk to Molotov about Iran. Didn't you realize that he had a resounding diplomatic defeat there? He is very sore with Iran. If you want to talk about it, talk to me. What is it?" Eden explained that it was time, in his opinion, to agree to a joint plan for removal of troops after the cessation of hostilities. Stalin nodded and said: "Yes, I understand. I'll think about it." [22]

This conversation had no effect on the immediate outcome of the Conference. The protocol of the proceedings noted only that the subject had been discussed and would be pursued through regular diplomatic channels. Despite Eden's persistence and Stalin's momentary willingness, the question of Iran remained unresolved.

THE DARDANELLES

The debate on the Straits question was less acrimonious than that on Iran but nonetheless it was just as indecisive. Stalin had indicated long before the Yalta Conference that he sought a revision of the Montreux Convention, which limited military use of the Dardanelles. Churchill responded sympathetically, but Eden did not. Eden wanted to use a possible revision of the Straits situation as a bargaining lever, especially in view of the general weakness of the Western negotiating position at Yalta.[23]

The issue was left untouched until the plenary session of February 10. While he was waiting for a translation of the British text on Polish boundaries, Stalin mentioned that he had a "few words" to say about the Montreux Convention. He began undermining its legality to show revision was necessary. The Convention, he pointed out, had been signed and partly created by the Japanese Emperor, whose role had been more significant than Soviet Russia's, and it was linked with the defunct League of Nations as well with the enemy Emperor. The Convention had been negotiated at a time when Great Britain was hostile to Soviet Russia, but now Great Britain certainly could not "wish to strangle Russia with the help of the Japanese." The Turks possessed unreasonable control over entry to the Black Sea, since, under the Convention, they could close the Straits even if there were only a *possibility* of war. Russia could not accept a situation in which Turkey had a stranglehold on Russia's throat. Stalin concluded that there should certainly be a revision of the Montreux Convention. Such a revision, he said, need not and should not harm the legitimate interests of Turkey. An appropriate organization, such as the Big Three foreign ministers, could consider this matter at their first meeting.

Roosevelt envisioned a harmonious relationship between Russia and Turkey and expressed a desire that their frontier should follow the example of the American-Canadian frontier—to be without forts and arms. Churchill supported Stalin and recalled that in Moscow he had been sympathetic to Stalin's ideas on revising the Montreux Convention. At that time the Prime Minister had asked Stalin to send a note on the revisions, but he had not yet received it. The Prime Minister emphatically agreed that Russia's present position was unsatisfactory. He considered discussion by the foreign ministers a wise step and hoped that the Russians would advance proposals at the ministerial meeting. He conjectured that perhaps the Turks, who would soon be entering the war on the Allied side, should be informed of the Soviet's interest.

Eden reminded Churchill that the Allies were already communicating with the Turkish ambassador and said he thought it advisable to give the Turks assurance of the Allies' intention to guarantee Turkish independence and integrity. Stalin agreed: it was impossible to keep anything from the Turks, he remarked, and it would be wise to reassure them as soon as possible. Roosevelt concurred.

Stalin proposed that the discussion take place at the United Nations Conference in San Francisco in April. Churchill asked for conversations on British soil. The issue was one of greatest interest to the British Empire, he said; therefore, London would be appropriate for this historic moment. Churchill reminisced that he had tried in World War I to get through the Dardanelles, but that, despite help from the Russian government, the campaign in Gallipoli had been unsuccessful. Stalin admonished Churchill for having given up too quickly, since the Turks and Germans had been on the verge of surrender. Churchill disavowed responsibility—he had been out of the Cabinet when the ill-fated decision was taken.[24] Returning to the problem of a decision on the Straits, Stalin asked who was recording the decisions of the Conference, and Eden replied that there would be an agreed-upon communiqué as well as a list of decisions.

On February 11, during the discussion of the Conference communiqué and protocol, Molotov proposed that the protocol brand the Montreux Convention as out of touch with the contemporary situation. Stettinius objected: he wanted the proposed changes in the status of the Straits to be considered by the foreign ministers before a public announcement was made. Eden suggested the protocol indicate that the foreign ministers would consider proposals put forward by the Soviet government, and that the British would inform the Turks at the appropriate moment. Molotov still tried to gain acceptance for his proposal, but Stettinius backed Eden's alternative formulation and it was incorporated in the final protocol.[25]

YUGOSLAVIA

Another problem in the same geographic area was Yugoslavia. Premier Subasic of Yugoslavia was supposed to fly immediately from London to Yugoslavia, but he was delayed by bad weather and by King Peter's obstinate refusal to co-operate with the new government. This delay led to a misunderstanding at Yalta between Britain and Russia. The British considered the Tito-Subasic Agreement to be in effect and wanted the Conference to consider two proposed amendments to it. The Soviets, on the other hand—either for purposes of bargaining or for fear of British motives—concluded that Britain was conniving with King Peter to keep Subasic in London and to sabotage the agreement with Tito. At the sixth plenary session, Churchill tried to discuss the British amendments to the agreement. Molotov instead insisted that the Tito-Subasic Agreement go into effect in spite of "King Peter's whims." He demanded that there be no consideration of any change until the present agreement was put into operation.

Churchill did not restrain his irritation: Was it too much to ask that the legislative acts of temporary authorities be subject to the confirmation of a democratic process, as Britain proposed? Stalin explained that the issue for the Soviet Union was one of British good faith in carrying out the present agreement. He insisted that there be no further delays and threatened to use his partial control * over Yugoslavia to introduce his own amendments if the British persisted with theirs. He charged Churchill with creating an unstable situation by delaying the formation of the Yugoslav government. Churchill retorted that the situation was not unstable since Tito was a dictator. Stalin disagreed—Tito was no dictator and the situation in Yugoslavia was indefinite.

Eden brought the situation into perspective. It was not a question, he emphasized, of amendments *before* the agreement went into effect. Great Britain only wanted the Conference to endorse the position which Subasic was going to propose to Tito and which Tito would surely accept. Stalin admitted that he did in fact support the additional agreements, but he demanded that the government be formed before any amendments were considered. Eden countered that if the Yalta Conference agreed to the amendments, Tito could be asked to adopt them after the government was formed.

Stalin agreed, but he wanted a telegram to be sent stating that the Three Powers backed the Tito-Subasic Agreement irrespective of King Peter's wishes. Churchill and Eden assured Stalin again that King Peter's wishes did not matter, that question had been settled long ago. Only the question of amendments remained. Stalin closed the discussion. He had already consented to the amendments, he said, and as a man of his word, he would not go back on it.[26]

By the time of the foreign ministers' meeting on February 10, Subasic was en route to Yugoslavia and Soviet suspicions were virtually dispelled. Eden and Molotov quickly agreed that an Allied statement supporting the Tito-Subasic Agreement should be included in the Conference communiqué, and they dispatched this statement as a telegram to the two Yugoslav leaders.

Eden also submitted two papers on the Yugoslav border between Austria and Italy. Since Britain would probably have an

* The fifty-fifty agreement was in effect, as described on p. 71.

occupation zone in Austria contiguous to the Yugoslav border, the British feared clashes between Yugoslav partisans who wanted to alter the prewar boundary and Austrians and British who wanted to retain it. Britain wanted the Allies to agree to maintain the 1937 boundary until the peace conference examined further claims. Eden asserted that Tito showed every sign of using his partisans to extend Yugoslav authority over territory beyond the former Yugoslav-Italian border. Britain wished to avoid clashes and sought some united policy to avert any unnecessary conflict. Molotov said the proposals needed adequate discussion, and the foreign ministers decided to explore the border question through diplomatic channels. Other minor issues relating to the Balkans were also discussed, generally without results.[27]

THE DECLARATION ON LIBERATED EUROPE

Roosevelt's Declaration on Liberated Europe was first discussed during the sixth plenary session. As we have previously seen, * in the course of an argument about Polish elections, Churchill objected to Stalin's discrimination between "fascist" and "non-fascist" elements. Stalin countered that his terminology was from the American's own Declaration on Liberated Europe, a draft of which Roosevelt had distributed earlier. Stalin said that "on the whole" he approved of it. He read the key sentence, which pledged the countries of liberated Europe "to destroy the last vestiges of Nazism and fascism." These were good words, he declared, for in them the distinction between fascist and non-fascist was clearly drawn.

Not surprisingly, Roosevelt was more interested in the Declaration's democratic guarantees than in its anti-fascist implications. He asked that the Polish elections be the first example of the practical implementation of the Declaration's promises.[28] After a further short discussion of Poland, the President returned to the text of the Declaration. Churchill, who had earlier seen sinister anti-colonialist designs behind the American

* See pp. 205–6.

proposal on trusteeships, immediately detected another threat to the British Empire in this document. He accepted the President's proposal, he said, but only so long as it was understood that the reference to the Atlantic Charter in the Declaration did not apply to the British Empire. Great Britain *already* followed the principles of the Charter, he said. Therefore, no reaffirmation of democratic guarantees for the Empire should be required, or, for that matter, would be permitted. Churchill added that he had already sent a copy of Britain's interpretation of the self-determination clauses of the Charter to Wendell Willkie. Roosevelt retorted, "Was that what killed him?"

In a calmer vein, Molotov proposed an amendment promising Allied support "to men in those countries who took an active part in the struggle against German occupation." Churchill seemed about to speak, but Stalin cut him off with the mischievous observation that the Soviet amendment did not apply to Greece, where, as was well known, British troops had just suppressed the Communist-led anti-German resistance. Churchill blandly replied that he was not anxious about Greece. Slapping at Soviet policy in Poland, he remarked that the Soviets were welcome to observe British conduct. Stalin declined, claiming that he had complete confidence in British policy in Greece. Churchill was duly grateful. After this interchange, Roosevelt rerouted Molotov's amendment to the usual body—the foreign ministers.[29]

At the foreign ministers' meeting on February 9, Stettinius, who had talked the matter over with the President, rejected Molotov's proposal. The Secretary stated succinctly that the amendment was irrelevant. Further, it represented a threat of intervention in the affairs of other countries and also raised the question of who had collaborated with the enemy. Eden fully agreed. On the following day, Stettinius repeated that the President and the American government could not accept the Soviet amendment because it would cause severe difficulties in American domestic politics. Molotov, undeterred, submitted a second amendment with an even more serious intent. The Soviets were delighted at the prospect of authorization to eradicate fascism, but the enforcement terminology in the Declaration seemed to them too restrictive. In the American draft, the Allies were to "immediately establish appropriate machinery for the carrying out of the joint responsibilities set forth in this declaration." Molotov proposed a formulation which allowed the Soviet Union more scope for unilateral action: "They will immediately take measures for the carrying out of mutual consultation." This amendment did not seem to be a radical alteration of the original text. Stettinius pronounced himself favorably impressed; Eden said it was an improvement. Stettinius then returned to Molotov's first amendment, which was withdrawn.[30]

Eden presented the revised Declaration to the seventh plenary session on February 10. However, he had changed his mind and recommended a substitute for Molotov's phrasing: they "shall consult together on the measures to discharge the joint responsibilities set forth in this declaration." Molotov reminded the conferees that there had been agreement on his wording, and he wanted it to stand. Roosevelt had the Soviet proposal read. Churchill complained that Molotov's proposal was unacceptable: how could you carry out a measure for consultation? Stalin, after listening to the discussion, overruled Molotov and agreed to Eden's wording, which, like the Soviet draft, substituted vague "consultations" for the more restrictive and inflexible "joint machinery." [31]

This ended the discussion of the Declaration on Liberated Europe. As noted before, Britain raised the possibility of France's associating herself with the Declaration* and used the issue to bargain for a seat for France on the postwar German Control Commission.

* See pp. 157–58.

PART III

THE FALSE DAWN

CHAPTER 8

SECOND THOUGHTS

AND CONCLUSIONS

AFTER YALTA: "THEY COULD GO TO HELL"

At the final plenary session on Sunday, February 11, the three heads of state discussed the draft communiqué of the Conference. No major changes were proposed. Churchill grumbled about the overfrequent use of "joint," which, he said, meant to him "the Sunday family roast of mutton." The offending word was accordingly stricken from six phrases in the text. At the end of the session, the President proposed that Stalin, who had been "such a wonderful host," should sign the communiqué first. Stalin objected. Churchill joked that, either by age or by alphabet, "I'll be first." Stalin, perhaps seriously, warned them that if he himself signed first, people would say he had led the Conference. He insisted on signing last. Churchill and Stalin both got their wishes. The communiqué was signed at lunch, in English alphabetical order *—Winston S. Churchill, Franklin D. Roosevelt, J. Stalin.[1]

After a last minute foreign ministers' session to hammer out the details of the Conference protocol, the conferees scattered to their various destinations, Churchill to the *Franconia*, Roosevelt to the *Catoctin*, both at anchor in Sevastopol harbor. Churchill was depressed about the results of the Conference, especially the failure to reach a solid agreement on Poland. He called the com-

* According to the Russian alphabet, the order would have been Roosevelt, Stalin, and then Churchill.

muniqué "this bloody thing" and said of the Conference, "Anyway, that's done with and out of the way." The Prime Minister was particularly unhappy about the obvious decline of British influence since Teheran. As a tonic, he decided to fly to Athens on the way home. In Greece, at least, the British did not have to bow impotently before the Americans and the Russians.[2]

The other members of the British delegation were reasonably satisfied, if not with the agreements, then at least with the atmosphere. Lord Ismay, Churchill's Chief of Staff, wrote home that the Conference had "been a great success, not so much because of the formal conclusions that were reached, but because of the spirit of frank cooperation which characterised all the discussions." The American delegation was openly pleased with both the results and tone of the Conference. Harriman considered the Far East agreement, which assured Soviet support for Chiang Kai-shek, to be a substantial success. He also felt that Stalin would fulfill his promise of free elections in Poland. Charles Bohlen thought the Polish settlement realistic, given the circumstances. Harry Hopkins was even more effusive. He told Robert Sherwood, "We really believed in our hearts that this was the dawn of the new day we had all been praying for and talking about for so many years. We were absolutely certain that we had won the first great victory of the peace—and, by 'we,' I mean *all* of us, the whole civilized human race. The Russians had proved that they could be reasonable and farseeing and there wasn't any doubt in the minds of the President or any of us, that we could live with them and get along with them peacefully for as far into the future as any of us could imagine." Edward Stettinius provided the most balanced statement: "The record of the Conference shows clearly that the Soviet Union made greater concessions at Yalta to the United States and Great Britain than were made to the Soviets." [3]

Unfortunately, the Soviet Union's co-operativeness was soon forgotten. Within a few months after the Conference, the United States attempted to undo those agreements at Yalta which reflected Soviet interests. America presented the Soviet Union with a choice between relinquishing her gains at Yalta or suffering ostracism and economic boycott in the postwar world.

The United States camouflaged its demands by accusing the Soviet Union of breaking the Yalta agreements, while, in fact, attempting to force the Soviet Union to make new agreements superseding Yalta. The agreements which Washington so diligently worked to overthrow were precisely the three in which Moscow had demonstrated an interest at Yalta. In effect, the West canceled the dismemberment provision of the Yalta agreement, made reparations at first difficult and then, later, impossible, and tried to renegotiate the Polish agreement. The Soviets, for their part, generally complied with the Yalta decisions sponsored by and beneficial to the West. The Russians accepted Britain's escalation of France to a major role in world affairs, even though initiation of a Western bloc to contain the Soviet Union was implicit in this arrangement. Moscow considered this potential threat less important than Western attempts to reverse the Polish agreement.

On April 12, 1945, Roosevelt died. He was succeeded by Vice President Harry S. Truman. President Truman, in considering co-operation with Russia and the proposed reorganization of the Polish government in the spring and summer of 1945, formulated his policy on this basis: "Our agreements with the Soviet Union have been a one-way street . . . it was now or never . . . (the Russians) could go to hell." Truman set out to implement the Yalta agreements by changing them. He told Molotov the United States insisted that "the Soviet government carry out the Crimea decision on Poland." He handed him a memorandum which equated fulfillment of the Yalta decisions with establishment of a "new" government. As we have previously seen, at Yalta the United States had agreed in writing to a "reorganized" version of the Polish Provisional Government "which is now functioning in Poland." Stalin noted the new direction of Truman's policy with some alarm: "You evidently do not agree that the Soviet Union is entitled to seek in Poland a government that would be friendly to it." [4]

At the end of May, Truman sent Harry Hopkins to Moscow and reverted—briefly—to the Yalta agreements, but the President's willingness to abide by the Yalta agreements was merely a delaying tactic to postpone a confrontation until the United

States was in a stronger position—or, as one historian has claimed, until the atomic bomb gave the United States the power to enforce its will on the Soviet Union. With the maximum bargaining leverage, the United States would at the proper time insist on free elections and a virtual return to the prewar situation in Poland. As to free elections, there was no reason to believe that Stalin—whose record included sponsoring free elections in Finland and Austria, backing the West's rightist régimes in France, Italy, and Belgium, and supporting Churchill's free hand in Greece against the powerful leftists—would not allow moderately free elections in Poland as promised. But when Western hostility threatened everything short of war with the Soviet Union, the Russians increasingly abandoned free elections and co-operation in favor of consolidation of a defensive perimeter in Eastern Europe. In effect, the Soviets responded to the West in kind; they closed the doors they had previously left open. The West created its own self-fulfilling prophecy of the dangers and goals of Soviet communism.

The West likewise attempted to undo the Yalta decisions on Germany, but with greater success. Motivated by political considerations, the United States prepared, despite earlier promises and the explicit intent of Congress, to cut off aid to the Soviet Union. Truman unilaterally used the possibility of postwar credits as a pressure tactic in the early months of his presidency. Further, Truman attempted to undo America's support for the Yalta reparations agreement. Although he admitted "morally [Germany] should have been made to pay," he decided that "America was not interested in reparations for anybody." Unfortunately, he could not simply refuse the Soviet Union reparations. The United States was committed, both morally and in writing. Truman would have to renegotiate reparations. As a start, he refused Soviet requests to hold a meeting of the Reparations Commission, agreed upon at Yalta, until the United States finally was able to alter the agreements at Potsdam. American hostility toward the Soviet Union was so obvious that Philip Mosely had to warn the Assistant Secretary of State about it: Moscow might get the impression that the United States sympathized more with the Germans than with the Soviet people by the end of the war.[5]

At Potsdam, Truman succeeded in watering down the previous agreements. At Yalta it had been agreed that the nature of reparations would include removal of capital equipment, "annual deliveries of goods from current production for a period to be fixed," and "use of German labor." Truman's Secretary of State, James F. Byrnes, insisted that reparations should come only from the zone under the control of the occupying power. His plan effectively denied the Soviet Union access to the industrial goods in the Western zones. Assistant Secretary Clayton told Byrnes that this "would be considered by the Russians as a reversal of the Yalta position in Moscow," which indeed it was. Despite this warning, Truman decided to bring reparations into line with emerging American policy and the Soviets accepted change rather than break with the West. The final Potsdam agreements stated that: "Reparations claims of the USSR shall be met by removals from the zone of Germany occupied by the USSR, and from appropriate German external assets."

The sum agreed upon as an initial consideration at Yalta was also altered. The State Department instructed the United States delegate to the Reparations Commission to scale down the total figure from $20 billion to $12 to $14 billion. Subsequently, reverting to Britain's position at Yalta, the State Department ordered the delegate to avoid any figure at all. Secretary Byrnes boasted that the United States "finally succeeded in eliminating from the agreed declaration any mention of the total amount." The final protocol of the Potsdam Conference allowed the Soviet Union only 15 per cent of the capital equipment in the Western zone not necessary for the German peace economy in exchange for raw materials of equivalent value, plus 10 per cent of the industrial equipment deemed unnecessary for the German economy.[6]

Washington, while rebuilding the German economy, insisted unilaterally that any imports into any zone would be the first charge against exports from current production. This procedure both reduced the amount of reparations due the Soviet Union and offset the unrest which, Washington feared, might lead to the bolshevization of Germany. General Clay, in accordance with Washington's orders, ceased deliveries to the Soviet Union from the American zone in May 1946. His action violated even the Potsdam accord, which stipulated that the first charge principle would not apply to reparations exports of capital equipment from the Western zones.

Washington's reversal of the Yalta decision on German dismemberment was accepted by Moscow; the Soviets had never been enthusiastic about the idea in the first place. When the British and American representatives in the European Advisory Council argued that dismemberment "was to be accomplished only as a last resort," the Soviets accepted this position and also came out against dismemberment. The West immediately charged that the Soviet Union was changing its position. Harry Hopkins asked Stalin why he had altered his previous stand. Stalin replied that it was because "both Great Britain and the United States were opposed to dismemberment." Dismemberment disappeared from the military instrument and from the Declaration issued on June 5 by the victorious powers.[7]

The United States and Britain delayed carrying out the zonal occupation agreement ratified at Yalta. In April, three weeks before Germany's surrender, Churchill proposed to Truman that British and American troops remain far within the future Soviet zone. He wanted to force the Soviets to provide food from their zone to the zones of the other three occupying powers. Ambassador John Winant "reacted strongly" to this "as a fatal blow to inter-Allied confidence, and to prospects of any measure of Allied co-operations in Germany." Churchill nonetheless insisted on altering the military surrender document because, as he told Eisenhower, he feared that the provisions for joint control gave Stalin a lever to demand Allied troop withdrawal from the Soviet zones. The surrender document was accordingly changed. The Allied Control Council was put on ice. Despite this, Stalin appointed Zhukov as the Soviet delegate to the Council when Hopkins advised him that Eisenhower would represent the United States. Eisenhower pressured for the withdrawal of troops from the Soviet zone, but the Joint Chiefs of Staff refused. Finally on June 12, Truman, responding to the position taken by Hopkins and Eisenhower, as well as to fear of a "strong public reaction," notified Churchill: "I am unable to delay the withdrawal of American troops from the Soviet zone in order to use pressure in the settlement of other problems." [8]

The West was not through tampering with the zonal agreement. The French zone, as decided earlier, was to be created from the existing American and British zones. Yet a new Anglo-American zonal protocol insisted that a French sector be created in Berlin by taking a *Bezirk* from the Soviet section. Philip Mosely found the War Department "adamant on the question of detaching one *Bezirk* from the Soviet sector in Berlin. The Western commanders had urged the Soviets to continue supplying all of Berlin with food and fuel for the economic needs of Berlin."

The Soviet government responded angrily to this breach of agreement. It complained in the E.A.C. that such a proposal was contrary to Yalta; it authorized General Zhukov to decline to supply all the Allies with food; it decided not to work with the Allies so closely and instead to establish the Soviet zone as a separate economic and political area. John Winant's warning of the consequences of America's unilateral policy was borne out: "I fear we may cause deep and deplorable discouragement on the British side and indifference on the part of the Russians and thereby jeopardize the chances of obtaining effective Anglo-Russian-American cooperation for the immediate post-war hostilities." [9]

The Far East agreement was similarly delayed. Following Yalta, American governmental circles openly debated whether the United States should fulfill its agreement. The American government began to believe that Russia should be kept out of the war against Japan because Soviet influence would unquestionably grow at the expense of American influence. They postulated that Russia might seize Manchuria and even Inner Mongolia. (She did not—nor is there any evidence that she had any such intention, except in official minds in Washington.) As a temporary expedient, Washington delayed notifying the Chinese of the Yalta agreement, as Roosevelt had agreed to do. But the Chinese, already eager for a favorable relationship with the Soviet Union, were ready to offer concessions beyond the Yalta recommendations. Alarmed by a possible Soviet-Chinese agreement not arranged by America, Washington maneuvered to postpone the proposed bilateral agreement as long as possible. But it proved impossible to keep the Soviet Union out of the Far Eastern war, and eventually the agreement reached at Yalta came into effect. The United States, however, was successful in rendering the Soviet role on the control commission for Japan virtually ineffective—as she had done in Italy, and as the Soviet Union in retaliation had done in Eastern Europe.

YALTA AS HISTORY

The conclusions reached in this work differ from the conclusions reached by previous American diplomatic scholars—both of "orthodox" and "revisionist" persuasions—on the nature of several decisions made at Yalta. Here we will attempt, through a comparison with several representative and serious studies, to delineate these differences. After this, the negotiating positions of the three sides will be examined and charted. The points of discrepancy referred to in this chapter are illustrated graphically on the chart on page 286.

John Snell, in *The Meaning of Yalta,* stated "the essential meaning of Yalta so far as Germany—and much of Europe—is concerned" was "how can the threat of German power be eliminated from Europe without leaving Soviet power dominant throughout the continent?" Snell intimated that this concern was reflected in the decisions of the Conference. He argued specifically that "the Russians failed to win full satisfaction on a single one of the demands they raised at Yalta concerning Germany's future." Thus triumphed a "hard rock of Anglo-American solidarity" and a policy of "moderation toward Germany." [10]

Gabriel Kolko, in his recent book, *The Politics of War,* similarly viewed the decisions on Germany as a "substantial accomplishment for the Americans and English, who alone obtained tangible concessions, and above all secured Russian approval to the formal postponement of a German problem." Therefore, "Germany represented a success for the English and Americans." [11]

These conclusions about Yalta cannot be substantiated. The position of the President of the United States regarding Germany coincided in almost every instance with the Soviet position. In fact, as we have seen, America's, and to a lesser extent, Britain's, policy, was the basis of Soviet policy itself. One can hardly visualize an Anglo-American "team," in this case: the conflict over Germany was as much between Churchill and Roosevelt as between Churchill and Stalin; Roosevelt and Stalin agreed. Certainly Roosevelt, who considered that he had made decisions on each one of the issues related to Germany, was not in this instance following a "policy of postponement." Further, Snell and Kolko assume a consistent Western anti-Soviet stance in the negotiations at Yalta. In fact, Yalta was more free of ideological content than has been supposed. The President did not follow a policy of "moderation toward Germany"; instead, he advocated harsh treatment of Germany. He sided with the Soviet Union *against* Great Britain on both dismemberment and reparations, with the result that Churchill acquiesced to a proposal on the first and agreed in principle to the second.

Snell, while citing the Soviet reparations plan as similar to the Morgenthau plan, hailed the Yalta reparations agreement as "a clear-cut rejection of the Morgenthau plan." [12] Yet the reparations agreement at Yalta, with only slight modifications, *was* the Soviet reparations proposal to which the United States agreed.

Snell claimed that Russia came out behind on reparations. Maisky, he wrote, weakened the concession received from Stettinius "by stating on February 10 that the proposed Russo-American draft 'did not commit the Allies to the exact figure' " [13] Since previous discussions and draftings of the protocol had always made clear that there was *no* exact figure, Maisky's remark must be seen as a restatement of the situation rather than a "weakening." The United States did not escape its responsibility; it endorsed the sum.

Snell concluded: "All in all, the reparations decisions were a thinly disguised defeat for the Russians." Roosevelt had "sidetracked the Soviet movement for American aid." He found that the "British and Americans put up a stiffer fight on reparations than on dismemberment," which was a victory for Roosevelt's policy, backed by Churchill, of "postponement." [14] This cannot be the case: the American delegation called the Soviet reparations plan reasonable and assured the Soviet Union that the United States supported it. Churchill and Eden disagreed but were unsuccessful in prying the Americans away from the Russians at Yalta. Their success in changing Roosevelt's policy came *after* Yalta. Further Soviet aid in other forms was hardly "sidetracked" at Yalta. The question was not officially raised by Stalin; however, Roosevelt did volunteer on February 8 that the United States intended to give substantial help to the U.S.S.R. after the war.

The official Soviet history of the war made a blanket statement without qualifying the circumstances: "At Potsdam the United States refused to follow the Yalta 'agreement' on the establishment of a specific sum of German reparations ($20,000,000,000), motivated by the fact that some parts of Germany suffered little destruction, namely, the parts occupied by the West." At Yalta this sum was agreed to as a basis of discussion or, in other words, it was agreed to establish it at a later date as a specific sum. As an indication of intention, the United States delegation did assure the Soviets that they found the sum equitable and intended to support it.

A harder look must be taken at the Soviet position on a French zone and French participation on the Allied Control Council. Herbert Feis, in *Churchill, Roosevelt, Stalin,* concluded that Russia resisted a zone for France "until the Conference was nearly over." [15] This is incorrect. On February 5, the first day France was discussed in tripartite session, Stalin at first followed Roosevelt's stand of the previous day and opposed a zone for France, but later that same day Stalin readily agreed to a French zone when Roosevelt did. Perhaps Feis had in mind the French role on the Allied Control Council, which was not decided until the final day of the Conference. In this instance the Soviet Union altered its position to harmonize with the Americans shortly after they learned what the President's position was.

In *The Politics of War* Kolko concluded, "Stalin was reluctantly prepared to let the English and Americans assign France an occupation zone." Stalin was a realist. He was prepared to grant the French a role; however, his reluctance was triggered by (and was perhaps entirely the result of) Roosevelt's stand. Kolko suggested: "The Allies resolved only one question pertaining to Germany at Yalta and that was France's role in the occupation." This is correct only in terms of *eventual* resolutions. In terms of the decisions made at Yalta, *two* questions were resolved—dismemberment and the role of France—and the basis of a third agreement—reparations—was created.

Forrest Pogue evaluated Stalin's strategy on the United Nations at Yalta in his essay, "The Big Three and the U.N.". He found Stalin's policy "like Roosevelt's on Germany and Poland, one of postponement." In this framework he viewed Stalin's statement that he had not had time to study the Dumbarton Oaks proposals as a postponement tactic. Molotov "persisted in his postponement tactics" the next day in the foreign ministers' meeting. Finally Churchill, he claimed, adopted Stalin's postponement tactics.[16]

Although postponing agreement does of course entail a delay, this delay did not constitute a grand policy. Stalin's delay initially resulted from questions about applying the voting formula. Since the State Department had altered its proposal a number of times, both the British and Soviets (as well as Roosevelt before Yalta) were confused by it. Stettinius appeared to make a further last minute alteration in it the very day when Stalin allegedly implemented his strategy of postponement.

Stalin hesitated for two reasons. First, he sought assurance. He was perfectly willing to agree to the President's proposal provided it did not isolate or disadvantage the Soviet Union. Churchill's acceptance (hardly adopting Stalin's tactics of postponement) helped convince Stalin. *After* Stalin decided to announce his acceptance of the formula, Molotov remained quiet in the foreign ministers' meeting. At the plenary session acceptance of the voting formula was announced and it was linked to the Soviet proposal on Poland.

Second, there were two *quid pro quos* implicit in the United Nations issues. The first has already been mentioned above, i.e. Roosevelt's favorable response to the Soviet's Polish proposal in return for Stalin's acceptance of the voting formula. But there was also Britain's: the Soviet Union accepted the voting formula; in return Britain supported the admission of two (reduced from sixteen) Soviet Republics to the General Assembly. Molotov announced, "We paid much attention to what Churchill told us." Churchill cabled the War Cabinet that it was "due to our explanation that they had found themselves in a position to embrace the scheme whole-heartedly." He strongly urged the War Cabinet to authorize adding the Republics: "I should like to be able to make a friendly gesture to Russia in this matter." [17]

These *quid pro quos* have generally gone unnoticed. In fact, the whole change in the Soviet position is often ignored. For example, Feis dismissed the Soviet acceptance of the American formula with one sentence: "Of a sudden on the day after this discussion, the Soviet Government made a surprising change of front." After a paraphrase of Molotov's brief statement, Feis dropped the issue.

The decisions on Poland have generally been viewed unfavorably by American historians. A variety of reasons for the decisions have been provided, ranging from Roosevelt's "sell-out" to his ill-health, to his disinterest, to other such voluntaristic appraisals. Among deterministic evaluations there is that of Feis, who asserted, "They were paying the full price for coalition and Soviet military cooperation." Charles F. Delzell, in his essay in *The Meaning of Yalta,* concluded, "Obviously, it was not a question of what they would permit him to do but what they could persuade him to accept." Quoting Admiral William D. Leahy, he reminded his readers the Russians could take the "elastic" agreement and "stretch it all the way from Yalta to Washington without ever technically breaking it." [18] These deterministic accounts at least touch on the facts as they existed at the time of the Conference.

Whatever the view one holds, another perspective must be considered in an appraisal of the Polish decision. The Soviet Union had been willing, for the sake of agreement with Britain, to come to terms with the Polish exile government, which was completely unco-operative and anti-Soviet. The London Poles had received verbal assurances from President Roosevelt that led them to believe their cause and its anti-Bolshevistic aims would eventually triumph. But Roosevelt, playing with the London group for reasons of domestic politics, was unconcerned with Polish affairs. Believing they had American support, the London Poles would not negotiate; the Soviet Union finally turned to the Poles who *would* negotiate. The tragedy of Poland is less the agreement at Yalta than that no agreement was reached *before* Yalta. Further, when the United States decided to reject its own Yalta policy following Roosevelt's death, it virtually went to war —albeit a "cold" one—like Don Quixote fighting his windmills. Washington, not Moscow, prevented a settlement which might have left Europe intact rather than divided into blocs and camps. Both Churchill and Stalin were realists; Roosevelt was a moralist, with intermittent periods of realism. In terms of decisions, Yalta was a brief and reasonable interlude rather than a consistent feature of American foreign policy.

Gar Alperowitz, in *Atomic Diplomacy: Hiroshima and Potsdam*, advanced two hypotheses to which some exception must be taken. First, he suggested that Truman's foreign policy was basically a departure from Roosevelt's. Due to Roosevelt's ambivalence and vacillations, a case can certainly be made for this conclusion, especially if Yalta is taken as a typical example of Rooseveltian policy. However, Roosevelt in Washington and in conversations with his advisers demonstrated many of the views and attitudes that found a logical conclusion in the Truman administration. It is hard to say in sum what Roosevelt's postwar policy would have been. Second, Alperowitz depicted the May 1945 talks between Harry Hopkins and Stalin as a new agreement or compromise. Actually, Hopkins's agreements with Stalin were Washington's *return* to the Yalta agreements, as Stalin well recognized. To some extent, there was before May a break between Truman and Roosevelt's Yalta policy. However, Hopkins' meeting with Stalin was not a compromise but an affirmation, albeit temporary, of the Yalta agreements.

YALTA AS A NEGOTIATING EXPERIENCE

Was Yalta the "dawn of the new day we had all been praying for and talking about for so many years," as Harry Hopkins stated as he left Yalta, or was it "the high point of Soviet diplomatic success and correspondingly the low point of American appeasement," as William Henry Chamberlin stated it? [19]

These judgments lie at either end of a spectrum of sentiment obscuring that fateful meeting in February 1945. For too long the Conference has been viewed as a success if the Americans won on every point and the Russians lost on every point. Even from this perspective interpretations differ, because estimates of what the Americans or the Russians wanted differ.

Perhaps the only realistic way to consider Yalta is as a traditional diplomatic negotiating situation, removed from its emotionally charged context. Toward the end of the war several issues were being unilaterally resolved by the various sides. At Yalta the Three Powers thrashed out their perspectives on these issues.[20]

There were five main issues that took up most of the time at Yalta, three of them problems related to a German settlement. It seems useful to recapitulate the process of reaching a decision on these issues in terms of what individual nations sought to accomplish by their negotiating positions. In this way some conclusion can be reached as to the reasonableness of the decisions and negotiating stances of the three nations at this tripartite meeting. The chart on page 286 shows the initial proposal by the sponsoring nation in the upper left hand corner; the opposing and subsequent positions over time can be followed in relation to this.

Reparations

The Soviet delegation presented a reparations plan (I-a) which Churchill opposed. Stalin was confronted from the onset with Churchill's pessimism and reluctance to accept a proposal for a specific payment in amount and kind by Germany because, argued the British Prime Minister, the Germans could not afford to pay. In contrast, Roosevelt's words were more lenient and, without a definite commitment, aligned him with the Soviets, who held a harsher view of Germany's responsibility. Readily agreeing to Churchill's suggestion to establish a Reparations

Commission in Moscow (I-b) as an interim solution, Stalin then argued in favor of establishing instructions for the Commission.

Molotov proposed that the Soviet principles be accepted by the three nations as a guideline in deciding reparations (I-c). Without contest, Eden added a new principle, and the principles seemed mutually acceptable. The United States again brought the question into prominence by offering a concrete proposal (I-d) in a foreign ministers' meeting two days later, and this plan, close to the original Soviet proposal, became the basis of final agreement. But this strong stand was again rejected by Britain. Molotov settled on the spot for a written agreement of American support (I-e).

The following day, Britain attempted once again, this time by introducing a counterproposal, (I-f) to alter the main features of the plan. When the heads of state met again in plenary session, Stalin immediately took umbrage at a remark made by Roosevelt which seemed to indicate a possible reversal of the American position and the adoption by the Americans of a British solution. Challenging both Washington and London to clarify their intentions, Stalin won further assurance from Roosevelt that he was completely in agreement with Soviet policy. Churchill continued to disassociate Britain from the agreement. Stalin then (I-g) sought minimal agreement from Britain, but when this also failed, he retreated to the Soviet-American agreement of a fixed sum for consideration by the Reparations Commission and the statement of principles.

The Dismemberment of Germany

Stalin altered the original agenda for February 5 (II-a) when he called for a discussion of Allied intentions to dismember Germany in light of the Morgenthau plan. Churchill reacted negatively to dismemberment, but Roosevelt positively. In the foreign ministers' meeting (II-b), Anthony Eden proposed that the word "dismemberment" be changed to "dissolution." Molotov vigorously disagreed and began to argue for an increased Allied commitment to dismember Germany. Stettinius stepped in (II-c), and the three nations were reconciled; they agreed to the inclusion of the word "dismemberment" in the protocol, the terms of surrender, and the immediate plan for postwar Germany.

The foreign ministers quibbled somewhat over the next question they had to resolve (II-d), namely, how the committee for dismemberment would work. Molotov envisioned that the committee should have the minimal function of studying procedure. Eden sought instructions that included France on the committee; and Stettinius suggested using the existing European Advisory Council. Unable to settle the question satisfactorily, the ministers agreed to let the Commission itself decide whether France was a member of it (II-e).

The Immediate Postwar Role of France

Through British initiative, the consideration of a zone for France was scheduled. Stalin, knowing from an earlier conversation with Roosevelt that America opposed elevating France to the role of a victor in the German settlement, played the antagonist. Tactically arguing the many (III-a) issues which this question provoked, Stalin assailed the proposal until Roosevelt announced (III-b) that American troops would leave Europe in two years. The immediate result of this announcement was that Churchill changed his argument from one that France should be an exception in the German settlement to the argument that France was necessary now to share in the protection of Europe. Stalin now moved to back Churchill. France could have a zone, he said, but not reparations.

In a foreign ministers' meeting, Molotov proposed that France be subordinate to the Control Council for Germany, but Eden insisted that France be an equal member of the Council (III-c). When Molotov (III-d) called for approval of the Soviet proposal, Eden refused. Stettinius and then Molotov supported postponing the question until it could be considered by the European Advisory Council. Eden remained adamant that the decision be made immediately. The stalemate continued until February 10, when Roosevelt decided to switch to the support of Churchill, and Stalin went along (III-e).

Questions Relating to Poland

Churchill and Roosevelt (IV-a) broached the issue of Poland on the second day of the conference. They indicated acceptance of the old Curzon Line as the Soviet-Polish border, granted certain Soviet principles as operative, and stressed their predominant concern for guaranteeing a democratic Polish government. Recognizing the predominant Soviet interest in Poland, they asked for concessions. Stalin replied, outlining a strong case for Big Three agreement on existing Soviet policy for reasons of both democracy and security.

Roosevelt (IV-b) sent Stalin a letter just prior to the next plenary session, suggesting that Stalin's recommendation to bring the Poles to Yalta be implemented; the Poles could then form a government recognizable by the three Allies. Stalin briefly rebutted the proposal, then displaced the issue with one far closer to Roosevelt's heart—the American voting formula for the United Nations (refer to V-b). In a dramatic shift of emphasis, Russia accepted Roosevelt's formula. Molotov then went back to the Polish question, putting forth a proposal (IV-c) which incorporated Stalin's position of the previous day with some modifications that took into account the requests made by Roosevelt and Churchill. Roosevelt announced that he was pleased with the compromise, while Churchill remained aloof.

The following day both Roosevelt and Churchill presented proposals on Poland at the plenary session (IV-d). Stalin responded by asking what substantively the three did agree upon? (For example, was the West prepared to abandon the exiled Polish government?) Next, Stalin rejected Roosevelt's proposed Presidential Council on the basis that a Polish government (Lublin) already existed.

Summarizing the issues already agreed upon, Stalin gained assurance (IV-e) that the Polish-Soviet frontier was not in question. The question of elections showing popular support for a government remained a key issue, although all agreed that there would be free elections. Heated exchanges between Soviet and British diplomats indicated that no agreement, implicit or explicit, could be reached without acceptance of the Soviet proposal in some form. In the course of debate, Roosevelt's position began to shift again toward the agreement he had expressed the previous day (refer to IV-c); he clarified it by stating that, since elections would be held within a month, disagreement on the interim government was not of great consequence. Thus the alignment by the end of February 8 (IV-f) in a sense completed the shift of balance.

The next day President Roosevelt proposed a compromise (IV-g) which embodied the Soviet proposal and the established points of agreement up to that point. Molotov took the initiative by launching an attack on Britain on an *ersatz* issue, but Churchill nonetheless withstood the combined pressure. Roosevelt (IV-h), assuming the function of mediator, insisted that remaining differences in posture were only slight. Without diminishing the breadth of Soviet-American agreement, Molotov rejected wording in the proposal that required active implementation of observation of the elections. Simultaneously, Stalin accepted Roosevelt's terminology for the expanded Lublin government. Almost as a measure of friction during the crystallization of this alignment, Churchill broke out in anger over his suspicions of Roosevelt's United Nations trusteeship concept (refer to V-k).

The special foreign ministers' session scheduled for the evening of February 9 centered on the British proposal to modify the emerging Polish solution. After stating a clear stand taken in London by the War Cabinet, Eden asked for major changes. He submitted a revised formula of the American proposal. Molotov countered this by altering the unacceptable points and restructuring it until it substantively returned to the Soviet original and American compromise proposals. (IV-i).

The final stage of agreement occurred on the next day, when the specific wording was agreed upon. Molotov incorporated into the Conference protocol the sum of agreements during different stages of the Conference. This was then the last agreement (IV-j).

Decisions Relating to the United Nations

Roosevelt raised the question of the United Nations, threatening trouble over the German peace unless the American voting formula for the United Nations were adopted (V-a). Stalin questioned the possible use of this formula against Russia, and Churchill insisted that Britain's imperial interests be protected.

Stalin (V-b) accepted the American voting formula (refer to scenario immediately above in chart to note timing, IV-b and c). The British also concurred. Stalin then requested United Nations membership for two or three Soviet Republics in addition. Churchill made a similar request by Britain (V-c). Roosevelt attempted to overlook this issue and moved on to the American list of nations to be invited to the San Francisco Conference and to the wording of the invitations. The three heads of state found they were unable to agree, so these issues were referred to the foreign ministers. Eden initiated the question of the two Soviet Republics (V-d); Stettinius followed Roosevelt's attempt to beg the question and move into invitations; and Molotov strongly stated his position, threatening discord on the question of invitations. Eden and Molotov (V-e) urged that the Republics be considered (Molotov favored immediate agreement on their treatment, but Eden wanted to delay agreement until the San Francisco Conference). Stettinius finally promised to take the question up with Roosevelt. After this meeting (V-f) and prior to the plenary session, Roosevelt agreed, stating that he did so because Britain backed the Soviet request.

Roosevelt (V-g) now could continue with his next item related to the formation of the United Nations, the list of nations to receive invitations to become original members. Stalin wanted the two Soviet Republics to be invited also and to become original members. Roosevelt (V-h) asked that his list be accepted. Parts of this session were confused, apparently because of the discrepancies in the criteria determining which nations would receive invitations. (Some had not signed the Declaration of the United Nations and yet would become original members, thus

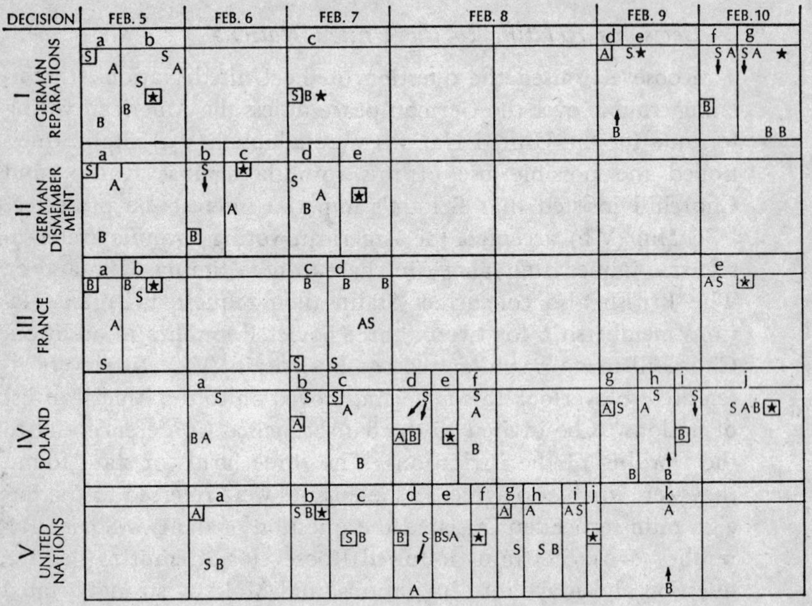

DECISION	FEB. 5	FEB. 6	FEB. 7	FEB. 8	FEB. 9	FEB. 10
I GERMAN REPARATIONS	a b		c		d e	f g
II GERMAN DISMEMBERMENT	a	b c	d e			
III FRANCE	a b		c d			e
IV POLAND		a	b c	d e f	g h i	j
V UNITED NATIONS		a	b c	d e f g h i j		k

KEY:
Placement from left to right signifies temporal sequence of statements. Placement from top to bottom signifies approximate distance between negotiating positions on a spectrum from unity (overlapping positions) ... to diametrically opposed positions. The original position of the nation initiating the proposal is placed in the upper left hand corner; opposition negotiating stances can be contrasted by scanning the chart.

A = USA   Ⓐ = USA Proposal   ✶ = Tripartite decision

B = GREAT BRITAIN   ↕ = Intense USA verbal attack   ★ = Bilateral decision

S = SOVIET UNION

Fig. II: Patterns of the Yalta Negotiations

individually receiving invitations.) Stalin, with Churchill's backing, sought acceptance of the two Soviet Republics as signers of the Declaration, to make certain that they would be original members. Granting that the Soviet Republics fulfilled the criteria for membership as well or better than some already listed, and yet unwilling to jeopardize the United Nations project, Roosevelt professed embarrassment (V-i); and Stalin, in deference, withdrew his request. By the end of the meeting (V-j), Roosevelt had agreed to membership at San Francisco of the Soviet Republics. Stalin continued to seek equal treatment of the Republics, and Churchill supported him.

Conclusions on the Diplomatic Process

A study of these decisions as they were made at Yalta indicates that several conclusions can be made about the Conference as a tripartite negotiating experience. Although the Great Powers differed in their initial viewpoints, a high incidence of consensus was reached at the Conference. The Allied coalition, which had been primarily military in nature, produced at last an impetus to nonmilitary agreement among all three parties—on the assumption that consensus was in the best interest of each of the parties. Most importantly, each nation had an issue of prime importance to it, and each gained support from its other two Allies. Britain's insistence on reviving France in the creation of a Western bloc was agreed to by Roosevelt and Stalin; America's voting formula for the United Nations, the subject on which the United States spent much of its diplomatic effort during the war, did not meet the opposition Washington feared; the Soviet Union, which was determined to prevent another hostile Polish government on its borders, gained support for the Lublin committee, although in a compromise form. But two Soviet desires, reparations and Poland's western frontier, remained unresolved, the former because of Churchill's instructions from the War Cabinet, and the latter because of an Anglo-American reluctance to make a frontier arrangement.

The Conference functioned reasonably on the basis of balanced diplomatic interaction. Agreement between two parties tended to assure agreement of the third, even if the third party was reluctant: Stalin used Roosevelt's support for dismemberment and reparations, and his agreement to an expansion of the Lublin committee as the basis for the government of Poland, in order to force British concurrence. (In the case of reparations, only a two-way agreement resulted on the details, but a three-way agreement was achieved on the establishment of a Reparations Commission.) British support for admission of two Soviet Republics to the United Nations led Roosevelt (by his own admission) to accept that proposal. Stalin's acquiescence to a zone for France in Germany promptly followed a shift by Roosevelt to the same position. When it seemed apparent that Britain would accept the American voting formula in the United Nations, Stalin also concurred.

A review of the contents of original proposals, compared with subsequent proposals and final agreements, indicates that the Soviet Union in particular tended to incorporate compromises and suggestions in order to achieve agreement. During the Conference the Soviet Union and the United States made six major proposals on prime topics and Britain made five. Of the five topics listed on the chart, the Soviet Union took the initiative on two issues, both on Germany and eventually a third, on Poland (although the first proposal came from Roosevelt). America took the initiative on one issue, and Britain on one. Considering the favorable military position of the Soviet Union as well as the disappointments of her earlier diplomatic encounters with the West, the Soviet Union showed a co-operative and conciliatory stance, which at the time of the Conference was recognized by many participants.

Soviet "stubbornness" or "obstructionism" can be argued only if one accepts the hypothesis that the Soviet Union ought to have accepted as just and superior any proposal which differed from the Soviet position.

In retrospect, we see a diplomatic encounter in which all sides, not without misgivings and harsh words, struggled to achieve their aims, but an encounter in which they prized agreement by traditional negotiation as preferable to unilateral action which might undermine international stability. Herein lies the meaning of the Yalta agreements, which provided an alternative to a "Cold War."

FINAL THOUGHTS

During World War II the United States was treading a path of expanding global "responsibility" and simultaneously fighting four wars to that end. The first was the military war against Germany, and the second the military war against Japan in the Pacific. The third was a struggle with Great Britain, allegedly to "defeat colonialism" (in American terms) but actually to determine which power would control Europe and Asia economically and politically. The last was the long-standing ideological struggle against "bolshevist" Russia, which continued, though intermittently, during the war. That struggle increased in focus and intensity as the Soviet Union emerged from the war with Great Power status.

Although American policy reputedly rested on the high-minded principles of the Atlantic Charter, those principles were invoked mainly to ward off British or Soviet threats to American plans. During the war, co-operation, the cornerstone of wartime diplomacy, was sorely pressed. Roosevelt gave the Soviet Union several "opportunities" to demonstrate its co-operativeness. One critical "opportunity" came up in 1942, when the President invited Molotov to Washington to plan a second front for that year. Simultaneously Roosevelt encouraged the Soviet Union to drop the provision in the proposed Anglo-Soviet treaty which recognized the incorporation of the Baltic states into the Soviet Union. Molotov did so, and in return he received a written commitment for the invasion of France—which Roosevelt dropped when Churchill objected. At the same time the President seized the initiative on Stalin's request for a postwar guarantee of co-operation—Roosevelt began to plan the United Nations, a slightly updated League of Nations with its membership dominated by America's allies. (Russia, of course, had been expelled by the League after attacking Finland.)

By 1943, both Anthony Eden and Ivan Maisky were openly discussing the two policy alternatives which the Soviet Union would decide upon after the war: unilateral action, or co-operation with her Western Allies. Eden informed Washington that the Soviet Union preferred the latter course. Maisky emphatically affirmed this judgment. Washington hindered Great Britain from adjusting Anglo-Soviet policy and held out to the Soviet Union promises of postwar aid, co-operation, and amicable adjustments, while resolving nothing. The few tripartite negotiating experiences, such as the Italian surrender and the European Advisory Commission, raised serious questions about American intentions. On the other hand, the Soviet Union during the war remained basically co-operative. American officials complained of the frustrations of dealing with the Soviet central bureaucracy, but this did not constitute Soviet unwillingness to co-operate.

In the wake of Soviet military victories, Roosevelt at last decided it was time to resolve issues which he had postponed for three years. The Yalta Conference met with a sense of deliberation. It was to be a test of the ability of the three nations to resolve the issues dividing them. It was a moment when American ideology, normally submerged in moralistic phrases uncharacteristic of its actual behaviour, was submitted to a traditional negotiating experience with binding results. Roosevelt and Churchill, when they met personally with Stalin, tended to treat the Soviet Union as the nation it was—an existing state with increasing influence in world affairs. The decisions at Yalta involved compromise by each nation, probably more by the Soviets than by the Western nations.

By abandoning the Conference agreements after Yalta, America created a self-fulfilling prophecy. Believing that the Soviets intended to take advantage of any opportunity at the expense of the United States, Washington tried to renegotiate the zonal agreements and held Western troops in Soviet occupation zones as a political pressure tactic. Further, the American government changed its interpretation of the Yalta decisions on Poland. After deserting the original American-Soviet viewpoint, the United States accused the Soviet Union of breaking the Yalta agreements. Finally, the Allies decided, contrary to Yalta, not to support reparations. In doing so they abandoned the Soviet Union. These decisions, and many others, left the Soviet Union with no alternative than to substitute unilateral action for a policy of co-operation which they had hoped for, but which had never emerged—except briefly, at Yalta.

The Yalta Conference has been more condemned than commended by Western commentators. Under most of these condemnations lies the implicit and unexpressed premise that the Soviet Union is in essence evil while the West embodies the virtues of the ages; and, further, a belief that the Soviet Union has and can have no interests which the West considers legitimate. American policy during the war and afterward has been studied in terms of what the United States failed to do to foil Soviet aims, or else in terms of what the United States could have done to alter a decision acceptable to the Soviet Union. The policies based on this ideological bent attributed false motives to the Soviet Union and created a situation in which the Soviet Union increasingly defended herself from Western hostility.

Roosevelt's departure from America's moralistic and anti-Soviet bias, combined with Churchill's usually consistent realism, served diplomacy for the week the leaders met at Yalta. But the postwar world bears little resemblance to what these men worked to achieve. Broken promises, bad faith, misperceptions, and self-righteousness have forced new and different policies upon the nations. We are living with the problems of a world that did not benefit from the experience at Yalta.

It is perhaps relevant to ask what the world would have been like if the spirit of Yalta had triumphed.

APPENDIX A

TRIPARTITE AGREEMENTS OF

THE YALTA CONFERENCE

The documents in this Appendix are taken from *Foreign Relations of the United States: Diplomatic Papers: The Conferences at Malta and Yalta, 1945*, pp. 968–84.

COMMUNIQUÉ ISSUED AT THE END OF THE CONFERENCE

REPORT OF THE CRIMEA CONFERENCE

For the past eight days, Winston S. Churchill, Prime Minister of Great Britain, Franklin D. Roosevelt, President of the United States of America, and Marshal J. V. Stalin, Chairman of the Council of Peoples' Commissars of the Union of Soviet Socialist Republics have met with the Foreign Secretaries, Chiefs of Staff and other advisors in the Crimea.

In addition to the three Heads of Government, the following took part in the Conference:

For the United States of America:

Edward R. Stettinius, Jr., Secretary of State
Fleet Admiral William D. Leahy, U.S.N., Chief of Staff to the President
Harry L. Hopkins, Special Assistant to the President

Justice James F. Byrnes, Director, Office of War Mobilization

General of the Army George C. Marshall, U.S.A., Chief of Staff, U.S. Army

Fleet Admiral Ernest J. King, U.S.N., Chief of Naval Operations and Commander in Chief, U.S. Fleet

Lieutenant General Brehon B. Somervell, Commanding General, Army Service Forces

Vice Admiral Emory S. Land, War Shipping Administrator

Major General L. S. Kuter, U.S.A., Staff of Commanding General, U.S. Army Air Forces

W. Averell Harriman, Ambassador to the U.S.S.R.

H. Freeman Matthews, Director of European Affairs, State Department

Alger Hiss, Deputy Director, Office of Special Political Affairs, Department of State

Charles E. Bohlen, Assistant to the Secretary of State

together with political, military and technical advisors.

For the Soviet Union:

V. M. Molotov, People's Commissar for Foreign Affairs of the USSR

Admiral Kuznetsov, People's Commissar for the Navy

Army General Antonov, Deputy Chief of the General Staff of the Red Army

A. Ya. Vyshinski, Deputy People's Commissar for Foreign Affairs of the USSR

I. M. Maisky, Deputy People's Commissar for Foreign Affairs of the USSR

Marshal of Aviation Khydyakov

F. T. Gousev, Ambassador in Great Britain

A. A. Gromyko, Ambassador in U.S.A.

For the United Kingdom:

Anthony Eden, Secretary of State for Foreign Affairs

Lord Leathers, Minister of War Transport

Sir A. Clark Kerr, H. M. Ambassador at Moscow

Sir Alexander Cadogan, Permanent Under Secretary of State for Foreign Affairs

Sir Edward Bridges, Secretary of the War Cabinet

Field Marshal Sir Alan Brooke, Chief of the Imperial General Staff

Marshal of the Royal Air Force Sir Charles Portal, Chief of the Air Staff

Admiral of the Fleet Sir Andrew Cunningham, First Sea Lord
General Sir Hastings Ismay, Chief of Staff to the Minister of Defense, together with
Field Marshal Alexander, Supreme Allied Commander, Mediterranean Theatre
Field Marshal Wilson, Head of the British Joint Staff Mission at Washington
Admiral Somerville, Joint Staff Mission at Washington
together with military and diplomatic advisors.

The following statement is made by the Prime Minister of Great Britain, the President of the United States of America, and the Chairman of the Council of Peoples' Commissars of the Union of Soviet Socialist Republics on the results of the Crimean Conference:

I THE DEFEAT OF GERMANY

We have considered and determined the military plans of the three allied powers for the final defeat of the common enemy. The military staffs of the three allied nations have met in daily meetings throughout the Conference. These meetings have been most satisfactory from every point of view and have resulted in closer coordination of the military effort of the three Allies than ever before. The fullest information has been inter-changed. The timing, scope and co-ordination of new and even more powerful blows to be launched by our armies and air forces into the heart of Germany from the East, West, North and South have been fully agreed and planned in detail.

Our combined military plans will be made known only as we execute them, but we believe that the very close working partnership among the three staffs attained at this Conference will result in shortening the war. Meetings of the three staffs will be continued in the future whenever the need arises.

Nazi Germany is doomed. The German people will only make the cost of their defeat heavier to themselves by attempting to continue a hopeless resistance.

II THE OCCUPATION AND CONTROL OF GERMANY

We have agreed on common policies and plans for enforcing the unconditional surrender terms which we shall impose together on Nazi Germany after German armed resistance has been finally crushed. These terms will not be made known until the final defeat of Germany has been accomplished. Under the agreed plan, the forces of the Three

Powers will each occupy a separate zone of Germany. Coordinated administration and control has been provided for under the plan through a central Control Commission consisting of the Supreme Commanders of the Three Powers with headquarters in Berlin. It has been agreed that France should be invited by the Three Powers, if she should so desire, to take over a zone of occupation, and to participate as a fourth member of the Control Commission. The limits of the French zone will be agreed by the four governments concerned through their representatives on the European Advisory Commission.

It is our inflexible purpose to destroy German militarism and Nazism and to ensure that Germany will never again be able to disturb the peace of the world. We are determined to disarm and disband all German armed forces; break up for all time the German General Staff that has repeatedly contrived the resurgence of German militarism; remove or destroy all German military equipment; eliminate or control all German industry that could be used for military production; bring all war criminals to just and swift punishment and exact reparation in kind for the destruction wrought by the Germans; wipe out the Nazi party, Nazi laws, organizations and institutions, remove all Nazi and militarist influences from public office and from the cultural and economic life of the German people; and take in harmony such other measures in Germany as may be necessary to the future peace and safety of the world. It is not our purpose to destroy the people of Germany, but only when Nazism and Militarism have been extirpated will there be hope for a decent life for Germans, and a place for them in the comity of nations.

III REPARATION BY GERMANY

We have considered the question of the damage caused by Germany to the Allied Nations in this war and recognized it as just that Germany be obliged to make compensation for this damage in kind to the greatest extent possible. A Commission for the Compensation of Damage will be established. The Commission will be instructed to consider the question of the extent and methods for compensating damage caused by Germany to the Allied Countries. The Commission will work in Moscow.

IV UNITED NATIONS CONFERENCE

We are resolved upon the earliest possible establishment with our allies of a general international organization to maintain peace and security. We believe that this is essential, both to prevent aggression and to remove the political, economic and social causes of war through the close and continuing collaboration of all peace-loving peoples.

The foundations were laid at Dumbarton Oaks. On the important question of voting procedure, however, agreement was not there reached. The present conference has been able to resolve this difficulty.

We have agreed that a Conference of United Nations should be called to meet at San Francisco in the United States on April 25th, 1945, to prepare the charter of such an organization, along the lines proposed in the informal conversations at Dumbarton Oaks.

The Government of China and the Provisional Government of France will be immediately consulted and invited to sponsor invitations to the Conference jointly with the Governments of the United States, Great Britain and the Union of Soviet Socialist Republics. As soon as the consultation with China and France has been completed, the text of the proposals on voting procedure will be made public.

V DECLARATION ON LIBERATED EUROPE

We have drawn up and subscribed to a Declaration on liberated Europe. This Declaration provides for concerting the policies of the three Powers and for joint action by them in meeting the political and economic problems of liberated Europe in accordance with democratic principles. The text of the Declaration is as follows:

The Premier of the Union of Soviet Socialist Republics, the Prime Minister of the United Kingdom, and the President of the United States of America have consulted with each other in the common interests of the peoples of their countries and those of liberated Europe. They jointly declare their mutual agreement to concert during the temporary period of instability in liberated Europe the policies of their three governments in assisting the peoples liberated from the domination of Nazi Germany and the peoples of the former Axis satellite states of Europe to solve by democratic means their pressing political and economic problems.

The establishment of order in Europe and the rebuilding of national economic life must be achieved by processes which will enable the liberated peoples to destroy the last vestiges of Nazism and Fascism and to creat[e] democratic institutions of their own choice. This is a principle of the Atlantic Charter—the right of all peoples to choose the form of government under which they will live—the restoration of sovereign rights and self-government to those peoples who have been forcibly deprived of them by the aggressor nations.

To foster the conditions in which the liberated peoples may exercise these rights, the three governments will jointly assist the people in any European liberated state or former Axis satellite state in Europe where in their judgment conditions require (a) to establish conditions of internal peace; (b) to carry out emergency measures for the relief of distressed people; (c) to form interim governmental authorities broadly representative of all democratic elements in the population and pledged to the earliest possible establishment through free elections of governments responsive to the will of the people; and (d) to facilitate where necessary the holding of such elections.

The three governments will consult the other United Nations and provisional authorities or other governments in Europe when matters of direct interest to them are under consideration.

When, in the opinion of the three governments, conditions in any European liberated state or any former Axis satellite state in Europe make such action necessary, they will immediately consult together on the measures necessary to discharge the joint responsibilities set forth in this declaration.

By this declaration we reaffirm our faith in the principles of the Atlantic Charter, our pledge in the Declaration by the United Nations, and our determination to build in cooperation with other peace-loving nations a world order under law, dedicated to peace, security, freedom and the general well-being of all mankind.

In issuing this declaration, the Three Powers express the hope that the Provisional Government of the French Republic may be associated with them in the procedure suggested.

VI POLAND

We came to the Crimea Conference resolved to settle our differences about Poland. We discussed fully all aspects of the question. We reaffirm our common desire to see established a strong, free, independent and democratic Poland. As a result of our discussions we have agreed on the conditions in which a new Polish Provisional Government of National Unity may be formed in such a manner as to command recognition by the three major powers.

The agreement reached is as follows:

A new situation has been created in Poland as a result of her complete liberation by the Red Army. This calls for the establishment of a Polish Provisional Government which can be more broadly based than was possible before the recent liberation of western Poland. The Provisional Government which is now functioning in Poland should therefore be reorganized on a broader democratic basis with the inclusion of democratic leaders from Poland itself and from Poles abroad. This new Government should then be called the Polish Provisional Government of National Unity.

M. Molotov, Mr. Harriman and Sir A. Clark Kerr are authorized as a Commission to consult in the first instance in Moscow with members of the present Provisional Government and with other Polish democratic leaders from within Poland and from abroad, with a view to the reorganization of the present Government along the above lines. This Polish Provisional Government of National Unity shall be pledged to the holding of free and unfettered elections as soon as possible on the basis of universal suffrage and secret ballot. In these elections all democratic and anti-Nazi parties shall have the right to take part and to put forward candidates.

When a Polish Provisional Government of National Unity has been properly formed in conformity with the above, the Government of the U. S. S. R., which now maintains diplomatic relations with the present Provisional Government of Poland, and the Government of the United Kingdom and the Government of the United States will establish diplomatic relations with the new Polish Provisional Government of National Unity, and will exchange Ambassadors by whose reports the respective Governments will be kept informed about the situation in Poland.

The three Heads of Government consider that the eastern frontier of Poland should follow the Curzon Line with digressions from it in some regions of five to eight kilometers in favor of Poland. They recognize that Poland must receive substantial accessions of territory in the north and west. They feel that the opinion of the new Polish Provisional Government of National Unity should be sought in due course on the extent of these accessions and that the final delimitation of the western frontier of Poland should thereafter await the Peace Conference.

VII Yugoslavia

We have agreed to recommend to Marshal Tito and Dr. Subasic that the Agreement between them should be put into effect immediately, and that a new Government should be formed on the basis of that Agreement.

We also recommend that as soon as the new Government has been formed, it should declare that:

(i) The Anti-fascist Assembly of National Liberation (Avnoj) should be extended to include members of the last Yugoslav Parliament (Skupschina) who have not compromised themselves by collaboration with the enemy, thus forming a body to be known as a temporary Parliament; and

(ii) legislative acts passed by the Anti-Fascist Assembly of National Liberation (AUNOJ) will be subject to subsequent ratification by a Constituent Assembly.

There was also a general review of other Balkan question[s].

VIII MEETINGS OF FOREIGN SECRETARIES

Throughout the Conference, besides the daily meetings of the Heads of Governments and the Foreign Secretaries, separate meetings of the three Foreign Secretaries, and their advisers have also been held daily.

These meetings have proved of the utmost value and the Conference agreed that permanent machinery should be set up for regular consultation between the three Foreign Secretaries. They will, therefore, meet as often as may be necessary, probably about every three or four months. These meetings will be held in rotation in the three Capitals, the first meeting being held in London, after the United Nations Conference on world organization.

IX UNITY FOR PEACE AS FOR WAR

Our meeting here in the Crimea has reaffirmed our common determination to maintain and strengthen in the peace to come that unity of purpose and of action which has made victory possible and certain for the United Nations in this war. We believe that this is a sacred obligation which our Governments owe to our peoples and to all the peoples of the world.

Only with continuing and growing co-operation and understanding among our three countries and among all the peace-loving nations can the highest aspiration of humanity be realized—a secure and lasting peace which will, in the words of the Atlantic Charter, "afford assurance that all the men in all the lands may live out their lives in freedom from fear and want."

Victory in this war and establishment of the proposed international organization will provide the greatest opportunity in all history to create in the years to come the essential conditions of such a peace.

WINSTON S. CHURCHILL

FRANKLIN D. ROOSEVELT

И. СТАЛИН

February 11, 1945

PROTOCOL OF PROCEEDINGS

PROTOCOL OF THE PROCEEDINGS OF THE CRIMEA CONFERENCE

The Crimea Conference of the Heads of the Governments of the United States of America, the United Kingdom, and the Union of Soviet Socialist Republics which took place from February 4th to 11th came to the following conclusions.

I. WORLD ORGANIZATION

It was decided:

(1) that a United Nations Conference on the proposed world organisation should be summoned for Wednesday, 25th April, 1945, and should be held in the United States of America.

(2) the Nations to be invited to this Conference should be:

(a) the United Nations as they existed on the 8th February, 1945 and

(b) such of the Associated Nations as have declared war on the common enemy by 1st March, 1945. (For this purpose by the term "Associated Nation" was meant the eight Associated Nations and Turkey). When the Conference on World Organization is held, the delegates of the United Kingdom and United States of America will support a proposal to admit to original membership two Soviet Socialist Republics, i. e. the Ukraine and White Russia.

(3) that the United States Government on behalf of the Three Powers should consult the Government of China and the French Provisional Government in regard to the decisions taken at the present Conference concerning the proposed World Organisation.

(4) that the text of the invitation to be issued to all the nations which would take part in the United Nations Conference should be as follows:

Invitation

"The Government of the United States of America, on behalf of itself and of the Governments of the United Kingdom, the Union of Soviet Socialist Republics, and the Republic of China and of the Provisional Government of the French Republic, invite the Government of _____ to send representatives to a Conference of the United Nations to be held on 25th April, 1945, or soon thereafter, at San Francisco in the United States of America to prepare a Charter for a General International Organisation for the maintenance of international peace and security.

"The above named governments suggest that the Conference consider as affording a basis for such a Charter the Proposals for the Establishment of a General International Organisation, which were made public last October as a result of the Dumbarton Oaks Conference, and which have now been supplemented by the following provisions for Section C of Chapter VI:

" 'C. *Voting*

'1. Each member of the Security Council should have one vote.

'2. Decisions of the Security Council on procedural matters should be made by an affirmative vote of seven members.

'3. Decisions of the Security Council on all other matters should be made by an affirmative vote of seven members including the concurring votes of the permanent members; provided that, in decisions under Chapter VIII, Section A and under the second sentence of paragraph 1 of Chapter VIII, Section C, a party to a dispute should abstain from voting.'

"Further information as to arrangements will be transmitted subsequently.

"In the event that the Government of _____ desires in advance of the Conference to present views or comments concerning the proposals, the Government of the United States of America will be pleased to transmit such views and comments to the other participating Governments."

Territorial Trusteeship

It was agreed that the five Nations which will have permanent seats on the Security Council should consult each other prior to the United Nations Conference on the question of territorial trusteeship.

The acceptance of this recommendation is subject to its being made clear that territorial trusteeship will only apply to (a) existing mandates of the League of Nations; (b) territories detached from the enemy as a result of the present war; (c) any other territory which might voluntarily be placed under trusteeship; and (d) no discussion of actual territories is contemplated at the forthcoming United Nations Conference or in the preliminary consultations, and it will be a matter for subsequent agreement which territories within the above categories will be placed under trusteeship.

II. DECLARATION ON LIBERATED EUROPE

The following declaration has been approved:

"The Premier of the Union of Soviet Socialist Republics, the Prime Minister of the United Kingdom and the President of the United States of America have consulted with each other in the common interests of the peoples of their countries and those of liberated Europe. They jointly declare their mutual agreement to concert during the temporary period of instability in liberated Europe the policies of their three governments in assisting the peoples liberated from the domination of Nazi Germany and the peoples of the former Axis satellite states of Europe to solve by democratic means their pressing political and economic problems.

"The establishment of order in Europe and the re-building of national economic life must be achieved by processes which will enable the liberated peoples to destroy the last vestiges of Nazism and Fascism and to create democratic institutions of their own choice. This is a principle of the Atlantic Charter—the right of all peoples to choose the form of government under which they will live—the restoration of sovereign rights and self-government to those peoples who have been forcibly deprived of them by the aggressor nations.

"To foster the conditions in which the liberated peoples may exercise these rights, the three governments will jointly assist the people in any European liberated state or former Axis satellite state in Europe where in their judgment conditions require (a) to establish conditions of internal peace; (b) to carry out emergency measures for the relief of distressed peoples; (c) to form interim governmental authorities broadly representative of all democratic elements in the population and pledged to the earliest possible establishment through free elections of governments responsive to the will of the people; and (d) to facilitate where necessary the holding of such elections.

"The three governments will consult the other United Nations and provisional authorities or other governments in Europe when matters of direct interest to them are under consideration.

"When, in the opinion of the three governments, conditions in any European liberated state or any former Axis satellite state in Europe make such action necessary, they will immediately consult together on the measures necessary to discharge the joint responsibilities set forth in this declaration.

"By this declaration we reaffirm our faith in the principles of the Atlantic Charter, our pledge in the Declaration by the United Nations, and our determination to build in co-operation with other peace-loving nations world order under law, dedicated to peace, security, freedom and general well-being of all mankind.

"In issuing this declaration, the Three Powers express the hope that the Provisional Government of the French Republic may be associated with them in the procedure suggested."

III. DISMEMBERMENT OF GERMANY

It was agreed that Article 12 (*a*) of the Surrender Terms for Germany should be amended to read as follows:

"The United Kingdom, the United States of America and the Union of Soviet Socialist Republics shall possess supreme authority with respect to Germany. In the exercise of such authority they will take such steps, including the complete disarmament, demilitarisation and the dismemberment of Germany as they deem requisite for future peace and security."

The study of the procedure for the dismemberment of Germany was referred to a Committee, consisting of Mr. Eden (Chairman), Mr. Winant and Mr. Gousev. This body would consider the desirability of associating with it a French representative.

IV. ZONE OF OCCUPATION FOR THE FRENCH AND
CONTROL COUNCIL FOR GERMANY

It was agreed that a zone in Germany, to be occupied by the French Forces, should be allocated to France. This zone would be formed out of the British and American zones and its extent would be settled by the the British and Americans in consultation with the French Provisional Government.

It was also agreed that the French Provisional Government should be invited to become a member of the Allied Control Council for Germany.

V. REPARATION

The following protocol has been approved:

1. Germany must pay in kind for the losses caused by her to the Allied nations in the course of the war. Reparations are to be received in the first instance by those countries which have borne the main burden of the war, have suffered the heaviest losses and have organised victory over the enemy.

2. Reparation in kind is to be exacted from Germany in three following forms:

a) Removals within 2 years from the surrender of Germany or the cessation of organised resistance from the national wealth of Germany located on the territory of Germany herself as well as outside her territory (equipment, machine-tools, ships, rolling stock, German investments abroad, shares of industrial, transport and other enterprises in Germany etc.), these removals to be carried out chiefly for purpose of destroying the war potential of Germany.

b) Annual deliveries of goods from current production for a period to be fixed.

c) Use of German labour.

3. For the working out on the above principles of a detailed plan for exaction of reparation from Germany an Allied Reparation Commission will be set up in Moscow. It will consist of three representatives—one from the Union of Soviet Socialist Republics, one from the United Kingdom and one from the United States of America.

4. With regard to the fixing of the total sum of the reparation as well as the distribution of it among the countries which suffered from the German aggression the Soviet and American delegations agreed as follows:

"The Moscow Reparation Commission should take in its initial studies as a basis for discussion the suggestion of the Soviet Government that the total sum of the reparation in accordance with the points (a) and (b) of the paragraph 2 should be 20 billion dollars and that 50% of it should go to the Union of Soviet Socialist Republics."

The British delegation was of the opinion that pending consideration of the reparation question by the Moscow Reparation Commission no figures of reparation should be mentioned.

The above Soviet-American proposal has been passed to the Moscow Reparation Commission as one of the proposals to be considered by the Commission.

VI. MAJOR WAR CRIMINALS

The Conference agreed that the question of the major war criminals should be the subject of enquiry by the three Foreign Secretaries for report in due course after the close of the Conference.

VII. POLAND

The following Declaration on Poland was agreed by the Conference:

"A new situation has been created in Poland as a result of her complete liberation by the Red Army. This calls for the establishment of a Polish Provisional Government which can be more broadly based than was possible before the recent liberation of the Western part of Poland. The Provisional Government which is now functioning in Poland should therefore be reorganised on a broader democratic basis with the inclusion of democratic leaders from Poland itself and from Poles abroad. This new Government should then be called the Polish Provisional Government of National Unity.

"M. Molotov, Mr. Harriman and Sir A. Clark Kerr are authorised as a commission to consult in the first instance in Moscow with members of the present Provisional Government and with other Polish democratic leaders from within Poland and from abroad, with a view to the reorganisation of the present Government along the above lines. This Polish Provisional Government of National Unity shall be pledged to the holding of free and unfettered elections as soon as possible on the basis of universal suffrage and secret ballot. In these elections all democratic and anti-Nazi parties shall have the right to take part and to put forward candidates.

"When a Polish Provisional Government of National Unity has been properly formed in conformity with the above, the Government of the U. S. S. R., which now maintains diplomatic relations with the present Provisional Government of Poland, and the Government of the United Kingdom and the Government of the U. S. A. will establish diplomatic relations with the new Polish Provisional Government of National Unity, and will exchange Ambassadors by whose reports the respective Governments will be kept informed about the situation in Poland.

"The three Heads of Government consider that the Eastern frontier of Poland should follow the Curzon Line with digressions from it in some regions of five to eight killometers in favour of Poland. They recognise that Poland must receive substantial accessions of territory in the North and West. They feel that the opinion of the new Polish Provisional Government of National Unity should be sought in due course on the extent of these accessions and that the final delimitation of the Western frontier of Poland should thereafter await the Peace Conference."

VIII. YUGOSLAVIA

It was agreed to recommend to Marshal Tito and to Dr. Subasic:

(a) that the Tito-Subasic Agreement should immediately be put into effect and a new Government formed on the basis of the Agreement.

(b) that as soon as the new Government has been formed it should declare:

(i) that the Anti-Fascist Assembly of National Liberation (AUNOJ) will be extended to include members of the last Yugoslav Skupstina who have not compromised themselves by collaboration with the enemy, thus forming a body to be known as a temporary Parliament and

(ii) that legislative acts passed by the Anti-Fascist Assemb[l]y of National Liberation (AUNOJ) will be subject to subsequent ratification by a Constituent Assembly;

and that this statement should be published in the communique of the Conference.

IX. ITALO-YUGOSLAV FRONTIER ITALO-AUSTRIA FRONTIER

Notes on these subjects were put in by the British delegation and the American and Soviet delegations agreed to consider them and give their views later.

X. YUGOSLAV-BULGARIAN RELATIONS

There was an exchange of views between the Foreign Secretaries on the question of the desirability of a Yugoslav-Bulgarian pact of alliance. The question at issue was whether a state still under an armistice regime could be allowed to enter into a treaty with another state. Mr. Eden suggested that the Bulgarian and Yugoslav Governments should be informed that this could not be approved. Mr. Stettinius suggested that the British and American Ambassadors should discuss the matter further with M. Molotov in Moscow. M. Molotov agreed with the proposal of Mr. Stettinius.

XI. SOUTH EASTERN EUROPE

The British Delegation put in notes for the consideration of their colleagues on the following subjects:

(a) the Control Commission in Bulgaria

(b) Greek claims upon Bulgaria, more particularly with reference to reparations.

(c) Oil equipment in Roumania.

XII. IRAN

Mr. Eden, Mr. Stettinius and M. Molotov exchanged views on the situation in Iran. It was agreed that this matter should be pursued through the diplomatic channel.

XIII. MEETINGS OF THE THREE FOREIGN SECRETARIES

The Conference agreed that permanent machinery should be set up for consultation between the three Foreign Secretaries; they should meet as often as necessary, probably about every three or four months.

These meetings will be held in rotation in the three capitals, the first meeting being held in London.

XIV. THE MONTREUX CONVENTION AND THE STRAITS

It was agreed that at the next meeting of the three Foreign Secretaries to be held in London, they should consider proposals which it was understood the Soviet Government would put forward in relation to the Montreux Convention and report to their Governments. The Turkish Government should be informed at the appropriate moment.

The foregoing Protocol was approved and signed by the three Foreign Secretaries at the Crimean Conference, February 11, 1945.

E R STETTINIUS, JR

B. МОЛОТОВ.

ANTHONY EDEN

PROTOCOL ON GERMAN REPARATION

PROTOCOL ON THE TALKS BETWEEN THE HEADS OF THE THREE GOVERNMENTS AT THE CRIMEAN CONFERENCE ON THE QUESTION OF THE GERMAN REPARATION IN KIND

The Heads of the three governments agreed as follows:

1. Germany must pay in kind for the losses caused by her to the

Allied nations in the course of the war. Reparation are to be received in the first instance by those countries which have borne the main burden of the war, have suffered the heaviest losses and have organised victory over the enemy.

2. Reparation in kind are to be exacted from Germany in three following forms:

a) Removals within 2 years from the surrender of Germany or the cessation of organised resistance from the national wealth of Germany located on the territory of Germany herself as well as outside her territory (equipment, machine-tools, ships, rolling stock, German investments abroad, shares of industrial, transport and other enterprises in Germany etc.), these removals to be carried out chiefly for purpose of destroying the war potential of Germany.

b) Annual deliveries of goods from current production for a period to be fixed.

c) Use of German labour.

3. For the working out on the above principles of a detailed plan for exaction of reparation from Germany an Allied Reparation Commission will be set up in Moscow. It will consist of three representatives—one from the Union of Soviet Socialist Republics, one from the United Kingdom and one from the United States of America.

4. With regard to the fixing of the total sum of the reparation as well as the distribution of it among the countries which suffered from the German aggression the Soviet and American delegations agreed as follows:

"The Moscow Reparation Commission should take in its initial studies as a basis for discussion the suggestion of the Soviet Government that the total sum of the reparation in accordance with the points (a) and (b) of the paragraph 2 should be 20 billion dollars and that 50% of it should go to the Union of Soviet Socialist Republics."

The British delegation was of the opinion that pending consideration of the reparation question by the Moscow Reparation Commission no figures of reparation should be mentioned.

The above Soviet-American proposal has been passed to the Moscow Reparation Commission as one of the proposals to be considered by the Commission.

WINSTON S. CHURCHILL
FRANKLIN D ROOSEVELT
И. Сталин

February 11, 1945.

AGREEMENT REGARDING ENTRY OF THE SOVIET UNION INTO THE WAR AGAINST JAPAN

TOP SECRET

AGREEMENT

The leaders of the three Great Powers—the Soviet Union, the United States of America and Great Britain—have agreed that in two or three months after Germany has surrendered and the war in Europe has terminated the Soviet Union shall enter into the war against Japan on the side of the Allies on condition that:

1. The *status quo* in Outer-Mongolia (The Mongolian People's Republic) shall be preserved;

2. The former rights of Russia violated by the treacherous attack of Japan in 1904 shall be restored, viz:

   (*a*) the southern part of Sakhalin as well as all the islands adjacent to it shall be returned to the Soviet Union,

   (*b*) the commercial port of Dairen shall be internationalized, the preeminent interests of the Soviet Union in this port being safeguarded and the lease of Port Arthur as a naval base of the USSR restored,

   (*c*) the Chinese-Eastern Railroad and the South-Manchurian Railroad which provides an outlet to Dairen shall be jointly operated by the establishment of a joint Soviet-Chinese Company it being understood that the preeminent interests of the Soviet Union shall be safeguarded and that China shall retain full sovereignty in Manchuria;

3. The Kuril islands shall be handed over to the Soviet Union.

It is understood, that the agreement concerning Outer-Mongolia and the ports and railroads referred to above will require concurrence of Generalissimo Chiang Kai-Shek. The President will take measures in order to obtain this concurrence on advice from Marshal Stalin.

The Heads of the three Great Powers have agreed that these claims of the Soviet Union shall be unquestionably fulfilled after Japan has been defeated.

For its part the Soviet Union expresses its readiness to conclude with the National Government of China a pact of friendship and alliance between the USSR and China in order to render assistance to China with its armed forces for the purpose of liberating China from the Japanese yoke.

И. Сталин
Franklin D Roosevelt
Winston S. Churchill

February 11, 1945.

APPENDIX B

UNITED STATES DELEGATION MEMORANDUM

PROPOSED FORMULA FOR VOTING PROCEDURE IN THE SECURITY COUNCIL OF THE UNITED NATIONS ORGANIZATION AND ANALYSIS OF THE EFFECTS OF THAT FORMULA

I. Proposed formula as communicated on December 5, 1944 to Marshal Stalin and to Prime Minister Churchill (with a minor clarification of the reference to Chapter VIII, Section C).

The provisions of Section C. of Chapter VI of the Dumbarton Oaks proposals would read as follows:

"C. *Voting*

1. Each member of the Security Council should have one vote.
2. Decisions of the Security Council on procedural matters should be made by an affirmative vote of seven members.
3. Decisions of the Security Council on all other matters should be made by an affirmative vote of seven members including the concurring votes of the permanent members; provided that in decisions under Chapter VIII, Section A and under the second sentence of paragraph 1 of Chapter VIII, Section C, a party to a dispute should abstain from voting."

II. Analysis of effect of above formula on principal substantive decisions on which the Security Council would have to vote.

Under the above formula the following decisions would require the affirmative votes of seven members of the Security Council including the votes of all the permanent members:

I. Recommendations to the General Assembly on
   1. Admission of new members;
   2. Suspension of a member;
   3. Expulsion of a member;
   4. Election of the Secretary General.

II. Restoration of the rights and privileges of a suspended member.

III. Removal of threats to the peace and suppression of breaches of the peace, including the following questions:

    1. Whether failure on the part of the parties to a dispute to settle it by means of their own choice or in accordance with the recommendations of the Security Council in fact constitutes a threat to the peace;

    2. Whether any other actions on the part of any country constitute a threat to the peace or a breach of the peace;

    3. What measures should be taken by the Council to maintain or restore the peace and the manner in which such measures should be carried out;

    4. Whether a regional agency should be authorized to take measures of enforcement.

IV. Approval of special agreement or agreements for the provision of armed forces and facilities.

V. Formulation of plans for a general system of regulation of armaments and submission of such plans to the member states.

VI. Determination of whether the nature and the activities of a regional agency or arrangement for the maintenance of peace and security are consistent with the purposes and principles of the general organization.

The following decisions relating to peaceful settlement of disputes would also require the affirmative votes of seven members of the Security Council including the votes of all the permanent members, except that a member of the Council would not cast its vote in any such decisions that concern disputes to which it is a party:

I. Whether a dispute or a situation brought to the Council's attention is of such a nature that its continuation is likely to threaten the peace;

II. Whether the Council should call on the parties to settle or adjust the dispute or situation by means of their own choice;

III. Whether the Council should make a recommendation to the parties as to methods and procedures of settlement;

IV. Whether the legal aspects of the matter before it should be referred by the Council for advice to the international court of justice;

V. Whether, if there exists a regional agency for peaceful settlement of local disputes, such an agency should be asked to concern itself with the controversy.

NOTES

The following abbreviations have been used in the Notes:

Corr *Correspondence Between the Chairman of the Council of Ministers of the U.S.S.R. and the Presidents of the U.S.A. and the Prime Ministers of Great Britain During the Great Patriotic War of 1941–1945.* (2 Vols.; Moscow: Foreign Language Publishing House, 1957.) Cited as *Corr*, volume number, document title, date, page(s).

DPSR Instytut Historyczary Imienia Generala Sikorskiego. *Documents on Polish-Soviet Relations, 1939–1945.* (2 Vols.; London: Heinemann, 1961, 1967.) Cited as *DPSR*, volume number, page(s).

SCD (Soviet Crimea Documents). U.S.S.R. "Documents: The Crimea and Potsdam Conferences of the Leaders of the Three Great Powers." *International Affairs.* Nos. 6–10 (Moscow: June–October, 1965). Cited as *SCD*, issue number, page(s).

YD (Yalta Documents). U.S. Department of State, *Foreign Relations of the United States: Diplomatic Papers: The Conferences at Malta and Yalta, 1945.* (Washington, D.C.: U.S. Government Printing Office, 1955). Cited as *YD*, name of minute-taker, page(s), for minutes; cited as *YD*, document title, date, page(s), for documents.

CHAPTER 1 CONFLICT AMONG "FRIENDS"

1. *Pravda Ukrainy*, February 3, 1970, p. 4; *Time*, March 9, 1970, p. 67; *DPSR*, I, p. 576 (italics added).

2. Ivan Maisky, *Memoirs of a Soviet Ambassador* (New York: Scribner's, 1967), pp. 169–71; *DPSR*, I, pp. 114–16.

3. *DPSR*, I, pp. 134–37, 140, 578–79.

4. Edward J. Rozek, *Allied Wartime Diplomacy* (New York: Wiley, 1958), pp. 60–61; *DPSR*, I, pp. 117–19, 134–37, 140–42, 581.

5. Stanislaw Kot, *Conversations with the Kremlin and Dispatches from Russia* (London: Oxford University Press, 1963), pp. 130–31; *DPSR*, I, pp. 244–45; Anthony Eden, *The Reckoning* (Boston: Houghton Mifflin, 1965), pp. 335, 347–48.

6. *DPSR*, I, pp. 277, 294–95, 301–10, 348–49, 351–52, 556n., 600; General Wladyslaw Anders, *An Army in Exile* (London: Macmillan, 1949), pp. 109–12.

7. *DPSR*, I, pp. 375–80, 384–91, 401–4, 407, 416–18, 421, 431, 434.

8. *DPSR*, I, pp. 171, 202, 211, 307, 353, 378, 384; Arthur Bryant, *The Turn of the Tide* (Garden City, N.Y.: Doubleday, 1957), p. 375.

9. *DPSR*, I, pp. 473–74, 480–91, 501–7; Eden, *The Reckoning*, p. 432; Robert Sherwood, *Roosevelt and Hopkins* (New York: Harpers, 1948), pp. 709–10.

10. J. K. Zawodny, *Death in the Forest* (University of Notre Dame Press, 1962), pp. 11–15; Winston Churchill, *The Hinge of Fate* (Boston: Houghton Mifflin, 1953) pp. 759–61; *DPSR*, I, pp. 523–25, 527, 529–34; Alexander Werth, *Russia at War, 1941–1945* (New York: Avon, 1965), p. 593.

11. *Soviet-Polish Relations—A Collection of Official Documents, 1944–1946* (London: Soviet News, 1946), p. ii.

12. Cordell Hull, *Memoirs of Cordell Hull* (2 Vols.; New York: Macmillan, 1948), II, p. 1269; *Corr*, I, Churchill to Stalin, 4/30/43, p. 125; *Corr*, I, Stalin to Churchill, 5/4/43, p. 128; M. K. Dziewanowski, *The Communist Party of Poland* (Cambridge: Harvard University Press, 1959), p. 166.

13. Stanislaw Mikolajczyk, *The Rape of Poland* (New York: McGraw-Hill, 1948), pp. 45, 265; Rozek, *Allied Wartime Diplomacy*, p. 146; Count Edward Raczynski, *In Allied London* (London: Weidenfeld and Nicolson, 1962), p. 172; Hull, *Memoirs*, II, p. 1306; Eden, *The Reckoning*, p. 483.

14. Hull, *Memoirs*, II, p. 1317 (italics added); Eden, *The Reckoning*, p. 495; Mikolajczyk, *The Rape of Poland*, pp. 46, 268.

15. Churchill, *Triumph and Tragedy*, p. 362–63; Hull, *Memoirs*, II, p. 1317; Herbert Feis, *Churchill, Roosevelt, Stalin* (Princeton: Princeton University Press, 1957), p. 285.

16. Eden, *The Reckoning*, pp. 503–4; Raczynski, *In Allied London*, pp. 178–79; Mikolajczyk, *The Rape of Poland*, p. 48.

17. Mikolajczyk, *The Rape of Poland*, p. 49; Dziewanowski, *The Communist Party of Poland*, pp. 171–72; Rozek, *Allied Wartime Diplomacy*, pp. 171–73.

18. *Corr*, I, Stalin to Churchill, 1/7/44, p. 182; Mikolajczyk, *The Rape of Poland*, pp. 51–53, 270–73; Eden, *The Reckoning*, pp. 507–8.

19. Mikolajczyk, *The Rape of Poland*, p. 56; Rozek, *Allied Wartime Diplomacy*, p. 219; Raczynski, *In Allied London*, pp. 197–98.

20. Rozek, *Allied Wartime Diplomacy*, pp. 222–23; Mikolajczyk, *The Rape of Poland*, pp. 59–62.

21. Rozek, *Allied Wartime Diplomacy*, pp. 219–20; Mikolajczyk, *The Rape of Poland*, pp. 64–65; Raczynski, *In Allied London*, pp. 226–27.

22. Eden, *The Reckoning*, pp. 539–40; Raczynski, *In Allied London*, pp. 227–28; Jan Ciechanowski, *Defeat in Victory* (New York: Doubleday, 1947) p. 313 (italics added).

23. *Corr*, I, Churchill to Stalin, 7/20/44, p. 241; *Corr*, I, Stalin to Churchill, 7/23/44, p. 242.

24. *DPSR*, II, pp. 306–8, 309–22, 325–33, 334–39.

25. Raczynski, *In Allied London*, p. 238.

26. Mikolajczyk, *The Rape of Poland*, pp. 93–97; Rozek, *Allied Wartime Diplomacy*, pp. 268–83; Churchill, *Triumph and Tragedy*, p. 237; *DPSR*, II, pp. 405–15, 416–22, 423–24.

27. Churchill, *Triumph and Tragedy*, p. 239; Lord Charles Moran, *Churchill: Taken From the Diaries of Lord Moran* (Boston: Houghton Mifflin, 1966), p. 213.

28. Rozek, *Allied Wartime Diplomacy*, p. 286.

29. *DPSR*, II, pp. 430–33.

30. Raczynski, *In Allied London*, pp. 239–40, 245–46; *YD*, Ciechanowski to Stettinius, 10/27/44, pp. 207–9; *DPSR*, II, pp. 437–38, 450–57, 468–69.

31. *YD*, Memorandum by Harriman, 1/20/45, p. 227; Eden, *The Reckoning*, p. 576; Rozek, *Allied Wartime Diplomacy*, pp. 325–27.

32. Milovan Djiles, *Conversations with Stalin* (New York: Harcourt, Brace, and World, 1962), pp. 114–15.

33. Eden, *The Reckoning*, pp. 335–36; Hull, *Memoirs*, II, p. 1167; Edward R. Stettinius, *Roosevelt and the Russians* (Garden City, N.Y.: Doubleday, 1949), pp. 8–9.

34. Eden, *The Reckoning*, pp. 432, 439; Sherwood, *Roosevelt and Hopkins*, pp. 711, 713, 720.

35. Eden, *The Reckoning*, p. 406; Hull, *Memoirs*, II, pp. 1233, 1266.

36. Gabriel Kolko, *The Politics of War* (New York: Random House, 1968), p. 36; *Corr*, I, Churchill to Roosevelt and Stalin, 8/19/43, p. 148; *Corr*, I, Stalin to Churchill and Roosevelt, 8/24/43, p. 150; *Corr*, I, Churchill to Stalin, 9/5/43, p. 154.

37. Sherwood, *Roosevelt and Hopkins*, pp. 714–15; Philip E. Mosely, *The Kremlin and World Politics* (New York: Vintage, 1960), p. 157.

38. Hull, *Memoirs*, II, pp. 1285, 1288.

39. Hull, *Memoirs*, II, pp. 1287, 1289.

40. Sherwood, *Roosevelt and Hopkins*, pp. 782–83, 797–98; Churchill, *Closing the Ring*, pp. 360–61, 400–403; Hull, *Memoirs*, II, pp. 1573–74.

41. George F. Kennan, *Memoirs 1925–1950* (Boston: Little, Brown, and Co., 1967), p. 166.

42. Kolko, *The Politics of War*, pp. 40–41; Mosely, *The Kremlin and World Politics*, pp. 160–61, 163.

43. Mosely, *The Kremlin and World Politics*, pp. 169–71.

44. Kennan, *Memoirs*, pp. 168–71; Cornelius Ryan, *The Last Battle* (New York: Simon and Schuster, 1966), pp. 144–45.

45. Mosely, *The Kremlin and World Politics*, p. 181.

46. Eden, *The Reckoning*, pp. 336, 432; Sherwood, *Roosevelt and Hopkins*, pp. 388, 713–14.

47. Hull, *Memoirs*, II, pp. 1286, 1303–4.

48. Hull, *Memoirs*, II, pp. 1614, 1618; Kolko, *The Politics of War*, pp. 325–32; *YD*, Memo to the President, 9/29/44, pp. 156–57.

49. Hull, *Memoirs*, II, pp. 1606–7, 1619; *YD*, The President to the Secretary of State, 9/29/44, p. 155.

50. Moran, *Churchill*, p. 208; Churchill, *Triumph and Tragedy*, p. 241; *YD*, Churchill to Roosevelt, 10/22/44, pp. 159–60.

51. *YD*, The Secretary of State to the President, 9/29/44, p. 158; *YD*, The Secretary of State to the President, 11/10/44, pp. 167–71

52. *YD*, Memorandum by Pasvolsky, 11/15/44, pp. 171–72; *YD*, The Secretary of State to the President, 11/29/44, p. 174; *YD*, The President to the Secretary of State, 12/4/44, p. 174; *YD*, Memo from the Treasury, 1/19/45, pp. 175–76.

53. *YD*, Briefing Book Paper: Economic Policies Toward Germany and Reparation and Restitution Policy Toward Germany, pp. 191–97.

54. *YD*, Briefing Book Paper: The Treatment of Germany, pp. 178–90.

55. Moran, *Churchill*, p. 208.

56. *YD*, Memorandum by Harriman, 1/20/45, pp. 176–78.

57. Harold Macmillan, *The Blast of War 1939–1945* (New York: Harper and Row, 1966) p. 242.

58. Hull, *Memoirs*, II, p. 1213; Eden, *The Reckoning*, p. 431.

59. *Corr*, I, Churchill to Stalin, 8/30/43, p. 152; *Corr*, I, Stalin to Churchill, 8/31/43, p. 152.

60. Churchill, *Triumph and Tragedy*, p. 252; Stettinius, *Roosevelt and the Russians*, p. 63; *YD*, Briefing Book Paper: France, pp. 300–301.

61. Sherwood, *Roosevelt and Hopkins*, p. 328.

62. Eden, *The Reckoning*, pp. 328, 343, 370. For details see Theodore Wilson, *The First Summit* (Boston: Houghton Mifflin, 1969).

63. Eden, *The Reckoning*, pp. 321, 324–27, 335–36; Maisky, *Memoirs*, pp. 200–203, 230–32; Sherwood, *Roosevelt and Hopkins*, p. 390.

64. Sherwood, *Roosevelt and Hopkins*, pp. 569, 572–73; Feis, *Churchill, Roosevelt, Stalin*, p. 68.

65. Eden, *The Reckoning*, p. 431; Feis, *Churchill, Roosevelt, Stalin*, p. 121.

66. Kennan, *Memoirs*, pp. 216–17; Feis, *Churchill, Roosevelt, Stalin*, p. 207; Churchill, *The Hinge of Fate*, p. 562.

67. Churchill, *Closing the Ring*, pp. 362–63; Sherwood, *Roosevelt and Hopkins*, pp. 784–90.

68. Eden, *The Reckoning*, p. 514; Kolko, *The Politics of War*, p. 272.

69. Hull, *Memoirs*, II, p. 1659.

70. Hull, *Memoirs*, II, p. 1677.

71. Hull, *Memoirs*, II, pp. 1682–84.

72. Kolko, *The Politics of War*, p. 273.

73. *Corr*, II, Stalin to Roosevelt, 9/7/44, pp. 158–59.

74. Hull, *Memoirs*, II, pp. 1679–80; Stettinius, *Roosevelt and the Russians*, p. 17.

75. Hull, *Memoirs*, II, pp. 1677–78, 1683; Sherwood, *Roosevelt and Hopkins*, p. 854.

76. Hull, *Memoirs*, II, pp. 1681, 1684; Feis, *Churchill, Roosevelt, Stalin*, p. 434.

77. Churchill, *Triumph and Tragedy*, p. 219; *YD*, Roosevelt to Churchill, 11/15/44, p. 56; Hull, *Memoirs*, II, p. 1685.

78. *YD*, Harriman to Stettinius, 12/19/44, p. 60; *YD*, Stalin to Roosevelt, 12/27/44, pp. 63–64.

79. *YD*, Memorandum by Pasvolsky, 1/8/45, pp. 67–68.

80. *YD*, Memorandum on Conversation between Gromyko and Pasvolsky, 1/11/45, pp. 68–69; *YD*, Stettinius to Roosevelt, 1/20/45, p. 77.

81. Stettinius, *Roosevelt and the Russians*, pp. 54–55, 62.

82. Eden, *The Reckoning*, pp. 342, 348–49; Churchill, *The Grand Alliance*, p. 631.

83. Hull, *Memoirs*, II, pp. 1309–10; Eden, *The Reckoning*, p. 485.

84. Sherwood, *Roosevelt and Hopkins*, p. 792.

85. N. N. Voronov, "The Exploitation of the Soviet People," *Istoriia SSSR*, No. 4, July–August, 1965, pp. 13–27.

86. Kolko, *The Politics of War*, p. 206.

87. Eden, *The Reckoning*, p. 565; Churchill, *Triumph and Tragedy*, p. 236.

88. *YD*, Harriman to Roosevelt, 10/17/44, pp. 370–71.

89. Churchill, *Triumph and Tragedy*, pp. 228–29; Eden, *The Reckoning*, pp. 536–37; Kolko, *The Politics of War*, p. 207.

90. *YD*, Harriman to Roosevelt, 12/15/44, p. 378.

CHAPTER 2 THE SETTING

1. *YD*, Roosevelt to Churchill, 11/2/44, p. 13.

2. Werth, *Russia at War*, p. 784.

3. Kolko, *The Politics of War*, p. 110.

4. U.S. Department of State, *Foreign Relations of the United States: Diplomatic Papers: The Conferences at Cairo and Teheran* (Washington, D.C.: U.S. Government Printing Office, 1961), p. 64; Kolko, *The Politics of War*, p. 22.

5. John R. Deane, *The Strange Alliance* (New York: Viking, 1947), pp. 149–51.

6. V. I. Chuikov, *The Fall of Berlin* (New York: Holt, Rinehart, and Winston, 1968), pp. 15–26.

7. Eden, *The Reckoning*, p. 376.

8. *YD*, Stalin to Roosevelt, 7/17/44, p. 3; *YD*, Harriman to Roosevelt, 7/18/44, p. 3.

9. Ciechanowski, *Defeat in Victory*, p. 63.

10. *YD*, Harriman to Stettinius, 12/19/44, pp. 219–21; *YD*, Harriman to Stettinius, 12/28/44, pp. 64–66.

11. *Corr*, II, Roosevelt to Stalin, 7/17/44, p. 150; *Corr*, I, Churchill to Stalin, 7/24/44, p. 242.

12. *Corr*, II, Stalin to Roosevelt, 7/22/44, p. 151.

13. Djilas, *Conversations with Stalin*, p. 114.

14. *Istoriia velikoi otechestvennoi voiny Sovetskogo Soiuza* (6 Vols.; Moscow: Voennoe Izd. Min. oborony, 1963–1965), IV, pp. 254–85.

15. Moran, *Churchill*, p. 173.

16. Stettinius, *Roosevelt and the Russians*, pp. 10, 22–23 (italics added).

17. *YD*, Harriman to Roosevelt, 9/24/44, p. 5.

18. *Corr*, I, Churchill to Stalin, 9/27/44, p. 257; *Corr*, I, Stalin to Churchill, 9/30/44, p. 258.

19. *YD*, Roosevelt to Stalin, 10/4/44, p. 6.

20. *Corr*, II, Stalin to Roosevelt, 10/8/44, p. 163.

21. Eden, *The Reckoning*, p. 555.

22. Churchill, *Triumph and Tragedy*, pp. 227–28.

23. *Corr*, II, Stalin to Roosevelt, 10/19/44, p. 165.

24. *Corr*, II, Roosevelt to Stalin, 10/25/44, p. 167; *Corr*, II, Stalin to Roosevelt, 10/28/44, p. 167.

25. *YD*, Roosevelt to Churchill, 10/4/44, p. 7; *YD*, Roosevelt to Churchill, 11/14/44, p. 14; *YD*, Churchill to Roosevelt, 11/16/44, p. 15; Eden, *The Reckoning*, p. 574. Moran, *Churchill*, p. 205.

26. *YD*, Harriman to Roosevelt, 12/26/44, p. 21; *YD*, Harriman to Roosevelt, 12/15/44, p. 21.

27. Interview with Philip E. Mosely on TV, September 17, 1964.

28. Marcel Gimot, *Combat*, 1/21/45.

29. Moran, *Churchill*, pp. 185, 204.

30. *Tass International*, 5/7/66.

31. J. V. Stalin, *On the Great Patriotic War of the Soviet Union* (Moscow: Foreign Languages Publishing House, 1945), 11/6/42, pp. 70–71; 11/6/43, p. 116; 11/6/44, p. 160.

32. V. L. Israelian, *Antigitlerovskaia koalitsiia: Diplomaticheskoe sotrudnichestvo SSSR, SShA i Anglii v gody vtoroi mirovoi voiny* (Moscow: Izdatel'stvo Mezhdunarodnye otnosheniia, 1964), p. 473.

33. Maisky, *Memoirs*, pp. 185–92; Eden, *The Reckoning*, pp. 317–21.

34. Maisky, *Memoirs*, p. 253 (italics added).

35. Stalin, *Great Patriotic War*, pp. 61, 65, 69; 11/7/42, p. 81; 2/23/43, p. 92.

36. Bryant, *The Turn of the Tide*, p. 373; *Corr*, I, Stalin to Churchill, 8/13/42, pp. 60–61.

37. Stalin, *Great Patriotic War*, 11/7/43, p. 134; 2/23/44, pp. 140–41; 5/1/44, p. 148.

38. Deane, *The Strange Alliance*, pp. 150–53.

39. Werth, *Russia at War*, pp. 775–76.

40. Stalin, *Great Patriotic War*, 11/6/44, pp. 167–73.

41. Werth, *Russia at War*, pp. 781–84.

42. Dwight D. Eisenhower, *Crusade in Europe* (Garden City, N.Y.: Doubleday, 1948) pp. 336–84.

43. Churchill, *Triumph and Tragedy*, p. 278.

44. *Corr*, I, Churchill to Stalin, 1/6/45, p. 294; *Corr*, I, Stalin to Churchill, 1/7/45, pp. 294–95; *Corr*, I, Churchill to Stalin, 1/9/45, p. 295.

45. Deane, *The Strange Alliance*, p. 156; Eisenhower, *Crusade in Europe*, p. 387; Churchill, *Triumph and Tragedy*, p. 280.

46. Marshal I. S. Konev, "From the Vistula to the Oder," in Seweryn Bialer (ed. and tr.), *Stalin and His Generals* (New York: Pegasus, 1969), pp. 480–83.

47. *Corr*, II, Stalin to Roosevelt, 1/15/45, p. 184; *Corr*, II, Roosevelt to Stalin, 1/18/45, p. 185.

48. Werth, *Russia at War*, p. 861; Israelian, *Antigitlerovskaia koalitsiia*, pp. 474–76.

49. Chester Wilmot, *The Struggle for Europe* (New York: Harper, 1952), pp. 580–614.

50. Erich Kuby, *The Russians and Berlin, 1945* (New York: Hill & Wang, 1968), p. 9.

51. *The New York Times*, 1/17/45.

52. Elliot Roosevelt, *As He Saw It* (New York: Duell, Sloan, and Pearce, 1946), p. 237.

53. V. I. Chuikov, "The Capitulation of Hitler's Germany," *Novaia i Noveishaia Istoriia*, No. 2 (February 1965), p. 6.

54. Chuikov, *The Fall of Berlin*, pp. 118–19.

55. S. M. Shtemenko, "In the General Staff," in Bialer, *Stalin and His Generals*, p. 478.

56. Shtemenko, "In the General Staff," p. 479 (italics added); Marshal G. Zhukov, "On the Berlin Axis," in Bialer, *Stalin and His Generals*, p. 507.

57. Marshal G. Zhukov, *Marshal Zhukov's Greatest Battles* (New York: Harper and Row, 1969), p. 263.

58. Shtemenko, "In the General Staff," p. 479.

59. Marshal V. I. Chuikov, "The Costly Delay," in Bialer, *Stalin and His Generals*, p. 502; Shtemenko, "In the General Staff," p. 495.

60. Chuikov, "The Costly Delay," p. 504; Zhukov, "On the Berlin Axis," p. 507.

61. Chuikov, "The Costly Delay," pp. 502–4; Chuikov, *The Fall of Berlin*, p. 120.

62. Kuby, *The Russians and Berlin, 1945*, p. 25; Shtemenko, "In the General Staff," p. 494; Zhukov, *Marshal Zhukov's Greatest Battles*, p. 265.

63. Chuikov, *The Fall of Berlin*, p. 120; Bialer, *Stalin and His Generals*, p. 617, n. 24.

64. Werth, *Russia at War*, p. 846; Eisenhower, *Crusade in Europe*, p. 422.

65. Shtemenko, "In the General Staff," pp. 499–500.

66. Kolko, *The Politics of War*, pp. 29–30; Kuby, *The Russians and Berlin, 1945*, p. 27.

67. Konev, "From the Vistula to the Oder," p. 521.

68. Viscount Montgomery of Alamein, *A History of Warfare* (Cleveland: World, 1969), p. 544.

69. YD, Roosevelt to Stalin, 11/18/44, p. 15; Stettinius, *Roosevelt and the Russians*, p. 13.

70. Moran, *Churchill*, pp. 205, 207.

71. *The New York Times*, 1/29/44, 2/4/44.

72. Moran, *Churchill*, pp. 247–48; Kolko, *The Politics of War*, p. 23; Stettinius, *Roosevelt and the Russians*, p. 62.

73. Eden, *The Reckoning*, p. 375; Stettinius, *Roosevelt and the Russians*, p. 8.

74. Moran, *Churchill*, pp. 173, 185, 197, 215–18.

75. Moran, *Churchill*, p. 209; Eden, *The Reckoning*, p. 560; Churchill, *Triumph and Tragedy*, p. 208.

76. Ciechanowski, *Defeat in Victory*, pp. 293, 334; Moran, *Churchill*, pp. 208, 215, 239.

77. John Toland, *The Last 100 Days* (New York: Random House, 1966), p. 40.

78. *The Economist*, 12/29/44, 1/5/45; *The* [London] *News Chronicle*, 1/5/45; Moran, *Churchill*, p. 171; Eden, *The Reckoning*, pp. 542–43.

79. Toland, *The Last 100 Days*, pp. 41–42; Eisenhower, *Crusade in Europe*, pp. 392–94; Stettinius, *Roosevelt and the Russians*, p. 74.

80. Eden, *The Reckoning*, p. 593; Toland, *The Last 100 Days*, p. 51.

81. *The New York Times*, 1/24/45.

82. Stettinius, *Roosevelt and the Russians*, pp. 52, 60–61; Eden, *The Reckoning*, p. 592.

83. Churchill, *Triumph and Tragedy*, p. 341; Stettinius, *Roosevelt and the Russians*, pp. 67–68; Moran, *Churchill*, p. 232.

84. Stettinius, *Roosevelt and the Russians,* pp. 69, 73; Moran, *Churchill,* pp. 234, 242–43, 247.

85. Eden, *The Reckoning,* p. 593.

CHAPTER 3 THE CONFERENCE OPENS

1. *YD,* Harriman to Roosevelt, 7/18/44, p. 4.

2. Sherwood, *Roosevelt and Hopkins,* pp. 844–45; *YD,* Deane to Joint Chiefs of Staff, 10/17/44, p. 8; *YD,* Stalin to Roosevelt, 10/19/44, p. 9; *YD,* Churchill to Roosevelt, 10/22/44, p. 10; Churchill, *Triumph and Tragedy,* p. 241.

3. *YD,* Roosevelt to Churchill, 10/22/44, p. 10; *YD,* Churchill to Roosevelt, 10/23/44, p. 11.

4. *YD,* Roosevelt to Stalin, 10/24/44, p. 11; *YD,* Stalin to Roosevelt, 10/29/44, p. 12; *YD,* Roosevelt to Churchill, 11/2/44, p. 12; *YD,* Roosevelt to Churchill, 11/3/44, p. 13; *YD,* Churchill to Roosevelt, 11/5/44, p. 13.

5. *YD,* Roosevelt to Churchill, 11/14/44, p. 14.

6. Sherwood, *Roosevelt and Hopkins,* p. 845; *YD,* Roosevelt to Stalin, 11/18/44, p. 15; *YD,* Stalin to Roosevelt, 11/23/44, p. 18.

7. *YD,* Roosevelt to Churchill, 11/26/44, p. 18; *YD,* Churchill to Roosevelt, 11/27/44, p. 19.

8. *YD,* Roosevelt to Churchill, 12/9/44, p. 79.

9. *YD,* Harriman to Roosevelt, 12/14/44, p. 20; *YD,* Roosevelt to Churchill, 12/23/44, p. 21; *YD,* Harriman to Roosevelt, 12/27/44, p. 22.

10. *YD,* Churchill to Roosevelt, 12/29/44, p. 23; *YD,* Roosevelt to Churchill, 12/30/44, p. 24.

11. *YD,* Churchill to Roosevelt, 12/31/44, p. 24; *YD,* Roosevelt to Churchill, 12/31/44, p. 25; Churchill, *Triumph and Tragedy,* p. 338.

12. *Corr,* I, Stalin to Churchill, 1/3/45, p. 290; *Corr,* I, Churchill to Stalin, 1/5/45, p. 293; *YD,* Roosevelt to Harriman, 1/6/45, p. 30; *Corr,* I, Stalin to Churchill, 1/10/45, p. 295; *Corr,* I, Churchill to Stalin, 1/12/45, p. 296.

13. Moran, *Churchill,* pp. 234–35; Churchill, *Triumph and Tragedy,* p. 345; William Daniel Leahy, *I Was There* (New York: Whittlesey House, 1950), pp. 295–96; Stettinius, *Roosevelt and the Russians,* pp. 79–81.

14. Deane, *The Strange Alliance,* p. 251; Stettinius, *Roosevelt and the Russians,* p. 81.

15. Stettinius, *Roosevelt and the Russians,* p. 82.

16. Moran, *Churchill,* pp. 238–39; Toland, *The Last 100 Days,* p. 51.

17. Churchill, *Triumph and Tragedy,* pp. 346–47; Moran, *Churchill,* pp. 236–37.

18. Moran, *Churchill,* pp. 237–38; Hastings Ismay, *The Memoirs of General Lord Ismay* (New York: Viking, 1960), pp. 386–87.

19. Churchill, *Triumph and Tragedy,* pp. 346–47; Toland, *The Last 100 Days,* p. 57; Moran, *Churchill,* pp. 237–51.

20. Churchill, *Triumph and Tragedy,* pp. 347–49.

21. *YD,* Bohlen, pp. 570–72.

22. *SCD,* 6, p. 92.

23. *SCD,* 6, p. 93; *YD,* Combined Chiefs of Staff, pp. 581–84.

24. *SCD,* 6, p. 94.

25. *SCD,* 6, p. 95; *YD,* Bohlen, pp. 576–77; *YD,* Combined Chiefs of Staff, pp. 585–86. The Soviet minutes give the only record of Marshall's remark about the bombing of German troop trains.

26. Stettinius, *Roosevelt and the Russians,* p. 101; Churchill, *Triumph and Tragedy,* p. 349; Eden, *The Reckoning,* p. 593; *YD,* Bohlen, p. 574.

27. *SCD,* 6, p. 95.

28. *YD,* Bohlen, p. 578; *YD,* Combined Chiefs of Staff, p. 587; *SCD,* 6, p. 95.

29. *YD,* Bohlen, pp. 578–79.

30. *YD,* Bohlen, p. 579; *YD,* Combined Chiefs of Staff, pp. 587–88; *SCD,* 6, p. 96; Stettinius, *Roosevelt and the Russians,* p. 109.

31. *YD,* Bohlen, p. 579; Admiral of the Fleet Viscount Cunningham of Hyndhope, *A Sailor's Odyssey* (London: Hutchinson, 1951), p. 627.

32. The main accounts are: Stettinius, *Roosevelt and the Russians,* pp. 111–15; *YD,* Bohlen, pp. 589–91; Moran, *Churchill,* pp. 239–40. Churchill omits the dinner, Eden mentions it only in passing; Leahy, Brooks, Ismay, and Hopkins were not present.

33. Eden, *The Reckoning,* p. 593.

34. Field Marshal Alexander, Earl of Tunis, *The Alexander Memoirs, 1940–1945* (London: Cassell, 1962), p. 133.

35. *YD,* Combined Chiefs of Staff, pp. 595–608.

36. *YD,* Combined Chiefs of Staff, pp. 640–55.

37. *YD,* Soviet Draft, pp. 416–18; *YD,* British Re-draft, pp. 694–97; *YD,* Joint Chiefs of Staff, pp. 687–88; *YD,* Combined Chiefs of Staff, pp. 751–52; *YD,* Memorandum, pp. 864–66; *YD,* Protocol, pp. 985–87.

CHAPTER 4 THE FUTURE OF CENTRAL EUROPE: GERMANY AND FRANCE

1. Moran, *Churchill,* p. 152; Arthur Bryant, *Triumph in the West* (Garden City, N.Y.: Doubleday, 1959), p. 180.

2. Kolko, *The Politics of War,* p. 339.

3. Moran, *Churchill,* p. 246.

4. Moran, *Churchill,* p. 241; Eden, *The Reckoning,* p. 573.

5. Eden, *The Reckoning,* p. 461 (italics added).

6. *YD,* Page, p. 610.

7. *SCD*, 6, p. 97; *YD*, Matthews, p. 624; *YD*, Bohlen, p. 611.

8. *SCD*, 6, pp. 97–98; *YD*, Matthews, p. 624; *YD*, Bohlen, p. 613.

9. *YD*, Matthews, p. 626; *SCD*, 6, p. 98. Bohlen omits the last statement.

10. *YD*, Bohlen, p. 614; *SCD*, 6, pp. 98–99. The Soviet minutes quote Churchill as saying thirty minutes.

11. *YD*, Bohlen, p. 615; *YD*, Matthews, p. 627; *SCD*, 6, p. 99.

12. *YD*, Matthews, pp. 627–28.

13. *YD*, Page, pp. 656–57.

14. *YD*, Bohlen, p. 660.

15. *YD*, Bohlen, pp. 616–17; *YD*, Matthews, p. 628.

16. *YD*, Matthews, p. 629; *YD*, Bohlen, p. 619; *YD*, Hopkins to Roosevelt, p. 634.

17. *YD*, Bohlen, p. 619; *YD*, Matthews, p. 630.

18. *YD*, Page, pp. 699–701. The other American minutes are fragmentary.

19. *YD*, Soviet Proposal, p. 707.

20. *YD*, Page, pp. 701–2.

21. *YD*, Bohlen, pp. 709–11; *YD*, Matthews, pp. 718–19.

22. *YD*, Bohlen, p. 854.

23. *YD*, Page, p. 873.

24. Sherwood, *Roosevelt and Hopkins*, p. 859.

25. *YD*, Bohlen, p. 899; *SCD*, 8, p. 113.

26. *SCD*, 6, p. 99. The American minutes only summarize the plan and lose the logical build-up Maisky was trying to establish.

27. *SCD*, 6, pp. 100–101; *YD*, Bohlen, p. 621; *YD*, Matthews, pp. 631–32. The American minutes do not record the Churchill-Stalin interchange in detail.

28. *SCD*, 6, p. 101. The only record of Churchill's acceptance is in the Soviet minutes.

29. *SCD*, 6, p. 102. Again, the only record is the Soviet minutes.

30. *SCD*, 6, p. 102; *YD*, Matthews, p. 633. The Soviet minutes omit Stalin's statement on France.

31. *SCD*, 6, p. 102; *YD*, Matthews, p. 633.

32. *YD*, Soviet Reparations Proposal, p. 707.

33. *YD*, Soviet Proposal on an Allied Reparations Commission, p. 708.

34. *YD*, Page, pp. 702–4.

35. *YD*, Page, p. 738.

36. Stettinius, *Roosevelt and the Russians*, pp. 229–30.

37. *YD*, Page, pp. 807–9; *YD*, Hiss, p. 812; Stettinius, *Roosevelt and the Russians*, pp. 230–32.

38. *YD*, Foreign Ministers' Report to the Sixth Plenary Session, p. 842; *SCD*, 8, p. 108, has only a summary.

39. *YD*, British Proposal on Reparations, p. 885.

40. *YD*, Page, pp. 874–75; Stettinius, *Roosevelt and the Russians*, pp. 253–55.

41. Stettinius, *Roosevelt and the Russians*, p. 265.

42. *YD*, Hiss, pp. 914–15; *YD*, Matthews, p. 909; *YD*, Bohlen, p. 903; *SCD*, 8, p. 114; Stettinius, *Roosevelt and the Russians*, p. 264.

43. *YD*, Hiss, pp. 915–16; *SCD*, 8, p. 114; Stettinius, *Roosevelt and the Russians*, p. 266.

44. *YD*, Bohlen, pp. 921–22; Stettinius, *Roosevelt and the Russians*, pp. 274–75.

45. *YD*, Protocol, p. 979.

CHAPTER 5   POLAND: "THE BEST HE COULD GET"

1. Churchill, *Triumph and Tragedy*, p. 314.

2. Raczynski, *In Allied London* (Introduction by John Wheeler-Bennet), p. xiv.

3. *Corr*, II, Stalin to Roosevelt, 12/27/44, p. 181.

4. *Soviet-Polish Relations . . . 1944–1946*, p. ii.

5. *Corr*, II, Stalin to Roosevelt, 12/27/44, pp. 180–81.

6. *Corr*, II, Roosevelt to Stalin, 12/31/44, p. 182.

7. Moran, *Churchill*, p. 235.

8. *YD*, Bohlen, p. 667; *YD*, Matthews, p. 677.

9. *SCD*, 6, p. 107.

10. *YD*, Bohlen, p. 668; *YD*, Matthews, p. 678; Stettinius, *Roosevelt and the Russians*, p. 152; James F. Byrnes, *Speaking Frankly* (New York: Harper, 1947), p. 29. The Soviet minutes omit Churchill's support for Roosevelt's proposal.

11. *YD*, Matthews, p. 679; *SCD*, 6, pp. 107–8.

12. *SCD*, 6, p. 108; Byrnes, *Speaking Frankly*, pp. 29–30.

13. *SCD*, 6, pp. 108–9; *YD*, Matthews, pp. 680–81.

14. *SCD*, 6, p. 109.

15. *YD*, Letter from Roosevelt to Stalin, 2/6/45, p. 727.

16. *SCD*, 7, p. 112.

17. Charles de Gaulle, *Salvation* (New York: Simon and Schuster, 1960), p. 79.

18. Kot, *Conversations with the Kremlin and Dispatches from Russia*, p. xxiii.

19. *DPSR*, I, p. 233.

20. *YD*, Matthews, p. 719.

21. Stettinius, *Roosevelt and the Russians*, p. 172.

22. *YD*, Hiss, p. 721. The Soviet minutes only summarize Molotov's statement.

23. *YD*, Bohlen, p. 716; *SCD*, 7, p. 114.

24. *YD*, Bohlen, p. 716; *SCD*, 7, pp. 112–14.

25. *YD*, Matthews, p. 720; *YD*, Bohlen, p. 716. The Soviet minutes omit the suggestion of Germans fleeing in terror from Soviet troops and only record Stalin's statement that the German population in that area was small.

26. *SCD*, 7, p. 114; *YD*, Bohlen, pp. 717–18; *YD*, Matthews, pp. 720–21.

27. *YD*, United States proposal, pp. 792–93; *SCD*, 7, p. 116.

28. The Soviet minutes omit Molotov's entire speech. The best accounts of it are: Churchill, *Triumph and Tragedy*, pp. 377–78; Stettinius, *Roosevelt and the Russians*, pp. 212–13; *YD*, Bohlen, pp. 776–77; *YD*, Matthews, pp. 786–87.

29. Churchill, *Triumph and Tragedy*, p. 378; *SCD*, 7, p. 117.

30. *YD*, Matthews, p. 788.

31. *SCD*, 7, pp. 117–18; *YD*, Matthews, p. 789.

32. *YD*, Matthews, p. 790.

33. *YD*, Matthews, p. 791; *SCD*, 7, p. 118.

34. Stettinius, *Roosevelt and the Russians*, pp. 223–24; *YD*, Page, pp. 803–5, 815–16.

35. *SCD*, 8, p. 108; *YD*, Bohlen, p. 842.

36. *YD*, Bohlen, pp. 842–43.

37. *YD*, Matthews, p. 850.

38. Churchill, *Triumph and Tragedy*, p. 382; *SCD*, 8, p. 108.

39. *SCD*, 8, p. 108.

40. *YD*, Bohlen, p. 846; *SCD*, 8, p. 110.

41. *YD*, Matthews, pp. 852–53; *SCD*, 8, pp. 110–11.

42. *YD*, Matthews, p. 853; *SCD*, 8, p. 111.

43. *YD*, Matthews, p. 854.

44. *YD*, British Proposal, p. 870.

45. *YD*, Bohlen, p. 867; *YD*, Matthews, p. 869; Stettinius, *Roosevelt and the Russians*, p. 247.

46. *YD*, British Revised Proposal on the Polish Government, pp. 870–71.

47. *YD*, Draft presented by Foreign Ministers to Plenary Session on February 10, p. 898.

48. Ibid.

49. *YD*, Bohlen, p. 868; Stettinius, *Roosevelt and the Russians*, p. 248.

50. Churchill, *Triumph and Tragedy*, p. 385.

51. Stettinius, *Roosevelt and the Russians*, p. 258.

52. Churchill, *Triumph and Tragedy*, p. 385.

53. *SCD*, 8, pp. 112–13; *YD*, Bohlen, pp. 898–99; Stettinius, *Roosevelt and the Russians*, pp. 260–61.

54. Stettinius, *Roosevelt and the Russians*, p. 260; *YD*, Bohlen, p. 899.

55. *YD*, Bohlen, p. 905; Stettinius, *Roosevelt and the Russians*, p. 271.

56. *YD*, Bohlen, p. 905; *YD*, Matthews, p. 911.

57. *YD*, Bohlen, pp. 905–6.

CHAPTER 6 THE UNITED NATIONS

1.   Macmillan, *The Blast of War*, p. 133.

2.   Sherwood, *Roosevelt and Hopkins*, p. 719.

3.   Moran, *Churchill*, pp. 33–34; Sherwood, *Roosevelt and Hopkins*, p. 718.

4.   *YD*, Bohlen, pp. 660–61; *YD*, Proposed Formula for Voting Procedure, pp. 684–86; Stettinius, *Roosevelt and the Russians*, pp. 140–41.

5.   *YD*, Bohlen, pp. 661–64; *YD*, Hiss, p. 674; *SCD*, 6, pp. 103–5; Byrnes, *Speaking Frankly*, p. 35. Only the Soviet minutes record Churchill's statement about the rights of the United States under the Monroe Doctrine.

6.   *YD*, Bohlen, p. 665; *YD*, Hiss, p. 674; *SCD*, 6, p. 105; Stettinius, *Roosevelt and the Russians*, p. 147; Byrnes, *Speaking Frankly*, p. 36.

7.   Byrnes, *Speaking Frankly*, p. 37.

8.   *SCD*, 6, pp. 105–6.

9.   *YD*, Hiss, p. 676; *SCD*, 6, p. 106.

10. Stettinius, *Roosevelt and the Russians*, pp. 171–72.

11. *YD*, Bohlen, pp. 712–14; *YD*, Hiss, p. 723; *SCD*, 7, p. 113.

12. Eden, *The Reckoning*, p. 598.

13. *SCD*, 7, pp. 113–14; *YD*, Hopkins to Roosevelt, p. 729; *YD*, Bohlen, pp. 715–16; *YD*, Hiss, pp. 724–25; Stettinius, *Roosevelt and the Russians*, p. 181. The Soviet minutes omit the discussion of Iran.

14. Stettinius, *Roosevelt and the Russians*, p. 190; *YD*, Page, pp. 734–35; *YD*, Hiss, pp. 742–43.

15. *YD*, Page, pp. 736–37; *YD*, Hiss, pp. 743–44.

16. Stettinius, *Roosevelt and the Russians*, pp. 195–97.

17. Stettinius, *Roosevelt and the Russians*, p. 198. For an example of the American attitude, see *YD*, Draft Message to Stalin, p. 990.

18. *YD*, Bohlen, p. 772; *SCD*, 7, p. 115.

19. *YD*, Bohlen, p. 773; *YD*, Hiss, pp. 782–83; *SCD*, 7, p. 115.

20. *SCD*, 7, p. 116; *YD*, Hiss, p. 784. The Soviet minutes omit Stalin's position on Denmark.

21. *YD*, Hiss, pp. 784–85.

22. *YD*, Hiss, p. 785; *YD*, Bohlen, p. 775; *SCD*, 7, p. 116. According to the Hiss minutes, Churchill eventually asked that the question of invitations to the two Republics be deferred until the United Nations Conference. Bohlen wrote that Churchill supported the Soviet Union to the end.

23. Stettinius, *Roosevelt and the Russians*, pp. 282–83.

24. *YD*, Hiss, pp. 812–13; *YD*, Page, p. 810; Eden, *The Reckoning*, p. 595; Stettinius, *Roosevelt and the Russians*, pp. 323–24.

25. *SCD*, 8, p. 109; *YD*, Bohlen, p. 844; Byrnes, *Speaking Frankly*, p. x.

26. Eden, *The Reckoning*, p. 595.

27. *YD*, Bohlen, p. 845; *SCD*, 8, p. 109.

28. *YD*, Protocol on World Organization, pp. 975–77.

CHAPTER 7 THE FAR EAST AND OTHER ISSUES

1. Macmillan, *The Blast of War*, p. 15.

2. Churchill, *The Grand Alliance*, pp. 406–7, 410.

3. Kolko, *The Politics of War*, pp. 298–99, 309–11.

4. *YD*, Instructions to Harriman and Memorandum to the President, pp. 331–32.

5. *YD*, Bohlen, pp. 768–71.

6. Churchill, *Triumph and Tragedy*, p. 363.

7. *YD*, Bohlen, pp. 770–71.

8. *YD*, Soviet Draft, p. 896.

9. *YD*, Harriman Memorandum, pp. 894–95.

10. Churchill, *Triumph and Tragedy*, p. 389.

11. *YD*, Kuter, p. 758.

12. *YD*, Kuter, p. 758; *YD*, Bohlen, p. 766; *YD*, Kuter, p. 834.

13. *YD*, Kuter, pp. 759–60.

14. *YD*, Bohlen, p. 767; *YD*, Kuter, p. 835.

15. *YD*, Kuter, pp. 759, 835.

16. *YD*, Kuter, p. 759; *YD*, Bohlen, p. 766; *YD*, Kuter, p. 836.

17. *YD*, Kuter, pp. 760, 836.

18. *YD*, Bohlen, pp. 767–68; *YD*, Kuter, p. 837.

19. *YD*, Hiss, pp. 744–45; *YD*, Page, p. 738–40; *YD*, Matthews, p. 741.

20. *YD*, Page, p. 810.

21. *YD*, Page, p. 877: *YD*, Hiss, p. 881.

22. Eden, *The Reckoning*, p. 596.

23. Eden, *The Reckoning*, pp. 587–89, 591.

24. *YD*, Bohlen, pp. 903–5; *YD*, Matthews, pp. 909–11; *YD*, Hiss, pp. 916-17. The Soviet minutes omit any mention of the Montreux Convention.

25. *YD*, Hiss, p. 933.

26. *YD*, Bohlen, pp. 845–46; *SCD*, 8, p. 109.

27. *YD*, Hiss, p. 879; *YD*, Page, pp. 873–74; *YD*, Eden to Molotov, pp. 964–65; *YD*, British Proposals, pp. 887–89.

28. *YD*, Bohlen, p. 848; *YD*, Matthews, pp. 853–54; *SCD*, 8, p. 111; *YD*, Hiss, p. 856.

29. *YD*, Matthews, p. 854; *YD*, Hiss, p. 857; *SCD*, 8, pp. 111–12; *YD*, Bohlen, pp. 848–49; Stettinius, *Roosevelt and the Russians*, p. 244. There is considerable confusion about the order and content of Churchill's tirade, Molotov's amendment, and the interchange on Greece. Hiss's and Matthews's accounts agree with the order followed here. Bohlen places Molotov's amendment first. Stettinius places Molotov's proposal first and Churchill's tirade last. The Soviet minutes omit the discussion of Molotov's amendment and Greece. Matthews caught only fragments of the remarks on Greece; for this I have followed Bohlen.

30. Stettinius, *Roosevelt and the Russians*, p. 249; *YD*, Bohlen, pp. 868, 873; *YD*, Hiss, p. 878.

31. *YD*, Hiss, p. 913; *YD*, Matthews, p. 908; *YD*, Bohlen, p. 899; *SCD*, 8, p. 113. The Soviet minutes refer to the final draft as a Soviet proposal.

CHAPTER 8   SECOND THOUGHTS AND CONCLUSIONS

1. Moran, *Churchill*, p. 248; Stettinius, *Roosevelt and the Russians*, p. 279; *YD*, Hiss, pp. 927–29; *YD*, List of Amendments to the Draft Communiqué, pp. 929–30; *YD*, Communiqué, pp. 968–75.

2. Moran, *Churchill*, pp. 248–50.

3. Ismay, *Memoirs*, p. 388; Toland, *The Last 100 Days*, pp. 115–16; Sherwood, *Roosevelt and Hopkins*, p. 870; Stettinius, *Roosevelt and the Russians*, p. 295.

4. Walter Millis (ed.), *The Forrestal Diaries* (New York: Viking, 1951), p. 50; Harry Truman, *Year of Decisions* (Garden City, N.Y.: Doubleday, 1955), p. 81; *Corr*, II, Stalin to Truman, 4/24/45, p. 220; *YD*, Communiqué, p. 973.

5. Truman, *Year of Decisions*, pp. 323, 398; Gar Alperowitz, *Atomic Diplomacy: Hiroshima and Potsdam* (New York: Vintage, 1967), p. 162; U.S. Department of State, *Foreign Relations of the United States: Diplomatic Papers: The Conference of Berlin (The Potsdam Conference) 1945* (2 Vols.; Washington, D.C.: U.S. Government Printing Office, 1960), II, p. 850.

6. *Conference of Berlin*, II, pp. 901, 1485–86; Byrnes, *Speaking Frankly*, p. 82.

7. *Conference of Berlin*, I, p. 456; Mosley, *The Kremlin and World Politics*, p. 153; Sherwood, *Roosevelt and Hopkins*, pp. 904–5.

8. Mosley, *The Kremlin and World Politics*, pp. 185–87; Truman, *Year of Decisions*, pp. 301–2, 391; Alperowitz, *Atomic Diplomacy*, pp. 82–84.

9. Mosley, *The Kremlin and World Politics*, pp. 182–85; Kolko, *The Politics of War*, p. 41.

10. John Snell, "What to Do With Germany?" in John Snell (ed.), *The Meaning of Yalta* (Baton Rouge: Louisiana State University Press, 1966), p. 72.

11. Kolko, *The Politics of War,* p. 356.

12. Snell, "What to Do With Germany?" p. 58.

13. Snell, "What to Do With Germany?" p. 61.

14. Snell, "What to Do With Germany?" pp. 57, 60.

15. Feis, *Churchill, Roosevelt, Stalin,* p. 532.

16. Forrest C. Pogue, "The Big Three and the U.N.," in Snell, *The Meaning of Yalta,* pp. 176–78, 181.

17. Churchill, *Triumph and Tragedy,* pp. 359–60.

18. Feis, *Churchill, Roosevelt, Stalin,* pp. 521, 553–54; Charles F. Delzell, "Russian Power in Central Eastern Europe," in Snell, *The Meaning of Yalta,* pp. 120, 124.

19. Sherwood, *Roosevelt and Hopkins,* p. 870; William Henry Chamberlain, "The Munich Called Yalta," in Richard F. Fenno, Jr. (ed.), *The Yalta Conference,* from the *Problems in American Civilization* series (Boston: D. C. Heath, 1955), p. 48.

20. This material has been previously published in Diane S. Clemens, "The Structure of Negotiations: Dynamics and Interaction Patterns of the Crimea Conference," *Peace Research Society: Papers, XI, The Budapest Conference, 1968.*

BIBLIOGRAPHY

This bibliography includes works cited in the text and those most instrumental in providing background and scope for this work. More comprehensive bibliographies, which this author consulted in trying to locate Soviet material, are listed at the end.

I. PRIMARY SOURCES

A. Memoirs and Recollections

1. CONFERENCE PARTICIPANTS

Alexander, Sir Harold, Field-Marshal, Earl of Tunis. *The Alexander Memoirs 1940–45*. London: Cassell & Co., 1962.

Bryant, Arthur. *The Turn of the Tide* and *Triumph in the West. A History of the War Years Based on the Diaries of Field Marshal Lord Alanbrooke, Chief of the Imperial General Staff*. Garden City, N.Y.: Doubleday & Co., 1957, 1959.

Byrnes, James Francis. *All in One Lifetime*. New York: Harper & Bros., 1958.

———. *Speaking Frankly*. New York: Harper & Bros., 1947.

Churchill, Winston S. *The Second World War*. 6 vols. Boston: Houghton Mifflin Co., 1948–1953.

Cunningham, Sir Andrew, Viscount of Hyndhope, Admiral of the Fleet. *A Sailor's Odyssey*. London: Hutchinson & Co., 1951.

Deane, John R. *The Strange Alliance: The Story of Our Efforts at Wartime Co-operation with Russia*. New York: Viking Press, 1947.

Eden, Anthony. *The Reckoning*. Boston: Houghton Mifflin Co., 1965.

Hiss, Alger. *In the Court of Public Opinion*. New York: Alfred Knopf, 1957.

Ismay, Hastings. *Memoirs*. New York: Viking Press, 1960.

Jacob, Ian. *United Kingdom Policy, Foreign, Strategic, Economic.* London: Royal Institute of International Affairs, 1950.

King, Ernest Joseph, and Walter Muir Whitehill. *Fleet Admiral King.* New York: Norton, 1952.

Kuter, Lawrence Sherman. *Airman at Yalta.* New York: Duell, Sloan, & Pearce, 1955.

Leahy, William Daniel. *I Was There.* New York: Wittlesey House, 1950.

Leasor, James. *War at the Top, Based on the Experiences of General Sir Leslie Hollis.* London: Michael Joseph, 1959.

Moran, Lord Charles. *Churchill: Taken from the Diaries of Lord Moran.* Boston: Houghton Mifflin, 1966.

Sherwood, Robert E. *Roosevelt and Hopkins, An Intimate History.* New York: Harper & Bros., 1948.

Stettinius, Edward R., Jr. *Roosevelt and the Russians: The Yalta Conference.* Garden City, N.Y.: Doubleday & Co., 1949.

2. MILITARY AND POLITICAL RECOLLECTIONS

Anders, General Wladislaw W. *An Army in Exile.* London: Macmillan, 1949.

Bialer, Seweryn (ed.). *Stalin and His Generals: Soviet Military Memoirs of World War II.* New York: Pegasus, 1969.

Bor-Komorowski, General Tadeusz. *The Secret Army.* New York: Macmillan, 1951.

Chuikov, V. I. "The Capitulation of Hitler's Germany," *Novaia i Noveishaia Istoriia.* No. 2 (Moscow: February 1965), 3–26.

———. *The Fall of Berlin.* New York: Holt, Rinehart and Winston, 1968.

Ciechanowski, Jan. *Defeat in Victory.* Garden City, N.Y.: Doubleday & Co., 1947.

De Gaulle, Charles. *War Memoirs: Salvation 1944–1946.* (Trans. by Richard Howard.) New York: Simon & Schuster, 1960.

Djilas, Milovan. *Conversations with Stalin.* New York: Harcourt, Brace & World, Inc., 1962.

Dulles, Allen. *The Secret Surrender.* New York: Harper & Row, 1966.

Eisenhower, General Dwight D. *Crusade in Europe.* Garden City, N.Y.: Doubleday & Co., 1948.

Grew, Joseph C. (ed. by Walter Johnson). *Turbulent Era, A Diplomatic Record of Forty Years, 1904–1945.* 2 vols. Boston: Houghton Mifflin, 1952.

Harriman, Averell W. *Peace with Russia?* New York: Simon & Schuster, 1959.

Hassett, William D. *Off the Record wih F.D.R., 1942–1945.* New Brunswick: Rutgers University Press, 1958.

Hull, Cordell. *The Memoirs of Cordell Hull.* 2 vols. New York: Macmillan, 1948.

Kennan, George F. *Memoirs 1925–1950*. Boston: Little, Brown, and Co., 1967.

Kot, Stanislaw. *Conversations with the Kremlin and Dispatches from Russia*. (Trans. by H. C. Stevens.) London: Oxford University Press, 1963.

Lane, Arthur Bliss. *I Saw Poland Betrayed: An American Ambassador Reports to the American People*. New York: The Bobbs-Merrill Co., 1948.

Macmillan, Harold. *The Blast of War, 1939–1945*. New York: Harper & Row, 1966.

Maisky, Ivan. *Memoirs of a Soviet Ambassador*. New York: Charles Scribner's Sons, 1968.

Manstein, Erich von. *Verlorene Siege*. Bonn: Atheralum, 1955.

Mikolajczyk, Stanlislaw. *The Rape of Poland*. New York: Whittlesey House, 1948.

Millis, Walter (ed.), in collaboration with E. S. Duffield. *The Forrestal Diaries*. New York: Viking Press, 1951.

Montgomery, Bernard, Viscount of Alamein, Field Marshal. *A History of Warfare*. Cleveland: World, 1969.

———. *Memoirs*. Cleveland: World, 1958.

Murphy, Robert D. *Diplomat Among Warriors*. Garden City, N.Y.: Doubleday & Co., 1964.

Nicolson, Harold. *The Diaries and Letters of Harold Nicolson, Vol. II, The War Years 1939–1945*. New York: Antheneum, 1969.

Raczynski, Count Edward. *In Allied London*. London: Weidenfeld and Nicolson, 1962.

Roosevelt, Elliot. *As He Saw It*. New York: Duell, Sloan & Pearce, 1946.

Smith, Walter Bedell. *Eisenhower's Six Great Decisions: Europe 1944–1945*. New York: Longmans, Green, 1956.

Standley, William H., and Arthur A. Ageton. *Admiral Ambassador to Russia*. Chicago: Regnery, 1955.

Stimson, Henry L., and McGeorge Bundy. *On Active Service in Peace and War*. New York: Harper & Bros., 1948.

Strang, William. *Home and Abroad*. London: Deutsch, 1956.

Truman, Harry S. *Year of Decisions*. Garden City, N.Y.: Doubleday & Co., 1955.

Vandenberg, Arthur H., Jr., and Joe A. Morris. *Private Papers of Senator Vandenberg*. Boston: Houghton Mifflin, 1952.

Voronov, N. N. "The Exploitation of the Soviet People," *Istoriia SSSR*. No. 4 (Moscow: July–August 1965), 13–27.

Welles, Sumner. *Seven Decisions that Shaped History*. New York: Harper & Bros., 1951.

———. *Where are We Heading?* New York: Harper & Bros., 1946.

Zhukov, Marshal G. (ed. by Harrison E. Salisbury). *Marshal Zhukov's Greatest Battles*. New York: Harper & Bros., 1969.

B. Speeches, Works, and Statements

Churchill, Winston S.   *The War Speeches of the Rt. Hon. Winston S. Churchill.* (Comp. by Charles Bade.)   3 vols.   London: Cassell, 1951–52.

Lenin, V. I.   *Selected Works.*   12 vols.   New York: International Publishers, 1935–38.

——.   *Sochineniia.*   38 vols.   4th ed.   Moscow: Gospolitizdat, 1941–58.

Molotov, V. M.   *Problems of Foreign Policy: Speeches and Statements.*   Moscow: Foreign Languages Publishing House, 1947.

Rothstein, Andrew.   *Soviet Foreign Policy During the Patriotic War.*   2 vols.   New York: Hutchinson & Co., 1946.

Stalin, J. V.   *On the Great Patrioic War of the Soviet Union.*   Moscow: Foreign Languages Publishing House, 1945.

——.   *Sochineniia.*   13 vols.   Moscow: Gospolitizdat, 1946–51.

Troyanovsky, Alexander A.   *For World Peace and Freedom: A Survey of the Twenty-five Years of Soviet International Policy.*   National Council of American-Soviet Friendship, Inc., 1943.

U.S. Senate.   "Statement of W. Averell Harriman, Special Assistant to the President, Regarding Our Wartime Relations with the Soviet Union, Particularly as They Concern the Agreements Reached at Yalta," 82nd Cong., 1st sess.   *Military Situation in the Far East, Hearing before the Committee on Armed Services and the Committee on Foreign Relations.* Part V, Appendix.   Washington, D.C.: U.S. Government Printing Office, 1951.

C. Documents

Correspondence Between the Chairman of the Council of Ministers of the U.S.S.R. and the Presidents of the U.S.A. and the Prime Ministers of Great Britain During the Great Patriotic War of 1941–1945.   2 vols. Moscow: Foreign Languages Publishing House, 1957.

Degras, Jane (ed.).   *Soviet Documents on Foreign Policy.*   3 vols.   London: Oxford University Press, 1951–53.

Documents on American Foreign Relations.   Boston: World Peace Foundation, annual, 1939–54.

Documents and Materials Relating to the Eve of the Second World War.   2 vols.   Moscow: Foreign Languages Publishing House, 1948.

Holborn, Louise Wilhelmine (ed.).   *War and Peace Aims of the United Nations.*   2 vols.   Boston: World Peace Foundation, 1943 and 1948.

Instytut Historyczny Imienia Generala Sikorskiego.   *Documents on Polish-Soviet Relations, 1939–1945.*   2 vols.   London: Heinemann, 1961, 1967.

Nixon, Edgar B. (ed.).   *Franklin D. Roosevelt and Foreign Affairs, January 1933–January 1937.*   3 vols.   Cambridge: Harvard University Press, 1969.

Rhode, Gotthold, and Wolfgang Wagner (eds.). *Quellen zur Entstehung der Oder-Neisse Linie in den diplomatischen Verhandlungen waehrend des Zweiten Weltkrieges.* Stuttgart: Brentano, 1956.

Roosevelt, Elliot (ed.). *FDR: His Personal Letters, 1928–1945.* 2 vols. New York: Duell, Sloan & Pearce, 1950.

Sontag, Raymond J., and Jones A. Beddie (eds.). *Nazi-Soviet Relations, 1939–1941.* Washington, D.C.: U.S. Government Printing Office, 1948.

United Nations Information Organization. *Documents of the United Nations Conference on International Organization, San Francisco, 1945.* 20 vols. New York: United Nations Information Office, 1945.

U.S. Department of State. *The Axis in Defeat, A Collection of Documents on American Policy toward Germany and Japan.* Washington, D.C.: U.S. Government Printing Office, 1945.

———. *Documents on German Foreign Policy.* 10 vols. Series D. Washington, D.C.: U.S. Government Printing Office, 1957.

———. *Foreign Relations of the United States: Diplomatic Papers: The Conference of Berlin (The Potsdam Conference) 1945.* Washington, D.C.: U.S. Government Printing Office, 1960.

———. *Foreign Relations of the United States: Diplomatic Papers: The Conferences at Cairo and Teheran, 1943.* Washington, D.C.: U.S. Government Printing Office, 1961.

———. *Foreign Relations of the United States: Diplomatic Papers: The Conferences at Malta and Yalta, 1945.* Washington, D.C.: U.S. Government Printing Office, 1955.

———. *The United States and Germany, 1945–1955.* (European and British Commonwealth Series, No. 47.) Washington, D.C.: U.S. Government Printing Office, 1955.

U.S.S.R. "Documents: The Crimea and Potsdam Conferences of the Leaders of the Three Great Powers," *International Affairs,* Nos. 6–10 (Moscow: June–October 1965).

Vneshniaia politika Sovetskogo Soiuza; dokumenty i materialy. Moscow: Gospolitizdat, 1945–46.

Vneshniaia politika Sovetskogo Soiuza v period Otechestvennoi voiny. 3 vols. Moscow: Gospolitizdat, 1946.

D. Newspapers

(December 15, 1944–February 15, 1945)

The Chicago Tribune
Combat
The *Christian Science Monitor*
The Economist
Evening Standard (London)
Jutro Polski
Krasnaia Zvezda

News Chronicle (London)
The New York Times
Pravda
The [London] *Times*

II. SECONDARY SOURCES

A. *Books and Articles*

Airapetian, M. E., and G. A. Deborin. *Etapy vnenshnei politiki SSSR.* Moscow: Izdatel'stvo Sotsial'no-Ekonomichieskoi literatury, 1961.

Akademiia nauk SSSR, Institut Istorii. *Ocherki istorii Velikoi otechestvennoi voiny, 1941–1945.* (Ed. by B. S. Telpukhovskii and others.) Moscow: Izdatel'stvo Akademii nauk SSSR, 1955.

Alperovitz, Gar. *Atomic Diplomacy: Hiroshima and Potsdam.* New York: Vintage Books, 1967.

Bailey, Thomas Andrew. *America Faces Russia: Russian-American Relations from Early Times to Our Day.* Ithaca: Cornell University Press, 1950.

Baldwin, Hanson W. *Great Mistakes of the War.* New York: Harper & Bros., 1950.

Barghoorn, Frederick C. *The Soviet Image of the United States.* New York: Harcourt, Brace and Co., 1950.

Beloff, Max. *The Foreign Policy of Soviet Russia, 1929–1941.* London: Oxford University Press, 1952.

———. *Soviet Policy in the Far East, 1944–1951.* New York: Oxford University Press (for the Royal Institute of International Affairs), 1953.

Betts, Reginald Robert (ed.). *Central and Southeast Europe, 1945–1948.* London: Royal Institute of International Affairs, 1950.

Bilainkin, George. *Maisky, Ten Years Ambassador.* London: Allen & Unwin, 1944.

Black, Cyril Edwin (ed.). *Rewriting Russian History.* New York: Praeger, 1956.

Boratynski, Stefan. *Dvplomacja orkresu drugiej wojnv swiatowej konferencje miedzynarodowe 1941–1945.* Warsaw, 1957. (Trans. in Russian as *Diplomatiia perioda vtoroi mirovoi voiny.*) Moscow: Izdatel'stvo inostrannoi literatury, 1959.

Bsuscaren, Anthony Trawick. *Soviet Foreign Policy: A Pattern of Persistence.* New York: Fordham University Press, 1962.

Burin, Frederick S. "The Communist Doctrine of the Inevitability of War," *American Political Science Review,* LVII, 2 (June 1963), 24–36.

Carman, Ernest D. *Soviet Imperialism: Russia's Drive Toward World Domination.* Washington: Public Affairs, 1950.

Clark, Alan. *Barbarossa: The Russian-German Conflict, 1941–45.* New York: William Morrow & Co., 1965.

Clauss, Max W. *Der Weg nach Jalta.* Heidelberg: Vowinckel, 1952.

Conte, Arthur. *Yalta ou le portage du monde.* Paris: Laffont, 1966.

Co-ordinating Committee of American-Polish Associations in the East. *Polish-Russian Problem.* New York: Co-ordinating Committee of American-Polish Associations in the East, 1945.

Dallin, David Y. *The Big Three.* London: Allen & Unwin, 1946.

Dean, Vera M. *The United States and Russia.* Cambridge: Harvard University Press, 1947.

Dedijer, Vladimir. *Tito.* New York: Simon and Schuster, 1963.

Dennett, Raymond, and Joseph Esray Johnson (eds.). *Negotiating with the Russians.* Boston: World Peace Foundation, 1951.

Department of the Army. *The Supreme Command.* (*The United States Army in World War II* series.) Washington, D.C.: U.S. Government Printing Office, 1954.

De Sola Pool, Ithiel. *Satellite Generals: A Study of Military Elites in the Soviet Sphere.* Stanford: Stanford University Press, 1955.

Deutscher, Isaac. *Stalin, a Political Biography.* New York: Vintage Books, 1961.

Divine, Robert A. *Roosevelt and World War II.* Baltimore: The Johns Hopkins Press, 1969.

Dulles, Foster Rhea. *America's Rise to World Power, 1898–1954.* New York: Harper & Bros., 1955.

———. *The Road to Teheran: The Story of Russia and America, 1791–1943.* Princeton: Princeton University Press, 1944.

Duroselle, Jean-Baptiste. *De Wilson à Roosevelt: Politique Extérieure des Etats-Unis, 1913–1945.* Paris: Colin, 1960.

Dziewanowski, Marian Kamil. *The Communist Party of Poland.* Cambridge: Harvard University Press, 1959.

Ehrman, John. *History of the Second World War: Grand Strategy.* Vol. 6. (6 vols., United Kingdom Military Series.) London: H.M. Stationery Office, 1956.

Feis, Herbert. *Between War and Peace: The Potsdam Conference.* Princeton: Princeton University Press, 1960.

———. *The China Tangle.* Princeton: Princeton University Press, 1953.

———. *Churchill, Roosevelt, Stalin: The War They Waged and the Peace They Sought.* Princeton: Princeton University Press, 1957.

Fenno, Richard F. (ed.). *The Yalta Conference.* (Problems in American Civilization, Readings selected by the Department of American Studies, Amherst College, Vol. 23.) Boston: Heath, 1955.

Garthoff, Raymond L. *Soviet Military Doctrine.* Glencoe, Ill.: Free Press, 1953.

———. *Soviet Military Policy: A Historical Analysis.* New York: Praeger, 1966.

Hayter, Sir William. *The Diplomacy of the Great Powers.* New York: Macmillan, 1961.

Hazard, John. *The Soviet System of Government.* Chicago: University of Chicago Press, 1960.

Hentsch, Guy. *Staline Négociateur: Une diplomatic de guerre.* Neuchâtel: La Baconnière, 1969.

Hoffman, George W., and Fred W. Neal. *Yugoslavia and the New Communism.* New York: Twentieth Century Fund, 1962.

Israelian, Viktor Leonovich. *Antigitlerovskaia koalitsiia (Diplomaticheskoe sotrudnichestvo SSSR, SShA i Anglii v gody vtoroi mirovoi voiny).* Moscow: Izdatel'stvo Mezhdunarodnye Otnosheniia, 1964.

————. *Diplomatisheskaia Istoriia Velikoi Otechestvennoi Voiny, 1941–45.* Moscow: Izd-vo Instituta Mezhdunarodnykh Otnoshenii, 1959.

Irving, David. *Accident: The Death of General Sikorski.* London: William Kimber, 1967.

Istoriia velikoi otechestvennoi voiny Sovetskogo Soiuza. 6 vols. Moscow: Voennoe Izdatel'stvo-Ministerstva Oborony SSSR, 1963–65.

Ivashin, I. F. *Ocherki istorii vneshnei politiki SSSR.* Moscow: Gospolizdat, 1958.

Jasper, Rootham. *Miss fire: The Chronicle of a British Mission to Mihailovich, 1943–1944.* London: Chatto & Windus, 1946.

Kolko, Gabriel. *The Politics of War.* New York: Random House, 1968.

Krzesin'ski, Andrzej J. *Poland's Rights to Justice.* New York: Devin-Adair, 1946.

Kuby, Erich. *The Russians and Berlin 1945.* New York: Hill and Wang, 1968.

Kusnierz, Bronislaw. *Stalin and the Poles.* London: Hollis & Carter, 1949.

Kutakov, Leonid Mikolaevich. *Istoriia Sovetsko-Iaponskikh Diplomaticheskikh Otnoshenii.* Moscow: Izd-vo Instituta Mezhdunarodnykh Otnoshenii, 1962.

Lukacs, John A. *The Great Powers and Eastern Europe.* New York: American Book Co., 1953.

Mackintosh, John Malcolm. *Strategy and Tactics of Soviet Foreign Policy.* New York: Oxford University Press, 1962.

Marriott, John A. A. *The Eastern Question.* Oxford: Oxford University Press, 1940.

McNeill, William Hardy. *America, Britain and Russia: Their Co-operation and Conflict, 1941–1946.* New York: Oxford University Press (for the Royal Institute of International Affairs), 1953.

McSherry, James E. *Stalin, Hitler, and Europe 1933–1939.* Cleveland: World Publishing Co., 1968.

Neumann, William Louis. *Making the Peace, 1941–1945: The Diplomacy of the Wartime Conferences.* Washington, D.C.: Foundation for Foreign Affairs, 1950.

Opie, Redvers, et al. *The Search for Peace Settlements.* Washington, D.C.: Brookings Insitution, 1951.

Reitzel, William, et al. *United States Foreign Policy, 1945–1955.* Washington, D.C.: Brookings Institution, 1956.

Repecka, Juozas. *Der gegenwaertige voelkerrechtliches Status der Baltischen Staaten unter Besonderer Beruecksichtigung der Diplomatischen Vor-*

geschichte der Eingliederung dieser Staaten in die Sowjet-Union. Goettingen, 1950.

Rozek, Edward. *Allied Wartime Diplomacy: A Pattern in Poland.* New York: John Wiley & Sons, 1958.

Ryan, Cornelius. *The Last Battle.* New York: Simon & Schuster, 1966.

Seton-Watson, Hugh. *The East European Revolution.* New York: Praeger, 1961.

Sharp, Samuel L. *Poland: White Eagle on a Red Field.* Cambridge: Harvard University Press, 1953.

Smith, Gaddis. *American Diplomacy During the Second World War, 1941–1945.* (America in Crisis series.) New York: John Wiley & Sons, 1965.

Snell, John L. (ed.). *The Meaning of Yalta.* Baton Rouge: Louisiana State University Press, 1956.

————. *Wartime Origins of the East-West Dilemma Over Germany.* New Orleans: Nauser Press, 1959.

Supnik, Robert M. "Poland and the Origins of the Cold War." Unpublished manuscript, on file with the Humanities Library, Massachusetts of Technology.

Telpuchowski, Boris S. *Die Sowjetische Geschichte des Grossen Vaterlandischen Krieges.* (Britisch erlautert von Andreas Hillgruber und Hans-Adolf Jacobsen.) Frankfurt am Main: Bernard u. Graefe, 1961.

Thayer, Charles Wheeler. *Hands across the Caviar.* Philadelphia: Lippincott, 1952.

Toland, John. *The Last 100 Days.* New York: Random House, 1966.

Towster, Julian. *Political Power in the U.S.S.R., 1917–1947.* New York: Oxford University Press, 1948.

Toynbee, Arnold Joseph, and Veronica M. Toynbee (eds.). *The Realignment of Europe.* 2 vols. London: Oxford University Press, 1955.

Triska, Jan F., and Robert M. Slusser. *The Theory, Law and Policy of Soviet Treaties.* Stanford: Stanford University Press, 1962.

Trukhanovskii, Vladimir Grigor'evich (ed.). *Istoriia mezhdunarodnykh otnoshenii i vneshnei politiki SSSR.* 3 vols. Moscow: Institut Mezhdunarodnykh Otnoshenii, 1961.

Umiastowski, Roman. *Poland, Russia, and Great Britain, 1941–1945: A Study of the Evidence.* London: Hollis & Carter, 1946.

U. S. Department of Defense. "The Entry of the Soviet Union into the War against Japan: Military Plans, 1941–1945." Mimeographed report released October 19, 1955.

Val'kov, V. A. *SSSR i SShA: ikh politicheskie i ekonomicheskie otnosheniia.* Moscow: Nauka, 1965.

Viorst, Milton. *Hostile Allies, Franklin Delano Roosevelt and Charles de Gaulle.* New York: Macmillan, 1965.

Vorontsov, V. B. "The Liberation Mission of the USSR in the Far East During World War II," *Istoriia SSSR.* No. 4 (Moscow: July–August 1965), 28–48.

Voroshilov, K. E. *Stat'i i rechi.* Moscow: Partizdat Tsk VKP (b), 1937.

Vygodskii, S. I. *Vneshniaia Politika SSSR—Politika Mira i Mezhdunarodnogo Sotrudnichestva*. Moscow: Gospolitizdat, 1958.

Wallace, Henry Agard, and Andrew J. Stiger. *Soviet Asia Mission*. New York: Reynal, 1946.

Weinberg, Gerhard L. *Germany and the Soviet Union, 1939–1941*. Leiden: Brill, 1954.

Werth, Alexander. *Russia at War, 1939–1945*. New York: Avon Books, 1965.

Wilmot, Chester. *The Struggle for Europe*. New York: Harper & Bros., 1952.

Wilson, Theodore A. *The First Summit: Roosevelt and Churchill at Placenta Bay 1941*. Boston: Houghton Mifflin, 1969.

Wittmer, Felix. *The Yalta Betrayal: Data on the Decline and Fall of Franklin Delano Roosevelt*. Caldwell, 1953.

Wolff, Robert Lee. *The Balkans in Our Time*. Cambridge: Harvard University Press, 1956.

Woodward, Sir Llewellyn. *History of the Second World War: British Foreign Policy in the Second World War*. (United Kingdom Military Series.) London: H. M. Stationery Office, 1962.

Yakhontoff, Victor A. *USSR Foreign Policy*. New York: Coward-McCann, 1945.

Zawodny, J. K. *Death in the Forest*. University of Notre Dame Press, 1962.

Zueva, F. G. (ed.). *Istoriia mezhundunarodnykh otneshenii i vneshnei politiki SSSR, (1870–1957 gg.)*. Moscow: Vysshaia partiinaia shkola pri Tsk KPSS, 1957.

B. Newspapers

The following have been selected from a large number of articles that the author has collected. These samples are of particular interest because they represent a wide range of reactions and concepts about the Yalta Conference before the publication of the American documents.

The *Christian Science Monitor*, January 31, 1946; February 1, 1946; November 21, 1946; March 27, 1947; February 7, 1953.

The *Daily Telegraph*, March 31, 1946.

Izvestiia, February 12, 1946; February 15, 1946.

The *Manchester Guardian*, March 26, 1947; February 5, 1953.

Le Monde, February 3, 1953.

The [London] *Times*, February 12, 1946; April 2, 1947; February 18, 1953.

Neue Zuericher Zeitung, January 28, 1946; February 13, 1946.

Neues Deutschland, March 26, 1947; February 3, 1953.

The New York *Herald-Tribune*, February 1, 1946; July 22, 1951; February 17, 1953.

The *New York Times*, January 30, 1946; March 1, 1946; August 3, 1952; March 10, 1953.

Nippon Times, February 15, 1953.

North China Daily News, March 21, 1947.

Sueddeutsche Zeitung, March 10, 1953.

Taegliche Rundschau (Newspaper of the Soviet sector in Berlin), February 12, 1946; February 13, 1946.

III. BIBLIOGRAPHIES HELPFUL IN LOCATING SOVIET MATERIALS

Akademiia nauk SSSR, Fundamentalnaia Biblioteka Obshchestvennykh nauk. *Istoriia SSSR; ukazatel' sovetskoi literatury za 1917–1952 gg.* (Comp. by I. P. Doronin and others.) 3 vols. Moscow: Izdatel'stvo Akademii nauk SSSR, 1956–.

The American Bibliography of Slavic and East European Studies. (Ed. by Joseph T. Shaw and others, Russian and East European Series.) Bloomington: Indiana University Publications, 1957–.

Columbia University, Russian Institute. *Report on Research and Publication.* New York: 1948–.

Egorov, V. N. (comp.). *Mezhdunarodnye otnosheniia: bibliograficheskii spravochnik. 1945–1960 gg.* Moscow: Izdatel'stvo Instituta mezhdunarodnykh otnoshenii, 1962–.

Foreign Affairs Bibliography: A Selected and Annotated List of Books on International Relations. 4 vols. New York: Published by Harper for the Council on Foreign Relations, 1933–64.

Hammond, Thomas T. (ed. and comp.). *Soviet Foreign Relations and World Communism: A Selected, Annotated Bibliography of 7,000 Books in 30 Languages.* Princeton: Princeton University Press, 1965–.

Harvard University, Russian Research Center. *Ten Year Report and Current Projects, 1948–58.* Cambridge: 1958–.

Mezhdunarodnyi politiko-ekonomicheskii ezhegodnik. 8 vols. Moscow: Gospolitizdat, 1958–.

U.S. Department of State, Bureau of Intelligence and Research, External Research Staff. *External Research, a List of Recently Completed Studies.* (Annual, published each spring.) Washington: Department of State, 1952–.

U.S. Library of Congress, Processing Department. *Monthly Index of Russian Accessions.* Washington: 1948–.

INDEX